Contents

List of illustrations   *page* ix
Notes on contributors   x
Acknowledgements   xiii

Introduction   Colonial and postcolonial plots in histories of
maternities and modernities   1
MARGARET JOLLY

1   Shaping reproduction: maternity in early twentieth-century
    Malaya   26
    LENORE MANDERSON

2   Modernizing the Malay mother   50
    MAILA STIVENS

3   'Good wives and mothers' or 'dedicated workers'?
    Contradictions of domesticity in the 'mission of sisterhood',
    Travancore, south India   81
    JANE HAGGIS

4   Maternity and the story of enlightenment in the colonies:
    Tamil coastal women, south India   114
    KALPANA RAM

5   The *dai* and the doctor: discourses on women's reproductive
    health in rural Bangladesh   144
    SANTI ROZARIO

6   Other mothers: maternal 'insouciance' and the depopulation
    debate in Fiji and Vanuatu, 1890–1930   177
    MARGARET JOLLY

7   Just add water: remaking women through childbirth,
    Anganen, Southern Highlands, Papua New Guinea   213
    LEANNE MERRETT-BALKOS

8   From sisters to wives: changing contexts of maternity on
    Simbo, Western Solomon Islands   239
    CHRISTINE DUREAU

Epilogue   Maternal experience and feminist body politics:
Asian and Pacific perspectives   275
    KALPANA RAM

Index   299

Feminist theories have focused on contemporary, Western, middle-class experiences of maternity. The present volume brings other mothers, from Asia and the Pacific, into scholarly view, aiming to show that birthing and mothering can be a very different experience for women in other parts of the world. The contributors document a wide variety of conceptions of motherhood, and drawing on ethnographic and historical research, they explore the relationships between motherhood as embodied experience and the local discourses on maternity. They reveal how the experience of motherhood has been influenced by missionaries, by colonial policies and by the introduction of Western medicine and biomedical methods, and raise important questions about the costs and benefits of becoming a modern mother in these societies.

Maternities and modernities

Maternities and modernities

Colonial and postcolonial experiences in Asia and the Pacific

Edited by

Kalpana Ram

Macquarie University, Sydney

and

Margaret Jolly

The Australian National University, Canberra

PUBLISHED BY THE PRESS SYNDICATE OF THE UNIVERSITY OF CAMBRIDGE
The Pitt Building, Trumpington Street, Cambridge CB2 1RP, United Kingdom

CAMBRIDGE UNIVERSITY PRESS
The Edinburgh Building, Cambridge, CB2 2RU, United Kingdom
40 West 20th Street, New York, NY 10011-4211, USA
10 Stamford Road, Oakleigh, Melbourne 3166, Australia

© Cambridge University Press 1998

First published 1998

Printed in the United Kingdom at the University Press, Cambridge

Typeset in Plantin 10/12 pt [VN]

A catalogue record for this book is available from the British Library

Library of Congress cataloguing in publication data

Ram, Kalpana, and Jolly, Margaret Anne.
  Maternities and modernities: colonial and postcolonial
experiences in Asia and the Pacific / edited by Kalpana Ram and Margaret Jolly.
    p.   cm.
  Includes index.
  ISBN 0 521 58428 0 (hardback). – ISBN 0 521 58614 3 (pbk.)
  1. Motherhood – Asia.   2. Motherhood Pacific Region.   3. Mothers –
Asia.   4. Mothers – Pacific Region.   I. Ram, Kalpana.   II. Title.
HQ759.J69 1997
306.874'3'095 – dc21   97-6813 CIP

ISBN 0 521 58428 0 hardback
ISBN 0 521 58614 3 paperback

Illustrations

Plates

1 Malaysian cartoons – about homework   *page* 64
2 Malaysian cartoons – actions speak louder than words   65
3 Midwife-cum-trader in fishing community, south India   130
4 Birthing mother being helped to sit up, Bangladesh   152
5 Birthing mother cutting her umbilical cord, aided by midwife,
   Bangladesh   153
6 Contemporary, collective mother love   191
7 Doctor and patient, Ba Hospital, Fiji, *c.* 1926   198
8 Anganen women working in a sweet potato garden   218
9 *Yasolu* (ceremonial pig-kill and exchange) – woman tending pig   218

Maps

1 Location of countries and regions in Asia and the Pacific
   discussed in this volume   xiv
2 Colonial British Malaya, Sraits Settlements and Federated and
   Unfederated Malay States as referred to in text   29
3 Fiji   184
4 Vanuatu   185
5 The Solomon Islands, showing location of Simbo in the west   240

Notes on contributors

CHRISTINE DUREAU is a Lecturer in Social Anthropology at the University of Auckland, New Zealand. She took her PhD at Macquarie University, after which she was a Postdoctoral Fellow in Pacific History in the Research School of Pacific and Asian Studies at The Australian National University. She has conducted extended field research on gender, Christianity and changing worldviews among Simbo communities in the Solomon Islands and archival research on Methodist missionary and colonial sources. She is currently working on an ethnographic history of Fijian Methodist missionaries and on a project on nineteenth-century Methodist missionary approaches to evolutionary theory.

JANE HAGGIS is a Lecturer in the Department of Sociology at Flinders University, Adelaide, South Australia. She has carried out research on British women missionaries in south India, and is currently working on a history of the women's missionary movement in Britain. She has a chapter in press in *Gender and Imperialism* (edited by Clare Midgley) on white women and women's history. Her major forthcoming publication is the book *Labours of Love: The Professionalisation of the 'Lady Missionary'*. A further book in preparation is *Culture and Development* (with Susanne Schech).

MARGARET JOLLY is a Senior Fellow and Convenor of the Gender Relations Project in the Research School of Pacific and Asian Studies, The Australian National University, Canberra. She taught feminist anthropology, illness and healing, Melanesian ethnography and the colonial history of the Pacific at Macquarie University in Sydney for seventeen years. She has published extensively on women in the Pacific and especially Vanuatu, on the Cook voyages, on gender in colonial history and on the politics of tradition. Her major publications are *Women of the Place: Kastom, Colonialism and Gender in Vanuatu* (1994); *Women's Difference: Sexuality and Maternity in Colonial and Postcolonial Discourses* (1994) (ed.); *Family and Gender in the Pacific: Domestic*

Contradictions and the Colonial Impact (1989) (ed., with Martha Macintyre); and *Sites of Desire, Economies of Pleasure: Sexualities in Asia and the Pacific* (1997) (ed., with Lenore Manderson).

LENORE MANDERSON is an anthropologist and social historian and is Professor of Tropical Health in the Faculty of Medicine, The University of Queensland. Her books include *Women, Politics and Change* (1980); *Australian Ways: Anthropological Studies of an Industrialised Society* (1985) (ed.); *Shared Wealth and Symbol* (1986) (ed.); *New Motherhood: Cultural and Personal Transitions in the 1980s* (1993) (with Mira Crouch); *Sickness and the State: Health and Illness in Colonial Malaya, 1870–1940* (1996); and *Sites of Desire, Economies of Pleasure: Sexualities in Asia and the Pacific* (1997) (ed., with Margaret Jolly). Her primary research interests and publications relate to infectious diseases in poor resource communities, and to gender, sexuality and women's health.

LEANNE MERRETT-BALKOS' fieldwork was undertaken among Anganen speakers near Poroma, Southern Highlands Province, Papua New Guinea from mid-1987 to early 1988. Her PhD thesis, 'New women: discursive and non-discursive processes in the construction of Anganen womanhood', was granted in 1992 through the University of Adelaide. She is now working on program management in the area of research and community group funding with the Commonwealth Department of Health and Family Services, before moving into public sector management improvement with the Department of Finance. Current interests are in public policy development and cultural change in public sector organizations.

KALPANA RAM is an Australian Research Council Research Fellow, attached to Anthropology and Comparative Sociology, Macquarie University, Sydney. She has published on gender, caste and class in contemporary India, as well as more general theoretical papers on feminism and modernity. Her major publication is *Mukkuvar Women: Gender, Hegemony and Capitalist Transformation in a South Indian Fishing Community* (1991). Her current research is on reproductive embodiment and gender in south India, and on the transformations of Indian dance and aesthetics in nationalism both within India and in the overseas Indian diaspora.

SANTI ROZARIO teaches Sociology and Anthropology at the University of Newcastle, Australia. She has undertaken extensive anthropological field research in Bangladesh, and has published *Purity and Communal Boundaries: Women and Social Change in a Bangladeshi Village* (1992).

Rozario's present teaching and research interests include women and development, women and reproductive health in South Asia; religious pluralism in South Asia and in the West, and community studies.

MAILA STIVENS studied Anthropology at the University of Sydney and at the London School of Economics. She has carried out research on middle-class kinship in Sydney and in Malaysia on 'matrilineal' Negeri Sembilan and on modernity, work and family among the new Malay middle classes. She has taught at University College London and at the University of Melbourne, where she is Director of Women's Studies. Her main publications include *Why Gender Matters in Southeast Asian Politics* (1991) (ed.); *Malay Peasant Women and the Land* (1994) (with Jomo Sundaram and Cecilia Ng); and *Matriliny and Modernity: Sexual Politics and Social Change in Rural Malaysia* (1996).

Acknowledgements

These essays are a selection from papers presented at a workshop on Maternity held by the Gender Relations Project in July 1992. We would like to thank the Research School of Pacific and Asian Studies, The Australian National University, for their visionary support of the project, in both research funds and in time for reflection, writing and editing. Kalpana Ram would also like to thank the Australian Research Council for their past and present support.

We would also like to express our warm thanks to all our contributing authors, who in successive drafts made their chapters better and better, and to the readers of the manuscript for their constructive comments and criticisms. Our thanks also to our editor at Cambridge, Jessica Kuper, and the production team.

Finally, our thanks to Annegret Schemberg for her continuing research assistance, for her sterling bibliographical work and her meticulous copy-editing and proofreading; to Ria van de Zandt, who has worked many long hours to render our inconsistencies, confusions and inelegancies into a beautiful manuscript, fit for publication; to Andrew Walker for excellent and fast work on our index; and to Coombs photographer Bob Cooper for superb reproduction of plates.

Plates 1 and 2 have been reproduced with the kind permission of S. Abdul Majeed & Co., Kuala Lumpur, from *Anak Anda Malas Belajar*; Plate 7 was made available by the Image Library of the State Library of New South Wales, Sydney (MOM 240); and the maps were produced by the Cartography Unit of the Research School of Pacific and Asian Studies, ANU, Canberra, except Map 2 which was reproduced by the University of Queensland. All other photographs are by the respective author of each individual chapter, with the exception of Plate 3, where the photo credit is to the late Roger Keesing.

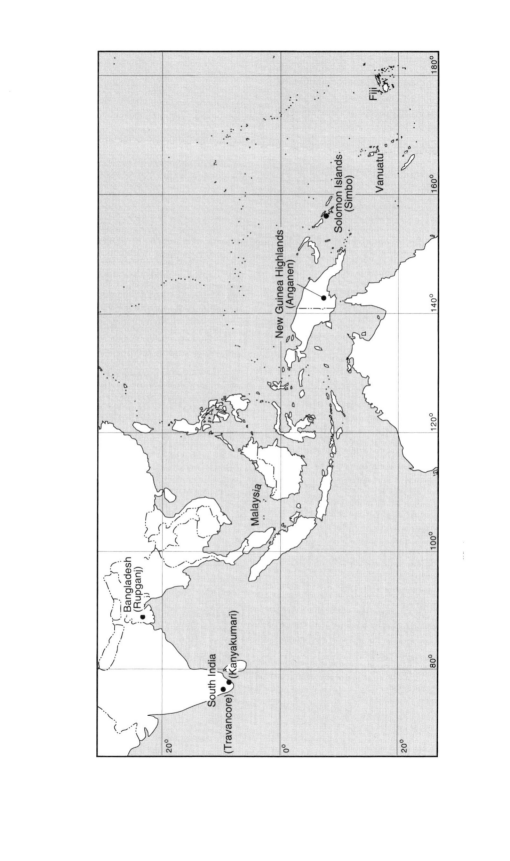

Introduction   *Colonial and postcolonial plots in histories of maternities and modernities*

Margaret Jolly

The link between maternities and modernities is more than an alliterative conjunction. These essays attest to how projects of modernity have also entailed remoulding maternity. But, whereas some recent studies have seen this relationship as singular and have typically privileged Euro-American experiences,[1] we pluralize understandings both of maternity and of modernity and problematize the way we plot their relation. More-over, the focus on Asia and the Pacific not only provides a different site for experiences of, and discourses about, maternity but suggests how these sites were and are connected in the processes of colonialism and post-colonial development. We highlight how class-based interventions in mothering in many countries of Europe and North America were parallel-ed by projects in European colonies where race, ethnicity and class compounded pre-existing local differences between women. In many Asian and Pacific countries indigenous patterns of mothering have been challenged and to some degree transformed, first in the colonial period and second in the postcolonial epoch, in the name of civilization, modernity and scientific medicine. But women in these places have not simply succumbed to the message of 'enlightenment' through maternal improve-ment, but have variously rejected or embraced such advice or accom-modated it selectively.[2] Such exercise of agency should not be construed as a matter of voluntaristic choices however, as if choosing between modes of mothering is akin to wheeling a supermarket trolley (Ram 1994:20). Indeed, this volume shows that such choices are saturated not just by the power of gender difference, but class and ethnicity. The embodied ma-ternal subject is pervaded by a profound tension, perhaps even a split, as the mother is sundered in contests between 'tradition' and 'modernity'.

Before I explore these themes through the several essays which follow, let me elaborate our key concepts – maternities and modernities. In talking of maternities, rather than mothering, we highlight the corporeal processes of being pregnant, giving birth and nurturing. But, although there is much here about the maternal body, the intimate practices of confinement and labour, sexual and dietary taboos during and after pregnancy, breast-feeding and early infant care, we are insistent on how these seemingly natural processes of swelling, bearing and suckling, the flows of blood, semen and milk are constituted and fixed not just by the force of cultural conception but by coagulations of power. And in such cultural conceptions and political coagulations we must not forget how many become mothers not through pregnancy but through processes of adoption and the labour of nurture.

Moreover, although the mother might appear to be the central subject of maternity, she is often evacuated from this position by a discursive focus on the child (see Manderson, this volume) or by an objectivist medical depiction which Manderson dubs 'the obstetric gaze'. Given how often the mother has been marginalized in debates about maternity, it is important to insist on her centrality. Assuming the subject position of the mother has a particular salience in the narratives of recent Western feminism where, as Stivens (this volume) suggests, the feminist has often situated herself as the angry daughter rather than the mother and rarely celebrates the maternal within herself. Indeed, it may be argued that the maternal has typically been denigrated within Western feminism (as in the surrounding culture) (e.g. Barrett and McIntosh 1982; Friday 1977) and that only recently has the maternal subject been embraced by Western feminists culminating in a belated burgeoning of research and writing in the 1980s–1990s (e.g. Irigaray 1985a, 1985b; Kristeva 1980, 1981; Ruddick 1989; see Adams 1995 and Ross 1995 for reviews of recent literature). By contrast Asian and Pacific feminists have more readily embraced the maternal subject position, although often to distinguish themselves from what are perceived as anti-family tendencies in Western feminism or as part of anti-colonial or nationalist movements (see Jolly 1994). This book thus explores not just how maternity is *experienced* by mothers and others but also how maternity is *constituted* in discourse and how it is valued or devalued. Indeed, despite the centrality of 'experience' in much Western feminist theory (see Scott 1991) and of testimony in the genres of both feminist life history and ethnography, we can never present the 'real life' mother, nor evoke her corporeality or subjectivity, except through an act of textual *re*presentation (cf. Ross 1995:399). There is no doubt that maternal subjects are often represented as absences in masculinist colonial texts, but even where mothers are more palpably present in the translations of contemporary feminist ethnography, they are still *re*presented, still 'given voice' through discourse.

Modernity, like maternity, has been the subject of much academic and political debate, from the earliest theories of modernization to the most recent controversies that have swirled around the concept of postmodernity. Older theories of modernization posited a linear progression, whereby allegedly 'traditional' societies become not only industrialized and urbanized, but rationalized, bureaucratized and secularized. This very partial view of historical transformations of Europe and North America from the eighteenth to the twentieth century was then projected on to the more recent experiences of those industrializing or 'developing' countries of Asia, Africa, South America and the Pacific. Apart from the dismal inadequacies of this view of historical processes in Europe or North America, such a linear concept of modernization has long been criticized as both teleological and Eurocentric.

Thus Stivens (this volume) suggests that the specificities of Malay modernity belie such a view – here a modern managerial state oversees the precipitous pace of industrialization, urbanization and commoditization but also the resurgence of Islam, and especially the espousal of a purer form of Islam on the part of some sections of the Malay middle classes. Malay modernity is expressly celebrated by its proponents as a form distinct and divergent from foreign forms and values, which some Malay intellectuals vilify as 'Westoxification'. As Stivens insists, modernity is gendered (cf. 1994) not just in the sense that male and female subjects experience it differently, but in how its discursive terms are constituted. Stivens suggests that the feminine is sometimes cast as the negative to the male modern, but can in other contexts shift to images of feminine modernity. Perhaps it is as mothers that Malay women most legitimately enter the modern. Malay middle-class women are thus enjoined to be modern mothers through a particular combination of Muslim chastity and discipline, energy in the office and at home, a persuasive psychology aimed at creating good obedient children rather than 'lazy natives' and the allure of a commodity culture which creates modern consumerist identities, as for the kids – Toys R Us.

But this particular trajectory of maternity in modernity, though distinctively Malay, is not disconnected from earlier processes in colonial history,[3] as Manderson (this volume) attests and it is to this earlier period of colonization that I turn at the outset. First I compare some of the colonial critiques of mothers in Asia and the Pacific, secondly I highlight the relation between processes within colonizing Europe and the places which were colonized and thirdly I ponder the relationship between religious and secular projects of enlightenment. I then query the impact of colonial and contemporary development projects on indigenous mothering and especially focus on persistence in the old ways, resistance to the new ways and forms of conflict and accommodation between them. This will then lead into a consideration of the allegedly 'postcolonial' character of contemporary maternity in Asia and the Pacific and a series of questions about narrativizing the past in the present.

Asian and Pacific mothers: the colonial critiques

For those of us familiar with the lore of more recent Western child-care manuals with their idyllic constructions of maternity in the 'state of nature' or female-centred childbirth in remote South America,[4] it is deeply shocking to confront the denigrations of Asian and Pacific mothers by earlier European observers. With tedious consistency most of these observers (male and female) accused Asian and Pacific women of lacking a maternal instinct or of being careless or incompetent mothers. Perhaps most predictably there were concerted attacks on indigenous forms of contraception, abortion and infanticide. But dietary and sexual abstinences in pregnancy and postpartum were ridiculed or lamented; modes of delivery, ways of cutting the cord or dealing with the afterbirth were attacked;[5] withholding colostrum or feeding pre-masticated food to neonates was admonished; suckling was often perceived as too protracted and sometimes the bottle and cows' milk was promoted in lieu of the breast. Maternal love was adjudged deficient – being portrayed as variously insufficient, too dispersed or too indulgent.

'Improving' or modernizing maternity thus not only meant the medicalization of pregnancy, birth and the postpartum period but also the discipline of mother love itself. Whereas various ancestral traditions constructed the maternal body and birthing in religious terms as sacred, dangerous or even polluting, the modernizing project aspired to 'clean up' and rationalize birth, not just by sanitary and hygienic injunctions at the moment of birth itself, but by forms of discipline of the pregnant body and surveillance of the new mother and her child. Antenatal and postnatal checks, attendance at clinics and home inspections were all part of such routines in colonial Malaya and Fiji for instance. No doubt sometimes some of these interventions saved lives – of mothers and of infants – by anticipating difficult presentations, by eliminating treatment of the umbilicus, which caused neonatal tetanus, or by helping to arrest postpartum haemorrhage or ensuring the placenta was rapidly evacuated. But such interventions also had the important effect of bringing the maternal body under the surveillance of others – and others often separated from the mother by race and class. And these others often aspired to change the maternal relation too – to ensure that babies were only fed at regular intervals, that mothers did not spoil their children but inculcated discipline, that mothers concentrated their attentions on their 'own' children and did not disperse their maternal affections unduly. There was thus from the colonial period new forms of 'rationality' applied to maternity and Eurocentric forms of psychology promoted which proclaimed earlier forms of mother love as sloppy, deficient or irrational (and thus gave issue to 'the lazy native'). Although such psychologisms mirrored the waves of fashion amongst the child experts 'back home' – psychoanalytic, behaviourist or object-relations theories – the 'modern mother' in the colonies was differently located – in more than her geographical locus. In aspirations towards modernity, Asian and Pacific women were often required to repress not just 'female feeling' but also archaic ancestral forms or anterior sacral traditions, some of which divinized rather than vilified the mother (see Ram, this volume: Chapter 4).

The chapters by Manderson and Jolly document the details of British colonial attacks on mothers in Asia and the Pacific – or more specifically Malaya, Fiji and Vanuatu. Some of the nuances and the timings differ, but there are striking commonalities – presumptions about 'bad mothers', mothers being blamed for depopulation and for high rates of infant mortality and being subjected to coercive and persuasive projects for maternal improvement. White women were often initially involved in such projects but then, when these failed, some indigenous women were trained as obstetric nurses or modern midwives while later many others were educated as modern mothers in domestic science courses.

Thus in colonial Malaya,[6] Manderson reports how the concern about mothering on the part of both indigenous Malay and migrant Indian and Chinese women emerged in the context of concerns about high rates of infant mortality and the need to arrest depopulation in order to maintain a labour force for plantations and mines. Not only infant but maternal mortality rates were incredibly high – in 1900 maternal mortality was about 16/1,000 and infant mortality about 250/1,000 (though varying by region). Although many causes were adduced, such as neonatal tetanus and malaria, diarrhoea spread by poor housing and sanitation, inadequate maternal and infant nutrition, colonial reports often focused on those proximate causes which could be traced back to midwives or mothers, and they were most often blamed.

Interventions in mothering were not just the benign feminine face of the civilizing mission however (see Manderson, this volume). They were, in colonial Malaya at least, pre-eminently a state rather than a mission project, and were foremost about assuring labour power for capitalist enterprise – since the costs of replacing labour from overseas was prohibitive, local reproduction was fostered. They were also about securing control over the diverse 'populations', attempting a modernization of social control, parallel to that which Foucault detects in eighteenth- and nineteenth-century Europe. But these new forms of capillary power had rather different venous connections in the colonies. The inspection of women's maternal and sexual being and the surveillance over the child here depended centrally on the hierarchy of race (cf. Stoler 1995). From the late nineteenth century in Malaya it was the English woman, nurse or not, who was enjoined to police the mothering of Malay, Indian and Chinese women. Other mothers were not, however, treated equally – the Malay woman, economically and geographically marginal to the colonial state, was always treated with more benevolent indulgence than the migrant woman. The Indian mother in particular was treated very badly (as she was in colonial Fiji), as if her being a mother and a labourer in a mine or on a plantation was aberrant and abnormal.

Fundamental to such interventions were attacks on indigenous modes of birthing and nurturing and on the traditional birth attendant (TBA), the *bidan* – the Malay midwife (who was used not just by Malay but by many Chinese and Indian women). Malay birthing was extremely culturally elaborated during pregnancy, labour and especially in the puerperium. After birth Malay women were 'roasted', took smoke baths and regulated their diets in order to revert the uterus, tone the vagina and ensure humoural balance in the body (Laderman 1983). From the late nineteenth century Malay women were enjoined to forego such sensual attentions to the maternal body, and to institute a more disciplined and rational form of birthing and postpartum nurture. Given the English practices of the period, home births were still favoured over hospital confinements. The latter was an unlikely choice, since in Singapore in 1907 there were only sixteen 'native' beds, and the medical staff were primarily male with no female doctors and few nurses. Moreover, as in colonial Fiji, given the notorious rates of cross-infection and poor rates of recovery of patients, hospitals were seen as sites of death, not birth (see below).

The main strategies of modernizing maternities, rather, involved control and inspection of home births – training for midwives in modern methods, regular inspections at the clinic and home visits by European women. But – despite the lectures on obstetric problems and difficult presentations, the inculcation of ideas of antiseptic procedure, attempts to reduce neonatal tetanus by care of the cord, the rituals of taking temperatures, giving inoculations and weighing babies at clinics after birth, and the incessant advice of 'home visitors' to offer regular feeds but refrain from handling infants too often – Malay mothers for the most part were not enthusiastic modernizers. They attended clinics irregularly, if at all, and remained unpersuaded by the models of English women as 'natural mothers', many of whom were single and childless anyway. The one exception seems to be, from the 1920s, the shift to bottle rather than breast-feeding, which, as was soon recognized, worsened rather than improved infant health.

Although the numbers of women attending clinics or receiving home visits steadily rose and these persuasions were later complemented by domestic science for all girls, 'modern mothering' did not supplant indigenous modes. As Laderman (1983) has documented, many distinctively Malay practices of birthing persist to the present: the rituals of the puerperium and elaborate dietary regulation during pregnancy and after most particularly. Moreover, many women still insist on taking the child's placenta home to plant, to maintain origins in and attachment to the ground (cf. Merrett-Balkos, this volume). Thus, as Stivens (this volume) suggests, many Malay women use both the government midwife and the *bidan*, but accurately perceive the first as focused on the child and the second as focused on the mother. She depicts Malay women as both compliant and resistant in the several interventions by colonial and independent state into their mothering and fertility control. Blaming mothers may co-exist with conferring on them the power to build the race, or the nation through 'happy families'.

The same paradox might be witnessed in the colonial states of Fiji and the New Hebrides (Vanuatu since Independence in 1980). They patently offer a Pacific parallel to the faltering attempts at modernizing maternity in colonial Malaya – but there are important divergences as well as convergences. Here, too, the concern about mothering emerged in the context of debates about depopulation around the turn of the century. Here, too, mothers and midwives were blamed for high rates of infant mortality, rather than addressing the more difficult and recalcitrant questions about the apalling impact of introduced diseases, combined with the continuing ravages of indigenous illnesses like malaria (in Vanuatu, but not Fiji).

But there were significant differences. Here Christian missions had an earlier and a continuing salience in attempts at remoulding maternity. Moreover, especially in Fiji, the imperial project was less about reproducing a labour force than social control of the indigenous population. Indeed, the population of migrant Indian mothers were not even mentioned in the earlier stages of this debate.

The event which heralded the British imperial concern with depopulation was the publication in Fiji in 1896 of the *Report of the Commission Appointed to Inquire into the Decrease of the Native Population*. As I attest in my chapter (Jolly, this volume: Chapter 6), this was an extraordinarily detailed and thoroughgoing document which canvassed a multitude of causes for the decline of the native population (the British rapaciousness and indifference to the survival and the health of migrant Indian labourers is perhaps testified here by their exclusion from this report, see Kelly 1991). But ultimately, when it came down to practical colonial policies in both Fiji and in Vanuatu, it was mothers who were blamed for the fact that the race was 'dying out'. A sequence of colonial strategies, coercive and persuasive, focused on improving mothers, maternity and midwives.

Attempts at reforming indigenous mothers did not originate with such colonial state reports and policies. From the first arrival of Christian missionaries in Fiji and Vanuatu from the mid-nineteenth century, indigenous mothers had been vilified for their contraceptive or abortive practices, for infanticide, for dirty procedures during labour itself, for feeding neonates pre-masticated tubers while withholding colostrum, and for variously being too indulgent or too indifferent towards their children (see Jolly 1991). Missionaries perpetuated their concerns and were involved in these colonial conversations about depopulation, along with state officials and anthropologists. In my analysis of some major texts in these debates (Jolly, this volume: Chapter 6) I argue that, despite the obsessive cataloguing of 'causes' and the relentless marshalling of them into 'indigenous' or 'exogenous', even those commentators who favoured exogenous causes (the introduction of alien diseases, grog and guns) considered that their effects were amplified by an indigenous malaise. The malaise in men was 'emasculation', in women the malaise was maternal 'insouciance' or carelessness.

In both Vanuatu and Fiji, the colonial state aspired to survey and police mothers, but given the weak and divided character of the state in Vanuatu (conjointly administered by England and France) this remained a rather pious hope and attempts at remoulding maternity remained pre-eminently a mission concern. In Fiji the colonial state was both stronger and had from the early colonial period intimate links to the indigenous hierarchy of male chiefs. It is in Fiji that we witness the more developed invasions into inspections of maternal experience. There were inquests into infant deaths to combat abortion and to allocate blame, where, as Lukere (n.d.a) has clearly documented, the pervasive premises were of maternal guilt, midwives' collusion and paternal irresponsibility. There were edicts passed to restrict the work and the mobility of pregnant women and enticements to men and to chiefs to promote the fertility of women. As in Malaya, white women were vaunted as educators in modern maternity, although here, given the sectarian rivalry between the Catholics and the Methodists, it was celibate and childless nuns who were the first models.

As for colonial Malaya, it is important not to credit these coercive and persuasive interventions with the efficacy their originators imagined. For the most part they were a miserable failure – inquests failed to implicate many mothers or midwives, women evaded the restrictions on their moving around or going fishing at night, and resisted attempts to control their sexuality on the part of male kin and chiefs. The Hygiene Mission of the Catholic sisters was shortlived and inconsequential (see Jolly, this volume: Chapter 6; and Lukere n.d.a, n.d.b). Of more consequence were the efforts at persuasion through the training of local women as nurses and, as in Malaya, the more generalized process of education in the science of domesticity. But importantly these both transpired in such a way that the combat between ancestral and biomedical traditions was softened and the imposition of colonial medicine was not so readily co-opted by high-ranking women who could terrorize others with their education and scientific rationality. The training of local women as nurses was perceived as a way of combating indigenous midwives here as in Malaya, but, according to Lukere (n.d.a), to some degree they co-operated more than combated and combined many aspects of indigenous and scientific medicines.

Echoes between Britain and the colonies

The examples in this book, though ranging widely across South Asia, Southeast Asia and the Pacific, are for the most part from countries colonized by the British (or as for Papua New Guinea, Australians). This poses questions not just about the distinctiveness of British colonialism (as against French or Dutch colonialism, on which see Stoler 1989, 1991, 1992) but also about the links between the so-called 'metropole' and 'peripheries'. Both Manderson and Jolly discern echoes between what was happening back in Britain and what was happening in the colonies. The resonances are many. The concern about 'population' was pervasive as was the blaming of mothers for the persisting high rates of infant mortality (cf. Klaus 1991 on depopulation debates in France and the US). But even more striking are the resonances in the discourses and the strategies of intervention in the lives of working-class mothers in Britain and colonized women in Asia and the Pacific. Both were singled out for maternal deficiency – for the dirt and dark of their houses, for their unhygienic forms of birthing and nurture, for their poverty, or for the simple fact that they were both workers and mothers. The focus in Britain was no doubt on *man*power, on those 'stalwart sons' who were required to man the machines of industry and of war. But in Malaya, too, the concern was also to reproduce enough healthy workers to *man* the plantations and the mines, for here, at least for the Indian population, their gender was eclipsed by their race – women were seen to be 'as men' (see Manderson, this volume). The same perception of Indian migrant mothers no doubt pertains in colonial Fiji, but importantly here the colonial intervention focuses on the indigenous or 'native' mother, who is not only to be exempted from colonial labour regimes, but ideally sequestered from most forms of indigenous hard work as well. Colonial officials tried to persuade Fijian mothers to remain in the house and devote their attention to weaving mats and making *tapa* (bark cloth), rather than exerting themselves in taro gardens or fishing. As I have intimated (Jolly, this volume: Chapter 6), sexual as well as maternal sequestration seems to have been at issue here.

But the concern for 'population' was not reducible to a concern with labour units. In both imperial Britain and the colonies there was a new form of control being assumed, a new kind of inspection afforded of those intimacies of 'population' – the familial and extra-familial relations of sexuality and fertility. Thus, we can witness an excess of power beyond the merely instrumental aspirations of reducing mortality. These interventions – in homes, schools and other institutions in both metropolitan and colonial sites – were, as Foucault has persuasively argued, about governing life (Foucault 1979, 1980; Mitchell 1988; Stoler 1989, 1991, 1992, 1995). And in both sites the ultimate aim was probably self-government through compliant citizen subjects, in this case through the 'native agency' of maternal subjects.

As Haggis (this volume) has brilliantly shown, a notion of 'native agency' had earlier linked the lower classes and the subject races in the constructs of Protestant missionaries on the Indian subcontinent. Her chapter challenges us to ponder further both the similarities and differences between the imperial centre and the colonies and between the religious and the secular in imperial notions of 'enlightenment'. She depicts the extraordinarily conflicted and difficult situation of those so-called 'Bible women' of Travancore, who were central to the proselytizing effort of the London Missionary Society (LMS) among Indian women. The missionaries perceived that conversion was best promoted by female 'native agency', but were singularly unable to penetrate the 'inmates of the *zenana*' (women's quarters), the sites and states of seclusion which pertained among high-caste women in this southern region. Although wary that working with the low-caste women might mean that they were cast at an even greater distance from their eventual goal, this was perforce their strategy. These 'Bible women' were not only poor, lower caste, even untouchable but also (unlike many of their English missionary women who 'superintended' them) married and with children. Haggis poignantly shows the strenuous exercises which were required of such 'Bible women' in evincing their commitment to Christ – itineraries which had them walking miles in the hot sun, delivering public lectures and sermons, and forsaking their own husbands and children for the sacred circuits of service of this foreign god. But they were the 'bright lights shining for Jesus', the 'rare flowers . . . purifying . . . the moral desert' (Haggis, this volume, pp. 91, 101). It was the transforming spirit of the convert, coupled with the discipline of the mission boarding school which was alleged to have effected this transformation from the dirty, stupid, low-caste heathen woman to the clean, intelligent and superior Christian woman. As Haggis so cogently demonstrates, more than a sanitary or moral transformation was effected – conversion was for many of these women ultimately a crucial step in class and caste mobility, in securing a professional female status as 'dedicated workers' rather than, and indeed often at the expense of being, 'good wives and mothers'.

But also of particular interest in Haggis' account is the way in which the concept of 'native agency' mediates the intersection of gender, class and racial presumptions in imperial and colonial loci. In the accounts of the period, the 'Bible women' are not so much assimilated to the working classes of England, but rather to those who work among them as 'visitors' or 'Bible women'. Mrs Ranyard, an Anglican 'visitor' to the urban poor of London, from the 1850s worked with 234 Bible women in her 'domestic female mission' to 'reach by female agency the wives and mothers of the working classes' (Ranyard 1856, cited in Haggis, this volume, p. 100). The primary inflection of 'native' here is an imputed female, rather than a class or racial essence. Ranyard also alleged that such women were 'the missing link between the upper and the lower classes of London' (Haggis, this volume, p. 101). As many have done before, Haggis here suggests the affinities between 'othering' by class and race and how missions in the slums of London or Glasgow were conceived as opposing a heathenism and a savagery almost as deep and dark as that pertaining in the exotic locales of Asia or the Pacific (Jolly 1991).

But the differences between the 'Bible women' in London and in Travancore are equally compelling. For the Indian Bible women were being asked to mediate between these foreign women who presumed their superiority and the indigenous women of the *zenana* who presumed theirs. Thus, although Indian 'Bible women' were in many ways akin to the 'respectable' working class of London and like them later aspired to middle-class status, they did so in a colonial configuration in which Christianity remained marginal and where the complexities of caste as well as class continued to divide Indian women (see Ram, this volume: Chapter 4).

The story of enlightenment in the colonies? Religious and secular narratives

But what of the second problem which this chapter highlights for us, the relation between these religious stories of enlightenment of Bible women 'shining like bright lights for Jesus' and those secular models, which stress the rational and scientific character of the enlightened 'modern mother'? Both Christian theologies and scientific teleologies deploy the trope of enlightenment to legitimate their projects – be it Christian dawning in heathen darkness or the light of reason dawning in the dark ages of religiosity and superstition. The tropes, like their associated projects, overlap and contend at different historical junctures and geographical sites. This is very clear in the overall project of 'modernizing maternity', but a regional comparison is instructive between Pacific experiences where adherence to Christian churches is now pervasive and Asia where it is a more marginalized, minority faith. Let me first consider Christine Dureau's fascinating material on Simbo, both here and elsewhere (Dureau, this volume and 1993). The imprint of the Christian mission and in particular Methodism in remoulding maternal subjectivity is here palpable. Women here, like many people throughout the Pacific, have assumed the 'enlightenment' language of the mission and the way in which it contrasts ancestral past and Christian present as epochs of darkness and light.[7] This language of temporal rupture is how women depict the difference between their experience of birthing and mothering and that of their forebears before 1900. One of her older friends on the island told her, 'I was born in the forest before the Light and Cleanliness.' Dureau herself portrays the change thus:

> Neli's mother sat on a boulder, banana leaves on the ground at her feet, her mother's female cognatic kin encircling her. When she was born, her mother cut the umbilical cord with bamboo, bound herself in her old *tapa* loincloth and then followed the women into the trees where she buried the placenta so the *tomate* (ancestral spirit) would not smell it. Then Neli and her mother went to the *savo* (postnatal hut) built by her father and for several months were cared for by Neli's female cognatic kin before returning to the village.
>
> Mari was born in 1989 in the clinic, where her mother lay prone on a delivery table while two other women held her and the Registered Nurse manipulated her labia to prevent tearing, delivered the baby, clamped and cut the cord with sterilized stainless steel instruments and checked the placenta before discarding it with other clinic waste. Next day she was inoculated for TB. After three days, a rush of dysentery cases were admitted to the clinic, so she was sent home with her mother where her MZD, her own sister, came to stay and see to household tasks. Mari and her mother were visited by large numbers of women, who brought small gifts of food or laundry soap. Six weeks later, her mother returned to work as a schoolteacher, leaving the same MZD to care for Mari during the day. (1994: 200)

The contrast seems stark. From a mother delivering in an active squatting position, in a forest setting, encircled by female kin, their fear of devouring ancestral spirits compounded by the dangers of tetanus and disease from proximity to the earth, to bamboo and old *tapa*, to a clinic, with sterilized medical procedures and instruments, a surfeit of soap, the mother prone and passive in delivering her baby and attended by the ministrations of the registered nurse as well as all those female kin. When Dureau enquired as to the cause of such changes in birthing, as in mothering generally, the response was usually 'the missionaries told us'. But she warns us not to accept either the confident teleology or the passive acceptance which such a narrative of the certain rupture from darkness to light implies.

Western medicine in the colonial context was often first associated with missionaries rather than secular scientists or doctors (see Comaroff 1993; Vaughan 1991). But, the 'Western medicine' which missionaries brought to the Pacific or Asia in the nineteenth century was not the same 'Western medicine' as pertains today. It lacked the antiseptic procedures, powerful drugs like penicillin and other antibiotics and anaesthetized surgery, all of which are indissociable from the practice and power of biomedicine in contemporary, affluent EuroAmerican centres today. Thus, as Lukere (n.d.a) stresses for colonial Fiji, early hospitals were quite legitimately dubbed – *vale ni mate* – places of death, since not only were Western medicines of the time inadequate for dealing with the pandemics of introduced diseases, but by concentrating the sickest patients in close proximity, they spread infections and disease more effectively. It is not surprising then that in the early colonial period few Fijian women chose to birth there, even in the cases of direst emergency.

Moreover, in the late nineteenth and early twentieth centuries, the practitioners of Western medicine in the colonies, missionaries and others, often deployed aetiologies which adduced supernatural as much as natural causes of illness. Thus in combating ancestral ideas of illness and the associated powers of the ancestors or indigenous deities, mission-aries in particular often proclaimed the rivalrous power of God to cure or to harm (see Jolly 1996). Thus, birthing mothers who relinquished the forest setting and the ideas of dangerous ancestral spirits for the benevol-ent protection of God in the missionary compound or later the clinic, and whose children survived, might be credited as proof of the miraculous effects of divine intervention. And as Lukere (n.d.a) further stresses, those Fijian women who trained as nurses and government midwives saw themselves as much as servants of God as of science. Bringing light to the mother shrouded by 'tradition' was as much a Christian vocation as it was an act of secular science or biomedicine.

The contrast with India is, as noted earlier, instructive; for here the class, caste and religious dimensions of the power of this 'enlightenment' are saliently different. As Ram (this volume: Chapter 4) depicts it, the power of scientific rationality has been arrogated by those who have class and caste power. Thus when low-caste Mukkuvar women have to resort to birthing in a hospital as a last resort in an emergency, they are subject to a violent exercise of scientific medicine over their bodies. Thus she argues that, from their perspective, the 'older forms of hierarchical discourse are simply mapped onto newer versions, with high-caste intolerance of "impurity", "pollution" and lack of learning being transposed on to the idiom of hygiene, rationality and scientificity' (Ram, this volume: Chapter 4, p. 139). It should be stressed that the proponents of this scientificity include both Christian and Hindu reformers, as well as medical personnel from the upper reaches of both caste and class hierarchies.

But the way in which the older and newer forms of power collude or compromise each other are quite variable in both colonial and contemporary patterns of birthing and mothering. It seems to depend partly on how birthing was ancestrally conceived and valued, how the process of 'modernizing maternity' has been effected in terms of pre-existing and novel hierarchies, and also how the status of the TBA relates to her seemingly implacable opponent, the registered nurse, or government midwife.

Traditional and modern birthing: romances and dangers

Both in the typifications of mothers themselves and in the language of analysis, there is a tendency to dichotomize birthing and mothering as 'traditional' versus 'modern'.[8] This reduces the diversity of birthing experiences at both ends – since both 'traditional' and 'modern' birthing patterns are quite various, not just in techniques but in their cultural conceptualization and evaluation.[9] In opposing traditional forms of birthing to the biomedical, we are, as Lumley and Astbury warned long ago, in danger of romanticizing the traditional as 'natural' (1980:2–3). As well as the very real corporeal dangers of maternal and infant mortality, birth was seen in many parts of Asia and the Pacific as an occasion of spiritual danger and sometimes also of pollution. This was the rationale for Anganen women in the Papua New Guinea Highlands and for Simbo women in the Western Solomons giving birth either alone or removed from the village (see Merrett-Balkos and Dureau, this volume) and for the Bangladeshi woman being assisted by a low-caste *dai*, who was already so polluted as to be less endangered by the blood and effluent of birth (Rozario, this volume). Thus, if birth was woman-centred, in that men were neither present nor allowed to intervene, it was not therefore a time of female collectivity or celebration. A number of authors in this volume caution against an undue romance about traditional birthing, and probably most forcefully Rozario writing on Bangladesh. Rozario (this volume) typifies the contrast between 'traditional' and 'modern' and indeed the confrontation of values in her study of birth in Bangladesh. As Rozario rightly suggests, this confrontation between the *dai* and the doctor gets saturated by the contest between the binaries not just of tradition and modernity, but of religion versus science, and of female-centred and male-centred birth. It is probably true that in opposing the masculinism of the medicalization of birth in Europe and North America some feminists have been in danger of romanticizing traditional childbirth, of eliding the pain, the dirt and the dangers, especially when things went wrong, and the lives of mother, baby or both were lost.

As Rozario depicts it, there is not much room for romance about birth in rural Bangladesh nor to reconstruct the traditional midwife, or *dai*, in the image of the 'wise women' of a feminist history of childbirth in Europe. Her view of birth in Bangladesh is signalled by two initial horror stories – of Tasmina and Zori. These suggest how birth itself is seen as a most polluting event – the body of the birthing woman, the baby, the placenta and umbilicus are all defiled and defiling. Only the low caste, already polluted *dai*, a poor menial more than a midwife, is powerful enough to withstand birth pollution. (Similar ideas about pollution and *dai* prevail in north and south India, cf. Jeffery *et al.* 1989; Jeffery and Jeffery 1993.) Given this, it is perhaps not surprising that Rozario sees only the biomedically trained Catholic nuns working at local dispensaries as having a significant potential to improve childbirth practices. But she insists this potential can only be realized if greater understanding prevails about the beliefs and practices surrounding birthing women and *dai*. Apropos WHO policy on the incorporation of TBAs she adjudges that literate and educated women are unlikely to take on the role of the *dai*, 'and the potential for substantial upgrading of the *dai* into trained TBAs is very limited' (Rozario, this volume, p. 168). Bangladesh might represent an extreme case of difficulty, denigration and danger in a 'traditional' birth. It offers an antidote to undue romancing about natural childbirth and the female-centredness of 'folk' practice. It also reveals the lines of class cleavage between the literate and educated, and the illiterate and uneducated, which in many ways parallels the old colonial cleavages of white nurse and indigenous midwife.

The view which Ram (this volume: Chapter 4) offers of the medicalization of childbirth for Mukkuvar women in Tamil Nadu is quite different. Here it seems that ancestral constructs of birthing were more benign. Ram prefers to gloss the anterior traditions as rendering birthing women (and indeed women's fertility in general) dangerous rather than polluting. Moreover, she argues women's fertility can be auspicious and not just polluting or dangerous (Ram 1991). Is this then to be explained in terms of cultural differences, the way in which the researcher plots her relation to maternal subjects in the narratives of modernity or progress, or are there important differences in the way in which the medicalization of birthing has been effected and is perceived? Now it may be that these Mukkuvar fishing communities, at the southern tip of India, are distinctive insofar as they avoid or mute the hierarchies of pollution which pervade birth elsewhere on the subcontinent in agrarian-based caste societies. They are distinctive insofar as here, as in other parts of coastal south India, Christian missions have had a very profound impact since the period of Portuguese colonization. The very marginality of these communities seems not only what made their indigenous evaluations of birth more benign but also what renders their experience of biomedically organized, and especially hospital, births so horrific. It seems that in this contest the full weight of caste and class oppression bears down on the birthing mother, as she experiences not just the pain of difficult childbirth but also the cruel humiliation of being scolded and lectured by impatient nurses and doctors, who look down on her as a 'dirty fishwife'.

The situation in Fiji offers another variant on how ancestral and colonial powers and values conjugate in modernizing birthing. First, the indigenous view of birth was not here a state of pollution nor of defilement, so much as one of danger and indeed sacral sequestration. Indeed, as Keesing (1985) has argued for the Kwaio, and Hanson (1982) more generally for the Polynesian parts of the Pacific, the menstruating or birthing woman was not so much sequestered because she was polluting, but because she was communing with ancestral spirits. Lukere (n.d.a) attests for Fiji that there was a deification of the products of birth and even of the aborted foetuses of chiefly women. Consonant with this view of birth, the midwife, or *bui ni gone*, was not a dirty menial, but rather a pathway to ancestral beings and to deities. She was, moreover, more than a midwife: she was a revered female healer who treated both female and male patients through a variety of techniques – herbs, massage, even surgery. Certain *bui ni gone* specialized in obstetrics and the treatment of particularly difficult birth presentations. Thus, when the British attacked such women as the incarnation of 'traditional superstition', they were not supported by an indigenous cosmology which rendered birth defiling and which constituted birth attendants as polluted or low status. In fact these older women healers were rather revered and celebrated, and the British attacks on them through inquests into infant deaths probably both sent them underground and in some ways amplified their power. Here, the analogies with the 'wise women' of European traditions seem somewhat more apt. But there the analogies cease, for ancestral and scientific medicine in Fiji seem to have secured a far more benign, feminine conjunction.

When the British authorities failed to reform Fijian mothers either by the draconian coercions or by the persuasions of white women in the Hygiene Mission, they plotted to modernize maternities from within by training Fijian women to become nurses – Native Obstetric Nurses (or NONs) who were to educate mothers and to combat the superstitions and ancestral practices of *bui ni gone*. This also failed initially; the young NONs educated in boarding schools and then in hospitals were not able to prevail over these 'wise women', but rather accommodated themselves to them, many moving back to villages and learning indigenous techniques from these older women.

Moreover, the way in which the NONs were constituted did not reinforce pre-existing hierarchical forms, which divided chiefly from commoner families. Nurses were not in the first place drawn from the chiefly families, since chiefly fathers were reluctant to expose their daughters to the sexual perils of a boarding school or hospital, or to lose them in marriage to foreigners. Thus, although chiefly women later became important, the nursing profession was distinguished by being an early route to education for commoner women. And such women seem to have consistently accommodated the experience of the older *bui ni gone* and incorporated indigenous and introduced techniques of birthing as equally 'Fijian'. Thus today, unlike the situation Ram describes for Mukkuvar women in south India, a Fijian mother from a remote village does not appear to experience the hospital as a place which is 'alien' and where the medical staff, both because they are more modern and more educated, subject the birthing mother to denigration. This more benign conjunction was perhaps afforded both by the more positive evaluation of birthing in the ancestral tradition and by the fact that the introduction of scientific medicine did not reinforce but rather cut across pre-existing social hierarchies.[10]

The past in the present

In the routine binary oppositions of 'traditional' and 'modern' mothering, there is a narrative structure presumed, a story told of then and now, or – in the words of the Anganen of the Papua New Guinea Highlands – of *bipo* and *nau* ('before' and 'now' in Tok Pisin (TP hereafter); Merrett-Balkos, this volume). In this particular example *bipo* (TP) and *nau* (TP) are very proximate, being the difference between the arrival of whites and the Catholic mission in 1964 and the time of the ethnography in the 1980s. In the case of Dureau's work on Simbo, the rupture is located around 1900. In the narrative structures of colonialism and Christian conversion in Southeast and South Asia, the temporality is deeper, and the language of tradition and modernity complicated by the successive if not cumulative waves of modernization. Stivens (this volume) stresses how in Malaysia the past and present keep resurfacing and resurging in debates about maternity, but in so doing their meanings constantly shift. Thus, there is no straightforward temporal progression, whereby the traditional mother is a 'relic' of a premodern past which progress leaves stranded on the shores of time. The past is no doubt constantly shifting as it is recreated by the present, but we still discern a tendency to stop the flow, and to narratize in terms of *bipo* (TP) and *nau* (TP). Such ruptures or punctuations of time seem compelling both for the women we write about and for ourselves.

But the complexities of these different stories of maternities and modernities must also make us highly suspicious of simplistic teleologies, moral sagas of 'improvement'/'enlightenment' or their degenerationist antitheses, how modernizing maternities are scientist violence to sacral traditions or masculinist horror stories against women's bodies. Let me again move between the Pacific and Asia to argue this.

First, there is Merrett-Balkos' study of those Anganen women of the Papua New Guinea Highlands, who very recently have encountered and negotiated a different mode of birthing offered by the Catholic sisters at the local aid post. Indigenously women birthed alone in the mother house – a birthing experience typified not just by isolation, but fear and disorientation. Merrett-Balkos stresses how in indigenous philosophies of the gendered body and of birthing, women are linked with ideas of connectedness and roads, while men are linked with ideas of rootedness and emplacement. The disorientation of birth is supposed to engender a loss of recognition of the world by women, but this moment of disorientation is addressed and redressed through dealing with the afterbirth – both placenta and umbilical cord. By burying the placenta the woman establishes her child's relation to place, through the father. By severing the umbilical cord, which signifies the connecting power of women, the new mother is in a sense also re-enacting her own severance of the road connecting herself to her natal kin, tied off and sealed like the cord of her infant.

Anganen women soon after contact by the Catholic mission in 1964 willingly started going to birth at the aid post rather than birth alone. The attractions of the nuns' care and nurture over the loneliness of the mother house are obvious. But this shift in locale did not mean that they embraced all the meanings and the values of biomedical birth. They asserted their own birthing ideals with the Catholic nuns who nursed them, by a mass protest in 1970, whereby hundreds of Anganen women sat down at the aid post, demanding that their placentas be returned. They wanted the placenta, or at least the umbilical cord, returned rather than being carelessly disposed of as impure medical waste. Eventually a compromise was reached: the sisters and protesting women agreed that a few inches of umbilical cord would be retained by new mothers.

The meanings of birthing for these women thus are in the process of being reconfigured in a complex pattern of past-in-present. Women seem desirous of a proximity to modernity which they associate with the mission and the Catholic nuns, and pursue this as vigorously as their husbands pursue the *bisnis* ('business' in TP) of cash and coffee. But they are also resistant to certain aspects of modernized birthing, or at least want to retain some power to generate their own metaphors of disorientation and reorientation in the experience of becoming a mother. Whether the power of the place of the mission (where the placenta is now buried or 'planted') will in any sense rival the power of the place of the father is in Merrett-Balkos' view a question still emergent.

It is hard, then, to construct this story of changed birthing in terms of a simple teleology of improvement or deterioration for women. And so Dureau has argued for both birthing in particular and mothering in general on Simbo. She suggests that the impact of Christianity on women in that island has indeed been a 'mixed blessing' and that, although the privileged relation between women and men has moved from that between siblings to that of spouses, this is not to be adjudged as a shift from the equality of the sister to the inequality of the wife (contra Sacks 1979). Thus, although women might have appeared to have more autonomy in the past in restricting and planning pregnancies without the interference of husbands, these seeming reproductive 'freedoms' were severely circumscribed, not just by the high risks of maternal and infant mortality, but by other kinds of death penalties. The premarital chastity of sisters and their marital fidelity were policed by their brothers, or *luluna*. Women were enjoined to be sexually continent – if not, they could be killed by their *luluna*. Alternatively, if their *luluna* died in battle, this was a sure sign of their sisters' premarital or extra-marital affairs, and also occasioned their death in retribution.

Although the surveillance and punitive sanctions associated with the *luluna* relationship have diminished with the combined effects of pacification, the diminution of chiefs and conversion to Christianity, the corporeal control which brothers once exercised over their sisters has in a sense shifted to that of husbands over their wives. Christian conjugality with its stress on nucleation, cohabitation, its strictures against indigenous contraceptives and abortifacients and its far greater number of children, has meant new burdens for Simbo women as mothers. There are not just more births and more children to care for, but also greater conflict with husbands over both. Men, though they might publicly expostulate on the importance of 'family planning', see their own wives using it as a sign of sexual licence, desertion of husband and children, and their planning to destroy the family. Despite the admonitions of the central Methodist hierarchy about conjugal harmony, equality and companionate marriage, men still quote the letter of St Paul to the Ephesians to proclaim their right to discipline their wives, violently if necessary. Thus 'modern' maternity for Simbo women, though it might mean birth which is safer and less likely to end in the death of mother, child or both, is also likely to be far more frequent, more burdensome and conflictual for women, especially in relations with their husbands.

Dureau stresses that how she narrativizes the benefits and gains of *bipo* (TP) over *nau* (TP) is not necessarily how most Simbo women construct their relation. In conversations with her, Simbo people often romanced the parenting of their ancestors, and whereas she stresses the difficulty and threatening tragedy of their grandmothers' maternity, they stress their forebears' freedom from childcare. This is perhaps a strategic romance, deployed to contrast with the lack of good contraception in the Solomons today (as against contemporary Australia where Dureau lives). And this gap between the narrative plotted by the ethnographer-author and that of her maternal subjects in the narratives of modernizing maternity signals the problems which Haggis poses in this volume, about how to write in this allegedly 'postcolonial' period of feminist scholarship. Haggis is alert to how the hierarchies of the colonial past have not disappeared but have assumed new guises in the present. In writing about the 'mission of sisterhood' in colonial India she ponders how to avoid the twin risks of rescuing white women from the masculinist historiography of empire or recuperating Indian women from the muting effects of the colonial archive. She has read too much Spivak (1987, 1988) not to perceive an 'uncanny resemblance' between the white woman in the colonies and herself, the Western feminist, in relation to the colonized/Third World woman. And although the problem of dealing with archival material is very different from that of contemporary ethnography, similar questions of the recuperation of the 'experience' of other mothers pertain even when we are dealing with women who are alive and anything but mute.

This seems most graphic in the work of Dureau and Merrett-Balkos, who work as contemporary 'white women' in the remote highlands or islands of the rural Pacific. But Stivens also perceives herself afflicted by the critiques of the persisting colonialisms of the Western feminist as author, even when her modern Malay mothers seem very proximate to her own class situation (juggling jobs and 'quality time' with children). Indeed, the problems in the power to represent and authorize narratives persist, even when the author is more proximate by reason of 'birth right', if less proximate by class or caste or diasporic dislocation (see the chapters by Rozario and Ram, this volume). As Ram sees it, her very commonality as a Tamil woman divides her from the women who are the subjects of her research, since she emanates from 'the upper Brahmanic reaches of the caste order' (Ram, this volume: Chapter 4). Thus, the projects of the 'mission of sisterhood' are complicated by class, and in this case caste difference as well as the racial hierarchies pertaining to the colonial period. Whether we have escaped from 'missions of sisterhood' into a more dialogical relation between our own subject positions and those of our ethnographic subjects is surely for our readers to judge. What does seem clear from telling these several stories about 'maternities and modernities' is that they are also entangled with our own several stories about our joys and sufferings, pleasures and pains of being women, feminists and even, for some of us, 'modern mothers'.

NOTES

1 A large number of texts might be cited here, but see in particular Everingham (1994); Martin (1987); Oakley (1980); Rich (1977); Stanworth (1987). The most recent reviews by Adams (1995) and Ross (1995) do, however, consider some exceptions to this cultural privilege in works about Afro-American (Bell-Scott et al. 1991), Amerindian (Boyer and Gayton 1992) and Brazilian mothering (Scheper-Hughes 1992). These works, however, are often divorced from the substantial comparative literature on developing countries (for recent collections see Ginsburg and Rapp 1995 and Greenhalgh 1995) and the works generated by the United Nations and its agencies, especially in the wake of the WHO Report of 1978 on traditional birth attendants, and culminating in journals like Safe Motherhood (WHO 1990–). A large international bibliography, recently published by the Gender Relations Project (Schemberg 1995), brings these literatures together.
2 From the viewpoint of the birthing mother the biomedical model has often been in Dureau's words 'a mixed blessing'. Given the high risks, the isolation and sometimes the denigration associated with birth in the past, rural women in Asia and the Pacific have often willingly gone to the clinic or the aid post. But in their eagerness to embrace some aspects of biomedical birthing practices, they have not embraced all. It is important to see women not just as passive recipients of biomedical routines.
3 There are some continuities between earlier colonial discourses about Malay mothers as cultivating laziness and lack of discipline through their indulgence and self-sacrifice. Manderson (this volume) finds these and other laments in early colonial critiques of Malay mothers. Stivens (this volume) discerns the same stereotype of Malay mothers in early anthropological works, and after

that in notions of national character. But the colonial inheritance is also there in the way in which the state has a vested interest in the maternal body, be it to curb or to urge maternal fecundity.

4 See for instance Arms (1975) and Kitzinger (1972). Of course both such denigrations and romances are projective evaluations, which typically universalize the Eurocentric adjudications of what is a 'good mother' prevalent at the time. Both constructs of other mothers are often quite innocent of indigenous practices.

5 The extension of scientific medicine in the training of doctors and nurses after Independence, in the postcolonial period, often perpetuated such criticisms of indigenous birthing practices as unclean or dangerous for the health of both child and mother. Thus for example for Malaysia, Manderson reports that the use of a bamboo knife and the application of wood ash and a paste of turmeric or ginger on the stump of the umbilicus is still opposed as a likely source of neonatal tetanus. This is probably true, but other aspects of indigenous birthing practices, such as the 'roasting of the mother' (by smoke baths and dietary regulation), are probably benign, and perhaps even beneficial in reverting the uterus and toning the vagina. But often such practices are dismissed in toto as 'traditional'; hence the WHO initiatives. Regardless of the veracity of these criticisms or the wisdom of such interventions, the political force of these 'modernizing' methods is still to instil in the very intimate bodily practices of birthing a sense of rupture between times past and times present, between the traditional and the modern.

6 That is, the Straits Settlements and the Federated and Unfederated Malay States.

7 Although it must be said that they have not assumed it completely, vaunting as they do many good things about their ancestors (and about *kastom*, tradition), these tensions are expressed in the inimitable phrase of one of Dureau's female friends, that her ancestors were 'good sinners'.

8 Moreover, in most contemporary situations there are several co-existing and contesting models surrounding birth. In the Papua New Guinea Highlands ancestral religious ideas about pollution and fertility confront Christian ideals of purification and confession merged with biomedical practices in the person of Catholic nuns at the birth clinic (Merrett-Balkos, this volume). In Bangladesh, there is a mix of beliefs in pollution, spirits, homoeopathic and herbal cures, the power of amulets, Islamic faith and, if it can be afforded, scientific medicine. This is of course not the pragmatic eclecticism critiqued by Ram (this volume: Chapter 4), but a hierarchy of 'choices' structured by poverty and power as much as belief.

9 As noted above, one of the problems with our singular category 'tradition' is that it homogenizes a great diversity of traditions, in opposition to what is presumed to be 'modern' or Western. In these several cases reported in this volume traditional birthing practices are quite various – in terms of whether the mother was alone or attended by a midwife or other female kin, in the birthing position assumed and in how difficulties in presentation or delivery were handled, in how the newborn babe, the umbilicus, the placenta and bodily exuviae were dealt with, and in the character and the length of postpartum sequestration and care of both mother and baby. There is thus no one form of traditional birthing practice which biomedicine encounters. The same diversity

could be stressed for 'medicalized' childbirth. Birthing in a remote clinic in Bangladesh or Simbo or an aid post in the New Guinea Highlands, though seemingly on a 'scientific' model, is rather different from birthing in a metropolitan hospital in Australia – either today or twenty years ago. The prone position of Australia's recent past is a disturbing similarity in Dureau's account of contemporary Simbo. But apart from the sterilized stainless steel instruments, intensive medical interventions and high-technology equipment are most likely absent (episiotomies, epidural anaesthesia, foetal heart monitors, caesarian sections are not performed, although they are in the capital). Second, the woman is likely to be accompanied not only during the labour but throughout her stay by close female kin – the attitude to visiting relatives has long been more relaxed in hospitals in Asia and the Pacific than it has been in Australia until very recently. Third, the actual delivery is most likely to be done not by a gynaecologist, but by a local female nurse, like the registered nurse who delivered Mari in Dureau's account. For most of the cases discussed in our volume, this is the norm.

10 I should stress that this benign conjunction Lukere perceives in the relation of female healers, but not in the relation of men in colonial medicine. Here there was a more stark opposition between white male doctors and Fijian native dressers, and a situation where indigenous and exogenous were associated with the racial hierarchy of men.

REFERENCES

Adams, A. 1995 Review essay: Maternal bonds: recent literature on mothering. *Signs* 20(2):414–27.

Arms, S. 1975 *Immaculate Deception: A New Look at Women and Childbirth in America*. Boston: Houghton Mifflin.

Barrett, M. and McIntosh, M. 1982 *The Anti-Social Family*. London: Verso.

Bell-Scott, P. *et al.* 1991 *Double Stitch: Black Women Write about Mothers and Daughters*. New York: Harper Collins.

Boyer, R.M. and Gayton, N.D. 1992 *Apache Mothers and Daughters: Four Generations of a Family*. Norman: University of Oklahoma Press.

Comaroff, J. 1993 The diseased heart of Africa: medicine, colonialism, and the black body. In S. Lindenbaum and M. Lock (eds.) *Knowledge, Power, and Practice: The Anthropology of Medicine and Everyday Life*. Berkeley: University of California Press, 305–29.

Dureau, C. 1993 Nobody asked the mother: women and maternity on Simbo, western Solomon Islands. *Oceania* 64(1):18–35.

1994 Mixed blessings: Christianity and history in women's lives on Simbo, Western Solomon Islands. PhD thesis, Macquarie University, Sydney.

Everingham, C. 1994 *Motherhood and Modernity: An Investigation into the Rational Dimension of Mothering*. Sydney: Allen and Unwin.

Foucault, M. 1979 *Discipline and Punish: The Birth of the Prison* (trans. A. Sheridan). New York: Vintage Books.

1980 *Power/Knowledge: Selected Interviews and Other Writings, 1972–1977* (trans. C. Gordon *et al.*, ed. C. Gordon). New York: Pantheon Books.

Friday, N. 1977 *My Mother/My Self: The Daughter's Search for Identity*. New York: Delacorte Press.

24   *Margaret Jolly*

Ginsburg, F. and Rapp, R. 1995 (eds.) *Conceiving the New World Order: The Global Politics of Reproduction*. Berkeley: University of California Press.

Greenhalgh, S. 1995 (eds.) *Situating Fertility: Anthropology and Demographic Inquiry*. Cambridge: Cambridge University Press.

Hanson, F.A. 1982 Female pollution in Polynesia? *Journal of the Polynesian Society* 91(3):335–81.

Irigaray, L. 1985a *This Sex Which Is Not One* (trans. C. Porter with C. Burke). Ithaca, NY: Cornell University Press.

1985b *Speculum of the Other Woman* (trans. G.C. Gill). Ithaca, NY: Cornell University Press.

Jeffery, P., Jeffery, R. and Lyon, A. 1989 *Labour Pains and Labour Power: Women and Childbearing in India*. London: Zed Books.

Jeffery, R. and Jeffery, P. 1993 Traditional birth attendants in rural north India: the social organization of childbearing. In S. Lindenbaum and M. Lock (eds.) *Knowledge, Power, and Practice: The Anthropology of Medicine and Everyday Life*. Berkeley: University of California Press, 7–31.

Jolly, M. 1991 'To save the girls for brighter and better lives': Presbyterian missions and women in the south of Vanuatu, 1848–1870. *Journal of Pacific History* 26(1):27–48.

1994 Motherlands? Some notes on women and nationalism in India and Africa. In M. Jolly (ed.) *Women's Difference: Sexuality and Maternity in Colonial and Postcolonial Discourses*. *Australian Journal of Anthropology* Special Issue 5(1&2):41–59.

1996 Devils, holy spirits and the swollen God: translation, conversion and colonial power in the Marist Mission, Vanuatu, 1887–1934. In P. van der Veer (ed.) *Conversion to Modernities: The Globalization of Christianity*. New York: Routledge, 231–62.

Keesing, R.M. 1985 Kwaio women speak: the micropolitics of autobiography in a Solomon Island society. *American Anthropologist* 87(1):27–39.

Kelly, J.D. 1991 *A Politics of Virtue: Hinduism, Sexuality, and Countercolonial Discourse in Fiji*. Chicago: University of Chicago Press.

Kitzinger, S. 1972 *The Experience of Childbirth*. London: Penguin Books.

Klaus, A. 1991 Depopulation and race suicide: maternalism and pronatalist ideologies in France and the United States. In G. Bock and P. Thane (eds.) *Maternity and Gender Policies: Women and the Rise of the European Welfare States, 1880s–1950s*. London: Routledge, 188–212.

Kristeva, J. 1980 Motherhood according to Giovanni Bellini. In J. Kristeva *Desire in Language: A Semiotic Approach to Literature and Art* (trans. T. Gora, A. Jardine and L.S. Roudiez, ed. L.S. Roudiez). New York: Columbia University Press, 237–70 .

1981 The maternal body. *m/f* 5&6:158–63.

Laderman, C. 1983 *Wives and Midwives: Childbirth and Nutrition in Rural Malaysia*. Berkeley: University of California Press.

Lukere, V. n.d.a Mothers of the Taukei. PhD thesis in preparation. The Australian National University, Canberra.

n.d.b Fijian women and the decrease of the race. Paper under consideration by a journal.

Lumley, J. and Astbury, J. 1980 *Birth Rites, Birth Rights: Childbirth Alternatives for Australian Parents*. Melbourne: Sphere Books, Thomas Nelson.

Martin, E. 1987 *The Woman in the Body: A Cultural Analysis of Reproduction.* Boston: Beacon Press.

Mitchell, T. 1988 *Colonizing Egypt.* Cairo: The American University in Cairo Press.

Oakley, A. 1980 *Women Confined: Towards a Sociology of Childbirth.* Oxford: Martin Robertson.

Ram, K. 1991 *Mukkuvar Women: Gender, Hegemony and Capitalist Transformation in a South Indian Fishing Community.* Sydney: Allen and Unwin.

1994 Medical management and giving birth: responses of coastal women in Tamil Nadu. *Motherhood, Fatherhood and Fertility. Reproductive Health Matters* Special Issue 4:20–6.

Rich, A. 1977 *Of Woman Born: Motherhood as Experience and Institution.* London: Virago Press.

Ross, E. 1995 Review essay: New thoughts on 'the oldest vocation': mothers and motherhood in recent feminist scholarship. *Signs* 20(2):397–413.

Ruddick, S. 1989 *Maternal Thinking: Towards a Politics of Peace.* London: The Women's Press.

Sacks, K. 1979 *Sisters and Wives: The Past and Future of Sexual Equality.* Westport: Greenwood Press.

Schemberg, A. 1995 *Motherhood and Reproduction: An International Bibliography.* Canberra: Gender Relations Project, The Australian National University.

Scheper-Hughes, N. 1992 *Death without Weeping: The Violence of Everyday Life in Brazil.* Berkeley: University of California Press.

Scott, J. 1991 The evidence of experience. *Critical Inquiry* 17:773–97.

Spivak, G.C. 1987 *In Other Worlds: Essays in Cultural Politics.* New York and London: Methuen.

1988 Can the subaltern speak? In C. Nelson and L. Grossberg (eds) *Marxism and the Interpretation of Culture.* Urbana: University of Illinois Press, 271–313.

Stanworth, M. 1987 (ed.) *Reproductive Technologies: Gender, Motherhood and Medicine.* Minneapolis: University of Minnesota Press.

Stivens, M. 1994 Gender and modernity in Malaysia. In A. Gomes (ed.) *Modernity and Identity: Asian Illustrations.* Bundoora: La Trobe University Press, 66–95.

Stoler, A. 1989 Making empire respectable: the politics of race and sexual morality in twentieth century colonial cultures. *American Ethnologist* 16(4):634–60.

1991 Carnal knowledge and imperial power: gender, race, and morality in colonial Asia. In M. di Leonardo (ed.) *Gender at the Crossroads of Knowledge: Feminist Anthropology in the Postmodern Era.* Berkeley: University of California Press, 51–101.

1992 Sexual affronts and racial frontiers: European identities and the cultural politics of exclusion in colonial Southeast Asia. *Comparative Studies in Society and History* 34(3):514–51.

1995 *Race and the Education of Desire: A Colonial Reading of Foucault's History of Sexuality.* Durham and London: Duke University Press.

Vaughan, M. 1991 *Curing their Ills: Colonial Power and African Illness.* Cambridge: Polity Press.

WHO (World Health Organization) 1990– *Safe Motherhood: Newsletter of Worldwide Activity in Maternal Health.* Geneva: WHO.

1 Shaping reproduction: maternity in early twentieth-century Malaya

Lenore Manderson

Defining maternity[1]

Over the past decade, the literature on maternity and motherhood has expanded dramatically. This has occurred not as a consequence or reflection of medical professional and state concern for maternal (and infant) health, but rather in the context of social, economic and ideological changes within industrialized societies, resulting in changes in the institutional settings of motherhood, in government policies towards reproduction and in the social meanings ascribed to it (Crouch and Manderson 1993). Concurrently, feminist scholarship has turned from the initial problem of the role of maternity in defining femaleness to interrogating its place in the social relations between men and women and among women, the meanings with which maternity as experience and status are imbued, and the tensions and accommodations of reproduction and production institutionally and personally in different places and under different systems of production. A driving concern has been to understand the macro-processes involved in maternity and motherhood, and the links between biology, psychology and culture, as addressed and problematized by writers such as Martin (1987) and Butler (1990).

This has resulted in numerous studies into the behaviours, practices and values of maternity (childbearing) and motherhood – child spacing, experiences of pregnancy, childbirth, confinement, breast-feeding, sexual practice and abstinence during pregnancy and lactation, child care, the medicalization of childbirth and mothering, foetal diagnosis and monitoring, in-vitro fertilization, infertility, 'late' or older motherhood, single motherhood, surrogacy, the choice not to have children, miscarriage, abortion, fertility control, postnatal depression – a list that might be endless, as reproduction and motherhood are documented, scrutinized and analysed (see e.g. Davis-Floyd 1992; Hull and Simpson 1985; Martin 1987; Michaelson 1988; Mitford 1992; Oakley 1980; Stanworth 1987). Yet for all this industry, much of the work over the past decade has centred on the industrialized (and English-speaking) world and has been driven by the local political concerns and agendas of Western feminisms. Meanings of maternity in other contexts, the ways in which these are shaped through the intersections of race, class and gender, and the relations of power over reproduction and production that are expressed in particular settings (including under colonialism), are ill-explored.[2]

Given the selectivity of our understanding of issues of reproduction and mothering, this volume's core concept – *maternity* – serves the ideal heuristic purpose, forcing us to tease out afresh the contrapuntal categories presumed to exist in 'being a mother'. Connotative of biology and the processes and experiences of pregnancy and birth as well as the broader cultural categories of mother and motherhood, incorporating the constitutive elements of biology and culture, process and status, identity and experience, the term maternity has global referents.

Does maternity have a history?

In an article on child health, Margaret Pelling (1988) points out the extent to which the published literature has focused on the health of younger children and maternal care of infants at the expense of older children.[3] And so it is with mothers, for even where aspects of mothering (breast-feeding, for example) are the objects of enquiry, the woman is invisible; her commentary on the nature of her relationship with her infant, or her perceptions of state interventions into domestic and personal affairs, are unrecorded and regarded as external to the enquiry. Such invisibility forces us, as we move from the present to the past, and from institutional history to the description of everyday life, to move from empiricism to an imagined reality in an attempt to give space and meaning to women, mothering and women's engagement with their children.

Maternity has received little attention in the written histories of colonial Malaya. That women conceived, gave birth and became mothers has been taken for granted or treated as static and 'natural', resulting in little commentary on women's maternal careers. The emotional and affectional dimensions of motherhood, too, have been presumed, or perhaps regarded as unimportant, although this is not unexceptional; the history of emotion, psychology and interpersonal relationships – like the broader field of the history of *mentalité* – is only now in the making, hampered by evidential problems. If we must rely on rare unpublished diaries and letters to supplement the thin published literature of women in the West to explore the meanings that they gave, in the past, to their social ties and emotional being, we have far less to draw on for other non-literate or otherwise silenced women to understand how they too might have regarded being a mother or being 'motherly'. For colonial Malaya, the fragmented and incidental comments on mothers and mothering in official departmental reports and in medical texts tell us more about colonial ideals and European ideologies than about the Malay, Indian or Chinese women purportedly described; in place of the behaviours, practices and values that might have been characteristic or constitutive of motherhood, we are offered an obstetric gaze that is synchronic, disembodying and technical. It is also male. Women's own commentaries exist, doubtlessly, in oral traditions and in the continued adherence to the rituals of pregnancy and birth that are elaborated and modified over time (Manderson 1981); for example, in women's stories of the past told to their daughters, granddaughters and others (Manderson 1984), and perhaps also in stories and songs. Their collection is another project.

The absence of women in the written record is not absolute, of course. In colonial writings and the discourse of medicine and administration the emphasis was always on pregnancy, the subjective focus the foetus and infant rather than woman. But with the discovery of the child, there was growing state interest in the behaviours of mothering, that is, how women fed, clothed and cared for their infants and children insofar as these were matters that might affect infant health. Other housekeeping activities too were subsumed and so subject to surveillance. Motherliness, as a set of behaviours and activities rather than emotions, was no longer taken for granted, and the state through the offices of its medical services questioned women's ability to mother 'naturally'. Mothering was medicalized, transposed to various colonial contexts, systematically incorporated into text and subject to state intervention.

The history of maternity, therefore, is shaped by the imbrication of ideologies of motherhood, empire and medicine. In this chapter, I focus on maternity and the intrusions of the state in colonial Malaya (the Straits Settlements, and the Federated and Unfederated Malay States; see Map 2).[4] The state's discovery of the child and its gradual consequent extension of interest, interference, surveillance and control in reproduction and mothering were linked to developments in the imperial centre; ideas were transferred to and imposed upon other peoples in very different settings and contexts for political, economic and ideological purposes. The interest in reproduction in Malaya by colonial authorities derived in part from a pragmatic concern, driven by the political economy of colonialism and aimed at reducing infant mortality to maintain a future workforce (Manderson 1987a and 1989), but related, too, to the processes that Stoler has termed 'the modernization of colonial control' (1989:639) and to state concern to temper the costs of imperialism by the provision of various welfare services (Manderson 1987b).

Map 2 Colonial British Malaya, Straits Settlements and Federated
and Unfederated Malay States as referred to in text

Government supervision and control of maternity took place via the surveillance of midwives and the provision of antenatal and postnatal services, home visiting and health education from the early 1900s. These initiatives were instigated in the United Kingdom in light of growing concern with reproduction, which resulted in programmes that emphasized the role of the middle class in policing working-class mothers; they were extended to colonial settings where they were predicated upon notions of the moral superiority of the colonizers as well as the technical superiority of their science. In colonial Malaya, state supervision of maternity took account of the existence of a system operating outside of biomedicine, and the aim of intervention was initially to control rather than replace village midwifery and maternity care. Early legislation and the training, registration and supervision of midwives served primarily to restrict and contain practices that occurred outside of the colonial medical services and colonial practice. The error, though, was to underestimate the extent and pervasiveness of these other practices and their cultural meanings.[5]

Discovering women

In a world dominated by men – the Malay male court elite, farmers and fishermen, British colonists, planters and adventurers, English and Indian troops, Chinese miners and rickshaw pullers, Indian merchants and rubber tappers – it is easy to see how a government might overlook maternity, an experience fundamentally antithetic and threatening to the homosociality and homosocial solidarity (Suleri 1992:80) of the early colonies. From the mid-nineteenth century, however, women emerge in small defined niches, most often as prostitutes, as venereal vectors rather than subjects. The lives of these women were described to preclude maternity, but this was a myth, and whilst stripped of free agency and confined by the racial and sexual geography of the colonial city, many prostitutes had children: the brothels of the ports and trading towns of the colony were also sites of conception, birth and mothering.

Women's work in prostitution was acknowledged, on the other hand, and those employed in brothels were subject to state interventions from the late nineteenth century; hence fragments of their histories exist in the archives of the state (see Lai 1986; Manderson 1996; Warren 1990). By contrast, other women living and working in the colonies, including peasant farmers, concubines, courtesans, traders, weavers, and others, were sometimes mentioned in passing, but the circumstances of their daily lives, the conditions of living and their health is subject to preemptory treatment. We know, for example, that on some estates as many as 25 per cent of Indian labourers were women; until well into the twentieth century they had no antenatal or other health care; they lived in crowded conditions, often sharing single rooms with other unmarried men as well as their husbands (Straits Settlements 1890). Other Chinese women worked as domestic servants, labourers, cleaners and in coffee shops, tea houses and hotels (Lai 1986; cf. Stoler 1989, 1992); their circumstances too received relatively little attention.

The sex ratio was extremely skewed among immigrants, although not for Malays. But Malay women, with their men economically as well as geographically marginal to the processes of the creation of the colonial capitalist state, were not subject to the colonial gaze during the nineteenth century; the circumstances of their maternity did not impinge upon imperial prospects. Those whose lives did intersect with the lives of the colonists in very specific ways – as the concubine-housekeepers of English men (Butcher 1979) – have shadowy, unspoken histories and maternities.

Late in the nineteenth century, English women arrived in Malaya as colonists' wives, feminizing the domestic space and establishing a more permanent colonial presence (Brownfoot 1984; Butcher 1979).[6] This provided for the emotional, sexual and daily reproductive needs of English men, thereby sharpening the divide between rulers and ruled, and by heading off further intermixture of race and blurring the categories of class and ethnicity, it sought to forestall the diminution of empire (Stoler 1989). At the same time, it facilitated the extension of the ideological arms of empire to all women. English women's concern with their own maternity, infant care and the health and education of their children flowed over to the maternity and mothering of other women, and state services were developed in response. In consequence, English nursing staff moved into the lives of other women as English men withdrew from them.

The sexual and cultural politics of colonial Malaya shaped the aims and objectives of maternal and child health services. The focus was on Malay maternity, and specific interventions were influenced by the negative imagery of Malay village life and conditions: dark, airless houses, a pathogenic environment, birthing women controlled by the village *bidan* cast as witch (old, stupid, ignorant, superstitious, dirty) (e.g. see Manderson 1987a, 1989, 1992). Government policy and programmes relating to midwifery services and infant health positioned the colonial state to the Malay polity in a way that was in line with general policies of governance and other areas of intervention (e.g. education, see Manderson 1978) – it was a benign, *maternal* administration. This benevolence to the Malay community contrasted with the government approach to immigrant groups: here the state was self-interested in the male workforce and

ambivalent to the women. Indian women worked with men on plantations in a space dominated numerically and physically by men, hence
(though paid less) they were *as if* men, not mothers; and Chinese women
were the whores (not mothers) of other subject men. Malay women,
despite occasional sexual liaisons, were least threatening (and threatened), their otherness was preserved not only through their separation
from English men but also from English homes. Malay, Chinese and
Indian men rather than women worked as 'houseboys' to provide the
labour to sustain the colonial residences, and they did some of the work of
mothering for English children, although Chinese women were employed
in this capacity also from the 1930s (Lai 1986:80). In general the links
between women were kept distant and English middle-class mothering
occurred too late in Malaya for wet-nurse ties to confound further the
emotional ties of the colonial economy. The employment of men as 'boys'
avoided, unintentionally or not, the possibility of shared mothering,
hence female solidarity across race and class. Suleri's 'economy of the
borrowed breast' (1992:81) was transmuted by the economy of the bottle
(Manderson 1982), and the mediating fluid of intercultural connections
in colonial Malaya was (still) semen, not breast milk.[7]

Imagining birth

Carol Laderman's work (1983, 1987), based on ethnographic research
undertaken in Trengganu in the 1970s, documents the 'traditional' management of pregnancy, birth and the puerperium, and in so doing draws
attention to the social importance of midwives and healers in Malay
society and clarifies the reluctance of women, at the time of her writing
and much earlier, to present to clinics and hospitals for maternal care.
The rituals of pregnancy, attendant care during labour and observation of
the puerperium highlight the social value as well as corporeal stresses of
reproduction. Among Malay women, the puerperium is especially elaborated and involves mother-roasting (*bersalin*), smoke baths and dietary
regulation to ensure return to equilibrium of humoural balance, to revert
the uterus and tone the vagina, and ensure continuing health, while also
providing the mother with time to adjust to the newborn and to establish
breast-feeding (Laderman 1983; Manderson 1981). Among Chinese and
Indian women similar observances, usually for a slightly shorter period,
pertain. This is a period largely ignored by early and much more recent
obstetric services where the emphasis has been on pregnancy and labour,
and the delivery of a live infant is the primary and final attainment.

In Singapore, a maternity hospital had been built in 1888 and by 1907
it provided sixteen beds for 'native' as well as thirteen beds for European

women (*Straits Times* 22 May 1907:8). Elsewhere in the colonies women were encouraged and able to deliver in government hospitals, but there were few beds, no women doctors and an inadequate number of nurses. Around the turn of the century, hospitals tended to be staffed by male hospital assistants and native dressers whose services were not regarded as appropriate by women. Women were wary too of hospitals as places of death, not birth, and the occasional closure of wards (because of infection among inmates or because of need for repairs) reinforced their views (Straits Settlements 1904:731).[8] European and Eurasian women tended to deliver in hospital, but few Tamil, Sikh and Chinese women did so, and virtually all Malay women had village births, usually in their natal home. Here, whilst the social and personal needs of the birthing woman were well met from the point of view of the health and medical officers of the state, infant health was compromised, particularly due to lack of antiseptic procedure for cord care, which resulted in neonatal tetanus.[9]

The circumstances of birth for many women in colonial Malaya lacked even the care and nurture that characterized safe midwife-tended village births. Indian and Chinese women may have called upon Malay *bidan* to assist, and government reports of the preference for Malay birth attendants by women from all backgrounds supports this contention (Manderson 1992). In some cases, though, women may not have had access to *bidan* care, or progressed in labour too quickly, or were too far away to summon for help, and they would have given birth alone. And so it must have been even in cities, where women feared or were suspicious of hospital services, where there were no women doctors, or where lack of personal mobility (under the quasi-slave circumstances of the brothel) or the need to maintain secrecy prevented them from seeking help. The health of registered prostitutes, and of other urban women, was poor. They were constantly reinfected with syphilis and gonorrhoea, abscesses and warts. While venereal disease such as gonorrhoea would have resulted in a high rate of infertility, some women must have conceived and sought illegal and dangerous abortions, or miscarried, or worked through pregnancy and given birth alone or with the help of a co-worker in unsanitary conditions. No less than any other women in the community, they would have sustained perineal and vaginal tears during labour.

Maternal mortality for women from all backgrounds was around 16 per 1,000 at the turn of the century and still 9.7 per 1,000 in 1931, with deaths primarily from postpartum haemorrhage and eclampsia, placenta praevia, septicaemia and various fevers; their infants died from prematurity, tetanus and convulsions (see e.g. Straits Settlements 1937:522).[10] Other factors, too, contributed to women's poor health, pregnancy losses, maternal and infant mortality. The poor health status of Tamil women provoked recurrent comment by health officers in contact with the estate population, and anaemia from malaria, hookworm and poor nutritional status would all have affected their pregnancies and pregnancy outcomes. Maternity-leave provisions meant too that women needed to work as long as possible through pregnancy, and low wages resulted in their early return to work after delivery. Compared with the infant mortality rate, however, maternal morbidity and mortality attracted little concern. 'Maternal and child health' was important predominantly because of the role of mothers as carers and nurturers, and the extent to which primary health care and public health programmes benefited women directly was largely incidental.

In this context it is important to emphasize women's general poor health and, hence, what giving birth – and other bodily processes and experiences – might have been like. A medical paper, published in the *Malayan Medical Journal* in the mid-1920s, offers some insight in this respect, as it draws our attention to the way in which disease literally ate away women's bodies, causing infertility and making maternity problematic (Galloway 1926). For those able to conceive and carry to term, ill health rendered childbirth fearful and painful. The material in this and similar texts is sensational, and one should not discount also its didactic moral subtext. But its value is its clinical explicitness; the material gives us some insight into those factors that enabled the medicalization of childbirth in the colonies, and that therefore brought about the connection of home and clinic.

The extent of venereal infection in the colony is impossible to assess; Galloway regarded it as so prevalent among men that it 'must appear in the anamnesis of nearly every illness' (1926:1). His description of lymph node infection in the groin, due to various venereal infections, is horrendous: internal and external ulceration, 'sloughy sore[s] with [a] hard base . . . creeping on at one part while healing at another' (1926:3). One woman presents with her urethral canal eroded by an ulcer. Other cases suffer 'more severe' internal infection, high temperatures, 'exquisite pelvic tenderness', fevers, swollen glands, badly inflamed cervix, rigid vaginal walls (p. 3). Some of these women would have been infertile, but the description draws our attention to the prevalence of untreated urogenital infections and forces us to imagine the effect of delivery and tearing for women with such infections. The imagery of midwifery-attended village birth is compelling (Jordan 1978), but it fails to accommodate the real risks faced by some women in the absence of even the limited technology that early obstetrics could offer (see also Dureau and Rozario, this volume).

The discovery of the child

By the early twentieth century, the child had been discovered. More precisely, as a result of a series of political events in Britain, infant mortality and child health had been subject to public scrutiny; in colonial Malaya, these events as well as the local political economy led to major changes in health policy and practice.

Both imperial history and the development of state demography contributed to the discovery of the child in Britain. The Boer War was a major impetus. Working-class men recruited to fight suffered from poor health and performed badly as soldiers. The 1901 census drew attention, too, to a declining birth rate and increasing infant mortality rate, leading in turn to scrutiny of conditions of urban and industrial life, infant and child health and welfare, and midwifery practice. Concern for the high infant mortality rate and poor child health in the United Kingdom, particularly among the industrial working class, occurred parallel to a new awareness of the links between child and empire: between infant health, child survival, physical well-being and the politics and economics of the state (Davin 1978; see also Fildes *et al.* 1992; Jolly, this volume: Introduction; Lewis 1980a and 1980b). This concern for infant mortality occurred at a time of enthusiasm for empire – hence the concern with the poor soldiering skills, stamina and physique of working-class army recruits. This was also a time when Britain was competing with other European states for control, power and prestige, when imperial power was dependent upon *man*power and when there was a perceived need for an expanding British population to fill the spaces of the margins of the Empire (Davin 1978). The high infant mortality rate and poor health of surviving children in the United Kingdom depleted the nation of a 'national asset' (Davin 1978:10–11), and eugenicists, politicians and doctors together argued for health interventions to ensure 'stalwart sons to people the colonies and to uphold the prestige of the nation' (Lewis 1988:307; also Szreter 1988, 1991). In addition, Britain needed an able-bodied workforce to feed its expanding industry. In response, a number of remedial steps were taken: the Midwives Act was introduced in 1902 to ensure that practising midwives were trained and births registered; subsequent regulations allowed for the provision of school meals and inspection of children; and in 1908, the Children's Act set out detailed provisions for child health and welfare.

In Malaya the need for labour – for mining and plantations – was paramount. Until around 1900 labour needs were met through adult immigration, but the high adult death rate (up to 50 per cent in the first year) meant that the cost of replacement was high, and the more efficient long-term strategy was to reproduce the labour force locally, hence placing both Malay and immigrant reproductive practice under imperial gaze. In this light, the infant mortality rate of 250–350 was of great concern and the governments of the Straits Settlements and Malay States took a number of steps to reduce infant mortality and to improve life expectancy. Interventions were aimed initially at midwifery services. In this, colonial doctors were much influenced by ideas in the United Kingdom. Health and medical officers from the colonies attended conferences in Britain, such as those of the National Association for the Prevention of Infant Mortality, and on their return submitted detailed reports of papers 'intended to show how the ignorance [of mothers] could be frustrated by means of instructed midwives, district nurses, and health visitors' (Clarke 1913:4).

As noted, the infant mortality rate was high at the turn of the century, around 250 per 1,000, although with considerable variation by year, between and within states, according to season and ethnicity. Variations occurred, too, as a consequence of the reliability of data, and whilst the Straits Settlements had a high infant mortality rate due to overcrowding and poor sanitation (hence a high incidence of acute respiratory infections and diarrhoeal diseases), it is also true that surveillance was greater and reporting of births and deaths nearer to accurate in these relatively small and dense administrative units. By contrast, in the Federated and especially the Unfederated Malay States, a substantial number of deaths (although also births) were unrecorded.

Causes of infant deaths are unclear. Many were uncertified and reported as due to *sawan* (convulsions), which would have included neonatal tetanus, but other causes also: in 1909, for example, 65 per cent of infant deaths recorded for Penang, Malacca, Singapore and environs were due to neonatal tetanus, malaria and deaths from 'dietetic errors' (Straits Settlements 1909:469). These reports drew attention to proximate causes, including those associated with midwifery practice and neonatal care, other social factors were implicated, and contemporary commentators recognized the extent to which illness was produced under specific sets of social, environmental and economic conditions. In Malaya, they included environmental conditions such as housing and sanitation, the prevalence of endemic diseases such as malaria, maternal and infant nutrition, midwifery training and practice, and child-rearing practices considered to compromise infant health.

Control of midwifery

Maternal and child health programmes were from the outset a government rather than a mission concern[11] and were introduced in the Malayan colonies from 1905. Village midwives or *bidan* received in-service training and were registered; other local women were also trained in basic nursing and midwifery to replace *bidan* as birth attendants and community nurses; home visits were instituted; and infant welfare centres were established. The first strategies were seen to facilitate the last, since midwives were regarded as gatekeepers, whose support or resistance to Western health services would determine community acceptance and compliance. Medical officers argued that birth attendance by registered and qualified midwives would have the immediate effect of bringing down the infant and maternal mortality rates, but also that the involvement of village midwives was an 'excellent method of furthering acquaintance of the kampong [village] Malay with Western medicine' (Kempe 1933:6).

As in the United Kingdom, the first steps taken to reduce the infant mortality rate focused on midwifery practice, directly addressing risks of death from 'accidents of childbirth' and neonatal tetanus. This was a pragmatic move, dictated by the preferred and possible circumstances of pregnancy and labour. Further, despite the trend towards medicalization of childbirth (for Britain, see Lewis 1980a; Oakley 1976), medical opinion at the turn of the century still tended to represent childbirth itself as normal rather than pathological, and in the United Kingdom as well as the colonies, primary emphasis was placed on improved domiciliary care.

Moves to train local Malay women were underway in the Settlements by 1910; this had occurred in all states, to some degree, by the late 1920s (Manderson 1989, 1992). Malay women were usually recruited to receive Western midwifery training, although some Chinese women were also trained; as already noted, the preference for Malay women related both to the reluctance of Malays to use non-Malay birth attendants and to the popularity of *bidan* among other women. Both practising midwives and other women desiring to become midwives were trained, although recruitment and retention of staff was poor. Women received lectures on antiseptic delivery practices, the diagnosis and referral of obstetric problems, cord care, and infant care and feeding. Registered midwives were classified and remunerated accordingly. In line with contemporary views about race, knowledge and standards of health and hygiene, their practices were supervised by other senior, and almost always European, women.

Home visiting

Alternative government strategies to reduce infant mortality centred on the mother and presupposed that infant mortality reflected women's inability, in light of lack of training, to be good and proper mothers. The first step in the supervision and education of mothers was home visiting.

Again, Britain provided the model. Home visiting was initiated in the United Kingdom in a number of towns, on a voluntary basis, from around 1860. From 1890 salaried home visitors were appointed in Manchester to inspect homes and provide advice on the management of common ailments, infant care and feeding (Davies 1988; Szreter 1988). Under these schemes, preference was given for women appointed as home visitors to be of similar class and background to those they would visit.

In Malaya, this was difficult, since no native woman was considered educated enough in infant care and mothercraft to undertake this role and even Eurasian women were regarded as unreliable; health visitors were ideally European (Selangor Secretariat (hereafter Sel. Sec.) 3006/1915:10, 13–14). The role of the home visitor was to provide the visited woman with minimal knowledge of health and hygiene to reduce infant deaths and to encourage her to attend the nearest infant welfare centre for continued advice regarding infant feeding and care and to enable the infant's health to be monitored. The first home visit occurred soon after birth, once it had been registered with the local police post, and the police in turn had notified the district health office. The first women health inspectors were appointed in urban areas of Singapore, Malacca and Penang from around 1911, and in 1914 a trained nurse was appointed to visit new mothers in Kuala Lumpur also (Sel. Sec. 3156/1915:20). This was extended to rural Malacca and Penang in 1927, and later in other states after infant welfare clinics attached to general hospitals had begun operation.

As noted, a major purpose of home visiting was to encourage women to attend the infant welfare clinic to enable their infants to be monitored and to increase their familiarity with the centre, staff and hospital services. It was hoped that this would increase women's use of the clinic, encourage them to present for antenatal care during future pregnancies, and seek biomedical advice and care when they or their infants were sick (Colonial Office (CO) 859/46/12101/4A, 1943:6). Health staff hypothesized that a proportion of infant deaths were the result of lack of immediate medical attention, and that early diagnosis and treatment would save lives. Home visitors also offered new mothers advice on the care and feeding of the well infant, transferring contemporary notions of the 'scientific' routine management of infants – regularized feeding, limited handling and so on[12] – ideas discordant with conventional Malay styles of mothering (Djamour 1965:100) and best suited to middle-class or elite English households where there was the least risk of disturbance or distress caused by a crying infant (Davin 1978:47–8).

A major concern was with the decline in the incidence and duration of breast-feeding and the practice of withholding colostrum and feeding infants rice water or banana until the let-down of milk (Manderson 1982, 1984). Reasons for the use of cow's milk, condensed milk and infant formula varied and included the increasing availability of tinned milk, baby formulas and other baby foods, and milk products, marketed by Nestlé, Glaxo and other milk companies from 1890 coincident with the arrival of English women and the establishment of the colonial family. This shift from breast to bottle was consolidated in the 1920s with the distribution of powdered and sweetened condensed milk by infant welfare clinics to improve infant nutritional status: doctors and nursing staff believed that the breast milk of Malay women was 'deficient' due to their restricted postpartum diet. Women were influenced, too, by the patterns of feeding followed by expatriate and wealthy local women, and the implied association of bottle-feeding and modernity; others bottle-fed because of the difficulties of nursing once they were working as wage labourers away from home, without nursery facilities or time off to breast-feed (Manderson 1982, and see Hunt 1988 for comparative material). By the early twentieth century bottled milk was readily available in urban centres, and even in remote rural areas of the states increasing numbers of women bottle-fed as well as breast-fed. This led to a rise in the number of infants brought to hospitals with diarrhoea caused by 'improper feeding' with tinned milk, from as early as 1907; the association between poor infant health and bottle-feeding was recognized widely much later (e.g. Carson 1940:6).

The clinics

Infant welfare centres were established by medical departments throughout the Straits Settlements and Federated Malay States by the late 1920s and in the Unfederated Malay States by the late 1930s. Singapore and Malacca municipalities also ran infant welfare clinics, and the Singapore Children's Welfare Society operated two more clinics for women factory workers. By 1936, there were seventy centres and nine subcentres in the colonies, each with a minimum staff of a health nurse, midwife and attendant. At clinics, health workers weighed the infant, followed up issues arising from home visits and gave advice on infant feeding and care. Ritual weighing and temperature-taking and the treatment of minor illness took up most clinic time, although the role of the clinics in preventive medicine and public health was given high value in the rhetoric of maternal and child health by government officials, as a means of justifying expenditure and effort in this area (cf. Reid 1984). Infant welfare centres resorted to various strategies to encourage women to bring their infants to the centres: providing transport, distributing milk and holding baby shows. Their success varied. In the Federated Malay States, for example, infant welfare centres were reported to be receiving good support from parents: 56,916 in 1925, 61,365 in 1926. But attendance was irregular even when clinic sessions were backed up by an extensive home visiting programme, and women's presentation varied according to availability of transport, agricultural and social obligations, and clinic staffing (Manderson 1992). In addition to monitoring infants and treating minor ailments, centres supervised local midwives and distributed basic obstetric equipment to them. They also offered basic health education by individual counselling to mothers and special displays and exhibitions at the centres and elsewhere, designed to teach mothers how to feed, clothe and care for their infants 'properly' and to avoid 'objectionable and injurious practices' such as feeding infants with rice water or banana from birth (Federated Malay States 1932:56 and 1937:20). Lack of time for preventive and promotive as well as curative work in the clinics, however, meant that this work was rarely given sufficient attention.

The clinic served other ideological purposes. It was the synecdoche of the beneficent face of colonialism, colonialism *as* mother, the setting where emotion work (the nature of mothering) and practice (the culture of motherhood) connected, even though increasingly the nature or naturalness of emotion was in question, and the need to train women to be mothers extended beyond bathing and feeding baby (for working-class women as well as colonized women). The role of the clinic sister was to anaesthetize the assaults of colonialism by supplanting relations of colonizer:colonized with those of mother:child, replacing the metaphor (and experience) of rape with that of nurture, male with female. The medium of change was that of commoditized friendship, which at least recognized that women might operate in ways which dissolved, ignored or challenged the boundaries between public and private. But the clinic was still English/colonial, dominated by expatriate women operating within their own time-bound ideas of mothering and maternity in urban, controlled spaces rather than the least colonized rural areas, and there were too many gaps for either the clinic sessions or home visits to be effective. As noted above, women were reluctant to go to hospitals or clinics, nervous of institutional medicine and warned off by the poor outcome of those who, presenting when seriously ill, did not survive. There was high staff turnover, too, and this and the overall lack of women doctors and nurses also discouraged presentation and compliance.[13] Further, the English nurses who provided advice were single and (presumably) childless – government regulations and the need for mobility ensured this. By the 1930s, the inadequacy of this was recognized, although the steps taken to resolve this underlined the gaps also between class and race, as colonial officers' wives were co-opted to help professional lady doctors and nurses.

Class and language must have operated to sustain the boundaries of the relations of colonialism, and the racism and fear of the most committed women infiltrated clinic encounters. Even liberal women (and men) accepted notions of racial difference that allowed for a European sensibility, which found the tropics antagonistic and enervating. The poor response of 'native' women to health services was explained in terms of their perceived intellectual shortcomings, resulting in the limited effectiveness of health education designed at behavioural change. The following text of maternal and child health work describes clinical care and health education in Kedah and Perlis in the late 1930s. It highlights the essentialism that informed understandings of native women (primarily as educable), as well as illustrating a medical model of the pregnant woman as reproductive equipment. Here the body is overhauled, teeth pulled; the products of maternity – babies – are registered, weighed, measured, reassessed:

Expectant mothers, who come in [to the maternity ward of the hospital] for a period beforehand, can be overhauled and given a certain amount of treatment before the child is due. The majority have intestinal parasites and some degree of anaemia. Many have dental cavities – but they have not yet been educated to part with their bad teeth while pregnant. All lying-in mothers, while in the ward, are urged to continue breastfeeding at home. They are given a card on which is the baby's weight and advised to return to the hospital or attend the Town Dispensary for further weighing and to take the card with them. A fair percentage do return, but it is not unusual to find that the babies have gained 4 or 5 pounds in the first month due to irregular and overfeeding. An attack of Colic or Diarrhoea then sends the mother to seek advice – and after a further homily on feeding, she seems to realise the mistake of giving the breast or the bottle to the child every time it cries . . . and that there is a limit to the capacity of a baby's stomach. (Dr M.G. Brodie, in Carson 1940:7)

Teaching maternity

During the first few decades of maternal and child health services in colonial Malaya, the number of women who presented and continued to use clinic services rose steadily. By the late 1930s, around 800,000 women were estimated to receive home visits or attend clinic sessions throughout the colonies, although clinic attendance was not predictable and, in the Unfederated States especially, local Malay communities remained suspicious of outpatient clinics and hospitals.

The utility and efficiency of maternal and child health services were evaluated on sessional attendance and compliance with clinic advice, rather than on the nature of the service; in a spirit of victim-blaming, resistance to biomedical health services and the adoption of 'hygienic practice' was explained as 'cultural'. According to the personal biases of those providing the evaluations – usually the same people as those offering the services – it was argued that Malay, Chinese, Indian or the 'poorer class' of women took least advantage of European medical and nursing services and advice. Disappointment in the success of the maternal and child health programme – that is, continued reliance on and support of village midwives and poor uptake of English ways of infant care – led to a shift in government programme emphasis from adult women to younger unmarried women. Although domestic science was included in the earliest curriculum for girls to encourage school attendance and to meet longer-term health goals (Manderson 1978), the incorporation of housecraft and mothercraft skills expanded in the twentieth century and included sewing, cooking, laundry, weaving, household cleaning, household management, hygiene and latrine use. This was in light of a heightened recognition of women's role in daily reproduction and, since acceptance of Western notions of health and ill health incorporated a particular ideology or logic, also for the social reproduction of colonial society (Manderson 1992). Greater emphasis was placed on domestic science and hygiene teaching in the 1930s, too, in response to criticism of colonialism and the nutritional and health status of its subject peoples, within British Malaya, by non-government organizations and from within the Colonial Office itself.[14]

The fullest representation of the value of education for maternity was made by Mary Blacklock of the Liverpool School of Tropical Medicine, who in 1935 toured the British colonies of Asia (and Palestine) to assess the welfare of women and children. She found that state interventions in maternal and child health had not been successful: mortality rates were still high; medical services for women were inadequate; and education rates and literacy were low, primarily because of the systematic reluctance of governments to allocate adequate resources or demonstrate their commitment to women's health and education (Blacklock 1936). Blacklock's proposal to strengthen clinical services for women and children, while improving their education opportunities and ensuring an appropriate curriculum, called for more maternity centres and wards, more women doctors to be recruited from Britain to the colonies, more local staff, and increased home visiting. These proposals had obvious continuity with earlier initiatives in colonial Malaya and reflected thinking of other colonists concerned to dilute the exploitative costs of empire and justify continued control (e.g. Great Britain 1939a, 1939b). The value of her report was its comprehensive treatment of the issues of maternity and the state, and the debate that ensued on the value and content of female education, infant welfare and the provision of maternal and child health services continued within the Colonial Office in London throughout the war.

Conclusion

Native Malay and other immigrant women were recipients of primary health care education, although some were also involved in the provision of home-based health care services and education, under the supervision of European women. But the activities of European women were no less circumscribed by gender, directing working women into these fields and presuming the responsibility of all women, whether or not in paid employment, for reproduction. Thus it was argued that all women going from the United Kingdom to the colonies should undertake a short course on hygiene, maternity, child welfare, cooking, elementary epidemiology, and that the course should be compulsory for any woman colonial officer, regardless of her actual post – school teachers, the wives of male colonial officers and women working with missionary societies in the field of education should all be so trained.[15] In addition, there was considerable discussion regarding the potential of women's voluntary associations such as the Women's Institutes to supplement the state in home visiting and other voluntary work in the areas of mothercraft, infant feeding and care, and primary health care.

The focus was on the child and infant health, but to effect change, preventive medical services and health education programmes were directed towards women, including health practitioners (*bidan*) and those responsible for family health on an everyday basis, in whose hands (or, rather, bodies) lay the responsibility of the reproduction of future generations. As noted, developments in colonial Malaya in the fields of education, health and medicine, and in social welfare, reflected ideological changes and practical developments in England as well as local circumstance. The surveillance of village midwifery practice and the incorporation of pregnancy and birth into hospital-based medicine, the establishment of home visiting, the development of maternal and child clinics, and the expansion of domestic science education all reflected developments in the United Kingdom, and built upon notions of reproduction informed by conventional understandings of gender, race and class. Maternal and child health care programmes were developed on the basis of understandings of the role of women in biological, social and daily reproduction, which assumed that some women, by virtue of class and race, were able to undertake these roles 'naturally'.

In Malaya, European women, or at least the middle-class wives of colonial officers, could be 'natural' mothers, but this was not necessarily so for Indian, Malay and Chinese women, who had to be taught to feed, care, nurture and treat their infants and children. There was further irony and confused reasoning, too, as culture and climate were collapsed as one; hence, conditions in the tropics were believed to 'react with particular severity upon the health of mothers and children', thus the high infant and maternal mortality rates also justified 'adequate supervision' by European health workers (CO 859/46/12101/4A, 1943:7–8). Training women to become mothers, it was hoped, would be the most effective intervention against the high infant mortality rate, and this was in Mary Blacklock's mind the *primary* function of the clinics (Blacklock 1936:224). The approach side-stepped economic and structural factors that had already been identified as contributing to poor health outcomes, and provided government with 'an easy way out': 'It was', as Davin (1978:26) has observed, 'cheaper to blame them [mothers] and to organize a few classes than to expand social and medical services.'

NOTES

1 Preliminary work for this chapter was undertaken whilst a Visiting Fellow at the Wellcome Unit for the History of Medicine, University of Oxford, 1992. I am very grateful to my colleagues in the Unit for their hospitality and their generosity with ideas, resources and time. The chapter draws on my earlier work in this area on midwifery, mothering and infant health, and education policy in Malaya, and from a chapter in my book *Sickness and the State* (1996); hence the unavoidable peppering of self-citation throughout the text. Archival research was supported financially by the Australian National University, the University of New South Wales, Tropical Health Program of the University of Queensland, and ARC Grant No.18015635.
2 Surprisingly, this lack of attention to historical variations has occurred despite anthropological interest in reproduction and difference (e.g. Davis-Floyd 1992; Jordan 1978; Kay 1982; MacCormack 1982; Martin 1987).
3 Pelling notes that 'as with other more or less "invisible" groups in history, the nature of the source dictates that we are forced . . . into discussing attitudes to the child and events happening to the child, rather than [describing and interpreting events from] the child's own point of view' (1988:138).
4 The Straits Settlements included Singapore, Malacca and Penang; the Federated Malay States incorporated Perak, Selangor, Pahang and Negri Sembilan; the Unfederated Malay States – where colonial rule was least direct – comprised Kedah, Perlis, Kelantan, Trengganu and Johore.
5 Malay childbirth, for example, involved not only *bidan* (traditional midwife) but also *bomoh* (healer), whose specific interventions in the case of obstructed labour (Laderman 1987) raises interesting questions of the psychology of birth whilst highlighting the integration of the physical and spiritual, corporeal and metaphysical in village Malaya.

6 A number of works describe the presence and role of white women in colonial societies, including Knapman (1986) and Callaway (1987), critiqued by Haggis (1990); see also Jolly (1993); Ramusack (1990); Stoler (1989, 1992); and Suleri (1992).

7 That is, between men, and between English men and indigenous/immigrant women, though not – according to the record – between English women and indigenous men.

8 The perception of the hospital as a site of infection and death was realistic, although not only in the colonies – hence the significance of Nightingale's reforms.

9 The umbilicus would be cut with bamboo or a household knife, the stump dusted with wood ash or a paste of pepper, ginger and turmeric. Infection often occurred.

10 In the Unfederated States, it remained around 16/1,000 throughout the pre-war period, due, according to official records, to 'early marriage and the ignorant native midwife' (Bridges 1930:12).

11 This compares with other areas, where maternal and child health services were primarily the work of missions and government health continued to focus primarily on the immediate health and medical needs of the labour force (see e.g. Beinart 1992; Denoon 1989; Vaughan 1991; and contributions in Fildes et al. 1992).

12 Popularized by Truby King in the 1930s; see Olssen (1981).

13 However, the Malayan colonies were better served than any of the other British colonies (see Colonial Office 859/1/1201/19, 1939).

14 See e.g. Fabian Colonial Bureau 1944; Great Britain 1939a, 1939b; Worboys 1988.

15 See e.g. Sel. Sec. G544/1937:1A, p. 3; cf. Denoon (1989:39) for Papua New Guinea, where missions were largely responsible for child health pre-World War II, in line with a government view that child health could best be handled in association with the missions.

REFERENCES

Beinart, J. 1992 Darkly through a lens: changing perceptions of the African child in sickness and health, 1900–1945. In R. Cooter (ed.) *In the Name of the Child: Health and Welfare, 1880–1940*. London: Routledge, 220–43.

Blacklock, M. 1936 Certain aspects of the welfare of women and children in the colonies. *Annals of Tropical Medicine and Parasitology* 30:221–64.

Bridges, D. 1930 Kedah and Perlis. *The Annual Report of the Medical and Health Departments for the Year 1347 A.H. (20th June 1928 to 8th June 1929)*. Alor Star: Government Press.

Brownfoot, J.N. 1984 Memsahibs in colonial Malaya: a study of European wives in a British colony and protectorate, 1900–1940. In H. Callan and S. Ardener (eds.) *The Incorporated Wife*. London: Croom Helm, 186–210.

Butcher, J. 1979 *The British in Malaya, 1880–1941: The Social History of a European Community in Colonial Southeast Asia*. Kuala Lumpur: Oxford University Press.

Butler, J. 1990 *Gender Trouble: Feminism and the Subversion of Identity*. New York and London: Routledge.

Callaway, H. 1987 *Gender, Culture and Empire: European Women in Colonial Nigeria*. London: Macmillan.

Carson, J.C. 1940 *Kedah and Perlis. Annual Report of the Medical Department for 1938*. Alor Star: Government Press.

Clarke, J.T. 1913 *Report on Conferences of the National Association for the Prevention of Infant Mortality and for the Welfare of Infancy, London 4–5 August 1913*. In Files of the Selangor Secretariat, Sel. Sec. 3006/1915.

Crouch, M. and Manderson, L. 1993 *New Motherhood: Cultural and Personal Transitions in the 1980s*. Chur, Switzerland: Harwood Academic Publishers.

Davies, C. 1988 The Health Visitor as mother's friend: a woman's place in public health, 1900–1914. *Social History of Medicine* 1(1):39–59.

Davin, A. 1978 Imperialism and motherhood. *History Workshop* 5:9–65.

Davis-Floyd, R.E. 1992 *Birth as an American Rite of Passage*. Berkeley: University of California Press.

Denoon, D. (with K. Dugan and L. Marshall) 1989 *Public Health in Papua New Guinea: Medical Possibility and Social Constraint, 1884–1984*. Cambridge: Cambridge University Press.

Djamour, J. 1965 *Malay Kinship and Marriage in Singapore*. London: The Athlone Press.

Fabian Colonial Bureau 1944 *Hunger and Health in the Colonies*. London: Fabian Colonial Bureau and Victor Gollancz Ltd.

Federated Malay States 1932 *Annual Departmental Reports 1930*. Kuala Lumpur: Government Press.

1937 *Annual Departmental Reports 1935*. Kuala Lumpur: Government Press.

Fildes, V., Marks, L. and Marland, H. 1992 (eds.) *Women and Children First: International Maternal and Infant Welfare 1870–1945*. London: Routledge.

Galloway, D. 1926 On inguinal lymphadenitis. *Malayan Medical Journal* 1(1):1–6.

Great Britain, Economic Advisory Council, Committee on Nutrition in the Colonial Empire 1939a *Nutrition in the Colonial Empire*. First Report, Part I (Cmd 6050). London: Her Majesty's Stationery Office.

1939b *Summary of Information Regarding Nutrition in the Colonial Empire*. First Report, Part II (Cmd 6051). London: Her Majesty's Stationery Office.

Haggis, J. 1990 Gendering colonialism or colonising gender? Recent women's studies approaches to white women and the history of British colonialism. *Women's Studies International Forum* 13(1/2):105–15.

Hull, V.J. and Simpson, M. 1985 (eds.) *Breastfeeding, Child Health and Child Spacing: Cross-Cultural Perspectives*. London: Croom Helm.

Hunt, N.R. 1988 'Le bebe en brousse': European women, African birth spacing and colonial intervention in breast feeding in the Belgian Congo. *International Journal of African Historical Studies* 21(3):401–32.

Jolly, M. 1993 Colonizing women: the maternal body and empire. In S. Gunew and A. Yeatman (eds.) *Feminism and the Politics of Difference*. Sydney: Allen and Unwin, 103–27.

Jordan, B. 1978 *Birth in Four Cultures: A Crosscultural Investigation of Childbirth in*

Yucatan, Holland, Sweden and the United States. Montreal: Eden Press.

Kay, M.A. 1982 (ed.) *Anthropology of Human Birth.* Philadelphia: F.A. Davis.

Kempe, J.A. 1933 *Perak Administration Report for the Year 1932.* Kuala Lumpur: Government Press.

Knapman, C. 1986 *White Women in Fiji 1835–1930: The Ruin of Empire?* Sydney: Allen and Unwin.

Laderman, C. 1983 *Wives and Midwives: Childbirth and Nutrition in Rural Malaysia.* Berkeley: University of California Press.

1987 The ambiguity of symbols in the structure of healing. *Social Science and Medicine* 24(4):293–302.

Lai Ah Eng 1986 *Peasants, Proletarians and Prostitutes: A Preliminary Investigation into the Work of Chinese Women in Colonial Malaya.* Research Notes and Discussion Papers, No. 59. Singapore: Institute of Southeast Asian Studies.

Lewis, J. 1980a *The Politics of Motherhood: Child and Maternal Welfare in England, 1900–1939.* London: Croom Helm.

1980b The social history of social policy: infant welfare in Edwardian England. *Journal of Social Policy* 9(4):463–86.

Lewis, M. 1988 The 'health of the race' and infant health in New South Wales: perspectives on medicine and empire. In R. MacLeod and M. Lewis (eds.) *Disease, Medicine, and Empire: Perspectives on Western Medicine and the Experience of European Expansion.* London and New York: Routledge, 301–15.

MacCormack, C.P. 1982 (ed.) *Ethnography of Fertility and Birth.* London: Academic Press.

Manderson, L. 1978 The development and direction of female education in Peninsular Malaysia. *Journal of the Malaysian Branch of the Royal Asiatic Society* 51(2):100–22.

1981 Roasting, smoking and dieting in response to birth: Malay confinement in cross-cultural perspective. *Social Science and Medicine* 15B(4):509–20.

1982 Bottle feeding and ideology in colonial Malaya: the production of change. *International Journal of Health Services* 12(4):597–616.

1984 'These are modern times': infant feeding practice in Peninsular Malaysia. *Social Science and Medicine* 18(1):47–57.

1987a Blame, responsibility and remedial action: death, disease and the infant in early twentieth century Malaya. In N. Owen (ed.) *Death and Disease in Southeast Asia: Explorations in Social, Medical and Demographic History.* Singapore: Oxford University Press for the Asian Studies Association of Australia, 257–82.

1987b Health services and the legitimation of the colonial state: British Malaya 1786–1941. *International Journal of Health Services* 17(1):91–112.

1989 Political economy and the politics of gender: maternal and child health in colonial Malaya. In P. Cohen and J. Purcal (eds.) *The Political Economy of Primary Health Care in Southeast Asia.* Canberra: Australian Development Studies Network and ASEAN Training Centre for Primary Health Care Development, 79–100.

1992 Women and the state: maternal and child welfare in colonial Malaya, 1900–1940. In V. Fildes, L. Marks and H. Marland (eds.) *Women and*

Children First: International Maternal and Infant Welfare 1870–1945. London: Routledge, 154–77.

1996 *Sickness and the State: Health and Illness in Colonial Malaya, 1870–1940*. Melbourne and Cambridge: Cambridge University Press.

Martin, E. 1987 *The Woman in the Body: A Cultural Analysis of Reproduction*. Boston: Beacon Press.

Michaelson, K.L. and contributors 1988 *Childbirth in America: Anthropological Perspectives*. South Hadley, MA: Bergin and Garvey.

Mitford, J. 1992 *The American Way of Birth*. New York: Dutton.

Oakley, A. 1976 Wisewoman and medicine man: changes in the management of childbirth. In J. Mitchell and A. Oakley (eds.) *The Rights and Wrongs of Women*. Harmondsworth: Penguin Books, 17–58.

1980 *Women Confined: Towards a Sociology of Childbirth*. Oxford: Martin Robertson.

Olssen, E. 1981 Truby King and the Plunket Society: an analysis of a prescriptive ideology. *New Zealand Journal of History* 15(1):3–23.

Pelling, M. 1988 Child health as a social value in early modern England. *Social History of Medicine* 1(2):135–64.

Ramusack, B.N. 1990 Cultural missionaries, maternal imperialists, feminist allies: British women activists in India, 1865–1945. *Women's Studies International Forum* 13(4):309–21.

Reid, J. 1984 The role of maternal and child health clinics in education and prevention: a case study from Papua New Guinea. *Social Science and Medicine* 19(3):291–303.

Stanworth, M. 1987 (ed.) *Reproductive Technologies: Gender, Motherhood and Medicine*. Minneapolis: University of Minnesota Press.

Stoler, A.L. 1989 Making empire respectable: the politics of race and sexual morality in 20th-century colonial cultures. *American Ethnologist* 16(4):634–60.

1992 Sexual affronts and racial frontiers: European identities and the cultural politics of exclusion in colonial Southeast Asia. *Comparative Studies in Society and History* 34(3):514–51.

Straits Settlements 1890 *Report of Commissioners Appointed to Enquire into the State of Labour in the Straits Settlements and Protected Native States*. Singapore: Government Printing Office.

1904 *Straits Settlements Annual Departmental Report for 1903*. Singapore: Government Printing Office.

1909 *Straits Settlements Annual Departmental Report for 1908*. Singapore: Government Printing Office.

1937 *Annual Departmental Reports for 1935, vol. I*. Singapore: Government Printing Office.

Straits Times 1907 (22 May). Singapore.

Suleri, S. 1992 *The Rhetoric of English India*. Chicago: University of Chicago Press.

Szreter, S. 1988 The importance of social intervention in Britain's mortality decline c.1850–1914: a re-interpretation of the role of public health. *Social History of Medicine* 1(1):1–37.

1991 The GRO and the Public Health Movement in Britain, 1837–1914. *Social History of Medicine* 4(3):435–64.

Vaughan, M. 1991 *Curing their Ills: Colonial Power and African Illness.* Cambridge: Polity Press.

Warren, J. 1990 Prostitution in Singapore society and the *karayuki-san*. In P.J. Rimmer and L.M. Allen (eds.) *The Underside of Malaysian History: Pullers, Prostitutes, Plantation Workers . . .* Singapore: Singapore University Press, 161–76.

Worboys, M. 1988 The discovery of colonial malnutrition between the wars. In D. Arnold (ed.) *Imperial Medicine and Indigenous Societies.* Manchester and New York: Manchester University Press, 208–26.

Unpublished sources
Colonial Office 859/1/1201/19, 1939.
Colonial Office 859/46/12101/4A, 1943.
Selangor Secretariat 3006/1915.
Selangor Secretariat 3156/1915.
Selangor Secretariat G544/1937.

2   Modernizing the Malay mother

Maila Stivens

This chapter looks at the modernizing of mothering in Malaysia, exploring the successive imaginaries of the 'mother' in both scholarly and political cultural production in the country, especially in the post-Independence, nation-building period. But as I shall argue, a series of uncertainties pervades any discussion of gender, women and mothering within Malaysian 'modernity'. To work on these issues in the context of my research, first in rural and then urban Malaysia,[1] has inevitably enmeshed me in a series of modern scholarly insecurities; these include furious debates about positionalities, the decentring of liberal humanist ideas and the scepticism of many 'Third World' scholars and activists about Western anthropological claims to know about and speak for its objects located beyond Euro-America.[2]

Exploring Malay mothering

To examine 'modern' mothering in Malaysia, we need first to attend to the particularities of modernity in the country. As I suggest elsewhere (1994b, n.d.b), imported Eurocentric models of 'modernization' project ideas deriving from Western social developments directly on to analyses of Malaysia. I argue that we cannot unproblematically apply to Malaysia assumptions about a standard linear progression from 'tradition' to the rationalization, bureaucratization, industrialization and secularism of mainstream Western models of modernity; this is to ignore both the specificities of the development process in the country and the problems within contemporary social theory with the increasingly unstable category of modernity itself.[3] Malaysian colonial and postcolonial processes have been marked by a highly directive state, with a reconstitution of the Malay peasantry through land legislation in the colonial period, continuing agricultural interventions (Lim Teck Ghee 1977; Stivens 1985, 1996) and an increasingly managerial state role in the economy with the implementation of the New Economic Policy in the 1970s.[4] Most particularly, the colonial reconstitution of a Malay peasantry cast as a 'yeoman idyll'

50

has reverberated down to the present politically and economically, forming a core imaginary for Malay nationalism: this core imaginary is only
now being challenged by the multiplying and fragmented meanings about
Malayness produced in relation to the new industrial and globalizing
orders.[5] In the context of resurgent Islam, the idea of modernity is
rendered even more unstable, because it is located within a series of
tensions surrounding the role of religion in the modern Malay world and
its relationship to 'tradition', 'family' and critiques of modernization and
Westernization. For a sizeable minority of contemporary Malays, modernity and its future is understood solely within a narrative about a
hoped-for Islamic modernity.

We have similar difficulties if we look against the masculinist grain of
the many debates about modernity (and postmodernity) from a gendered
standpoint. I have argued elsewhere that feminist theory's profound
critique of the main assumptions of masculinist social theory can be
applied to the category of modernity, revealing it to be a thoroughly
masculinist construct, based on a series of highly dubious, socially and
historically specific and gendered binary oppositions that pose women,
woman and the female as always negative: in such theorizing the processes producing modernity are seen as taking place in a male public
sphere from which women are excluded (cf. Felski 1995; Stivens 1994b,
n.d.b).

A dominant storyline about the development of mothering in Malaysia
within government and some social science rhetoric accepts such linear
models of modernity. It sees ever-increasing health arising from colonial
and postcolonial medical and infant welfare services, and, with industrialization, increasingly nuclearized urban families and individual mothering
replacing the allegedly more collective earlier patterns and a new purpos-
ive parenting replacing the previous over-indulgence and nurturance. For
most commentators, such developments have been seen as *effects* of the
larger forces of modernization. But as Lenore Manderson's work has
shown (1981, 1982, 1987a, 1987b, 1989, 1992 and this volume), in fact
the colonial state largely allocated the task of producing 'modern' health
for the Malayan populace to women, with a range of pressures and
exhortations applied to them. Other versions growing in importance
recently pose a dystopic vision, seeing the 'problems' produced by
women going out to work – the failings of mothers – as directly responsible for some of the ills of modernity, especially over-sexed and lazy
youth 'hanging out' and 'loafing'.

The Malaysian context poses a particular tension for would-be feminists in writing about mothering because of the explicit critique of Western
feminist perspectives by some recent Islamic commentators there. *Dak-*

wah groups in Malaysia (missionary, so-called fundamentalist groups, although they disown the term) argue that women's true vocation is motherhood and child care. Islam, it is held, upholds and values motherhood and child rearing as part of women's full participation in society, while the West devalues such activities. Some scholars have also argued that Western feminism is inappropriate in the Malaysian context, and that the veil and Islamic practices confer equal but separate power. In this account, then, a somewhat different 'public' and 'private' is created from that argued for by the modernists, with women more firmly located within the 'private'. It is debatable, however, how far such avowedly Islamic 'womanist' discourses (e.g. Roziah Omar 1996) will be 'free' to distance themselves from hegemonic North Atlantic perspectives. Some Islamic feminists have worked for a reinterpretation of 'fundamentalist' ideas, through a rereading of the Koran (e.g. Mernissi 1991, writing from a Middle Eastern context; Amina Wadud-Muhsin 1992, writing from Malaysia). They suggest that the Koran can be read as a text setting out a social justice agenda whose gender egalitarianism has been suppressed historically. Many of my present middle-class informants' representations of their everyday lives are deeply embedded in religion in its highly specific local manifestations.

The *Dakwah* critique rightly objects to the ways Islam has been represented in some Western feminist discourse. This has sometimes pictured the veiled Muslim woman, in a highly Orientalist and reductionist way, as representative of all that is oppressed (cf. Lazreg 1988).[6] But the various versions of a supposedly purer Islam, both in modernist and revivalist versions, have great appeal for modern Malay women of both the middle and working classes (cf. Ong 1987). This is apparent in the mass of writing by middle-class women – journalists and others – within the proliferating magazines aimed at the modern Malay market. For example, there are large numbers of articles outlining the correct ways to conduct Muslim family life. For some middle-class Malay women, some of the greatest adherents to the model of modern Muslim womanhood, the veiling and covering of their bodies has become a potent symbol not only of 'modern' womanhood but of ethnic and class situation. In the contemporary period, the veiled Malay woman has become a significant site of (Malay) nationalist symbolization (cf. Ong 1990), the very embodiment of a highly specific Malay modernity, although there are many veils and as many versions of the new Malay woman (see Stivens n.d.b). The long development of this discursive production of the Malay woman within Malay nationalist thought and education is apparent in Malaysian history (see Manderson 1980).

An added dimension to a discussion of these issues is the subjective position of mothers researching maternity. I have had to ask myself why my own position as a mother seems to be so important to me in trying to write about Malay mothering, why I feel tempted to privilege this experience. Am I trapped within a maternalist essentialism based on the intense emotions of the whole experience of being a mother in my time and place? Some escape from this anxiety about essentialism may come from looking critically at my supposed 'difference' in time and place: this is an issue very much to the fore in recent feminist concerns about positionalities. But such an insistence on 'difference' threatens to reify culture, seeing it as some portable attribute of the person which can be quantified and compared from an uninspected, authoritative, epistemological basis. Indeed, we could well see equal problems with middle-class researchers like myself over-identifying with middle-class informants' everyday life dilemmas of juggling children and jobs, and not wanting to lose precious 'quality time' with their children by being interviewed in their homes.

These anxieties are compounded by a degree of ambivalence I feel about Western feminist writing on mothering in general: this body of work has often been rather unreflectively negative about the whole institution of motherhood – starting with Nancy Friday's self-positioning as the feminist-as-angry daughter (Friday 1977) and continuing into what I see as an often uninspected inheritance of mother-blaming (cf. Ross 1995) and anti-child discourses.[7] As Snitow (1992) suggests, early second-wave feminism either questioned motherhood as destiny for all women, seeing child-care provision as a solution to the 'problem' or else ignored motherhood entirely. The second half of the 1970s saw sceptical probings of the social and subjective meanings of motherhood (Chodorow 1978; Rich 1977), but this, she argues, was displaced by a degree of celebration of motherhood in the 1980s. Snitow (1992) sees a trajectory within feminist discussion that gives less and less voice to women without children.[8] But I would argue that we have in fact seen comparatively little interest in mothering as a social institution in the central texts of recent Western feminist theorizing, apart from such work as Ruddick's *Maternal Thinking* (1989), until the 'torrent' of new work in the 1990s (Ross 1995:402).[9] Mothers' bodies (and children's bodies) even seem to be less common than we might expect in writing about the body, which has often concentrated on a narrow understanding of 'sexuality'.[10]

These have been interesting developments for a movement drawing so strongly on the politics of 'experience'. Although a number of influential texts in the early 1980s produced calls for renewed debate and action around the family (Segal 1983; Thorne and Yalom 1982), the 'family', mothering (and children) seemed to become somewhat marginal within feminist theorizings preoccupied with postmodernism and difference. In particular, there have been few attempts to face up to the relative absence of children in feminist theory, and their marginal place when they do appear,[11] in spite of child-care campaigns having been so central to second-wave feminist political activity. The family does come back in new guises, of course, deconstructed and fragmented into a series of related issues, including continuing attention to male violence in the family. (It is noteworthy that family history has continued to keep its distance from feminist history.) In spite of the well-established critiques of the reified heterosexual nuclear family of family ideology, much Western feminist writing outside of anthropology has evaded the intellectual and political challenge of dealing with the family and kinship in all their diverse forms and practices in a global context.[12] The problems within Euro-American feminism about presuming to speak for 'woman' / all women and a persistent privileging of First World women's concerns were all too apparent in the way that critiques about the family addressed a reified 'nuclear' family based on a Western ideology of family, rather than actual family and kinship practices both in the West and elsewhere.[13] The importance of family as support for women and its political significance in a range of overtly political actions (as among the mothers of the disappeared in some Latin American countries, for example) speaks to these complexities.[14] The narrow understandings of 'family' in Euro-American discourse may be partly due to the ways that the right in the United States has monopolized the 'family' as the site of celebration and contest: in the process it has become a no-woman's land for much North American feminism.[15]

Susan Bordo has claimed that the growth of Women's Studies programmes, and of feminist intellectuals, has contradictorily produced raw hostility to discussions of the 'female' virtues of mothering and empathy in feminist writing. She attributes this to the university setting's emphasis on the meritocratic exercise of Reason (1990:148–9). But poststructuralist work in flight from Reason has often similarly avoided mothering.[16] In its embrace of the idea of the body in an often idealist or at best neo-Feuerbachian materialist mode (Turner 1994), it is clear that feminist theory, like any other theory, is unavoidably a child of its time, even as it self-consciously affects to be taking up a contestatory stance.

It is of immediate concern here to determine whether local Malaysian cultural productions of the modern Malay mother are in fact partaking of a global cultural emphasis on the 'body' within late modernity, and hence might engage with such 'Western' theorizing. At present, there is a considerable distance between these theorizations within the West and most concerns of Malaysianists (see Stivens 1992), although an emphasis on body care and enhancement is highly visible within contemporary consumption patterns in the country.

The modernizing of Malay mothering

My recent project exploring work and family in the Malay middle classes grew directly out of my earlier work in the 'matrilineal' society of Rembau, in the small Malaysian state of Negeri Sembilan: that study focused on the relationships between gender and successive social transformations in the peasant economy. It described and analysed the restructuring of gender relationships in the colonial and postcolonial periods, the role of the colonial state in reconstituting matrilineal kinship practices, including land inheritance patterns and clan structure, and the significance of women's political action to preserve 'matriliny'. A special focus of interest was the effects of recent extensive outmigration on labour processes in the peasant economy, and household and family structure. The 1970s and 1980s saw industrialization and urbanization undermining the rural economy and a mass exodus to the cities (see Stivens 1996). The recent project has moved on to explore the formation of the Malay middle class historically and the everyday lives of the middle class, including migrants from the rural exodus. As part of this project, extensive interviews with about a hundred households in Seremban (Negeri Sembilan), Kuala Lumpur and Penang have been conducted.

The nature of the Malay middle classes is an important context for this discussion. My present study has been looking at the historical development of these classes, concentrating on a range of class fractions from the clerks, school teachers and public servants of the colonial era to the burgeoning professionals, entrepreneurs and bureaucrats of the contemporary period. Middle classes have always been awkward classes in European social theory, and the importation of these concepts to Malaysia produces further awkwardness. It is important again to look at the specificities of these processes of class formation and their impact on everyday life in contemporary Malaysia, without assuming simple parallels with the fortunes of North Atlantic middle classes. We cannot, for example, assume a homogeneous class identity or politics among these disparate fractions. It would also be misleading to see the rapid transition of many rural Malays into living within fully commodified middle-class capitalist culture in the last twenty years as simply part of a homogeneous, global, universalized pattern. Similarly, we cannot portray Malay women in their situations as wives and mothers co-ordinating consumption and producing an elaborated domesticity as simply entering a global economy and culture. This would be yet again to see Malay

modernity through Western lens, ignoring the specificities of developments in the country.

Contemporary Malay mothering can only be understood in terms of its
history. It is clear that the social processes structuring Malay women's
childbearing have been subjected to increasing interventions by the state,
medical authorities and advice-givers as central parts of the colonial and
postcolonial modernizing projects. Lenore Manderson's work has detailed some of the modernizing of mothering and the saving of the child in
colonial Malaya (1981, 1982, 1987a, 1987b, 1989, 1992), processes
which paralleled similar developments in Britain and elsewhere in the
Empire (Davin 1978; see Jolly, this volume: Chapter 6). These interventions are particularly apparent in the long history of encroaching medicalization redefining appropriate management of maternal and child
health.[17] Ann Stoler's (1991) analysis of gender, race and mortality in
colonial Asia points to the obsessive concern with censuses, measures of
infant mortality and so on in the modernizing of state control by colonial
regimes, and Malaya was no exception. But, as I have argued elsewhere
(1987), while these regulatory practices set the parameters for 'family',
they by no means determined the form these social relations took.

We have a very limited number of studies of Malay mothering and child
rearing, although there is some discussion of child rearing in a number of
the standard anthropological studies of rural and urban Malay society.[18]
This literature has tended to represent Malay parental ideology as relatively unchanging and as uniformly highly altruistic and sentimental (cf.
Djamour 1965; Firth 1966:107ff; Malaya (Fed) 1951). The scholarly
representations of the Malay mother have often overlapped with popular
cultural pictures of the long-suffering, self-denying Malay mother and the
sentimentalization of her relationship with her children. The historical
development of these cultural images of the mother is unclear, although
there is ample poetic evidence alone.[19] Such attributed qualities have
been common in some earlier pronouncements about the supposed gen-
eralizations possible about mothering and child-rearing practices, rapidly
leaping from maternal practices to 'national character' to explain economic backwardness. The idea of Malay 'laziness' induced by 'in-breeding' (Mahathir bin Mohamad 1970) and over-indulgent parenting has
been a recurrent theme within both colonial and nationalist writings.[20]

Such ahistorical and homogenizing discourses were of course direct
heirs of colonial discourses constructing the 'lazy native' (cf. Syed Hussein Alatas 1977), even as they on occasion critiqued them. Prime Minister Mahathir's own (formerly banned) book *The Malay Dilemma* (1970),
for example, attributed Malay 'backwardness' to, among other factors,
failures in child rearing. The Malays' inherent capacities and character

traits, which he saw as responsible for their economic failures, were due to the 'incapacity of parents to take care of their children and the upbringing of children . . . distorted by the well-known excessive indulgence of the grandparents' (1970:29). Mahathir's controversial views were a clear example of the internalization of the 'lazy native' discourse, embedded in a version of Social Darwinism (Khoo Boo Teik 1995:32–4).

A Malayan government committee report on Malay education in 1951 (compiled by a fourteen-person committee, which included only one woman, Miss N.B. MacDonald, the principal of the Malay Women's Training College, Malacca), suggested that

observers agree that Malays of all classes show great tenderness towards children, especially towards infants and toddlers. Small children are constantly fondled and caressed by the older members of the family, including grandparents and by friends and acquaintances who visit the home. Parents who slap and shout at their children may come under sharp criticism from relatives and neighbours; and the misbehaviour of a child is more apt to be ascribed to its parents' failure in kindness and forbearance than to their over-indulgence . . . Thus the Malay home is normally a place of much good feeling and reciprocal affection. It would seem admirably adapted to give the growing child that fundamental emotional security, that sense of being permanently wanted and valued which is the starting point for healthy and balanced development of the person. Indeed, it is a typical strength of the Malay character that its growth is not stunted or distorted by repression. It may be remarked on the other hand, that Malay ideas on bringing up children do not appear to include any view of the process known to western parents as spoiling. (Malaya (Fed) 1951:15–16)

The report, however, then goes on to suggest that Malay children get a less favourable start in life, due to economic and medical reasons. It details the failings of Malay parents (for which we can read mothers), including irregular and unsuitable feeding, poor hygiene and toilet training, Malay girls becoming mothers before they have reached physical maturity, poor discipline, lack of awareness about education and failure to teach children to tolerate frustration. Later, it remarks that it is

quite possible for parents to be too rigid and exacting. Much harm is probably done in Western countries, for example, by associating cleanliness training with feelings of guilt. But when the balance between laxity and strictness is judiciously held, the child is well on the way to learning one of the crucial lessons of life, namely to take no for an answer without sulking or losing his temper. (1951:17)

The report moves on to rhetoric about how 'the under-nourished and fatalistic kampong dweller will have to scrape, save, work and produce as he never has before' in order (to bring a new school system into existence) (1951:14). To this end, the report suggests the need to bring the very different beliefs and desires of home and school together, with teachers 'trained as soldiers of initiative and determination in this war . . . to combat the harmful circumstances we have detailed' (1951:19).

Rosemary Firth (1966) and Judith Djamour (1965), 'expatriate' anthropologists whose work has had considerable authority to set agendas and fix images, both provided accounts of child rearing that closely paralleled this colonial report's emphasis on the indulgence of Malay parenting. Firth's study in Kelantan in the late 1930s, for example, suggested that '[b]y some of our standards, it might seem that Malay children are spoilt by their parents' (1966:107), but she goes on to suggest that 'the prevalent idea seems to be that as a child grows older he will realize that he must accept social responsibility and obligations like anyone else' (1966:107–8). She details the mild rebukes and patient cajoling of children that form part of the Malay parent's child-care routines. Djamour, writing about Singapore in the 1950s, also repeated the claims about Malay children being spoiled.

Lenore Manderson argues that the blaming of mothers has been a dominant feature of the giving of advice during the colonial period (1987a and this volume). We can see something of this in the colonial report above and also in some of my Rembau informants' experiences. A wife of a former soldier, for example, told me how she had been blamed by a British army doctor in Singapore in the 1950s for the death of her newborn baby (her second birth, after a first stillbirth). He told her that she had caused the infant's death by feeding it the then customary rice gruel at so early an age.

Commentaries on Malay 'culture' have repeatedly pointed to the power of pronatalism within Malay culture over at least the last one hundred years. With 'modernization' the desired number of children has steadily declined, but not the wish for children. All studies report that involuntary childlessness has been greatly pitied. Among my informants in my earlier study in Rembau, for example, women had often been divorced when no child was forthcoming; those with no children were anxious to adopt one and women often provided a sister with one of their daughters to raise as her own. I was constantly questioned about how Westerners could possibly have only one or two children; genealogies indeed revealed many families with twelve or more children. Today, three or four children are seen as the ideal in Rembau, so there has been a sizeable shift in desired numbers.[21]

Such pronatalisms have no doubt been complex phenomena; they cannot simply be read as evidence of highly oppressive state, patriarchal or Islamic ideologies reducing women to their child-bearing function, as the Western feminist movement has sometimes alleged in a somewhat essentialist fashion. Similarly, they are better understood not as unchanging, 'traditional' cultural persistences, but as constantly recreated beliefs and practices, specific to their time and place. In the Negeri Sembilan context, for example, I saw pronatalism in the 1970s and 1980s as an ideology celebrating motherhood in a reconstituted 'traditional' matrilineal social order.[22] Although the government was energetically promoting birth control until the mid-1980s, I have heard much more about difficulties in conceiving from women in Rembau.

One woman (doing 'home duties' and married to a school teacher) had been constantly in tears for two years after her marriage, because she had failed to become pregnant. The extreme heartache of another (middle-class) acquaintance who had failed to produce a child was obvious in her transformation from a cheerful, outgoing person during my first fieldwork to a depressed and dejected one seven childless years later, engaged in a continuous round of medical tests and painfully jealous of my own child, even though her husband was hurtling through the upper levels of the bureaucracy and they now lived in elegant Damansara Heights in Kuala Lumpur.

In the first twenty-five years or so after Independence, Malay pronatalisms operated against some state pressure to limit families. In line with economic demands for greater growth unimpeded supposedly by a high birth rate, the Malaysian state apparatus subscribed to the population policies promoted by international organizations like the World Bank, which saw unchecked population growth as a cause of poverty and underdevelopment. Consequently, Malaysian women became subject to increasing pressure from programmes funded by the World Bank and United Nations Population Fund (UNFPA) to control the size of their families. Whether it was the programmes or other factors which reduced the crude birth rate from 46.2 in 1957 to 30.6 in 1976 (Nor Laily Aziz and Tan 1978) is open to debate.

But after this period of stress on family limitation, there was a reversal of policy: in March 1984 it was announced as part of the Fourth Malaysia Plan Mid-term Review that the country was now aiming for a population of seventy million by the beginning of the twenty-second century. Government officials have stated that the policy is not pronatalist in intent, because a reduction in overall fertility is still hoped for. The committee set up to implement it, however, apparently hoped for more women marrying, and for them to combine large families with continued workforce participation. Prime Minister Mahathir was even more pronatalist, suggesting that Malaysian women should 'go for five children' and if the family was well-off, women should not work but stay at home to raise them (*Star* 28 July 1984, quoted by Rashidah Abdullah 1993:67). This policy could be seen as an attempt by the state to secure the conditions of reproduction of a greatly expanding industrial labour force and a con-

prominently in some of the contrasting images of the march towards modernity, as chaste, modern Muslim wives, glamorous and/or energetic business and career women, hard-working housewives, doting mothers and keepers of the family, particularly of the family's health, and indeed of Malay modernity. A major arena for these representations is the growing number of magazines targeted at the middle-class market. Random selections from the plethora of images picturing women to themselves illustrate the representations of mothers: a back cover of *Ibu* (Mother) magazine in 1991 shows a boy, probably Indian (although his ethnicity seems to be deliberately fudged), astride the picture, neatly dressed in grey school pants, with blocks of flats in the middle distance. The caption celebrates the Selangor Development Corporation, taking part in a government campaign exhorting 'happy families', 'We build housing, you build happy families.' *Jelita*, a more up-market production, ran a special issue on mothers and children in May 1993, featuring a folio of beautiful mothers and their children of varying ages pictured in 'designer' clothes – Western and up-market refigured Malay 'traditional' dress, with only one of the women veiled – and articles about how a safe house makes for a happy family. The multiplying and diverse images of women are clearly not simply reflections of a monolithic state or Islamic ideology or discourse governing the lives of women, in spite of the many crude state messages about the happy family making for a happy country. They express, rather, the very clear tensions between the varying versions of state, market and religious modernities.[26]

However diverse popular representations of contemporary women are, they are notable for their emphasis on the energy and industry of mothers and women in general. This has moved women on in some ways from the 'lazy native' discourse, although it may be a subliminal response to it. The ever-growing cultural production of 'domesticity' suggests that women (as wives-mothers) are being groomed to take a crucial role in producing the everyday practices of modern Malays. The detailed instructions on household decor, advice bringing women up-to-date (sic) with 'modern' views about child rearing and interpersonal relationships, and the re-invention of cuisine all apparently accord women a key part in the 'domestic' construction of Malay middle classness. This may seem predictable to observers of consumer capitalist culture in the West, where women are seen to occupy a similarly focal role as co-ordinators of consumption and the producers of an elaborated domesticity. But, as noted, the embeddedness of a range of Islamic practices in the material manifestations of becoming modern lends a highly specific set of meanings to women's place in producing domesticity. Thus magazine articles (often written by male 'experts') regularly instruct women on the duties of

Muslim parents and give full instructions, complete with numerous glossy pictures, to help readers produce all the reworked trappings of preparations for Muslim holy days and festivals.

The commoditization of child care accompanying the emergence of the recently modern mother is remarkable. To be a modern mother is to be an active consumer under great pressure to acquire all the commodities necessary for the satisfactory performance of motherhood. The smaller number of children has coincided with an enormous expansion of expenditure on children. Today, the market for baby goods has boomed dramatically, with cots, pushchairs, disposable nappies, a huge range of feeding equipment, toys and clothing sold in glossy new stores in the post-modern shopping centres in urban areas, including the giant US toy chain Toys R Us. Disposable nappies and pushchairs were rare even in 1982, when I took my first child, then nearly two years old, to Malaysia: now disposable nappies are ubiquitous. The relative absence of footpaths in 1982 made the use of a pushchair difficult even in Petaling Jaya (the 'satellite' area of Kuala Lumpur), and ours was constantly commented on. The commoditization of child care is expressed in a number of ways, including masses of new shops and the growing role of servants (often allegedly Indonesian illegal immigrants), childminders and nurseries. As noted, many middle-class women have become avid employees, backed up by complex and sometimes fraught arrangements of kin help and servants and childminders. But we need to be careful about generalizing these patterns for all sections of the middle class: only a minority of the sixty middle-middle-class households interviewed on a Seremban housing estate, for example, actually employed servants, although over 80 per cent of the Kuala Lumpur sample had some form of paid domestic help.

The expansion of women's magazines and advice books has brought a whole new arena for the cultural production of ideas about child bearing and child rearing. Again, these ideas have become closely linked to other burgeoning cultural productions surrounding religion and nation building. There is a strong strand of exhortation: a recent publication for example is titled *Mengapa Anak Anda Malas Belajar?* (Why is Your Child Lazy about Studying?),[27] which is amusingly illustrated with cartoons almost all featuring boys, although the cover shows a picture of a girl (see Plates 1 and 2). Albert Gomes has suggested that this title speaks to a continuing internalization of the colonial lazy native discourse (pers. comm.). This and the earlier example of the link between nation and happy families both feature maternal efforts as being directed at sons in particular. I suspect this focus on boys may be general, but my analyses of the magazines are still in process. My present informants tell me that they have usually not consulted the 'bibles' of Western child rearing such as

Ibu bapa membuat kerja rumah anak-anak.

Main hingga ke malam, kerja rumah tidak siap.

1 These two cartoons point to the pitfalls of parents being too easy on their children. One set of parents is doing the child's homework for *him* (my emphasis), the other two are letting the child play on into the night, so that the homework never gets done.

Anak-anak mencontohi kelakuan ibu bapa..

2 These two cartoons convey the message that actions speak louder than words. The father in the car is telling the policeman that 'the car drove itself [through] the red light, sir'.

Dr Spock and Penelope Leach (available in all the big bookstores), but do rely heavily on newspaper and magazine articles. The discourses of the latter are very much in line with the imported modernist psychological ideas of those books, however, stressing the development of the child in a loving, child-centred atmosphere, but not one of 'over-indulgence'. It is notable that such ideas represent a marked contrast to the state school system's emphasis on relatively disciplinarian practices that appear to be a direct descendant of the quasi-military school practices of the British colonial era. This suggests some disjunction between the actual child rearing practices of home and state, although both are addressed in the state discourses about a direct and necessary link between family, child rearing and nation building.

It is worth stressing the simultaneous creation of and living in and criticism of their own cultural forms by the contemporary Malay middle classes. The 'authentic' voice of the middle-class woman herself will always be a mediated one: the journalists, doctors, writers, lawyers, TV producers, teachers and academics who are part of the elaborate production of the 'modern' mother are simultaneously living the processes that they are imposing on other women who lack their voice – for example, nurses, secretaries, clerks and housewives.

Power, 'tradition' and modernity in Malay mothering

Some feminists have interpreted the continuing growth of modernist interventions in the mothering process, especially state interventions (both in Malaysia and elsewhere), as elaborate male-dominated mechanisms of social control (Laderman 1983; Manderson 1987a; Oakley 1980). Such interventions can be seen as only partially effective, however; women have not simply acquiesced or been complicit with such impositions, although these resistances often brought new contradictions. The power of 'expert' advice has not been uniform: thus while much advice about infant care seems to have been imposed, most notably by the maternal health clinics, pregnant women have sometimes been able to successfully resist the new regimes. And, as we saw, women have also resisted the imposition of some family planning schemes.

Some of the ideological contests about managing life-cycle events were well illustrated by the ceremonial display which I observed of the baby of a Rembau school teacher who had flown home from Sabah to her village to give birth.

Like other newborns, her baby was presented for visitors in a highly uniform ritualized display of newly acquired 'modern' consumer goods. He was placed on a cushion on the floor, flanked by one or more plastic laundry baskets stacked with cloth nappies, Johnson's baby powder, other items of clothing, and a feeding bottle (*nota bene!*). In this case, the mother had left hospital after one day, because she could not get any sleep. A number of neighbours and the government midwife were in attendance to visit the new arrival. The government midwife on her daily visit saw to the mother's perineum and the baby's umbilicus and then tried unsuccessfully to get the baby's swaddling loosened. The mother was observing all the food taboos which are 'traditionally' supposed to preserve women's health under the humoural system of beliefs. 'You must eat dry foods', said a thirty-seven-year-old neighbour. 'The *orang tuo* [old folk] are very much against fruit and vegetables' (which are believed to cool the body). The government midwife retired, defeated. The *bidan* (village midwife) later made her appearance, supervising the binding and massage of the mother's abdomen.

My informants represented the relationship between the two midwives as a simple division of labour, with the government midwife there to look after the child, the village midwife to look after the mother, which was not strictly the case. The scene represented an interesting conjunction of the impositions of commoditization and modernizing state control, only some of which were being resisted.[28]

The new 'modern' mothers among my informants were decidedly ambivalent about the control exercised by the *orang tuo*, the 'old folks', in spite of the apparent success of the latter in imposing food taboos. Some of the young women grumbled a lot about these taboos, saying that they felt unable to resist the social pressure within the village. This ambivalence was also manifest in the case of the young school teacher mentioned above. She had planned to leave her baby with her mother while she and her husband went back to East Malaysia, but her husband persuaded her to take the baby with them, because he had become very attached to him. She was not feeling very confident:

I'm worried about looking after the baby myself. My sister's baby who's a month older weighs fifteen pounds and mine still only weighs seven pounds. It's because she breast-feeds. Mine is bottle-fed, because I thought that I was leaving him. The doctors prefer you to breast-feed. I'm very worried about taking him. My mother knows how to stop him crying. He cries every night. What if he cries on the plane? I can't stop him . . . I would have liked to leave him for a few months longer.

These anxieties suggest to me that romantic naturalizing views about the supportiveness of the women's community are not necessarily apposite. They can overlook the considerable ambivalence present about the older women's control and competence. The younger woman in this case obviously felt that her competence as a mother had been called into question by the failure of the baby to thrive like her sister's, and by her mother's much greater ability to stop the baby crying. That this anxiety was to be resolved by leaving the baby with her mother also suggests an absence of 'modern' ideologies and subjectivities about 'maternal deprivation'. We might, however, see her lack of confidence overall as deriving from the loss of maternal power through the medicalization of childbirth and by the new conjunctures in which mothering after the birth period has become an activity carried out in individual households often removed from kin support.

The management of childbirth in the industrializing era has been marked by a series of conflicts – between, on the one hand, the pronatalist 'old' ways with a high level of female control over everyday events and, on the other hand, the state's zealous efforts in first limiting, then, later, encouraging fertility, medicalizing birth and improving nutrition. I do not think, however, that we can see the 'persistence' of the 'old' ways as merely a cultural transmission from the past. Rather, the 'traditional' ways can be seen as constantly recreated within 'modern' cultural practices. There has obviously been some undermining of women's ideological control of biological reproduction with attempts to strengthen modernist health practices. Women's 'traditional' knowledge has been more and more devalued by 'moderns' and the state, although we also see many of these practices still firmly adhered to. In Negeri Sembilan in the 1970s, for example, the placenta was often retrieved in hospital births, so that the home-delivery-based ritual surrounding it could be performed. But not everyone bothered, although some reportedly still bring the placenta home even from urban centres. Some religious officials and *Dakwah* groups have also been attempting to discredit such practices as un-Islamic, which ties religion again into a version of modernity and against 'un-Islamic', premodern tradition. Those attached to the modern ways, whether the 'young', representatives of the modern sectors (such as nurses and teachers) or migrants to the city, marshal ammunition from the media and their experience of the urban world about vitamins and 'correct' ways of looking after babies. But even young proponents of some of the new ways among my informants have found their contacts with modern medicine profoundly alienating; for example, one young mother deeply resented the episiotomy and stitching with her first baby, feeling it was worse than the whole labour. She also found the government midwife *sombong* (arrogant) and in fact resolutely refused all the vitamins and iron given to her at the *mukim* (young women engaging in 'free sex') maternal health clinic during the pregnancy. On the other hand, stories are widespread of the battles some urban middle-class parents have engaged in to follow the new ways in having the father present at the birth.

The sexual politics of child care has been another important aspect of the power relations surrounding mothering. It appears that women have done and continue to do much of the work in looking after children, although it is possible that there was some spreading of this labour to men and other children in the more communal contexts of village life in the past. This is not simply a 'traditional' sexual division of labour. It has, of course, been endlessly reconstituted. As in the past, power in household relations can be seen as linked to the larger forces of economy and polity. It is clear that the social changes of the industrial era have imposed enormous new strains on women. The elaboration of child care and the consumption necessary to motherhood have produced complex new domestic regimes. Such work often has to be carried out within a period of time strongly circumscribed by paid work regimes. School arrangements were a real headache for the Seremban households interviewed, for example: one neighbouring couple, with four children at four different schools on different shifts (Malaysian schools run two shifts) and with no servant, had complex and often fraught arrangements for both parents and some friends to pick up the children. On the other hand, my village study showed how many middle-class migrants have relied on grand-motherly care of children sent back to the village over the last few decades – about a quarter of all village households had been involved in such care at some point (see Stivens 1996). Such kin care obviously has often helped out, but has provided full care for only a small proportion of working parents in the middle-class populations I studied in Seremban, Kuala Lumpur and Penang.

The politics of child care has other dimensions. The absence of proper maternity leave has left many salaried women returning to work after six weeks. This gives them little respite from the pregnancy and birth and forces many of them to hand over some of the child's care to kin and servants long before they actually wish to. (There are as yet few well-run nurseries.) They have also experienced problems with breast-feeding because of this. The absence of any developed state ideology of maternal deprivation over the last couple of decades is especially interesting, com-pared to its force in the West, for example. Thus there seemed to be little public discussion about the supposed guilt that 'working mothers' might feel until recently, although there has been much publicity about prob-lems with servants and their care of children. (There is very little dis-cussion, however, about the problems servants have with their em-ployers.) And it is only comparatively recently that we have seen a developed campaign about working mothers and their effects on teenage children, although ideas of maternal deprivation have been deployed in some of the Muslim critiques of modern life.

The extent of the sheer hard work (and mostly female work) that goes into child rearing cannot be exaggerated. The extended family, mainly mothers or sisters, can also provide some help, but it is less clear that they actually provide sustained periods of relief from the hard slog of motherly care, apart from cases where the grandmother was looking after the children. It is significant, for example, that only a small number of interviewees were living in extended family households, and the majority had kin living far away in other states.

Some Malaysian feminists have been expressing real despondency about the potential for men to change, particularly on the domestic front. While I know of some academic men doing a larger share of domestic labour, and some of the magazines are now running stories about fathers cooking and doing night feeds for their bottle-fed babies, there appears to be little evidence of real changes in urban housework patterns. Among my Kuala Lumpur sample, for example, most informants – male and female – thought that fathers should 'help' with child care and feeding. It is much harder to measure how much they actually did do, however. The forces of conservatism are not just the national production of the housewife or intransigent, individual men, however. In Rembau older women occasionally disparaged a few such pioneers. It is also possible that the availability of servants for some sections of the middle class has lessened the pressures on men to 'help' their harassed 'working wives', forestalling renegotiation of domestic masculinity.

The postcolonial state has clearly seen mothers as having the power to build happy families and a happy nation. Such attributions of power carry with them, as we saw earlier, equal potential for the state's blaming mothers. These interweave in interesting ways with the received everyday ideologies and practices of mothering, which also attribute considerable power and blame. In Rembau, for example, people told me that a mother was to blame if her children quarrelled among themselves. Whether we can see this particular development as a move towards an increasingly individualistic 'modern' attribution of blame and responsibility within a rural context of growing individualization of production is debatable and probably outside the scope of this discussion.[29] But the state and media campaigns at the national level to exhort parents – both fathers and mothers – to greater efforts in raising their children suggest some elaboration of these ideas. This has been especially noticeable in recent moral panics about *boh sia* (young women engaging in 'free sex') and *lepak* (loafing, hanging out): the behaviour of teenagers has become a site for the negotiation of anxieties about the possible ills of modernity, the embodiment of parental and societal failures to produce the right kind of Asian family values and Islamic modernity, or at least to be able to resist the worst of 'Westoxification'.[30] Child abuse, which has also received a lot of attention recently from academics, journalists and government, is similarly represented in some quarters as one of the by-products of 'development', collapsing family values and general social decline.

Conclusions

I have suggested that the unrecognized gendering and specificities of Malaysian modernity have been embedded in writing about the 'family', motherhood and childbearing in the country. We cannot simply and authoritatively pronounce about the 'effects' of successive stages of Malaysia's divergent modernity on women's mothering. Women have had complex and multiple relationships as mothers to the modernizing patterns and practices described: these relationships have been open to various interpretations, positioned differently by different sets of commentators.

I suggested above that earlier models of Malay mothering were constructed within the colonial discourses of mothers and others as indulgent, loving and nurturant, but perhaps too indulgent and, as Lenore Manderson shows (this volume), unhygienic, fatalistic and somewhat unindustrious. Much of this body of earlier work presumptuously claimed to be providing authoritative accounts of the relationships between parents and children and their respective subjectivities. Yet for all this authoritativeness, there was comparatively little about the conditions and experiences of mothering in this work (cf. Introduction, Manderson, this volume). These views led directly to a contemporary modernist storyline that sees increasingly nuclearized urban families arising with industrialization, individual mothering replacing the more collective earlier patterns and a new purpose in life replacing the previous over-indulgence and nurturance. Women are to be transformed into energetic creators of happy families and a happy nation.

A different version of contemporary narratives of motherhood, however, sees 'traditional' child rearing as peculiarly vulnerable to the ills of Westoxification, collapsing family values and general social decline. This scenario is prominent in some resurgent Islamic versions of 'modern' discourse, which to some extent collapse family and society into each other, granting family a central place as the building block of society. The 'Asian Family' of government rhetoric becomes a nostalgia-laden repository for reinvented versions of family life, motherhood and morality.

A third, feminist version can pronounce that modernity and modern motherhood mean a loss of earlier female power or autonomy, that ever-increasing modernity and commoditization erodes women's situation in multiple ways. Women are seen as suffering under their responsibility for increasing production of the commodity-like product, the happy, smiling, clever, industrious, religious and indeed nation-building child, while on occasion slowly going mad in their expensive, if not especially large, town houses or burning out with the dual demands of work and home. The child in such accounts, however, can veer dangerously towards being depicted as the main villain, as in Barrett and McIntosh's account of the 'tyranny of motherhood' (1982:62). The child per se can appear to be held responsible for the institution and the woes it may confer on women.

These competing claims to give an authoritative account of Malay mothers' experiences of mothering return us to the opening remarks about the problems facing any such account. It is clear that scholarly and media agendas have often mirrored the overt impositions of first colonial, then nation building and now resurgent religion's and globalizing culture's concerns and agendas. The competing narratives about the transformations of mothering from 'traditional' to 'modern' and the place of mothering in the modernizing process echo the tensions in women's lived experiences of modernity. I highlighted in particular the embeddedness of much discursive production of Malay mothering in the tensions surrounding the relationship of Malaysian Islam to modernity. Thus some of my informants in the present study have been living the religious resurgence in very intense ways, finding religion to be their main support in such stressful situations as negotiating single parenthood after divorce. I am not happy about representing these experiences as simply a governance of women as 'victims' by an ultimately repressive religion (as Ong (1990) does). Indeed, we could equally see their religious practice as representing a form of social and political agency: the support for revivalist Islam among sections of the new middle classes, especially university students (Narli 1986), can be seen as a means for women to confront Malaysian modernity on terms somewhat more of their own making.[31]

The dominant representation of the many tensions surrounding the modernizing process as a conflict between the purported 'old' and the 'new' creates a false duality out of what are in fact shifting meanings. This opposition is represented as a straightforward temporal one: the 'traditional' is posed as some relic of the 'premodern' 'past', which 'progress' – in whatever version is favoured by the observer – will displace. I would see 'tradition' rather as a highly complex, continuous development of discursive and social practices, constantly recreated in the 'present'. The discursive opposition between 'tradition' and 'modernity' has constantly shifted, tying one or other or both terms to various other areas of discourse, as in the widespread linkage of 'modernity' with 'Westernization' / 'Westoxification'. For my informants, these shifting instabilities are everpresent as they negotiate the complex intersections of mothering, class, nation and religion.

NOTES

1 My original research in Negeri Sembilan, Malaysia, was carried out in three
adjacent villages in Rembau District from 1975 to 1976, funded by a student-
ship in the Department of Anthropology, London School of Economics, from
the then Social Science Research Council (SSRC) (UK). Further visits were
made in 1982 (funded by the (UK) Hayter Fund), 1984, 1985, 1986 and
1987–8 (the latter funded by the Australian Research Grant Scheme). The
focus of the original research was on gender and transformation of the agrarian
economy. Later research visits have centred more on macro-level change. My
research on Negeri Sembilan appears in my book *Matriliny and Modernity*
(Stivens 1996). See also Stivens (1987). In the last few years I have been
engaged on an Australian Research Council funded project on Work and
Family in the New Malay Middle Classes. This has involved a two-month
period of residence on a Seremban middle-class housing estate in 1987–8 and a
number of trips since gathering materials in Malaysia, Singapore and the UK,
including several series of interviews with samples of middle-class households
in Seremban, Kuala Lumpur and Penang (1990–3). I am extremely grateful to
Lucy Healey, Goh Beng Lan, Hah Foong Lian, Zainab Wahidin, Linda Pang,
Azizah Kassim, Norani Othman, Clive Kessler and Joel Kahn for their help
during this current project.
2 Such work has raised pertinent questions about the categories West, non-
Western and Third World, which essentialize and homogenize highly diverse
patterns and reproduce colonial categories (cf. Said 1986). See di Leonardo
(1991); Fox (1991); Mani (1990); Mascia-Lees *et al.* (1989); Mohanty *et al.*
(1991); Moore (1988, 1994); Nencel and Pels (1991); Ong (1989). The
insecurities are acute in writing about the so-called 'Third World', although
Malaysia's version of modernity has probably removed it from that category.
See Stivens (1994b).
3 There is clearly a growing instability surrounding the category of modernity,
produced mainly by the debates around postmodernity and postcolonialism.
Elsewhere, I have argued that we have many problems in theorizing Malaysian
modernity, especially the all too common conflation of modernity and Westernization in much of the development literature (1994b, n.d.a, n.d.b). This is
a further twist on the undoubted Eurocentrism of most of the sociological
debates about modernity and postmodernity.
4 The New Economic Policy, introduced in 1970 after communal riots in 1969,
has been particularly important in subsequent restructuring of the economy:
this aimed to progressively redistribute wealth to the poorest sections of
Malaysian society, the Malays. The target of the New Economic Policy was a
30 per cent *bumiputra* (Malay or indigenous) ownership of the economy by
1990 (compared to 2.4 per cent in 1970, and 10.3 per cent in 1978). Other
Malaysians were to own a 40 per cent share and foreign interests 30 per cent
(compared to 63.3 per cent in 1970; Majid and Majid 1983:69).
5 See Stivens (n.d.b).
6 Lazreg (1988) has argued that this is common in writing on the Middle East
(cf. Ahmed 1992; Sabbah 1988). Mather (1985) is a clear example of this
demonizing of Islam. See Stivens (1992).
7 It is perhaps invidious to concentrate on Barrett and McIntosh's writings on the
family as an example of the anti-child writing of the time (and it was firmly

autocritiqued for its 'ethnocentrism', Barrett and McIntosh 1985). But their analysis of the 'family' has been central and, I would argue, indicative. Although they concede some of the passionate emotions involved, they see the woman's love for her children as tying the woman down. As they say, 'This is what we mean by the tyranny of motherhood' (Barrett and McIntosh 1982:62). Under the heading *Avoid oppressive relationships* they tell us that '[e]ach woman who is coquettish with men and each mother who indulges her child with excessive attention and toys makes it harder for other women to resist the pressures from men and children' (1982:143). We can only describe this as constituted within an overtly anti-child discourse.

8 See Ross' (1995) and Adams' (1995) reviews of recent writing about mothering for bibliographies of this literature.

9 The more empirical work looks at fertility and infertility, feeding practices, pregnancy, the medicalization of childbirth, older mothers, foetal imaging and diagnosis, surrogacy, and so on. See Phoenix *et al.* (1991) for summaries and discussion of this body of work. See also Kaplan (1992); Oakley (1980); Stanworth (1987). The most influential theoretical texts include Chodorow (1978) and Riley (1983). For discussions of Kristeva and Irigaray on mothering, see Grosz (1989).

10 But see among others Kristeva (1981, 1986); Martin (1987); Young (1990).

11 See, for example, Riley's excellent book *War in the Nursery: Theories of the Mother and Child* (1983), where the child none the less is presented mainly within the terms set by psychoanalytic theory, and the tensions between some feminist views of mothering as oppression and a literature about the needs of children are not addressed.

12 Feminist anthropology has had a somewhat tense relationship with other feminisms. See Moore (1994); Stivens (1994a).

13 Such uncritical acceptance of a homogeneous 'Western' family can also be detected in Asian constructs. In the Malaysian context, we have a hegemonic discourse of the 'Asian family' which is operated both by the state and by my present middle-class informants for example. This derives its meaning from an explicit contrast with and critique of the alleged decline of the family in the West (see Stivens 1987, n.d.b).

14 I find the neglect of children in recent feminist theory especially interesting. There seems to have been very little real discussion within the central theoretical texts of children as a subordinate group and of the contradictions posed by trying to be attentive as feminists to the needs of both women and children. I am tempted to see this as an unreconstructed inheritance of a long-standing (Western) cultural hostility towards children. Elsewhere I am working on a project exploring the cultural complexities of the subordination of children.

15 See, among others, Stacey (1986).

16 I personally regard the prominence of the 'body' within contemporary social theory with some suspicion. Terry Turner, for example, in the course of a developed discussion, sees the emergence of the discourse on the body in contemporary social theory as one of the major manifestations of a crisis in the intellectual politics and epistemology of Western social thought. He argues that in the flight from the social in this thought we have seen a replacement of

the subject with the body as the more or less passive object of disciplines and representations. He sees much contemporary discourse on the body as an expression of the individualistic social ideology of the middle-class professional intellectuals who have developed it as an alternative to class – and other socially based political and intellectual perspectives (Turner 1994; cf. Introduction, di Leonardo 1991). The importance of the body, in social theory, he suggests, is associated with the prominence of body-related themes in the culture of contemporary late capitalism (Turner 1994).

17 See Manderson (1987a, this volume).
18 See Djamour (1965); Firth (1966); Karim (1984); Laderman (1982, 1983); Swift (1965). See also Noor Laily Abu Bakar and Hashim (1984).
19
Kami mengunjungi pusara bonda	We went to mother's grave
Sunyi pagi disinari suria	On a quiet sunlit morning
Wangi berseri puspa kemboja	The fragrant *kemboja* blossoms
Menyambut kami mewakili bonda	Welcome[d] us on mother's behalf
Nisan batu kami tegakkan	We erected tombstones for her
Tiada lagi lalang menjulang	Cleared the tall wild grass
Ada doa kami pohonkan	Then we said a simple prayer
Air mawar kami siramkan	And sprinkled rose-water on her grave
Begitu bakti kami berikan	Whatever we may do to serve her
Tiada sama bonda melahirkan	Can never repay her gift of birth
Kasih bonda tiada sempadan	And her boundless love for us
Kemuncak murni kemuliaan insan.	The peak of human nobility.

Excerpt from Usman Awang's *Ke Makam Bonda* (Mother's Grave). Selections from *Contemporary Malaysian Poetry* (Muhammed Haji Salleh 1978).

Ibu dan Anakku	**Mother and My Child**
Ibu,	Mother,
Kenangan inin bukan merindumu,	This tribute bears no sorrow,
Hati sekadar terusik melihat anakku,	Only, I am moved by the sight of my child,
(Ibu tak pernah menyaksikan persandinganku)	(The child you have never seen)
Wajahnya wajah ibu yang melahirkan daku.	Who bears your face.
Ibu,	Mother,
Jika benar ia menyerupaimu,	Would that she resembled you,
Bukan wajahnya membelai hatiku,	It is not her face that saddens me,
Sipat dan jiwanya membanggakan daku,	Her demeanour and spirit make me proud,
Sipat ibu yang selalu merestu,	For they bear your blessing,
Damai sejahtera manusia selalu.	The blessing of eternal peace.
Ibu,	Mother,
Panggillah ia disampingmu,	Be there to guide her,
Jika anakku ke lain tuju.	Should my child be led astray.

From Usman Awang (1961:61).

20 See Shaharuddin Maaruf's (1988) discussion of some aspects of this.
21 See, for example, Nor Laily Aziz and Tan (1978).
22 See Stivens (1996) for further discussion.
23 Fong Chan Ong 1986 'Industrialisation and manpower implications' in *Population and Demographic Issues in Malaysian Industrialisation*, compiled by Khong Kim Hoong and Salleh Ismail, Population Studies Unit, Universiti Malaya, cited by Rashidah Abdullah (1993).
24 As Rashidah Abdullah (1993) notes, few of these concerns have been expressed publicly, due to the (political) sensitivity of the issue. She cites one of the most critical reports from the Population Studies Unit of the University of Malaya.
25 The figures from the 1990 census (censuses are conducted at ten-year intervals) which differentiate birth rates by ethnicity are not yet available, so it is not yet possible to assess the effects of the policy.
26 Elsewhere I look at what we might see as a postmodernization of the many images of women within contemporary Malay cultural productions (Stivens n.d.b).
27 This book was published in 1991 in Kuala Lumpur, but the author, Heryanto Sutedja, appears to be Indonesian from his name. The front cover has a different title from the frontispiece, namely *Anak Anda Malas Belajar*.
28 See Karim (1984) for a descriptive account of Malay midwives. See Manderson (1981, 1982, 1987a, 1987b, 1989, 1992).
29 See my book *Matriliny and Modernity* (Stivens 1996) for discussion.
30 'Westoxification' is, I understand, a term first used by the Ayatollah Khomeini, which has some currency in the region. There was, in fact, a conference exploring its meanings in Singapore in December 1993.
31 See, for example, Akbar Ahmed (1992) who argues for an understanding of Islamic resurgence as a quintessentially postmodern form of political practice. See Sabbah (1988); Stivens (n.d.b).

REFERENCES

Adams, A. 1995 Review essay: Maternal bonds: recent literature on mothering. *Signs* 20(2):414–27.
Ahmed, L. 1992 *Women and Gender in Islam: Historical Roots of a Modern Debate.* New Haven: Yale University Press.
Akbar Ahmed 1992 *Postmodernism and Islam: Predicament and Promise.* London: Routledge.
Amina Wadud-Muhsin 1992 *Qu'ran and Woman.* Kuala Lumpur: Penerbit Fajar Bakti.
Barrett, M. and McIntosh, M. 1982 *The Anti-Social Family.* London: Verso.
    1985 Ethnocentrism and socialist-feminist theory. *Feminist Review* 20:23–47.
Bordo, S. 1990 Feminism, postmodernism and gender-scepticism. In L. Nicholson (ed.) *Feminism/Postmodernism.* New York: Routledge, 133–56.
Chodorow, N. 1978 *The Reproduction of Mothering: Psychoanalysis and the Sociology of Gender.* Berkeley: University of California Press.
Davin, A. 1978 Imperialism and motherhood. *History Workshop* 5:9–65.
di Leonardo, M. 1991 (ed.) Introduction: Gender, culture, and political economy: feminist anthropology in historical perspective. In M. di Leonardo (ed.) *Gender at the Crossroads of Knowledge: Feminist Anthropology in the Postmodern Era.* Berkeley: University of California Press, 1–48.

Djamour, J. 1965 *Malay Kinship and Marriage in Singapore*. London: The Athlone Press.

Felski, R. 1995 *The Gender of Modernity*. Cambridge, MA: Harvard University Press.

Firth, R. 1966 *Housekeeping among Malay Peasants*. London: The Athlone Press.

Fox, R. 1991 (ed.) *Recapturing Anthropology*. Santa Fe: School of American Research Press.

Friday, N. 1977 *My Mother/My Self: The Daughter's Search for Identity*. New York: Delacorte Press.

Grosz, E. 1989 *Sexual Subversions*. Sydney: Allen and Unwin.

Heryanto Sutedja 1991 *Mengapa Anak Anda Malas Belajar?* (Why is Your Child Lazy about Studying?). Kuala Lumpur: Syarikat S. Abdul Majeed.

Jamiah binti Bador 1974 *Rancangan keluarga di Kampung Gadung* (Family planning in Kampung Gadung). BA (Hons) thesis, University of Malaya.

Jomo, K.S. and Tan Peck Leng n.d. *Not the Better Half: Malaysian Women and Development Planning*. Kuala Lumpur: Integration of Women in Development, Asian and Pacific Development Centre.

Kaplan, E.A. 1992 *Motherhood and Representation: The Mother in Popular Culture and Melodrama*. London: Routledge.

Karim, W.-J. 1984 Malay midwives and witches. *Social Science and Medicine* 18(2):159–66.

Khoo Boo Teik 1995 *Paradoxes of Mahathirism: An Intellectual Biography of Mahathir Mohamad*. Kuala Lumpur: Oxford University Press.

Kristeva, J. 1981 The maternal body. *m/f* 5&6:158–63.

1986 (French orig. 1977) Stabat mater. In J. Kristeva *The Kristeva Reader* (ed. T. Moi). Oxford: Basil Blackwell, 160–86.

Laderman, C. 1982 Putting Malay women in their place. In P. van Esterik (ed.) *Women of Southeast Asia*. Occasional Paper No. 9. [De Kalb]: Center for Southeast Asian Studies, Northern Illinois University, Detroit, 79–99.

1983 *Wives and Midwives: Childbirth and Nutrition in Rural Malaysia*. Berkeley: University of California Press.

Lazreg, M. 1988 Feminism and difference: the perils of writing as a woman on Algeria. *Feminist Studies* 14(1):81–107.

Lim Teck Ghee 1977 *Peasants and their Agricultural Economy*. Oxford: Oxford University Press.

Mahathir bin Mohamad 1970 *The Malay Dilemma*. Singapore: Donald Moore for Asia Pacific Press.

Majid, S. and Majid, A. 1983 Public sector land settlement: rural development in West Malaysia. In D.A.M. Lea and D.P. Chaudhri (eds.) *Rural Development and the State: Contradictions and Dilemmas in Developing Countries*. London and New York: Methuen, 66–99.

Malaya (Fed) 1951 *Report of the Committee on Malay Education, Federation of Malaya*. Kuala Lumpur: Government Printer.

Manderson, L. 1980 *Women, Politics and Change: The Kaum Ibu UMNO Malaysia, 1945–1972*. Kuala Lumpur: Oxford University Press.

1981 Traditional food beliefs and critical life events in Peninsular Malaysia. *Social Science Information* 20(6):947–75.

1982 Bottle feeding and ideology in colonial Malaya: the production of change. *International Journal of Health Services* 12(4):597–616.

1987a Blame, responsibility and remedial action: death, disease and the infant in early twentieth century Malaya. In N. Owen (ed.) *Death and Disease in Southeast Asia: Explorations in Social, Medical and Demographic History*. Singapore: Oxford University Press for the Asian Studies Association of Australia, 257–82.

1987b Health services and the legitimation of the colonial state: British Malaya 1786–1941. *International Journal of Health Services* 17(1):91–112.

1989 Political economy and the politics of gender: maternal and child health in colonial Malaya. In P. Cohen and J. Purcal (eds.) *The Political Economy of Primary Health Care in Southeast Asia*. Canberra: Australian Development Studies Network and ASEAN Training Centre for Primary Health Care Development, 79–100.

Manderson, L. 1992 Women and the state: maternal and child welfare in colonial Malaya, 1900–1940. In V. Fildes, L. Marks and H. Marland (eds.) *Women and Children First: International Maternal and Infant Welfare 1870–1945*. London: Routledge, 154–77.

Mani, L. 1990 Multiple mediations: feminist scholarship in the age of multinational reception. *Feminist Review* 35 (Summer):24–41.

Martin, E. 1987 *The Woman in the Body: A Cultural Analysis of Reproduction*. Boston: Beacon Press.

Mascia-Lees, F.E., Sharpe, P. and Cohen, C.B. 1989 The postmodernist turn in anthropology: cautions from a feminist perspective. *Signs* 15(1):7–33.

Mather, C. 1985 'Rather than make trouble, it's better just to leave': behind the lack of industrial strife in the Tangerang region of West Java. In H. Afshar (ed.) *Women, Work and Ideology in the Third World*. London: Tavistock Publications, 153–80.

Mernissi, F. 1991 *Women and Islam: An Historical Enquiry*. Oxford: Blackwell.

Mohanty, C., Russo, A. and Torres, L. 1991 (eds.) *Third World Women and the Politics of Feminism*. Bloomington and Indianapolis: Indiana University Press.

Moore, H. 1988 *Feminism and Anthropology*. Oxford: Basil Blackwell.

Moore, H. 1994 *A Passion for Difference: Essays in Anthropology and Gender*. Bloomington: Indiana University Press.

Muhammed Haji Salleh (ed.) 1978 *Contemporary Malaysian Poetry* (trans. Adibah Amin). Kuala Lumpur: Universiti Malaya Press.

Narli, A.N. 1986 Malay women in tertiary education: trends of change in female role ideology. PhD thesis, University Sains, Penang.

Nencel, L. and Pels, P. 1991 (eds.) *Constructing Knowledge: Authority and Critique in Social Science*. London: Sage Publications.

Noor Laily Abu Bakar and Hashim, R. 1984 Child care for working women. In Hing Ai Yun, Nik Safiah Karim and Rokiah Talib (eds.) *Women in Malaysia*. Petaling Jaya: Pelanduk Publications, 78–93.

Nor Laily Aziz and Tan, B.A. 1978 *Methods of Measuring the Impact of Family Planning Programmes on Fertility in the Case of Malaysia*. Kuala Lumpur: Lembaga Perancang Keluarga Negara (National Family Planning Board).

Oakley, A. 1980 *Women Confined: Towards a Sociology of Childbirth*. Oxford: Martin Robertson.

Ong, A. 1987 *Spirits of Resistance and Capitalist Discipline: Factory Women in Malaysia*. Albany: State University of New York Press.

1989 Colonialism and modernity: feminist re-presentations of women in non-western societies. *Inscriptions* 5:79–93.

1990 State versus Islam: Malay families, women's bodies, and the body politic in Malaysia. *American Ethnologist* 17(2):258–76.

Phoenix, A. Woollett, A. and Lloyd, E. 1991 (eds.) *Motherhood: Meanings, Practices and Ideologies*. London: Sage Publications.

Rashidah Abdullah 1993 Changing population policies and women's lives in Malaysia. *Reproductive Health Matters* 1(1):67–77.

Rich, A. 1977 *Of Woman Born: Motherhood as Experience and Institution*. London: Virago Press.

Riley, D. 1983 *War in the Nursery: Theories of the Mother and the Child*. London: Virago Press.

Ross, E. 1995 Review essay: New thoughts on 'the oldest vocation': mothers and motherhood in recent feminist scholarship. *Signs* 20(2):397–413.

Roziah Omar 1996 *State, Islam and Malay Reproduction*. Working Paper No. 2. Canberra: Gender Relations Project, Research School of Pacific and Asian Studies, The Australian National University.

Ruddick, S. 1989 *Maternal Thinking: Towards a Politics of Peace*. London: The Women's Press.

Sabbah, D.A. 1988 *Woman in the Muslim Unconscious*. New York: Pergamon Press.

Said, E.W. 1986 Intellectuals in the post-colonial world. *Salmagundi* 70–1:44–64.

Segal, L. 1983 (ed.) *What Is to be Done about the Family?* Harmondsworth: Penguin Books.

Shaharuddin Maaruf 1988 *Malay Ideas on Development: From Feudal Lord to Capitalist*. Singapore and Kuala Lumpur: Times Books.

Snitow, A. 1992 Feminism and motherhood: an American reading. *Feminist Review* 40 (Spring):32–51.

Stacey, J. 1986 Are feminists afraid to leave home? The challenge of conservative pro-family feminism. In J. Mitchell and A. Oakley (eds.) *What is Feminism?* Oxford: Basil Blackwell, 219–48.

Stanworth, M. 1987 (ed.) *Reproductive Technologies, Gender, Motherhood and Medicine*. Minneapolis: University of Minnesota Press.

Stivens, M. 1985 The fate of women's land rights: gender, matriliny, and capitalism in Rembau, Negeri Sembilan, Malaysia. In H. Afshar (ed.) *Women, Work and Ideology in the Third World*. London: Tavistock Publications, 3–36.

1987 Family and state in Malaysian industrialisation. In H. Afshar (ed.) *Women, State and Ideology: Studies from Africa and Asia*. London: Macmillan, 89–104.

1992 Perspectives on gender: problems in writing about women in Malaysia. In J. Kahn and F. Loh (eds.) *Fragmented Vision: Culture and Politics in Contemporary Malaysia*. Sydney: Allen and Unwin, 202–24.

1994a The gendering of knowledge: the case of anthropology and feminism. In

N. Grieve and A. Burns (eds.) *Australian Women: Contemporary Feminist Thought.* Melbourne: Oxford University Press, 133–41.

1994b Gender and modernity in Malaysia. In A. Gomes (ed.) *Modernity and Identity: Asian Illustrations.* Bundoora: La Trobe University Press, 66–95.

1996 *Matriliny and Modernity: Sexual Politics and Social Change in Rural Malaysia.* Sydney: Allen and Unwin.

n.d.a Introduction: Theorising gender, power and modernity in affluent Asia. In K. Sen and M. Stivens (eds.) *Gender and Power in Affluent Asia.* London: Routledge (forthcoming).

n.d.b Sex, gender and the making of the Malay middle classes. In K. Sen and M. Stivens (eds.) *Gender and Power in Affluent Asia.* London: Routledge (forthcoming).

Stoler, A. 1991 Carnal knowledge and imperial power: gender, race and morality in colonial Asia. In M. di Leonardo (ed.) *Gender at the Crossroads of Knowledge: Feminist Anthropology in the Postmodern Era.* Berkeley: University of California Press, 51–101.

Swift, M. 1965 *Malay Peasant Society in Jelebu.* London: Athlone Press.

Syed Hussein Alatas 1977 *The Myth of the Lazy Native: A Study of the Image of the Malays, Filipinos and Javanese from the 16th to the 20th Centuries and its Function in the Ideology of Colonial Capitalism.* London: Cass.

Thorne, B. and Yalom, M. 1982 *Rethinking the Family.* New York: Longman.

Turner, T. 1994 Bodies and anti-bodies: flesh and fetish in contemporary social theory. In T. Csordas (ed.) *Embodiment and Experience: The Existential Ground of Culture and Self.* Cambridge: Cambridge University Press, 27–47.

Usman Awang 1961 *Gelombang.* Kuala Lumpur: Oxford University Press.

Young, I.M. 1990 Pregnant embodiment: subjectivity and alienation. In I.M. Young *Throwing Like a Girl and Other Essays in Feminist Philosophy and Social Theory.* Bloomington: Indiana University Press, 160–74.

3 'Good wives and mothers' or 'dedicated workers'? Contradictions of domesticity in the 'mission of sisterhood', Travancore, south India

Jane Haggis

Recent feminist reassessments of the historiography of European colonialism have identified a gendered quality intrinsic to colonizing endeavours across a range of imperial settings (see for example Callaway 1987; Chaudhuri and Strobel 1992; Grimshaw 1989; Hunter 1984; Jolly and Macintyre 1989; Knapman 1986; Strobel 1991). In particular, these studies have revealed a cultural agenda directed at transforming the ideologies and practices of indigenous gender orders into versions of metropolitan norms. This gendered dimension of colonialism is embodied, in much of this literature, in those 'colonizing women'[1] who not only provided potent symbolic images for the 'recasting' of indigenous women,[2] but were significant agents in articulating and conducting a project of domestication aimed at colonized women. Through the influence of their own exemplary femininity and domesticity, white women sought to remodel indigenous women into the 'good wives and mothers' they themselves were assumed to personify. Missionary women, as wives and single women, are prominent in this revisionist history, reflecting the intimate connections between nineteenth-century evangelical Christianity, dominant gender ideologies and imperialism.

Interestingly, given Britain's imperial and evangelical past, it is the North American women's missionary movement which has attracted most research attention to date. In particular, the book-length studies by Jane Hunter (1984) and Patricia Grimshaw (1989) and a growing periodical literature have begun to document missionary women's involvements in proselytizing a 'gospel of gentility', to use Hunter's term, in an overt programme to 'convert' indigenous women not only to Christianity but to conventions of 'true womanhood' embodied in the exemplary figure of the missionary women themselves (see especially Flemming 1992; Grim-

81

shaw 1989; Hunt 1990a, 1990b; Hunter 1984; Jolly 1991; Ramusack 1992). Irony tinges the accounts of these conversion efforts, as the women, in their roles as wife or single missionary, sought to breach the divide between their activism and the ideal of domestic femininity. Moreover, the consequences of this effort were often quite contrary to those intended by the missionary women. Their endeavours too often reinforced the disintegration of indigenous norms and values in a context which did little to facilitate or make desirable the imitation of the missionary women's 'true womanhood'. At best, their educational efforts and organizational initiatives might offer opportunities for new public roles and occupational endeavours to some of the women they came in contact with. Margaret Jolly (1993) and Nancy Hunt (1990b) have demonstrated how a maternal idiom was used to structure the relationships between the colonizing women and those they hoped to 'uplift'. Jolly extends this observation to define the concept of 'maternalism' to express the peculiar location of white women in the colonial hierarchy: 'For white women although race and class might intersect to accumulate her power, her sex did not' (1993:115). Representing the relation between colonizing and colonized women as that between mother and daughter was a 'strategic expression of the tension . . . between detachment and agonized intimacy, between other and self' (1993:115).

In this chapter I consider the trope of domesticity informing the historical account of 'colonizing women' in the light of material drawn from the archive of the London Missionary Society's (LMS) mission in Travancore, south India, during the second half of the nineteenth century.[3] The chapter traces the construction of a 'mission of sisterhood' as a project of domestication in the missionary periodical literature, illustrating how this domesticating agenda fractures around the mediating agency of the Indian Christian 'Bible woman' in the writings of the missionaries serving in the Travancore mission. Drawing on the representations of 'women's work' in the missionary texts I illustrate how a rubric of domesticity – the making of 'good wives and mothers' of Indian Christian women – was imbricated with an imagery of intellectual and professional development. Paradoxically, the missionary narrative produces images of dedicated workers rather than good wives and mothers. The Travancore material thus challenges any straightforward assumption of 'domestication' as the singular project of missionary women's colonizing endeavours. Instead, I argue, a trope of emancipation organizes a contradictory imagery of domesticity and professionalism indicative as much, or more, of the shifting locations of the missionary women within British 'home' culture as of any actual colonizing efforts or effects. The final section of the chapter considers this trope of emancipation and 'mission of sisterhood' in terms of the concept of 'maternalism' suggested by Hunt and Jolly as expressive of the awkward location of 'colonizing women'.

Writing a feminist postcolonial history

As a number of writers have pointed out, feminist interventions in colonial historiography cannot avoid confronting the dilemmas of representation caught in the narratives of the past and a contemporary politics of difference within and beyond feminisms (see for example Carby 1982; Haggis 1990; Jolly 1991, 1993; Mohanty 1991; Nair 1990). Such an awareness has been further stimulated by the postcolonial critique of current academic discourses as colonizing.[4]

Rescuing Western women from the masculinist stereotypes of the existing historiography of empire runs the risk of continuing a colonizing discourse in reverse essentialist terms – the benevolent white woman softening the dominating agency of the European male's imperial ambitions. Writing a postcolonial feminist history of imperialism, however, involves more than capturing the complex qualities of hierarchy embedded in past narratives. It must also engage with the hierarchies of the present. The image of the 'colonizing white woman' revealed in colonial history bears uncanny resemblance to the image of the contemporary Western feminist in relation to her 'other' – the 'Third World' woman. As Spivak acerbically describes her own 'ideological victimage' to 'International Feminism', at best the latter is informed by the question 'what can I do for them?' (1987:135). Writing a postcolonial feminist history of imperialism must therefore engage directly with Western feminism's discursive relationships to Third World feminisms.

This chapter is a preliminary attempt to explore the dimensions of writing a text which tries to build into its mode of representation an awareness of both these aspects of the politics of difference – past and present. In that sense, it straddles uneasily the divide between what Jolly identifies as a realist history, one claiming an authentic recuperation of the 'real' lives of white women, and one concerned with discourse and the constructed, fictional quality of colonial narratives (1993:103ff). To simply re-present the missionary accounts of the 'mission of sisterhood' as an effort to 'free' Indian women risks a double jeopardy of colonizing authority. The colonized continue to be caught in the colonizer's gaze, now also overlaid with the contemporary reflection of First/Third World dissonance. Yet, to deconstruct the colonizing effect of the missionary texts, revealing its imperialist and racist declensions, compounds this contemporary author's colonizing authority – as 'liberator' of the Indian historical subject and custodian of the 'real' meaning of the historical evidence.

The dilemmas of representation and meaning are not made easier by the sources; missionary texts remain my primary material to date, an archive in which 'subject' voices are rarely authentic or vocal, precluding straight-forward recuperation of Indian voices and narratives. What do I 'liberate' the Indian subject to – Third World recipient of First World feminist enlightenment? And on what grounds can I simply dismiss the missionary narrative of sisterhood as fiction – I/we know better? A way through these discursive dilemmas is suggested in the notion of translation I have assembled from the several ways in which Haydn White (1978) and Talal Asad (1986) have utilized the term for, respectively, history writing and ethnography.

Drawing on an anthropological model of textual production, White utilizes the notion of translation to provide a poststructuralist dismantling of positivist historiography. For White there is no 'real' history beyond the historian's text. Her/his product is a translation of the exotic past (itself a construct of the historian's own questions) into a comprehensible fiction for the present. There is no one 'true' history, only competing fictions, a plurality of stories all equivalent in their verisimilitude. Thus, rendering the 'mission of sisterhood' as a colonizing discourse rather than an effort of emancipation is legitimated as an available mode of transla-tion – inscribing the past in the narrative forms of the contemporary world.

This persuasive dismantling of realist history (ruthlessly summarized here) receives a salutary check, however, in Talal Asad's critique of the anthropological notion of translation White draws on. Asad argues that the cultural translation of the ethnographer is inevitably caught in rela-tions of power, such that the ethnographer is not 'translator' in the sense of transparent mediator, but author.[5] As such, the ethnographic 'transla-tion' attains a powerful authority to inscribe meaning, locked as it is into arenas of professional, national and global power relations. While White's 'exotic past' can never offer the promise of dialogic discursivity held by the anthropological exotic, his image of a plurality of historical stories all equally prescient fails to acknowledge the worldliness of the historian's discursive product and its placement in a hierarchy of authorization. Moreover, as Edward Said has pointed out, the historical texts White unproblematically ascribes to the historian's imaginary scope are in them-selves 'worldly, to some degree they are events, . . . a part of the social world, human life, and of course the historical moments in which they are located and interpreted' (1983:4).

However, with the provisos offered by Asad and Said respectively, White's notion of translation nevertheless offers a way through my di-lemmas of representation and authority. I attempt to dissect the missionary narrative, 'translating' its religious idiom and colonizing subjectivity into my late twentieth-century narratives. In so doing I seek to convey the authenticity of the missionary accounts, and the sense they make of their task, while respecting my late twentieth-century sensibility of the nineteenth century not as a narrative of 'true religion' and civility, but as one of secularization, capitalism and imperialism. It is in this sense I try and straddle the realist–discourse divide. I make no singular 'truth' claim for my narrative or that of the missionaries; rather, both are available versions of the past. However, while I try and avoid dismissing the missionary text, I nevertheless privilege my translation of the 'mission of sisterhood', from a tale of emancipating Indian women to a story of professionalization and liberation of English 'ladies'. To do otherwise would risk ignoring precisely those issues of power and worldliness Asad and Said raise. At best, by making explicit how the two narratives meet, I indicate the ways in which the missionary view had a sense not only different, but inaccessible and unacceptable to my own.

At the same time, White's depiction of writing history as an act of translation provides a way of locating Indian women outside either my fiction or the story of the 'mission of sisterhood'. I am able to provide a provisional space for them within my account, one that I hope avoids the 'information retrieval' epithet,[6] by suggesting their 'fiction' turns on an as yet untranslatable historical narrative, a narrative which cannot be assumed to be that of 'true religion' or of secular capitalism.

The chapter begins the task of trying to write such a text by tracing the construction of the 'mission of sisterhood' in the pages of the Protestant missionary periodicals aimed at a popular audience in Britain. This provides the framework for considering how the 'mission' is portrayed within the accounts of 'women's work' in a specific mission locale in south Travancore. By revealing the discursive praxis of these texts as they shift ambiguously between domestic ideal and 'women's work' their colonizing authorization of the Indian woman is displayed. Yet at the same time, the figure of the Indian Bible woman dislocates this colonial capture, suggesting an active agency of her own while turning the missionary discourse back on itself, its subject not the Indian 'other' but itself, or rather herself: the English lady.

The 'mission of sisterhood'

In the periodical literature of the British Protestant missionary societies British women are cast as the saviours of Indian women, liberating them from the degradation of a vindictive Hindu culture and religion. 'The daughters of India', ran one oft-quoted assessment by a veteran missionary wife, 'are unwelcomed at their birth, untaught in childhood, enslaved when married, accursed as widows, and unlamented at their death' (*India's Women* 1880, 1:3).[7] The institutional context of this pitiful state was the *zenana* (or 'women's quarters')[8] – a prison in every sense of the word, its 'walls' are portrayed as real barriers to any significant change in the condition of Indian women, spiritually or materially. The 'inmates' of these *zenana* prisons are portrayed as innocent and passive victims of a merciless system that uses and abuses them as daughters and, especially, as wives. The plight of the child-brides and child-widows of India is a constant refrain, with descriptions of how even the youngest of 'brides' is forbidden to remarry, dragged off to have her hair cut; her bangles removed and pretty clothes exchanged for widow's cloths; neglected and accursed.

In sharp counterpoint to these pathetic creatures, English women bear the virtues and responsibilities of their free-born and independent situation. Not for them the walls of a domestic prison; instead they are portrayed as intelligent, respected help-meets in male endeavours, secure also in their own sphere of usefulness and purpose: 'women's work'. It is in the setting up of this opposition of stereotypes that the 'mission' of English women to their Indian counterparts is constructed, and they are, in emotional and graphic language, urged to respond:

> Hear the wail of India's women!
> Millions, millions to us cry,
> They to us for aid appealing,
> . . .
> 'Come to us!' with hands uplifted
> And with streaming eyes they plead.   (*IW* 1882, 2(9):134)

These two contrasting stereotypes – the passive, pitiable Indian woman and the active, independent English lady missionary – were nevertheless brought together in a very close relation indeed. For it is as sisters that English ladies are urged to respond to India's call. There is an odd juxtaposition about the depth of difference constructed between Indian and British women: the heathen and perishing against the Christian and secure; the free and the unfree; the cherished and the unwanted; and a characterization of a close, familial bond, that of sisterhood, surely based on a recognition of identity or similarity.

Both Indian and British women, by virtue of being women, are seen alike as innately religious, spiritual and moral, in ways that men (by implication and regardless of race) are not. The model of the Victorian lady as the 'angel in the house', providing the moral and spiritual influence around which domestic civilization turned, was drawn on both to define the effective qualities of the lady missionary and the potential of

Indian women: 'if won for Christ all their self-sacrificing devotion' would be pitted against 'ignorance [and] superstition' (*IW* 1887, 7(40):186). This combination of religiousness and domestic influence, especially in the upbringing of young children, produced the rallying slogan 'Get the hearts of the women of India . . . and you will win India' (*IW* 1887, 7(39):41). Those best able to win these hearts were English ladies, suited by temperament and personality and, as well, able to enter beyond the walls of the *zenana* into the 'heart of home and culture' into which the male missionary could not go (*IW* 1887, 7(40):187).

However, at the same time as 'sisterhood' is constructed on a shared womanly identity, a set of differences around axes of class, religion and race-nation are drawn, which break down this assumed identity into constituent parts in keeping with the dichotomous stereotypes described above. Class serves to cement a sense of sisterhood between English ladies and their assumed counterparts in the (usually) upper-class/caste *zenanas* of India, whose members are acknowledged as ladies, or at least potential ladies, and thus as ideal recipients of lady missionaries' enlightening influence, and as the key to winning over to Christianity the influential male members of their class. It was to this group that lady missionaries were enjoined to adopt a friendly 'sisterly' approach and to share their educational benefits and sense of social and religious responsibilities. To the 'village woman' on the other hand 'the appearance of a female evangelist must be as it were the vision of an angel from heaven' (*IW* 1887, 7(37):6). Class also distinguished British women; working-class women were drawn as self-sacrificing contributors to the financial fund enabling the agency of the 'lady'.

English ladies were also accorded a superior gendered authority, as better women. There is an identifiable split made between the all-embracing inclusion of women by nature and the socialized female: all women are sisters, but some have a superior femininity. The endeavour women missionaries are involved in becomes not one simply to convert, educate or enlighten, but to impose/introduce a very specific set of gender roles and models belonging to Victorian middle-class culture.

The aim was not only to convert Indian women to Christianity but 'to convert Indian *zenanas* into "true homes", moulded after the Christian pattern' (*IW* 1887, 7(40):180).[9] This ambition was reinforced by the explicit linkage made between the evangelical aims of the missionary movement and British imperial rule: 'This great empire has . . . been delivered into our hands . . . not, surely to gratify us, but to use our influence in elevating and enlightening the vast myriads of her people' (*IW* 1884, 4(22):180). In particular, '[i]t is to alleviate that misery as God may enable us and bless our efforts, and to deliver our sisters out of it, that we Englishwomen are called and selected in the providence of God – a wondrous honour [and] responsibility of the deepest solemnity' (*IW* 1880, 1 (preliminary issue):3).

The 'mission of sisterhood' is, in this literature, defined as a project of domestication – of transforming the Indian home into a mirror image of the Victorian middle-class ideal by 'emancipating' the *zenana* victim into 'Christian womanhood'. The agency of the 'lady', organizationally expressed as 'women's work', constitutes sisterhood across a hierarchy not only of race and class but also femininity. The irony is, of course, that this 'mission' presupposes the removal of the lady herself from the haven of domesticity – 'the true English home' legitimated in the periodical literature by the higher call of God (*IW* 1887, 7(40):180).

This ironic edge assumes a deeper ambiguity in the organizational history of the 'mission of sisterhood'. 'Women's work', as a distinct sphere of missionary endeavours, developed during the first quarter of the nineteenth century out of the labours of women operating largely outside of the missionary societies themselves. In India, the wives of missionary men saw a sphere of labour for themselves in providing education services to those – usually poor – Indians who were among their local contacts. The missionary wives drew upon their own female networks in Britain to raise funds for, and publicize, their efforts and needs. By the 1820s 'Ladies Associations' formed a web of effort throughout Britain, dedicated to raising funds for 'the work'.[10] In 1834 the scope of this 'women's work' had expanded sufficiently to inspire the formation of the Society for the Propagation of Female Education in the East (SPFEE) to send single women to the mission-field as teachers to their heathen 'sisters', a service the mainstream missionary societies had consistently refused to sponsor.

This public and highly successful female activism caught the missionary societies and their male membership in a quandary. While evangelical Christianity gave great weight to female 'influence' in spiritual and moral matters,[11] the missionary societies had conceived of their task, in the initial stages of establishment, as a mission of ordained men to evangelize the heathen. Even educational work amongst heathen boys could, by many conservative supporters of the missionary endeavour, be defined as outside the reach of this mission, the power of preaching seen as the only strategy appropriate to 'evangelizing the world'. The very presence of a missionary wife had been a subject of debate within missionary societies – as a possible hindrance rather than a help to the ordained preacher's tasks. The founding of the SPFEE gave institutional expression to the gendered quality of the missionary movement's purpose, indicating the inability of female agency to be encompassed within the generalized male one, at the same time as it provocatively enshrined the need for a 'division of labour' (SPFEE 1847:4).

The founding of the SPFEE also indicates the ways in which female agency was eventually integrated into the institutional frameworks of the mainstream missionary societies. During the 1860s and 1870s most of the British missionary societies began recruiting, training and sending women to their overseas mission-fields as 'lady missionaries'. By 1899 the number of women in the 'foreign field' outnumbered men substantially. In fact, if not in popular perceptions, the 'missionary' was more likely to be an educated single woman than an ordained male preacher.[12] In the process, 'women's work' in the mission-field shifted from a voluntary 'labour of love' conducted primarily by the wives of missionaries largely outside the organizational frameworks of the missionary society to a professional and paid employment of unmarried women by those societies to conduct a still distinct 'women's work', although now brought into a more formal correspondence with the 'work' of the male missionary. While the missionary wife remained an important presence within 'women's work', the central focus of agency and image was on her single colleague, 'freed' from the constraints of marriage and maternity to devote herself to the 'work' more fully.[13]

By setting this institutional history of 'women's work' alongside the portrayal of that work within the narrative of the 'mission of sisterhood' the self-referencing quality of these texts is discernible. The domesticating intent of the 'mission of sisterhood' requires the rupturing of the very image it relies on for its coherence: the 'angel in the house' gives way to the agencies and effects of, first, the working wife and then, more subversive still, the highly trained presence of the 'lady missionary'. The remainder of this chapter explores how these shifts in focus are dealt with in the representations of the 'mission of sisterhood' and its conduct in the LMS mission in south Travancore. In particular it is the imbricated images of Indian women with their missionary 'sisters' that draws out the ambiguous quality of the emancipatory effort of the 'mission of sisterhood'.

'Bright lights shining for Jesus'

This 'mission of sisterhood' took on a specific Travancore character in the writings of the missionaries who served there. The idioms of Hinduism and caste frame 'women's work' in their writings, reflecting the mission's presence in a Hindu kingdom only indirectly under British authority. On the one hand, an institutional nexus of state and religion formed a powerful barrier to missionary aspirations. On the other, this nexus provided their major constituency – the large population of nominal Christians who converted en masse in a strategic move to avoid upper-caste oppressions and gain access to missionary economic patronage and political protection.

The portrayal of the missionary endeavour in south Travancore bifurcates around the dual demands of converting the Hindu state and society while 'uplifting' the thousands of nominal Christians whose low-caste origins, poverty and deprivation threatened to label Christianity, in the eyes of the upper-caste communities, as the religion of the 'untouchables', thus thwarting the grander missionary ambition. The demands of this 'uplift' effort, which dominated the time and resources of the Travancore mission from its establishment in the 1810s, were reconciled with the aspiration of converting high-caste Hindu society by seeing a reformed and 'respectable' Christian community as a major 'native' agency in the conversion effort.

The critical medium in this transformation was the acquisition of a Christian education based on literacy. The *zenana* workers offered Hindu women a version of this agency: literacy and Scripture. The boundaries of 'women's work' formed in this emphasis on educational work as the transmission belt of both faith and civility. Initially a dual focus forms: both the convert and Hindu woman are portrayed as victims in need of Christian light. A difference intervenes with the successful transformation of convert women into the *zenana* worker or 'Bible woman' by the middle of the century. The Bible woman becomes an active agent, transcending the status of victim to become – almost – heroic in her attempts to bring her Hindu sisters into the light of Christianity. In the missionary writings the raw material of nominal Christians are transformed by the efforts of 'female education' into 'dedicated workers' rather than 'good wives and mothers'.

This transformation was the result of an educative aim and breadth of effort which, by the last quarter of the nineteenth century, had developed a range of institutions to carry out its goals. A network of village schools, staffed by 'native' teachers under the overall superintendence of the missionary women, provided a basic education for Christian girls in Scripture, literacy and numeracy as well as manners and morals, the essentials of the 'good wife and mother'. Separate 'caste schools' were established also. Designed for the young daughters of high-caste Hindus, they sought to pursue the aim of conversion by yet another strategy, aimed at the young.

More ambitiously, the girls' boarding schools, established at each station where a missionary wife was based, sought to provide a longer and more substantive education for selected Christian girls. It was the graduates of the boarding schools who provided many of the Bible women upon which 'women's work' in the mission relied. Initially, an holistic education was envisaged, usually lasting about four or five years, at the end of which the girls 'are in a very important sense of the term "new creatures"' (CWM/LMS/India/South India/Travancore/Reports/Box 5/ 1892 (Mr Allen)). A daily timetable was designed to instil 'habits of neatness, order and industry', a mixture of domestic training, academic and religious study and Christian outreach (CWM/LMS/India/Odds/ Box 16/Folder 1852–5/Letter 17.11.54/Mrs Whitehead) – this last in keeping with the hope that these girls would become 'bright lights shining for Jesus' (CWM/LMS/India/South India/Travancore/Reports/Box 3/1886 (Mrs Duthie)), once back in their communities, amongst the heathen and the nominal believer.

For much of the period such a syllabus was considered appropriate not only for the girls' religious development but also as preparation for a role as teacher – of both literacy and the Scriptures – to their Christian and heathen sisters. By the last quarter of the century, however, especially with the development of 'zenana visitation', it was felt that while '[t]he wives of former missionaries did a great work in training Christian women . . . the advance of education, and the growing importance of the work now demand teachers who are more thoroughly qualified' (CWM/LMS/ India/South India/Travancore/Reports/Box 3/1887). Major changes were implemented in the Nagercoil school, the oldest, largest and most sophisticated of the schools, giving increasing emphasis to training the girls for this Christian 'work'. By 1897 the school had in effect become three schools: an English-language middle school, a Tamil-language middle school and the Normal School for teacher training. In the same year the first batch of Nagercoil girls to attempt a public examination in English passed their Lower Secondary Exam (CWM/LMS/India/ South India/Travancore/Reports/ Box 5/1897).

Dedicated workers

The presentation of the missionary endeavours to make 'good wives and mothers' as distinct from their efforts to train 'good workers' is my separation – the two themes are intertwined in the missionary texts. Alongside comments about the need for better qualified boarding school graduates to take up 'women's work' there are vociferous statements about the importance of educating for Christian motherhood. The linkages between the two are explicit in the accounts of the Bible woman and her work. A product of the transformatory influence of the missionary wife's boarding school herself, she provides the effective break through the barrier of caste. The account of her labours gives the reportage of 'women's work' its empirical veracity.

The Bible women were recruited because they were judged to be 'good Christian women', the quality that also established their power of influence and effect. Mrs Knowles pointed out about the work of her Bible woman Eley:

[H]er gently kindly ways are invaluable . . . They see too what a woman can become through the grace of God & that is no small part of the benefit. I was present at the opening of the Puthoor church and as I watched Eley and my little Checha [another Bible woman and ex-boarding school pupil] among the other women it was difficult to believe they could belong to the same race & sex. (CWM/LMS/India/South India/Travancore/Reports/Box 3/1886)

The magnitude of the difference Mrs Knowles observes draws attention to the extent of the transformation wrought by the boarding school and the identification of its graduates with that 'other' feminine ideal, the English Christian lady. As the work grew, however, Christian conviction and a model femininity, while still crucial, no longer seemed sufficient to maintain the Bible women's effectiveness:

We require Christian women, who can speak and sing well . . . we require superior teachers. Truly Christian women they must be, with a good knowledge of the bible and its truths – nothing can make up for the lack of this, and earnest desire and devotion to the work; but they should also be well trained, apt to teach, and, with a good general knowledge, know something of the religious Books, ways of thinking, customs and superstitions of the people. *Training Classes* are very important . . . higher general training is necessary for our Christian workers, if they are to keep their hold upon these Hindu women. (CWM/LMS/India/South India/Travancore/Reports/Box 5/1893 (emphasis in original))

In short, by the closing decade of the century, Bible women required a specialized and 'professional' training beyond their qualities of femininity and Christian faith. This was a training the missionary wives increasingly strove to provide in the boarding schools under their supervision.

The Bible women's conduct of the work did not alter radically during this period, despite the perception that a more thorough training was required. The emphasis on teaching and reading the Scriptures to the *zenana* inmates remained the core of the 'work', though always attached to the need to gain entry and win, as well as maintain, the attention of the women.

The opportunity for contact afforded through medical assistance was quickly appreciated. During the 1870s Bible women were receiving midwifery training from the medical missionary at Neyoor (CWM/LMS/India/Odds/Box 17/Printed Annual Report 31.12.84/File 19). In 1887 two Bible women were sent for two years medical training at the recently established Victoria School of Medicine in Quilon with the intention that they return to the Pareychaley station as medical workers cum Bible women (CWM/LMS/India/South India/Travancore/Reports/Box 3/ 1886). In 1892 the first missionary nurse appointed to Neyoor established training classes for nurse-Bible women, while other Bible women received a basic training in midwifery and first aid, skills auxiliary to their teaching and evangelical duties.

This impression of a systematic and increasingly professional preparation of the Bible women for the work is reinforced in the rigorous schedule of work expected of them. One missionary wife reported that the '*Zenana* Teachers leave for work at 10 o'clock and return at 4 p.m. Often they are weary and footsore, for, they have to bear the "burden & heat of the day". On Sunday evenings they go out "two by two" into different villages specially to read & explain the Scriptures' (CWM/LMS/India/South India/Travancore/Reports/Box 2/1882). While sent out in pairs, each of the women was responsible for a certain number of houses and required to give a monthly written report. In addition 'at the large annual [Hindu] Festivals our Bible women preach the Gospel both to men and women, sell books, and distribute hundreds of tracts among the thousands who flock together from all parts' (CWM/LMS/India/South India/Travancore/Reports/ Box 3/1887). This considerable mobility was not restricted to the immediate locality. A scheme was established at Nagercoil to reach outlying villages, where two or three Bible women were sent on 'itinerating tours'. They would stay at a large central village and make daily trips to the surrounding villages.

The 'work' of the Bible women involved not only a spatial pattern extending well beyond the environs of home but also a range of highly visible public activities calling for considerable stamina and self-confidence:

[They] may be found at work in the surrounding villages and hamlets, in the markets where women assemble for domestic purchases, in private houses, and in the hospital – visiting the afflicted and the dying, . . . They are found reading and explaining the Holy Scriptures . . . teaching a few to read – answering puzzling or impertinent questions – comforting the widow and the poor and the bereaved . . . reasoning with those who are afraid of demons . . . administering simple medicines – distributing handbills . . . conducting women's prayer meetings, and in other benevolent labours, amongst Sudras, Ilavars, and Pulayars, mostly sunk in the deepest spiritual ignorance and superstition. (CWM/LMS/India/Odds/Box 17/Travancore/Report 1889/Folder 19 (Mr Mateer)).

This was made clear to the audience 'at Home' in extracts from the Bible women's own reports of the opposition and difficulties they met in their

professional 'worker' is encapsulated that shift of emphasis which, for missionary women, had to bifurcate between wives and 'lady missionaries' around the boundary of marriage. Yet, almost without exception, the Bible women (and other 'native Christian women' involved in 'women's work') were wives or widows. Many, including the latter, were still actively involved in the duties of motherhood. If being a 'good wife and mother' set limits on the involvement of missionary wives, how could 'native Christian women' appear to surmount such barriers? How does the dual image of 'good wives and mothers' – the expressed purpose of the transformatory goal of 'women's work' – and 'dedicated workers' come together in the spatial and public quality of the Bible women's duties?

A different kind of wife

The involvement of married women and widows in the 'women's work' of the mission represented both the strength of indigenous conventions of femininity and the local realities lying behind the missionary image of the *zenana*.

In south Travancore the strict seclusion of women was practised primarily by Brahman communities. Most non-Brahman castes appear to have allowed much greater freedom of movement, particularly to married women. The weight of seclusion norms fell on young women post-puberty, but before they married. Missionaries complained of the 'foolish prejudice' which encouraged parents even among the Christian communities to withdraw their daughters from school, and forbid them to engage in activities outside the home, even the voluntary evangelical work missionary women tried to encourage through establishing branches of the YWCA and other similar Christian youth associations; sometimes even church attendance was discouraged for young unmarried girls.[16]

For many low-caste and relatively poor convert families, the new opportunities for work available through 'women's work' represented an extension of previous employment in agricultural labour rather than a major innovation or 'liberation' from the confines of the home. Moreover, while missionaries railed against the restrictions on the activities of young single women, and tried to raise the customary age at which girls married among the Christian communities, their educative efforts were always firmly couched in a rhetoric of domesticity – the training of good wives and mothers, thus confirming marriage as the primary relationship for adult women. Involvement in 'women's work' did not of itself represent a contradiction. It was, after all, the duty of the Christian woman; how much more so for those women who were often the wives of the pastors, catechists, evangelists and teachers of the indigenous church.

Part of the mission's brief was precisely to ensure the female half of this new church assumed their rightful role.

What is surprising is the way in which they carried out their duties, a contradiction made more explicit in that most of these workers were paid employees of the mission, even where their husbands were also employed as church workers, reinforcing the apparent similarity of their relationship to the 'work' with that of lady missionaries.

The strength of indigenous conventions and the relative failure of missionary efforts to change the pattern of female involvement in public life were not the only factors which drew married women into 'women's work'. The missionaries themselves, both men and women, did not temper their expectations or demands of the women in the light of their domestic or marital responsibilities. Indeed, the archives reveal little of the practices of their domestic lives or of their maternal experiences. They demanded a dedication, mobility and public visibility which appeared to ignore the domestic, maternal or marital commitments the Bible women had. A stark opposition is drawn between the constraints on the Hindu inmates of the *zenana* and the ease with which the Bible women are shown carrying out their Christian duties. Whether married or widowed, familial bonds or concerns of propriety were clearly not meant to stand in the way of the 'work'. One missionary rather proudly related the story of Rachel, a favoured graduate of his wife's boarding school, who was sent under his auspices to Quilon to undertake a midwifery course at the Medical School for Women in 1887:

As she had a family of four young children it was not an easy matter for her to leave her home and go for two years with only occasional holidays to a place over sixty miles off. However I knew her spirit and she herself felt quite with me that . . . [it] seemed a providential arrangement designed to qualify her more fully for her work. She felt sure too that if my dear wife had been alive she would have wished her to strive and obtain the extra preparation now offered. Her husband who is a schoolmaster at Martandam felt it very difficult of course to spare his wife for two years and take charge himself for so long a time of three or four young children but he finally decided to do so. (CWM/LMS/India/South India/Travancore/Reports/Box 3/1888)

Little patience was spared for those women who would not or could not live up to the demands of the job. Miss MacDonnell expressed exasperation when one of the nurses she had trained, at the end of her course on midwifery, refused to go and work at a dispensary some eighteen miles away from Neyoor and her home. We are told only that the woman complained that '[A]mmal was cruelly sending her to foreign lands to die amongst strangers' (CWM/LMS/India/South India/Travancore/Reports/ Box 6/1897). It is very unlikely the woman was single, although she may well have been widowed. Miss MacDonnell had previously stated, 'We have still much difficulty in getting suitable women for this work, for past experience shows that they must be of about 40 years of age and of sufficient education and intelligence to adapt themselves readily to new ideas and methods' (CWM/LMS/India/South India/Travancore/Reports/Box 6/1896).

A sharp contrast is drawn, in the depiction of the conduct of 'women's work', between the Bible women (as successfully transformed into 'free' and Christian women) and the women of the *zenana*. The 'mission' of the women missionaries, as wives and ladies, was precisely to carry out such a transformation – a transformation explicitly couched in terms of changing the *zenana* inmate into a Christian lady in the image of her British 'sister', a 'sister' who throughout most of this period was drawn firmly in the image of the 'good wife and mother' – the missionary wife. Yet the 'good Christian wives and mothers' of south Travancore are drawn into the conduct of 'women's work' in ways which compare with the lady missionary rather than the missionary wife. The demands of 'women's work' supersede the demands of domesticity or marriage, particularly in the level of commitment and mobility expected of its indigenous practitioners.

Images of distance

Lurking around the idioms of transformation used to chart and describe the training and 'work' of the Bible women are several important qualifiers which create several senses of distance between the prevailing motif of the Christian 'lady'/'wife' and the images of the Bible women. A patronizing tone pervades the accounts of the efforts of the Bible women – a 'nearly but not quite' aspect to the apparent identity between the 'new' Christian women and the missionary wives and ladies.

The 'superintendence' of an indigenous workforce carried out by both the wives and lady missionaries of the south Travancore District constructs a firmly colonial discourse within which the conduct of 'women's work' is told. It is this overarching authority which contains the obvious agency of the Bible women's endeavours. In effect, they become the voice, hands and feet of the missionary women, who retain the organizing initiative. Thus, while it is the Bible women who actually reach out and break down the walls of caste and heathen opposition, who teach the *zenana* inmates to read and know the Scriptures, it is the missionary women who provide them with the knowledge, expertise and resources to carry out their duties.[17] This is not expressed as a simple division of labour, but one based on the authority of race, to the necessity of a *European* presence, a distinction which assumed an expert civil, moral and spiritual influence, bolstered by a persistent view of the 'native': 'Any work done by an European lady would be likely to render the work of native assistants far more effective and useful' (CWM/LMS/Home and General/Candidates Papers/Box 5/Envelope 5/Memo: Travancore District Committee, September 1881). This 'European' authority adhered as much to the women of the race as the men, going beyond an exemplary presence to embrace an active engagement in the 'work'.

The intermediary location of the Bible women confirmed their consistent qualification as 'native'. It was precisely their 'native' language and constitution which made them essential for the conduct of the work. Few missionaries, even those who spent many years in the field, were able to acquire an easy facility with either the Tamil or Malayalam language, particularly the localized idiomatic speech of the mass of the population. The 'native Christian' workers, whether male or female, were thus critical communicators between the missionaries and the people they sought to influence. The Bible women 'guided' the missionary women through the alien environment, having that stamina required to 'bear the "burden & heat of the day"', reflected in the difference between the Bible women's hours of '10 o'clock and return at 4 p.m.' and the hours the missionary women and men were careful to observe, usually with a long afternoon rest. Yet this assumption of physical stamina (or environmental compatibility) and linguistic ability was firmly caught in a necessary but not equivalent relation to the 'work', an adjunct to that distinctive 'European' presence that gave the 'work' its effect.

The representation of the conduct of 'women's work' was not without its lacunae, however. As the previous discussion of the Bible women's own representations of their 'work' illustrates, even as part of the missionary text they convey a strong sense of themselves as powerful interlopers into the *zenana*. The colonial capture of their agency is not complete. The Bible women maintain a strong and cogent effect within the account of 'women's work', one that obtains its power from the subversive inverting of caste their confident agency achieves.

These Bible women felt superior women to their 'heathen' sisters, as they make clear in their accounts. One unnamed Bible woman reported to Mrs Duthie: 'We began to speak to her of Jesus and both the men and women listened attentively. "What you say is good", the women said, "but what can we do? As high-caste women, we cannot mix with others and get an education, as you Christians do"' (CWM/LMS/India/South India/Travancore/Reports/Box 6/1897). '[T]hey treat the Christian teachers kindly,' wrote the Bible woman Paramie, 'listen to our teaching, and speak of the value of learning and civilization' (CWM/LMS/India/South India/Travancore/Reports/Box 6/1897). Even Brahman women began to ask why they 'could not be taught to read, so that they, too, might learn the things Christian women did. They were all sorry when we left, and regretted that they were without the privileges which Christians enjoy.'[18] The ultimate authority was, however, the knowledge of the path to salvation. An unnamed Trivandrum Bible woman reported: 'One woman said I believe the Christian religion is the only way to heaven and I desire to embrace it. But my relatives will not consent. Do you think I can go to heaven? I showed her that she should by all means seek Salvation now. She went away sorrowfully' (CWM/LMS/India/South India/Travancore/Reports/Box 2/1877 (Mr Mateer)).

The abstracted and translated words of the Bible women still convey such an image because of the direct relationships the missionaries constructed within their portrayal between the 'workers' and their audience 'at Home'. Individual subscriptions were constantly sought to support particular Bible women, who, it appears from occasional references, were sometimes drawn into a separate correspondence with their benefactors.[19] The relationship of 'superintendence' itself meant the Bible women must necessarily form a positive part of the prism of appeal through which the missionaries constructed their texts.

Another line of difference was also drawn around the conduct of 'women's work', further hedging the agency of the Bible women. It was a difference which may well have had a greater resonance with the 'Home' readership, most of whom, apart from the ever more certain chauvinisms of an imperialist society, had no direct experience of the colonial relationship or its 'native'.

The title of 'Bible woman' was not specific to the 'native Christian woman', but a term which seems to have come into use in England during the 1850s as part of an innovation in the evangelical and philanthropic effort directed by Christian ladies to the urban poor. Mrs Ranyard, an Anglican 'visitor' to the poor in London, is generally credited with forming 'the idea of the Bible woman' as a means of reaching the poorest of the poor women of the city while enjoying a summer walk through St Giles, a notorious London slum, in 1857. By 1867 her 'Bible and Domestic Female Mission' had 234 Bible women working in the poor districts of London (Prochaska 1980:126–7; Stock 1899, II:31).

Mrs Ranyard located her initiative firmly within that Victorian concern with 'the moral and religious condition of our labouring classes . . . an agency commensurate with the necessity must reach and purify the foundations of social influence, by penetrating the *home-life* of our people . . . We need especially to reach by female agency the wives and mothers of the working classes' (Ranyard 1856 (emphasis in original)). It was the Bible women who were to provide this 'native agency brought by a woman to the women who make those places what they are, and who alone can raise them to what they should be. She is admitted at times and seasons when no *man* would find entrance, nor any *lady*, and she sees "life as it is" in the rookeries' (Ranyard 1859 (emphasis in original)). The Bible women were to be 'the missing link between the upper and lower classes in London', for the battle being fought was not only against immorality and irreligion, but an empty 'Socialism' whose void the Bible was to fill. Drawn from the ranks of the poor themselves, the Bible women were the newly converted, 'the rare flowers of St. Giles, silently purifying the air of the moral desert' (Ranyard 1856).

While their insider knowledge and status (as 'native') provided the Bible women with their particular 'agency', Mrs Ranyard was quick to reassure the 'Lady Visitors' their efforts were far from replaced: 'The labour of a Bible-woman can never supersede any previous effort of a true kind, . . . her work is only supplementary, but the supplement was sadly wanting . . . *a lady* . . . may follow and hold a mother's class in one of the altered rooms' (Ranyard 1861 (emphasis in original)).

It would be labouring the point to detail the similarity here in the portrayal of the 'Bible women' and 'Lady Visitors' of London and their counterparts in south Travancore. Mrs Ranyard's repeated use of 'native agency' to categorize the London Bible women's distinctive quality duplicates the phraseology of the missionary literature. The analogy of distance is precise. That 'Other' country of the working classes seems almost as far from the 'Lady' as the exotic location of south Travancore and its inhabitants. I say almost, however, since there was of course a difference between Mrs Ranyard's Bible women and those of the mission. For while the London Bible woman's 'native' identity is complete, save for salvation, with that of her 'labouring' sisters, the Travancore Bible woman remains apart from her compatriots of the *zenana* by the divides of caste and class. It is the colonial context which condones the presumption, inverting the 'missing link' from that between low and high class to that between 'European (Christian) lady' and the 'native (heathen) lady' of the upper-class *zenana* – an inversion not without its tensions, however.

In a way the working-class referent of the 'Bible woman' fitted with the missionary emphasis on the low-caste, poor and labouring background of the Travancore Bible women – both image and emphasis reinforced by their relationship as paid employees of the mission. The missionary women rarely miss an opportunity to draw their readers' attention to the quality of the transformation the Bible women represent: how much 'brighter', 'cleaner' and 'superior' their 'workers' are compared with the less uplifted converts and the low-caste heathen. A further comparison is, however, frequently made between the Bible women and the high-caste

women of the *zenana*s, particularly in regard to the Brahman and Sudra
(Nair) women, who are invariably depicted in more prosperous situations. The transformation wrought through the *zenana* teaching is not
one of hygiene, but of intellectual stimulation and awakening. This
indicates the class agenda informing the missionary efforts. To win a
high-caste (presumed higher-class) convert fitted missionary notions
both of contemporary Indian society and of that 'right society' they hoped
to establish. Evangelizing the high-caste elite was the path to ultimate
success, while Christianity alerted that same elite to its rightful duty: the
moral and spiritual guidance of the 'labouring classes' – precisely Mrs
Ranyard's burden.

To the readers 'at Home', the presence of the Bible women in the
conduct of 'women's work' is thus secured within a familiar idiom which
reinforces the assumptions of colonial difference. The twinning of 'native'
with 'respectable' working class underpins the depiction of the Bible
women's involvement in the conduct of the work, and the ease with which
the boundaries of marriage, maternity and propriety are able to shift
between the missionary wives, ladies and 'native Christian women'.

By the end of the century the missionaries' complacent analogue between the 'Home' and 'foreign' mission in the figure of the Bible woman
was not always one shared by their 'native' constituency. The missionary
women, wives and ladies, increasingly complained of the difficulties they
had recruiting 'suitable' Christian women to take up the duties of Bible
women. The more highly educated graduates of the boarding schools
were reluctant to take on such duties. Christian women preferred employment as teachers in state and private schools, suggesting a changing
assessment of their social aspirations and status. This was an assessment
which went beyond that of being the 'respectable poor', aspiring rather to
a nascent 'middle-class' status, an ambition shared by many – Christian
or otherwise – who were likewise negotiating the reconstitution of colonial society in India at that time.

Ironies at work

This chapter describes the series of differences through which the relations which structured the conduct of 'women's work' were represented
in the missionary accounts. However, the notion of 'women's work' did
not only indicate the ways in which these differences were ordered and
brought into an effective picture of action. There is also an underlying
uniformity in the ways the respective groups of women – missionary
wives, lady missionaries and 'native Christian women' – are each related
to the 'work'.

An *a priori* quality of 'woman' gives each her relative role: each is constitutive of the 'heart of culture', as one commentator put it, of love and affection; of spiritual and moral influence. This organic or natural characteristic crosses the bounds of both class and race, extending even to the heathen 'sister' in the *zenana* – requiring redemption precisely to enable her cultural influence to be harnessed for good rather than evil. Structuring the portrayal of the conduct of 'women's work' in south Travancore was thus the same assumption of a universal 'woman' discussed earlier with reference to the broader missionary genre. It was, as I argued there, precisely this 'natural' identity of 'woman' that gave 'women's work' its distinction. A distinction, however, which did not signify a contingent or partial notion of 'work' as much as a *separate* 'work' from that of the male missionary.

This sense of separate rather than partial 'work' is reinforced by the way in which the conduct of the 'work' in no way easily fits our assumptions of the 'separate spheres' of private and public activity. The one visible containment, that of the missionary wife, does not, during this period, fall across such a divide, but turns on a spatial proximity to the missionary husband – embodying the particular relation of marriage. It is only with the arrival of the single-lady missionary that this way of organizing a wife's involvement appears as a constraint; even then, the wife does not yet do less work, neither do her efforts appear to be evaluated as partial 'work' in any way.

The career of Mrs Baylis Thomson, a long-serving missionary in the LMS Travancore mission indicates how this spatial aspect did not signify domesticity in any straightforward way. Twice widowed and twice employed as a 'lady missionary' by virtue of the absent marital tie, she served out the bulk of her service as a working mother, her children distributed among relatives in Australia and England. No wifely tie served to justify the motherly absence, yet at no point does it appear to have seemed exceptional or undesirable that she remain 'in the field' on the death of her husband, rather than return 'home' and resume her maternal role more directly. Quite the contrary, her familial responsibilities qualify her for an extra £50 per annum over and above the regular salary of a 'lady missionary'.

As we saw, a similar ease glided over the maternal responsibilities of the Bible women, whether widows or wives. However, an additional factor in the 'native Christian' wives' participation in 'women's work' was the relative undermining of their husbands' influence, countermanded by the more authoritative colonial relationship, as the account of Rachel's husband's eventual capitulation (p. 97) suggests.

'Women's work' assumed a unity around an organic category of 'woman', superseding bounds of class or race, marriage or maternity, in ways which differentiated rather than impinged on the notion of 'work'. This also gave it its legitimating focus. For it is clear from this discussion of the conduct of 'women's work' in south Travancore that it was as women working with and for women that the missionary wives, lady missionaries and Bible women conducted themselves as such committed, effective and professional workers.

The whole notion of 'women's work' within the separate spheres ideology coalesced around a distinction of space and activity. Whether a missionary wife or lady – even a 'working-class' Bible woman – entered spheres of endeavour outside the home or the constraints of domesticity and maternity mattered less than that the object of that endeavour be other women – in this case: the *zenana* inmate.

Such a 'separate sphere' bears a surprising resemblance to Indian ideologies of gender segregation, particularly as they were practised in Travancore. The women of Travancore were not excluded from 'public' life, as much as constrained to those spheres of activity considered female, a distinction that did not always stop at the door of the house. A recent study of popular culture in colonial Bengal suggests a similar category of 'woman' operated to include women regardless of caste and class boundaries (Banerjee 1989). A unity capable of penetrating strict norms of upper-caste *purdah*, facilitating a contact that, under the rubric of 'women's matters', occasionally brought the *purdah* women out of their secluded quarters. I am not suggesting the 'separate spheres' of British culture were those of India, whether in Travancore or Bengal. Certainly, the missionaries identified significant points of difference and were prepared to acknowledge little or no identity between their own notion of 'appropriate spheres' and that of the Indian.

A hint of irony tinges the account of the conduct of 'women's work' in respect of this evaluation, however. At the heart of the missionary's critique of Indian gender relations was a deeply critical view of Indian marriage, particularly the segregation of wife and husband within the home. This became a more strident claim during the later decades of the century, as the ideal of companionate marriage took a firmer hold on the orthodoxies of gender within British middle-class culture. This was the ideal held up as the desirable consequence of 'women's work' in the *zenana*: an image of the Indian husband, wife and child taking an evening carriage ride *together*. It was this same ideology of companionate marriage which was helping to redraw the acceptable boundaries of missionary wives' involvement in the work; just as 'women's work' was undoubtedly helping some Indian women enter new spheres of higher education and employment.

Without dislodging patriarchal norms of masculine priority, the wifely 'companion' in the missionary marriage was in danger of becoming even more closely tied by a literal 'nearness' to her husband's presence and requirements. Such a marriage might bind more tightly than some forms of marriage within Indian cultures, not least the matrilocal and matrilineal liaisons available to some communities, such as the Nairs, in Travancore. The wifely relation in such 'marriages' assumed a lesser significance that, potentially at least, offered a wider realm of social and emotional engagement than that of the 'angel in the house'.

But the missionary wife was not yet confined to her bungalow, nor did she focus solely on her husband. Neither was she expected to. Another claim – of a very different ilk – joined her, along with the lady missionaries and Bible women, to the conduct of 'women's work', a 'work' which demanded of them all a commitment in no way partial, nor viewed by themselves or others as secondary or lesser. For it was the power of God, and in 'His' service, that each participated in 'women's work', as they make clear in their various accounts included here. It was this transcendent claim which overcame the boundaries of ideology and brought together the portrayal of 'women's work' in a way which forged its own orthodoxy:

I know of no work in India more trying to body, mind and spirit than that of a *zenana* Missionary and her helpers – exposed daily to the oppressive heat – going from house to house through crowded unsanitary streets – meeting pupils in small unventilated rooms – noise, unsavoury smells – oppositions and hindrances of various kinds on every hand, and the depressing consciousness, or, at least, fear in time of weakness, that all may be in vain. Honour, everlasting honour, to all noble ladies and women of India who, amid all trial, persevere in this Christ-like service. (CWM/LMS/India/South India/Travancore/Reports/ Box 7/1900)

Conclusion

I want briefly to return to the themes of domestication and maternalism raised at the beginning of the chapter. The representations of the 'mission of sisterhood' in the texts of the south Travancore missionaries portray the 'dedicated workers' of the Indian Bible women as the products of missionary endeavours to transform the Indian home into an English ideal. Distinctions of femininity construct the relationship of power and authority between the missionary and Bible women not as one of maternalism but one of work and employment. Fractured through discourses of race and class, the missionary women appear able to assume an authority by virtue of a superior womanhood which seems to obviate the tension 'between detachment and agonized intimacy' Jolly detects in the maternalism of other colonizing women (1993:115).

The image of the '*zenana* inmate' likewise assumes a contradictory location in these texts. As I have argued elsewhere (Haggis 1991), over the course of the nineteenth century 'women's work' in the LMS was progressively transformed from a 'labour of love' conducted by missionary wives to a professional employment carried out by single women – a process mirrored in British society as a whole, as single middle-class women entered paid employment in significant numbers for the first time during the second part of the century. Rather than a trope of domestication, it is a trope of emancipation which organizes the representations of the 'mission of sisterhood' within the missionary texts. The 'mission of sisterhood' turns on a comparison between the 'unfree' *zenana* victim and the 'free' English counterpart, portrayed most starkly in the contrast between the confining *zenana* and the freedoms of the British home, portrayed as the harmony of companionate marriage. Such a picture assumes an artificial gloss in the light of our contemporary feminist understanding of the Victorian middle-class home and family to be a place of confinement and site of rebellion for many Victorian women, an image more nearly like that of the '*zenana*' than the ideal of 'home' expressed in the missionary writings.

Across the distance of time, the image of the Indian home and family is an artifice with which the narrative of 'women's work' is able to negotiate the boundaries of a Victorian gender order, rather than a rendition of south Travancore circumstances. Despite the rhetoric of domesticating the *zenana* inmates, as I have illustrated, the interventions of 'women's work' do not produce images of marriage and motherhood, but the figure of the Bible woman. It is a picture that most nearly captures the agency of the missionary women themselves, as wives and then as single ladies, both likewise hardly the 'good wives and mothers' of the stereotypical 'home', embroiled as they each were in the demands of the 'work'. As I have indicated, it is the religious rubric of the higher 'call' to God which legitimates this trope of emancipation.

By turning the missionary representations of the 'mission of sisterhood' back on themselves, as negotiating shifts in English social history and gender ideology, I do not mean to characterize their accounts as anything other than 'colonizing'. Not least the power of their representations of Indian circumstances were major contributors to an imperialist culture in Britain. I do not intend to imply the trope of emancipation in any way reflects an actual 'liberation' of Indian women by their missionary 'sisters'. As I have indicated at several points in this chapter, the Bible women drew on the power of 'true religion' to empower themselves in an indigenous milieu of complex and shifting politics around caste and community rather than being subjects of, and mediums for, the emancipatory goals of the 'mission of sisterhood'.[20] Perhaps this is a further reason why the missionary texts which form the basis of my account are so devoid of any focus on 'maternity' as lived experience or discourse, despite the overt rhetoric of domesticity and making 'good wives and mothers'. It is tempting to conclude that a conventional idiom of domesticity and maternity (conventional, that is, for the British missionary women and their audience) serves as a textual device to explain and explore the cogent agencies of both the Bible women and their missionary 'sisters', agencies which turned on other bases of experience.

NOTES

1 The term 'colonizing women' is borrowed from Jolly (1993).

2 Sangari and Vaid (1989) use the term 'recasting' to conceptualize the ways in which notions of Indian womanhood were reinscribed through the debates between Indian nationalist and colonial authorities over defining Indian history, culture and 'tradition'. In the process the Indian woman assumed central symbolic importance as a 'measure' of Indian backwardness from the colonialist perspective. From the perspective of the nationalists the Indian woman became a measure of modernity and authenticity. The cross-currents of these debates, especially amongst nationalist groupings, were complex, but as the essays in the volume indicate, notions of gendered 'respectability' drawn from the colonizing culture were important, if often unacknowledged, measures by which Indian nationalist discourse recast both 'traditional' and 'modern' ideals of womanhood.

3 Travancore was the name of the princely state running down the south-west coast of India from south of Cochin to Kanyakumari at the very tip of India. Today this territory is divided on linguistic lines between Malayali-speaking north and central Travancore, now part of Kerala state, and the Tamil-speaking south Travancore now Kanyakumari District of Tamil Nadu state. The bulk of the LMS activities centred around Nagercoil in contemporary Kanyakumari District and the mainly Tamil-speaking territory north to Trivandrum – now the capital of Kerala.

4 Most particularly by the writings of Bhabha (1985, 1986); Mohanty (1991); Said (1985); Spivak (1987, 1990); Trinh T. Min-ha (1989).

5 For a more extensive and extended critique of the notion of translation as it has been deployed within the Western philosophical tradition to contribute to colonizing discourses see Niranjana (1992). She also attempts to formulate a postcolonial translation practice suitable for translation studies and literary theory.

6 This is a term of accusation which Spivak applies to much feminist research on 'Third World women' (1987:135).

7 Hereafter, references to *India's Women* will occur in the text abbreviated as *IW*.

8 The term *zenana* was used in the missionary literature about India to refer to the home and women's locations within it. It was a stereotype evoking images

of thickly veiled and strictly secluded women in Eastern harems for its British audiences. Used indiscriminately to refer to all Indian situations, it collapsed the great diversity of confinement practices and discourses operating in India then as now into the one crude image of the *purdah* victim. However, as Santi Rozario's chapter in this volume argues, seclusion and the confinements of the *zenana* were not simply exaggerations of the missionary imagination. They have long been and still are central components in Indian discourses about gender and sexuality, variously shared by the three religious traditions of Hinduism, Islam and Christianity.

9 The sentence is taken from a speech given by a Chairman of the Church of England Zenana Missionary Society, Sir Monier Williams, at an Annual General Meeting of the Society. In another part of the same speech he elaborates the ideal of home India lacked:

> [T]rue English homes are not to be found in India . . . there exists no word . . . in any Indian language exactly equivalent to that grand old Saxon monosyllable 'home' . . . that little word . . . which is the key to our national greatness and prosperity . . . For home is not a mere collection of rooms . . . home is not a place where women merge their personal freedom and individuality in the personality of men; still less is home a place where husbands and wives do not work, talk and eat together on terms of equality, . . . Rather it is a hallowed place of rest and of unrestrained intercourse, where husbands and wives, brothers and sisters, male and female relatives and friends, gather together round the same hearth in loving confidence and mutual trust, each and all working together like the differently formed limbs of one body, for the general good and for the glory of the great Creator.

10 Clearly the links between women's activism in missionary work – as wives of missionaries and as fundraisers – and the development of that enormous female effort of organized philanthropy during the nineteenth century are very close. As Prochaska (1980) has argued, in many respects the missionary movement pioneered the field. Certainly, the development of female philanthropy provided the context within which 'women's work' in the missionary movement was institutionalized.

11 As Davidoff and Hall succinctly put it:

> There was . . . some ambiguity among evangelicals as to the strict definitions of male and female responsibilities. It was clear that women were subordinate, yet they had influence; . . . It was this ambiguity on the finer points of detail that made the precise delineation of woman's role a matter of negotiation, rather than a fixed code. Between the recognition of influence and the marking out of a female sphere there was contested ground. (1987:117)

The missionary movement was one such piece of contested ground within which a female sphere was constituted.

12 By 1899 it was estimated that approximately 8,000 women were serving in the

'foreign field', outnumbering men by over 1,000 (Dennis 1899, vol. II:46). One writer calculated that in 1879 there were no more than 400 single women serving in the entire foreign mission-field (covering the Protestant missions from Britain, USA and Europe) (Pitman n.d.:7). Between 1887 and 1894, the Church Missionary Society (affiliated to the Church of England), which had previously refused to directly sponsor single women overseas, alone sent 214 women overseas (Stock 1899, vol. II:369).

13 For a fuller exposition of this argument see Haggis (1991).

14 Mrs Duthie quoting an anonymous Bible woman.

15 Travancore, Cochin and Malabar, the three administrative regions which now form Kerala state and Kanyakumari District of Tamil Nadu, appear to have had a particularly rigid structure of distance and pollution norms backed up, in the Travancore and Cochin instances, by the princely state systems, whose own legitimations to rule were intimately linked with the Hindu religious code and temple system (see Bayly 1984). Failure to keep strict dress and distance codes, including limits to using public footpaths and roads, could bring severe physical retribution and economic sanctions for low castes. Christian converts and their missionary protectors as well as Hindu low-caste communities waged a long series of struggles against such proscriptions such that by the 1940s such overt practices and punishments, particularly their state sanction, had largely disappeared (Gladstone 1984; Hardgrave 1968, 1969; Jeffrey 1976, 1987, 1992; Tharamangalam 1981; Yesudas c. 1980). One elderly Salvation Army Captain, born into a Pulayar community at Nayatinkara, south of Trivandrum, recalled how in the 1920s as a youth he had had to wait outside shops until a kind upper-caste person would enter the store and bring out his small wants – necessities such as salt and sugar. The goods would be pushed towards him with a stick and he would respond by pushing money to the 'good samaritan' – an exchange which echoes the Bible women's experiences of teaching their high-caste 'sisters' by pointing to the book with a stick. Over sixty years later he still vividly felt a burning indignation and sense of injustice at being so treated (interview with author, Trivandrum, June 1987).

16 There have been no historical studies focusing on gender relations or the experiences of women in this region of India with which to compare the missionary accounts. However, Kalpana Ram's (1991) study of Catholic fisherwomen in contemporary Kanyakumari District, Tamil Nadu, suggests the complexities and subtleties of norms of mobility and seclusion operating in an area immediately adjacent to the agrarian communities the LMS tended to. While the Mukkuvar community of her study are differently situated, not only occupationally and by caste but also in terms of their Christianity and mission experience, their practices around female puberty and norms of mobility over the female life-cycle strongly echo the missionary accounts.

17 Forbes (1986) in her study of Protestant women missionaries in Bombay in the mid-nineteenth century also makes the point that it was not the missionary women who educated Indian women, but Indian women themselves. However, Forbes bases her argument on empirical evidence rather than on an analysis of missionary discourse. Her empirical sample suggests that the missionary women were ineffectual and unable to conduct the work.

18 An anonymous Bible woman quoted in an article by Mrs Duthie, missionary wife at Nagercoil, published in *Quarterly News of Women's Work* (1888:11).
19 Unfortunately I have come across no examples of such letters in the archives as yet.
20 Susan Bayly's (1989) study of religion, community and caste in the context of the changing socio-political, economic and cultural conditions of colonial South India is suggestive of the milieu the Bible women of south Travancore were operating within.

REFERENCES

Asad, T. 1986 The concept of cultural translation in British social anthropology. In J. Clifford and G.E. Marcus (eds.) *Writing Culture: The Poetics and Politics of Ethnography*. Berkeley: University of California Press, 141–64.
Banerjee, S. 1989 Marginalisation of women's popular culture in nineteenth century Bengal. In K. Sangari and S. Vaid (eds.) *Recasting Women: Essays in Colonial History*. New Delhi: Kali for Women Press, 127–79.
Bayly, S. 1984 Hindu kingship and the origin of community: religion, state and society in Kerala 1750–1850. *Modern Asian Studies* 18(2):177–213.
    1989 *Saints, Goddesses and Kings: Muslims and Christians in South Indian Society 1700–1900*. Cambridge: Cambridge University Press.
Bhabha, H.K. 1985 Signs taken for wonders: questions of ambivalence and authority under a tree outside Delhi, May 1817. *Critical Inquiry* 12(1): 144–65.
    1986 The other question: difference, discrimination and the discourse of colonialism. In F. Barker *et al.* (eds.) *Literature, Politics and Theory: Papers from the Essex Conference, 1976–1984*. London: Methuen.
Callaway, H. 1987 *Gender, Culture and Empire: European Women in Colonial Nigeria*. London: Macmillan.
Carby, H.V. 1982 White woman listen! Black feminism and the boundaries of sisterhood. In University of Birmingham, Centre for Contemporary Cultural Studies *The Empire Strikes Back: Race and Racism in 70s Britain*. London: Hutchinson, 212–35.
Chaudhuri, N. and Strobel, M. 1992 (eds.) *Western Women and Imperialism: Complicity and Resistance*. Bloomington and Indianapolis: Indiana University Press.
Davidoff, L. and Hall, C. 1987 *Family Fortunes: Men and Women of the English Middle Class, 1780–1850*. London: Hutchinson.
Dennis, J.S. 1899 *Christian Missions and Social Progress: A Sociological Study of Foreign Missions*. Vol. II. Edinburgh and London: Oliphant, Anderson and Ferrier.
Flemming, L.A. 1992 A new humanity: American missionaries' ideals for women in North India, 1870–1930. In N. Chaudhuri and M. Strobel (eds.) *Western Women and Imperialism: Complicity and Resistance*. Bloomington and Indianapolis: Indiana University Press, 191–206.
Forbes, G. 1986 In search of the 'pure heathen': missionary women in nineteenth century India. *Economic and Political Weekly* 21(17):WS2–WS8.

Gladstone, J.W. 1984 *Protestant Christianity and People's Movements in Kerala 1850–1936*. Trivandrum: Trivandrum Seminary Publications.

Grimshaw, P. 1989 *Paths of Duty: American Missionary Wives in Nineteenth Century Hawaii*. Honolulu: University of Hawaii Press.

Haggis, J. 1990 Gendering colonialism or colonising gender? Recent women's studies approaches to white women and the history of British colonialism. *Women's Studies International Forum* 13(1/2):105–15.

1991 Professional ladies and working wives: female missionaries in the London Missionary Society South Travancore District, south India, in the nineteenth century. PhD thesis, Manchester University.

Hardgrave, R.L. 1968 Breast cloth controversy: caste consciousness and social change in south Travancore. *Indian Economic and Social History Review* 5(2):171–87.

1969 *The Nadars of Tamilnad: The Political Culture of a Community in Change*. Berkeley: University of California Press.

Hunt, N.R. 1990a Domesticity and colonialism in Belgian Africa: Usumbura's foyer social, 1946–1960. *Signs* 15(3):447–74.

1990b Single ladies on the Congo: Protestant missionary tensions and voices. *Women's Studies International Forum* 13(4): 395–403.

Hunter, J. 1984 *The Gospel of Gentility: American Women Missionaries in Turn-of-the-Century China*. New Haven: Yale University Press.

India's Women: Journal of the Church of England Zenana Missionary Society. London.

Jeffrey, R. 1976 *The Decline of Nayar Dominance: Society and Politics in Travancore 1847–1908*. Brighton: Sussex University Press.

1987 Governments and culture: how women made Kerala literate. *Pacific Affairs* 60(3): 447–72.

1992 *Politics, Women and Well-Being: How Kerala Became 'A Model'*. Basingstoke: Macmillan.

Jolly, M. 1991 'To save the girls for brighter and better lives': Presbyterian missions and women in the south of Vanuatu, 1848–1870. *Journal of Pacific History* 26(1): 27–48.

1993 Colonizing women: the maternal body and empire. In S. Gunew and A. Yeatman (eds.) *Feminism and the Politics of Difference*. Sydney: Allen and Unwin, 103–27.

Jolly, M. and Macintyre, M. (eds.) 1989 *Family and Gender in the Pacific: Domestic Contradictions and the Colonial Impact*. Cambridge: Cambridge University Press.

Knapman, C. 1986 *White Women in Fiji 1835–1930: The Ruin of Empire?* Sydney: Allen and Unwin.

Mohanty, C.T. 1991 Under Western eyes: feminist scholarship and colonial discourses. In C.T. Mohanty, A. Russo and L. Torres (eds.) *Third World Women and Politics of Feminism*. Bloomington: Indiana University Press, 51–80.

Nair, J. 1990 Uncovering the *zenana*: visions of Indian womanhood in English-women's writings 1813–1940. *Journal of Women's History* 2(1):8–34.

Niranjana, T. 1992 *Siting Translation: History, Post-Structuralism, and the Colonial Context*. Berkeley and Los Angeles: University of California Press.

Pitman, E.R. n.d. *Heroines of the Mission Field: Biographical Sketches of Female Missionaries Who Have Laboured in Various Lands among the Heathen.* London: Cassell, Petter and Galpin and Co.

Prochaska, F.K. 1980 *Women and Philanthropy in Nineteenth Century England.* Oxford: Oxford University Press.

Quarterly News of Women's Work 1888 London.

Ram, K. 1991 *Mukkuvar Women: Gender, Hegemony and Capitalist Transformation in a South Indian Fishing Community.* Sydney: Allen and Unwin.

Ramusack, B.N. 1992 Cultural missionaries, maternal imperialists, feminist allies: British women activists in India, 1865–1945. In N. Chaudhuri and M. Strobel (eds.) *Western Women and Imperialism: Complicity and Resistance.* Bloomington and Indianapolis: Indiana University Press, 119–36.

Ranyard, E.N. (pseud. L.N.R.) (ed.) *The Book and its Missions Past and Present,* issues 1856, 1859, 1861. London.

Said, E.W. 1983 *The World, the Text, and the Critic.* Cambridge, MA: Harvard University Press.

 1985 *Orientalism.* Harmondsworth: Penguin.

Sangari, K. and Vaid, S. (eds.) 1989 *Recasting Women: Essays in Colonial History.* New Delhi: Kali for Women.

SPFEE (Society for the Propagation of Female Education in the East) 1847 *History of the Society for Promoting Female Education in the East.* London.

Spivak, G.C. 1987 *In Other Worlds: Essays in Cultural Politics.* New York and London: Methuen.

 1990 *The Post-Colonial Critic: Interviews, Strategies, Dialogues* (ed. S. Harasym). New York and London: Routledge.

Stock, E. 1899 *The History of the Church Missionary Society: Its Environment, its Men and its Work* (3 vols.). London: Church Missionary Society.

Strobel, M. 1991 *European Women and the Second British Empire.* Bloomington: Indiana University Press.

Tharamangalam, J. 1981 *Agrarian Class Conflict: The Political Mobilization of Agricultural Labourers in Kuttanad, South India.* Vancouver: University of British Colombia Press.

Trinh T. Min-ha 1989 *Woman, Native, Other: Writing Postcoloniality and Feminism.* Bloomington: Indiana University Press.

White, H. 1978 *Tropics of Discourse: Essays in Cultural Criticism.* Baltimore: Johns Hopkins University Press.

Yesuda, R.N. *c.* 1980 *The History of the London Missionary Society in Travancore, 1806–1908.* Trivandrum: Kerala Historical Society.

Unpublished sources

References to primary sources in the text are to the LMS records in the Couuncil for World Mission (CWM) Archives, School of Oriental and African Studies, University of London. Each reference specifies the location of the documents as in the CWM handlist.

CWM/LMS/Home and General/Candidates Papers/Box 5/Envelope 5/Memo: Travancore District Committee, September 1881.

CWM/LMS/India/Odds/Box 16/Folder 1852–5/Letter 17.11.54/Mrs Whitehead.

CWM/LMS/India/Odds/Box 17/Printed Annual Reports 31.12.84/File 9.

CWM/LMS/India/Odds/Box 17/Travancore/Report/Folder 19/1889 (Mr Mateer).

CWM/LMS/India/South India/Travancore/Reports/Box 2/1877 (Mr Mateer).

CWM/LMS/India/South India/Travancore/Reports/Box 2/1877 (Dr Thompson).

CWM/LMS/India/South India/Travancore/Reports/Box 2/1882.

CWM/LMS/India/South India/Travancore/ Reports/Box 3/1886.

CWM/LMS/India/South India/Travancore/Reports/Box 3/1886 (Mrs Duthie).

CWM/LMS/India/South India/Travancore/Reports/Box 3/1887.

CWM/LMS/India/South India/Travancore/Reports/Box 3/1888.

CWM/LMS/India/South India/Travancore/Reports/Box 5/1892 (Mr Allen).

CWM/LMS/India/South India/Travancore/Reports/Box 5/1893.

CWM/LMS/India/South India/Travancore/Reports/Box 6/1896.

CWM/LMS/India/ South India/Travancore/Reports/ Box 5/1897.

CWM/LMS/India/South India/Travancore/ Reports/Box 6/1897.

CWM/LMS/India/South India/Travancore/ Reports/Box 6/1897 (Miss Derry).

CWM/LMS/India/South India/Travancore/Reports/ Box 7/1900.

4 Maternity and the story of enlightenment in the colonies: Tamil coastal women, south India

Kalpana Ram

On confronting a hysterectomy: Australia 1993

Gynaecologist 1: Of course, on the other hand, you may be emotionally attached to your uterus. Some women are . . . .

Gynaecologist 2: Once a woman has had her children, the uterus is useless and often a downright nuisance. And I am not being sexist . . . .

The antinomies of the practical and the emotional, of the use value of our bodies and the psychic investment we place on it, continues to structure the way in which biomedicine is interpreted to the female subject by even the most sympathetic practitioners in Australia today. Choices structured by these discursive oppositions compel women to participate in conceptually dissecting their reproductive bodies even before they experience the surgical dissection. Fertility is reduced in its meanings to the finite and concrete behavioural actions and decisions as to whether or not to have a(nother) child, and the focus is placed on the uterus as a purely mechanical organ, now impaired in its functioning. To continue to experience one's body as a more integral unity becomes a matter of emotional attachment to an organ that is clearly impaired – an allowable scenario, but one closely aligned with the irrational.

Meanwhile, as the woman wrestles with the 'choices' she becomes a participant in a process where, more than ever, she comes to view her own body as an object of visualization and spectatorship. Technologies of visualization, of ultrasounds, place on the screen before her, not the glamorized female body that surrounds her in media and filmic images, or even in the world of feminist film theory, but the hitherto secret reproductive body known only to herself, and then through the medium of intimate sensations rather than vision. She is now one of an audience of the many who participate in this viewing process, of others more adept than she is at interpreting the meaning of these fluid images.

It is a struggle to retain or even to begin to articulate a perspective which does some justice to the woman's lived experience of her reproduction and fertility, not as an experience situated in particular organs, or even in a series of decisions to reproduce, but in the way in which she situates herself in the world as a woman, in relation to other women, and to men and to children.

If this is the predicament even for women occupying positions of relative privilege, as I do, what then is the current situation of lower-caste rural Tamil women as they negotiate a far more complex terrain, with far fewer resources deriving from class, caste or a metropolitan location within world capitalism? Rural low-caste women confront a powerfully class-based challenge to their understandings of their reproductive bodies. In and through the medicalization of pregnancy and childbirth, in the implementation of sterilization, in their constitution as the object of reform by government and non-government organizations, and by postenlightenment discourses that seek to rid women of superstitious beliefs, the anterior world of sacral, quasi-divine and quasi-demonic meanings, which places the female body on a continuum with goddesses and demons, is sharply challenged, if not fragmented.

My attempts to represent their world in this chapter inevitably heightens that fragmentation by virtue of the distances that separate me from the world of these women. My very commonality with them, as a Tamil woman, is another divisive factor. Tamil culture itself places my familial culture at the upper Brahmanic reaches of the caste order. Only a few generations ago the women of my family would have strenuously shunned all contact and sympathetic understanding of the lower-caste and 'untouchable' women among whom my work is located. The problems this would normally have caused for me were mitigated by two factors. First, the particular community among whom I undertook extensive fieldwork had for their part historically distanced themselves from the caste hierarchy through their occupation as fisherpeople, and through conversion to Christianity. As I have described elsewhere (1991:81), they were therefore less affected by my Brahman status than would have been the case in an agrarian labouring community. Secondly, my generation of Brahman women can afford to disregard caste norms of purity and pollution in pursuit of a profession. However, the very processes of modernity which make this indifference possible have in their turn established new forms of social distance between upper- and lower-caste women. These new forms of social distance stem from a differential access to Western forms of education, to jobs and to the resources of urban professional life. They therefore dictate unequal relationships to the resources of modernity itself.

In Tamil-speaking country, there is a particular history to modernity's contribution to the social polarization of Brahman and non-Brahman castes. Colonial power disrupted the intricate alliances between Brahman and non-Brahman kingly castes, with the British displacing or rendering 'hollow' the institution of Hindu kingship while at the same time drawing Brahmans into the state as bureaucrats and as active agents in the creation of an official discourse about native tradition (Dirks 1987; Mani 1989). Such a devaluation of non-Brahmanic sources of power occasioned a powerful anti-Brahman movement in the twentieth century (Irschick 1986), and brought pressure on the state government to adopt affirmative action policies for non-Brahmans in education and in government employment. The outmigration of educated Tamil Brahmans away from Tamil Nadu is another consequence of this historical process. Thus the existing inequality between Tamil Brahmans and rural low-caste women is intensified by the social distance between metropolitan and peripheral location.

The metaphorical language of fragmentation and distancing has been overdrawn in contemporary theory however – particularly at this time when new groups of subjects are moving into the position of shaping anthropological theory and, more generally, making their voices heard. For it must also be said that as I live with such women, reflect upon and write about the experiences of fieldwork – a process enriched by the new questions posed by life itself – I become aware of a shared cultural universe which I inhabited as a matter of birthright, from childhood through to puberty in India, long before adopting the role of anthropologist. This is a shared universe peopled by gods, goddesses and demons, a common language, and common symbols, metaphors and structures of emotion which inform ways of mothering and being mothered in a Tamil extended family. The experience of fieldwork has, therefore, the power to unlock areas of knowing and emotion in a migrant woman that are particularly intense, and otherwise suppressed by dominant Western paradigms of academic knowledge.

In this chapter I seek to utilize both my differences and commonality with the rural Tamil women in order to elicit an account of their subjectivity in the specific domain of maternity and birth. The chapter explores their responses to a complex series of historical interventions, singling out for attention key elements of modernity which have a specific bearing on rural women's experience of maternity. I focus on rural women's experiences of the biomedical transformations of birth, but also examine the more broad-based discourses of enlightenment which seek to reform religious understandings of the sexual and maternal body, in the name of scientific rationalism. In the first part of this chapter I document one contemporary variant of this intellectual agenda, tracing the continuities with the nineteenth-century intellectuals' particular adaptation of rationalism and enlightenment values to the demands of anti-colonial nationalism (Panikkar 1995:1–33). In the second half of the chapter I explore one of the crucial ways in which scientific rationalist endeavours to transform maternity are realized in practice, namely, in and through the medicalization of birth. I depart, at this point, however, from a perspective which talks exclusively of the discourses of modernity, and attempt instead to render with equal complexity and force the pre-existing discourses on birth and maternity which inform the understandings and experiences of the women.

'The politics of enlightenment in the colonies': the Catholic church and the fishing caste

The situation of the non-elite or 'subaltern' caste I consider in this chapter presents challenges all its own to ethnographic renditions of Indian culture. Ethnographic traditions of representation tend to be agrarian based, and for the most part do not take up the perspective of minority religious communities. The Mukkuvars, a fishing caste, became Catholics in the sixteenth century with the missionary efforts of the Portuguese Jesuits. I have previously detailed the extent to which the Mukkuvar version of Christianity modifies the religion in order to fit in with pre-existing understandings (Ram 1991). Equally, however, no ethnographer is permitted to stay unaware for long of the central force of Christianity in the lives of the people. Fishing villages have their entire life dominated by the church, to an extent that any outsider must find extraordinary. The church has functioned as a virtual state, running the villages' internal politics, and their ritual life, as well as extracting economic revenue for its own upkeep. Parish priests are automatically invested with a wide range of leadership roles – an extension of a much earlier nexus between the Portuguese state and the clergy, as characterized by Pearson, historian of the Portuguese in India: 'The *padroado* gave the state considerable influence over the clergy. On the other hand, in rural areas the state was often represented solely by the parish priest' (1987:120).

Such traditions continue today. Villagers refer to a parish priest as a *kuṭi rācā*,[1] or 'petty prince'. Until recently (and still, in some fishing villages) the church arrogated the right to levy taxes on the fishing catch, which may be as high as 25–30 per cent of a good day's catch. The church owns nearly all the land in and around the fishing villages, and lays claim to the produce of all coconut trees and associated produce thereof (see Ram 1991:29ff for details).

The presence of the Roman Catholic church and of several other Christian sects in the district gives some very particular meanings to the local discourses of reform, social action and modernization. The missionary discourses which provide the framework for such local understandings have an institutional history dating back to the sixteenth century.

Roman Catholic fisherpeople live on the western coast of the cape that brings the Indian subcontinent to a tapering end. Although their space has been officially incorporated since the mid-50s into the state of Tamil Nadu, their cultural and political history is more accurately described as alternating between Tamil and Malayalam-speaking kingdoms and partaking of both sets of traditions. During the colonial period, their country was part of the 'princely state' of Travancore, permitting a certain degree of autonomy from direct British control in matters of economic budgeting and policy.

I will begin with the historical background to this region's exposure to discourses of reform, particularly in the sphere of medicine and health. Given the peculiarities in the historical definition of 'the region', the history relevant to this account of reform and modernization is both that of (post-eighteenth-century) Kerala, as well as what is today defined as 'Tamil Nadu'. During this period, the Travancore region was already incorporated into a world plantation economy. The princes who ruled the region represented a combination of highly self-conscious custodianship of Hindu values, and displayed an openness to encouraging reforms such as taking over land-holdings and granting tenants ownership rights.

Christian missions represented an important aspect of this general process of exposure to new discourses (see Haggis, this volume). In a recent history of reform and social change in the area, Jeffrey (1992) tells us that in the 1840s there were more than a dozen European missionaries. By 1938 this had increased to more than a dozen Christian sects, ranging from the Salvation Army to the Seventh-Day Adventists. In the 1980s the list has grown to twenty different sects (Jeffrey 1992:31, 99–100).

The aspect of modernization of most direct relevance to this chapter is the equally long history of exposure to biomedical institutions – an exposure which partly grows out of a longer tradition of indigenous medicine, a south Indian branch of Ayurveda, known in both Tamil Nadu and Kerala as Siddha medicine. According to statistics issued for the state of Tamil Nadu by the Ministry of Health and Family Welfare in 1991, the degree of rural exposure to doctors, nurses and hospital beds is considerably higher than the all-India average:

	Tamil Nadu per 100,000 of population	All-India average per 100,000 of population
Doctors	81	43
Nurses	70	47
Hospital beds	88	73

Source: Ministry of Health and Family Welfare 1991.

The Tamil Nadu government understands itself to be providing the largest, most comprehensive state-mediated support to social services.

Today, some 64 per cent of all births occur in hospitals. The figure is as high as 90 per cent for women in urban areas. But even in rural areas, the figure for hospital births is 46 per cent. Of these hospitals, less than 35 per cent of women are giving birth in government-operated facilities. The rest are attended by doctors in private hospitals.

Even these figures do not give a full picture of the extent to which biomedical treatment has transformed birth practices. About 94 per cent of women consulted by the National Family Health Services Survey in 1992, of whom the majority were in rural areas, had tetanus toxoid injections during their pregnancies. Another 84 per cent received iron/folic acid tablets (Ministry of Health and Family Welfare 1993). Visits to hospitals and clinics during pregnancy therefore casually weave in and out of the accounts given by the poorest of fisherwomen in coastal Kanyakumari. Such a widespread use of biomedical facilities is unevenly distributed through Tamil Nadu. Although a district-wise breakdown of medical facilities is not available, when my close friend Stella, from the Mukkuvar community, who has worked as a health co-ordinator for a Christian non-government organization, took up a similar position in the hinterland of Chenglepet District after working twenty years in Kanyakumari District she was quite dismayed at the lack of hospital facilities as well as the roads and adequate transport to get to the nearest ones.

At the same time the conditions on the coast are a source of social embarrassment for an area continually exposed through kinship and regular interstate travel to the kind of example of success that the 'Kerala model' of development has become for planners, reformers and activists. Conditions of extreme overcrowding, poor sanitation and high rates of bowel and intestinal problems are cyclically exacerbated during the peak fishing seasons and by the slow spread of fish and flies to every corner of the coastal villages. To reformers and activists within the church community, then, 'the coast' is synonymous with 'backwardness'. To church groups that are the bearers of an increasingly activist conscience the challenge is a potent one. Coastal villages have, as a result, been for the last twenty years the site of a number of reformist initiatives undertaken by parish priests and numerous Christian activist social welfare groups in the district.

A good example of such initiatives comes from what is one of the largest of these organizations, the Kottar Social Service Society (KSSS) begun by Belgian Catholic missionaries in the district. The organization has been taking a particular interest in the coast since its inception in 1971, due to the efforts of the Belgian sister who is its head. The organization is now in some disarray due to the collapse of overseas funding. At its peak, however, the organization ran twenty-six health centres, each of which covered between one and three villages. Health teams (one guide and two workers) were recruited from among village girls, trained at the centre in health care, hygiene, social awareness (to use the commonly employed terminology), and employed back in the villages in clinic buildings that are set aside with the co-operation of parish priests. Village women attended these clinics for the purpose of weighing their babies, the occasional talk about health care, some of the inoculations for mother and child, and for receiving the food supplies of bulghur wheat and oil sent by overseas Christian groups.

What is significant about these moves is that discourses about biomedicine and reform of practices to do with the body are no longer situated purely in the space of a hospital or clinic that a village woman must consciously decide to visit. The human agents propagating such discourses are now relocated right inside the space of the village itself. The social agents of reformist endeavours are thus no longer restricted to women and men from the elites, but are to be found among a newly trained younger generation of women from the village.[2] The stake in the wider framework of discourses regarding reform is much higher than getting people to attend hospitals or adopt more sanitary measures. In its broadest sense the stake is no less than the project of transforming the human subject. I will attempt to delineate the contours of the contemporary Christian projects of reform and their internal tensions by examining one of the many forms of evidence relevant here, namely, the kinds of texts that circulate in the district and are widely read and cited by social activists and reformers. I will confine myself to a couple of very recent examples (Alphonse 1991; Prakash 1991) of specifically Christian discourses of reform which are of particular significance in the Catholic coastal belt. I have elsewhere (Ram 1995) discussed these priests and their texts of reform in the context of an extended discussion of 'state intellectuals' in India, all sharing a common vocabulary of reform, rationalism, development and cultural nationalism. The contemporary tracts analysed here share their commitment to an intervention into 'traditional superstitions' with their nineteenth-century missionary predecessors, but in their blend of reform with nationalism they partake of numerous Tamil political projects in the region. These include the Tamil parties which have dominated politics since the 1930s and base their appeal on regional and caste identity rather than religion, as well as various left parties and groupings.

The books written by the priests Fr Alphonse and Fr Prakash are published by small local publishing houses in Tamil Nadu and sold at low cost (Rs. 14 and 17 respectively). They are read and utilized by several Christian non-government organizations in the district of Kanyakumari, but also in the state more widely. I found Fr Alphonse's book (1991) being used by my old research assistant, who is now a schoolteacher in the local village primary school. She mentioned the book to me, praising it and saying she found it extremely useful in counselling girls in the village.[3] The book's title *Aṉpu Itayaṅkaḷ, Iṉpa Utayaṅkaḷ* may be translated as 'Love Between Two Hearts, the Rise [as in sunrise] of Happiness'.

Fr Alphonse argues for a more liberated version of interpersonal relations between the sexes, involving companionship, the sharing of life's problems and love. He likens marriage without love to the kind of union befitting cattle, but not human beings. Sexuality, even within marriage, becomes, if unaccompanied by love, a base form of union. Such sex (*pāl uṟavu*) is likened to prostitution (*vēcittaṉam*). The book is intended, as he states in the foreword, to fill a gap. Indians should be encouraged to reimagine what married life is or ought to be about. He sees his intended audience as being teachers, social workers and religious activists as well as ordinary married and unmarried men and women. Through a campaign for enlightened approaches to sexuality which is embedded within loving marital relations, he argues that one can combat the spread of pornography and prostitution, as well as sexual ignorance. Among the false and superstitious beliefs he spends time in dispelling are beliefs that frequent sex is dangerous, that men are more sexually motivated than women, and that sex is unsafe during menstruation and pregnancy.

I do not wish to minimize the break that this set of teachings represents in relation to the harshly punitive attitudes and practices of the Roman Catholic church towards sexuality. This was seen most clearly in attitudes towards sex outside the institution of marriage. Illegitimate children are refused baptism and burial in the village cemetery, a practice which can only be interpreted locally as the kind of incomplete death which produces restless and dissatisfied spirits. Until recently, couples found guilty of adultery had to expiate their behaviour by publicly parading around the village with a cross in hand (known as *koti piṭikaraṭu*), and by paying a fine to the church. Divorce is prohibited, as are abortions.

However, the texts of reform mark only a partial break with this institutional history. First, they are as concerned as the church ever was to emphasize the marital basis for sexual relations, wishing only to introduce a more modern basis for relations between husband, wife and children. Secondly, these texts wage battle not only with the official orthodoxies of the church but also with the kinds of underground beliefs with which villagers have sustained a certain autonomy with respect to church teachings. Life crises such as birth, death and illness are understood by coastal villagers in ways that connect them with an alternative understanding of the body. In this schema, the trajectory of one's life is determined not only by Christian divinities but also by the Hindu goddess and her minions. Life crises demonstrate with particular acuteness the continued vulnerability of Christian bodies to the powers of Hindu deities (see Ram 1991 for details). The texts of reform express as much distaste for this set of unofficial understandings as their church forebears did.

This becomes clearer in another series of widely quoted texts by Fr Prakash (1991). The titles of his series are all organized by the binary trope of enlightenment versus superstition, and phrased in the alliterative mode approved by Tamils:

Pēya? Noyva?	Demon? or Illness?
Uṭala Maṇamā?	Body or Mind?
Matiyā Vitiyā?	Wit or Fate?
Mantiramā Tantiramā?	Mantra or Trickery?

Of these resoundingly entitled works, I deal only with the first. The book contains an elaborate attack on a widespread tendency in popular belief: the linking of human illness with divine and demonic possession. To this tendency he opposes concepts that focus on the individual and 'his' psychology – imagination (*karpaṇai*), fear (*payam*) and guilt (*kuṟṟa unarvu*). In the schema of Manichaean opposition of tradition and enlightenment, tradition becomes the site of falsehood and stupidity – of *muṭa nampikkai* (false beliefs). Along with the importation of individualistic psychological models comes the familiar figure of Western psychology, the guilty mother. In singling out for criticism the problem of erring lifestyles (*tavāraṇa vāḻkkai*), Fr Prakash sets out to demonstrate that this category has everything to do with erring mothers. He begins by quoting a folk saying which links the infant's persona with the mother:

tāyaip pōlap piḷḷai	The child is as like the mother
nū laip pōlac cilai	As the thread is to the sari

The period in the womb, he argues, affects the qualities of the child, and the years before schooling are critical for child development. Up until the age of ten, the mother is everything to the child, and a child separated from the mother at an early age is liable to have mental disorder and may become anti-social (*camuka viroti*).

Fr Prakash's text must be read as a complex and, above all, an unequal cross-cultural intertextual conversation. The conversation and adaptations are in part developed from indigenous models which strongly posit the centrality of the maternal to human subjectivity, a theme which I take up for more extended treatment later in this chapter, but which has already received critical amplification and scrutiny from feminists in India.[4] However, the claim to modernity and reform comes from a process of borrowing and adopting tenets from Western manuals of guidance for familial and maternal development. In a survey and analysis of contemporary parenting manuals in English, Marshall (1991) describes the overwhelming responsibilities placed on the mother to actively ensure, through a process of monitoring and intervention, the child's physical, intellectual, emotional and moral development into a normal, disciplined, adjusted adult.[5] Fr Prakash readily adopts the characteristic tendency of such manuals to list among the factors contributing to bad upbringing every possible behaviour: both neglect and over-attention, control as well as indulgence.

Fr Prakash is eclectic. Freudian psychoanalysis, the maternal deprivation schools of behavioural psychology and sociology are all actively culled in order to create this local variant of enlightenment discourse. Unlike their Western psychological counterpart, however, texts such as Fr Prakash's operate under an additional imperative – that of distinguishing themselves from and waging war on tradition. Thus, the kind of ideal subject imagined by the text is an individual who will take responsibility for his or her own actions and exercise self-restraint. This is opposed to traditional subjects who attribute causality and responsibility for their actions to *pēy* (demons) or, as in the choice of one's marriage partners, to social institutions of kinship.

Yet it would, I suggest, be a mistake to take the self-presentation of these discourses at face value. Even in their own terms, they do not in fact imagine a subject who is unified as an individual. Instead, texts of reform such as the two quoted from above are themselves discursively split by an

internal tension that seems common to many postcolonial projects of
modernization and subject formation. For along with the lack of faith in
'tradition' goes a fear of becoming over-modernized. Here the Western
subject stands as a constant reminder of the hazards of an overly modernized population. Thus Fr Alphonse is not only an advocate of the subject
who can think rationally for himself. He is just as concerned to warn
against the immorality of couples who decide not to have children for
purely selfish desires (*cuyanalam*). Such couples become enemies of
society by putting an end to a new generation. The only defensible
reasons for not having children are clearly listed – hereditary genetic
disorder and the illness of the parents. Overpopulation legitimizes only a
cutting back on the number of children to two or three. The values of
childbearing remain intact, values which, like Fr Prakash's notion that
children acquire qualities from the mother even while in the womb, are
derived from the very cultural traditions ostensibly under attack.

Other examples could be given which can also be attributed to tensions
raised by the spectre of the excessively Westernized subject – and of the
female subject in particular. For example, Fr Alphonse (1991) regards
the woman who does not breast-feed her children but feeds them with
milk powders from a bottle in the same light as the couple who will not
have children for 'purely selfish reasons'. He urges his readers to regard
maternal milk in a way they would be well accustomed to from the
traditions of Tamil religious devotionalism – as the liquid of pure love,
itself a form of transcendence over female suffering entailed in pregnancy,
birth and nurturance. Under the subheading *Tāyp pālē piḷḷaikku amutam*,
or 'The mother's milk itself is nectar to the child', he exhorts readers: 'To
embrace the child close to one's body, to give milk which is at once the
giving of body and of blood to one's child, this is the sacrifice of a *devi*
(Skt) [goddess].'

And yet such ideas, which are directly continuous with a long historical
tradition which has 'feminized' Hinduism by emphasizing the importance of suffering, of emotional love and of surrender to the loved object,
cannot be allowed to have their antecedents acknowledged in this fashion
– for this would be to surrender to an unreconstituted tradition. In the
project of reform and enlightenment, they must necessarily be buttressed
by reference to Western science – which here takes the form of studies
demonstrating the importance to the infant of close bodily contact with
the care-giver. Other strands of Western psychology also play an important role.

Even Freud, who is often cited, may be employed to buttress notions
that are in fact quintessentially south Indian, such as ideas on female
comportment. In arguing for a greater degree of interaction between the

sexes before marriage and a greater liberalization of sexual norms, reformers such as Fr Alphonse run the risk of upsetting not only Christian church ideals but the symbols of purity that have become part of the rhetoric of Tamil identity. Tamil norms set enormous store by female chastity and a variant of seclusion which is less rigorous than its north Indian counterpart, but crucial to ideas about femininity. It is in compliance with these norms that Fr Alphonse argues for increasing the value placed on the individual's control over his/her own actions and sexual impulses. To this end he invokes Freud's idea that civilization is built on the repression of sexual drives. This is the new ingredient borrowed from the scientific rationalist West; but the rest is pure Tamil cultural ideology as it has been shaped by the cultural nationalism of the Tamil regionalist movement since the turn of the century. The authoritative texts for the rhetoric of regional nationalism are most often drawn from periods of Tamil literary efflorescence when the incursions of Sanskrit (a north Indian import in this discourse) are negligible. Female chastity, readily identifiable with the purity of the language, and with the intimacy of the identity which binds one to the land through the mother, has been a key signifier in this movement (see Lakshmi 1990 and Pandian 1982).[6]

Fr Alphonse's text bears witness to a dilemma: how is reform possible without courting the risk of an uncontrolled female sexuality? He finds a resolution by turning to the code of ethics in Tamil culture which emphasizes the *devi*-like example of the female subject taking responsibility for her own chastity. One of the truly authoritative sources of the cultural tradition is the *Tirukkural*, a manual of ethics written by Tiruvalluvar somewhere between AD 400 and 500. Couplets from this text are typically displayed on buses in Tamil Nadu. The couplet quoted in this context by Fr Alphonse is a famous one, which I translate literally, keeping the Tamil idiom: 'Of what use is it to the girl to protect her by placing her and watching her in a prison-like home? To control chastity with one's mind is the highest form.'

In his analysis of Indian nationalism as a 'derivative discourse', Chatterjee (1986) has clearly delineated the internal tensions that split the discourse in two. On the one hand, nationalists acceded to the universalist and rationalist claims of Western thought; on the other, they resented the inferior place assigned to them in the light of such claims. He calls the resultant oscillation between these two extremes 'the story of Enlightenment in the colonies' (1986:168).

Contemporary Christian projects of reform are shaped by similar dilemmas. First, they must distinguish themselves from the zealously condemnatory stance adopted in the inaugural moments of the mission enterprise which, actively backed by the Portuguese state, saw Hindu temples destroyed, 'orphans kidnapped and converted, and rice Christianity flourish' (Pearson 1987:117). References to the values of Tamil classical literature and to the emotional core of recent identity politics are therefore not simply born out of an innate conservatism, but are a necessary part in the move by reformers themselves to 'indigenize' and make themselves part of the nationalist (or regionalist nationalist) project. Tamil cultural nationalism has always found it necessary to contrast the good Tamil woman – virtuous, maternal and chaste – with the bad Westernized woman who does not experience maternal desires and is sexually unchaste, which may simply mean unsecluded and unrestrained in behaviour (see also Lakshmi 1990 and Pandian 1982).

The Tamil film industry, intimately associated with the politics of regional nationalism, has produced dozens of films which revolve around this opposition. Several of these films, dating back to the sixties and attended by avid audiences, star the couple who went on to become the previous and the current chief ministers of Tamil Nadu, namely, MGR and Jayalalitha. The plots repeat a familiar trajectory: the transformation of the 'modern' woman into the love-struck, and hence modest and recognizably 'Tamil' woman. Once again, the films also craft together a mixture of themes both new and very old. The transformation of the independent and powerful woman through love and marriage is enshrined, for instance, in the very pantheon of goddesses themselves, within which unmarried powerful goddesses are opposed to and sometimes transformed into the loving and benign married ones.[7] The modern woman who espouses a variant of women's liberation takes on the mantle of the soon-to-be-tamed warrior goddess. The films do not rest content, however, with simply insisting that she be conquered: her modern identity must also be de-legitimized through the admixture specific to the regional indigenist 'Dravida' movement. Viewed through this populist lense with its anti-elite sentiments, the modern woman is portrayed as upper class (residing in incredible mansions), bereft of firm male control and 'Western'. In an early film entitled *Kaṇavaṉ*, or 'Husband' (which I viewed on a makeshift screen along with coastal villagers on a moonlit beach), the modern woman (Jayalalitha) demonstrates her alien and spurious identity by wearing Western clothes, indulging in activities that are at once frivolous and Western: dashing off mini-skirted to play tennis, attending charitable 'social work' clubs that are patently devoid of any serious purpose and displaying a 'childish' antagonism to marriage and maternity. Feminism is thus de-legitimized by aligning anti-bourgeois and anti-Brahman politics with the threat of the liberated woman.[8] Tapping into this preoccupation with the Tamil woman is one of the surest ways of vindicating the 'native' status of any project of intervention.

Such projects exhibit, then, a regionally peculiar version of 'enlighten-ment in the colonies'. They attempt to blend, if not simply oscillate between, the values of Reason and science while enshrining simulta-neously a version of Woman as the repository of traditional virtue. The implications for de-legitimizing middle-class feminism are perhaps more readily apparent, however, than the contradictory effects such political discourses have on rural poor women. The local discourses of modernity fuel appeals both to woman as bearer of tradition, and to woman as the object of reform. Electoral politics tends to be built on existing signifiers of identity (caste, region, religion), in which woman-as-mother is a key identity. Appeals to the rural poor address women simply as 'Mother' (*tāy*) and implicitly ask them to support parties that recognize their moral worth as mothers (Lakshmi 1990). On the other hand the discourses also fuel projects of social reform among rural poor. In these, rural women are necessarily 'interpellated' or addressed in ways that involve them in coming to 'recognize' themselves in descriptions of themselves as the site of illiteracy, ignorance and superstition before they can go on to being refashioned into enlightened subjects.

The very interviews that I conducted with the coastal women provided a vivid instance of the way in which enlightenment values can in fact require the most abject acknowledgement of inferiority precisely on the part of the women being inducted for liberation. The interviews were centrally mediated by the help and co-operation of Stella, whom I have already described as a woman of the coastal area, as well as long-term health co-ordinator for a leading non-government organization (KSSS) in the district. One of our interview questions, 'How would you explain the onset of menstruation to your daughter?', was adapted from Martin's book *The Woman in the Body* (1987:205).

Women usually responded to this question in terms of a discourse of a specifically feminine morality involving values of seclusion and contain-ment of bodily and social comportment. The interview I am about to describe was no different.

The woman, Antoni Āmmaḷ, had other women friends grouped around. Like most other women, she answered the question in terms of telling her daughter not to wander around any more, no longer to display qualities of fierceness and rebellion. Stella persisted in the question. Her years of educating women in precisely this area spurred her on in wishing to elicit a correct (biomedically framed) answer. She asked Antoni Āmmaḷ, 'But do you know where the blood comes from, how it gets produced?' Antoni Āmmaḷ's lively friend Soosamma interjected at this point. 'When menstruation starts, different women have differ-ent responses. For some, there is stomach ache, giddiness. At this point a girl may ask "What is this?". And an adult woman responds by saying, "Look *Āmma*, this is periods (*māta vilakku*) and this is how it affects you.'''

Stella repeated the original question and Antoni Āmmaḷ began to perceive that all their responses were being regarded as inadequate. Soosamma held out for a while. 'No one', she stated, 'not even a *vitvāṉ* [scholar] can accurately predict when a girl's periods are to start.' Finally Antoni Āmmaḷ cut her short. 'You and I', she said to Soosamma, 'we cannot teach in the way Stella suggests. But Stella can – she is educated. We do not know, but those who have read [studied], they know (*nammaḷukku teriyatu, paticṭa ālukku teriyum*).'

Some aspects of coastal women's responses to the projects of modernizing the 'management' of pregnancy and birth[9]

The project of reform involves, as we have seen above, two contradictory strains. On the one hand, the aim is to produce a subject who will take responsibility for her own actions and not rely on pre-given discourses of religion and tradition. But on the other hand, this very project of acquiring this competence requires of women who are already prefigured as inferior by virtue of their caste, illiteracy and poverty that they acknowledge their inferiority. Simultaneously, then, they are made to take on board their presumed *in*capacity to accept responsibility for their own belief systems.

Many illustrations could be given of the ways in which coastal women negotiate these complex sets of demands. Here I will focus on only one aspect, namely, women's acutely concentrated experience of such a politics in the space of hospitalized births. Coastal women have available to them, apart from the *carkār* or government hospital, a couple of local clinics run by Catholic nuns of the Presentation (Kāṇikkai Mātā) convent in the main settlement of Colachel.

Women's exposure to and utilization of biomedical practices in relation to pregnancy and birth is varied and selective. The complexity of the distinctions made by the women, both verbally and in practice, challenges any conveniently simple notion of a unitary attitude dictated by congealed 'tradition'. Most have not taken on the notion that pregnancy itself is to be regarded as a time when a continuous process of monitoring and reporting to biomedical authorities should occur. However, the idea of visiting for specific purposes does occur to some. Thus, some women will avail themselves of *taṭuppu ūci*, the local term for an injection against tetanus given at six to eight months of pregnancy. Others may turn up at the Catholic clinic with specific complaints, such as water retention, or in order to obtain supplies of tonics. Even if they do attend a 'check-up' during pregnancy, very few will present for the birth itself. Yet others will distinguish different pregnancies, and the different kinds of help sought in each of them. The Christian non-government organization, the KSSS, has been emphasizing hospitalization for the first birth, and this is reflected in the practice of some of the women. The range of distinctions can appear in a single woman's narrative, as in the following excerpt from a village woman called Alphonse, who was brought to my attention by other women because she has had thirteen live births in the last eighteen years:

> I can't work during pregnancy. I get swelling. I also have nausea for five to six months and cannot eat a thing. I do not go to the hospital for births, because they do not allow anyone from home to be there with you. I have had all my births at home. But I do go to the Kāṇikkai [Presentation] Hospital or the carkār hospital to get tonics, and I take Horlicks.

To hazard a generalization, a number of the distinctions operative in women's actions and behaviour towards biomedical facilities seem to revolve around the degree of change it involves in their older ways of experiencing pregnancy and birth, and daily life in general. Visits to the clinics for particular ailments are relatively unexceptionable, since they do not involve major disruption to women's daily routine or prolonged relocation in a space controlled by medical staff. Women can come away from there having received treatment, consisting of an injection, or sometimes they report a saline or a glucose drip (see Rozario, this volume, on the enormous efficacy attributed to saline drips). They may also avail themselves of packets of pills or bottles of Horlicks. The same cannot, however, be said for birth in hospitals. At this point, the woman is at her most vulnerable, and the power of the medical staff – most of them recruited from other castes – simultaneously at its height. I will come back to this point about recruitment of staff.

For all their tolerance and utilization of biomedical facilities, women's mistrust of modern management of birth comes to a climax in the matter of presenting for hospitalized birth. For most, hospitalization is encountered not as a first choice, but as a transition which often occurs half-way through the birth itself. The first preference of most women is to have the birth at home, attended by traditional midwives. Hospitalization is therefore most often an emergency resort.

The contrast could not be more stark. Midwives are recruited from within the same fishing community (see Plate 3). They are not to be distinguished from other women of the village by caste or even by their specialization. The former point requires a little elaboration. Births among the middle and upper castes of rural south India tend, as in the rest of the subcontinent, to be organized by the hierarchy of pollution. Given

3 The photo, taken for me by the late Roger Keesing, shows Kirtina – the midwife-cum-fish trader – seated with her group of co-traders. Unlike many other South Asian communities, the role of the midwife among the fisherpeople is not lower in status, but is completely integrated into the general lifestyle of the older women who trade.

the pollution attendant upon birth and death, well-to-do castes will employ service castes (the washer woman, the barber), to attend upon them in ritualized fashion in birth and in death. The idea is that the service caste then takes upon itself the attendant pollution and removes it from the higher community (see also Rozario, this volume).

Mukkuvar fishing communities employ a very muted idiom of pollution in most contexts – I have argued previously that the archaic notions of danger rather than of impurity are more relevant in organizing constructions both of caste identity and of the female body (Ram 1991). This comes across most strikingly in the organizing of birth, where various precautions are taken for protecting the birthing woman against the dangers of ghosts and demons, including the device of seclusion and the placing of iron objects in the hut as well as various Christian prayers to the Mātā (Virgin Mary, referred to simply as Mother) and to Jesus. However, there is no notion of birth pollution affecting either the birthing woman or the midwife.

This muting of pollution ideology – which carries important and positive consequences not only for the midwife and the birthing woman, but for the self-perception of a community placed low in the caste hierarchy – is a feature I have explored in my ethnography of the Mukkuvars (1991). I have argued that it is to be understood as embedded within important features of the material relations of production governing the work of fishing and the sexual division of labour within the fishing community. Put briefly, fishing does not involve the community in the personalized relations of dependency and servitude to higher castes in agricultural society – instead, the relationships to higher castes are based on trade. The work of trade, as of the associated spheres of credit and finance, is in turn squarely the domain of women who thus enjoy the kind of complementary (though unequal) status and power common to fishing communities from many parts of the world (Abraham 1985; Acheson 1981:297–9; Alexander 1982; Cole 1991; Firth 1943).

By contrast, outsiders' perceptions of the fishing community *are* organized by idioms of pollution and untouchability. Although this no longer takes the form of imposing absolute taboos on commensality, it has been transposed to the idiom of dirt, lack of hygiene and the lingering odour of poverty itself. This is of particular relevance in the hospital context, which is centrally organized around the discourse of sanitation and the separation from dirt and impurity. The midwife who accompanies the birthing mother to the hospital is in stark contrast to the nursing staff of the clinics – usually dressed in an old blue sari, hair carelessly tied back in a knot, wiry and dark with the sun. Such midwives are not even occupationally separated from other fisherwomen. Most of them are in fact elderly women who also work as vendors – many will proudly relate how they rush from their work at any time when women of the village need their help, without even pausing for niceties such as having a bath. In their eyes, such actions are all evidence of their care and concern. To hospital staff, they look the epitome of the dirty fish-wife responsible for furthering the deplorable state of the coastal health situation.

In part, this is due to the caste distance between hospital staff and the fisherwomen. Few nurses are recruited from the coastal villages, which have had very poor rates of education (see Ram 1991). This is in sharp contrast to the neighbouring caste of Nadars, once exclusively agricultural labourers and toddy tappers. Large sections of the Nadar caste group were converted by the nineteenth-century Protestant missionaries, and their subsequent climb through education to social and political prominence is legendary in the area and the subject of scholarly attention (Hardgrave 1969; see also Haggis, this volume).

Nursing sisters in the local Christian clinics are direct heirs to the tradition of the Protestant Nadar 'Bible women' described by Haggis (this volume) for nineteenth-century Travancore. They may belong to castes that have their own history of oppression, but they are seeking to leave that historical memory behind them. Membership in the higher community offered by Christianity and Western knowledge has long operated as a means to combat low ranking within the local status system. Even by the end of the century the Nadar Bible women were aspiring to middle-class status (Haggis, this volume). In the 1990s, Christian women employed as nurses or even doctors are far less likely to identify with Mukkuvar women either on the basis of caste or class experience. Nurses in government hospitals from Hindu castes would bring to this social distance the additional distaste for the pollution carried by fisherwomen.

Whatever the social recruitment of nursing staff, tales of the withering scorn of hospital staff towards birthing mother and midwife are legion. This is Antoni Āmmaḷ from the fishing community:

Yes, we do believe in English *maruntu* [medicine] and do use the *carkār* hospital. But God willing, I have managed to have nearly all of my births at home and avoid hospitals. There is *aṟutal* [calmness, comfort, reassurance] at home.

With my last birth, the cord was caught around the baby's neck and Kirtina [the midwife] was with me for hours. Finally we went to the hospital. In there, people say such cruel things: 'You knew how to sleep with him and have fun. So why are you making such a big noise now? Shut your mouth.'

Whereas at home, the midwife and the [women] neighbours will say things like: 'It is all right, my dear. This is the way things are, we have all experienced this kind of pain. Bear with it. In a very short time it will all be over. It will be over with now. Call out to Mātā. Call out to Jesus.'

Midwives such as Kirtina, who willingly accompany women to hospital as well as turn to hospitals where they cannot manage themselves, are liable to be given a stern lecture by hospital staff, 'Why have you left it so late to bring her? Did you bring her here to die? Do you want to pin the blame on us?'

Mary, aged thirty-two, has had six births. She was taken to the government hospital during the sixth and, as it turned out, last birth:

I was taken there after Kirtina found it impossible: the uterus itself seemed to be coming out, but yet there was no baby. I do not usually go there – the *carkār* hospital has no *piṭi* [no 'hold'] over the birth.

The hospital staff abused the midwife for waiting so long, and they also lectured me for having another baby, before they performed a tubectomy on me, saying my life would be at risk with another pregnancy. In hospital, though, there is no one to even give you food or water when you need it. They leave it to the family to come and visit and do these things for you. But I do not have close women relatives in the village, and my husband is a brutish drunk. My mother-in-law's family does not want to know us because of his drinking.

Mary's statements bring out another aspect of hospitalized birth or, indeed, hospitalization in general, which is problematic for those who do not enjoy kin support. It seems fairly common for hospitals to leave much of the care required after major medical intervention to the kin of the patient. In many private hospitals this is rendered official by providing a space where the family can come and cook meals for the patient, and there is often a little space where the kin can sleep alongside the patient at night. In other words, the biomedical staff and facilities do not aim to provide complete care – they assume the existence of kin support and care, which in Mary's case is nearly non-existent.

However, an even greater source of bewilderment and anguish for the women is in the harsh attitudes of hospital staff towards pain. Pain incurred in pregnancy and in birth are integral parts of the local constructions of femininity. They are opportunities for other women to demonstrate the qualities of comforting and understanding with which femininity is itself closely associated. Village midwives see their tasks as an extension of these feminine virtues. Since my earliest contact with the coastal midwives in the early eighties, they have been concerned to stress to me that what they offer the birthing woman is a quality of patience and endurance. They contrast this with what they find to be the polar opposite quality of hospitalized treatments of birth – *im*patience. Hospital staff are impatient with the birthing woman's experience of pain, they are impatient when a baby is overdue. This characteristic impatience is evinced (still according to the midwives) in an over-hasty resort to 'tearing open the woman's stomach and vagina' – that is, to caesarians and episiotomies. Needles, forceps, scissors – these are all seen as fearful instruments by most women and as reason enough to avoid hospitalized births.

Coastal women's perception that the pain and suffering of pregnancy
and birth are somehow connected intrinsically to the emotional qualities
of femininity – patience, endurance and love – links them to the specifically Catholic attributions of the worship of the Virgin Mary. In this
coastal area it is Mātā who presides over women's experience of maternity, she is a 'woman' who understands the sufferings of women on earth
and can be called upon – just like a midwife or like other female kin and
neighbours who attend coastal births – to sustain the woman in pain.

The themes are, however, of wider cultural resonance in Tamil Nadu,
where Hinduism has long been inflected by the idiom of *bhakti* (Skt), or
emotional love and surrender to the divine Other. Religious experience
becomes redefined to exceed the previously available *trimargaha* (Skt), or
three paths to salvation: the *marg* (path, Skt) of correct techniques, that is,
yoga (Skt); the *marg* of acquiring correct knowledge, *gnana* (Skt); and the
marg of following the correct moral/ethical codes specified by caste,
gender and stage of life, that is, one's *dharma* (Skt). Instead, religious
salvation becomes constituted by internal subjective transformations that
occur through the path of love and suffering. The *bhakti* movement begins
very early among the Tamils, by the tenth century AD (Hardy 1983).

My particular interest is in the way it orients religion towards those who
can claim to have experienced the birth of love through suffering and
abjection. Suffering becomes the place where one learns to tame one's
own ego and selfish desires in order to experience the joy of transcendence. Subject positions such as that of the woman, and more specifically
the mother, along with the position of other 'subaltern' groups such as
untouchables, and those considered marginal to caste agrarian society
such as the tribals – all acquire new significance in this reformulation of
religion. Subsequently, these are the social groups who go on to produce a
significant body of poetic literature that has as much claim to constituting
a source of pan-Indian thematic unity as the elite textual traditions of
Sanskritic ritual.

Maternity brings such meanings to a head. *Āmma eṉrāle aṉpu*, a Tamil
aphorism, instructs us that 'to say "mother" is to say "love"'. *Aṉpu*
(love), *poṟumai* (patience) are repeatedly mentioned as the qualities of
maternity – which many formulate as beginning with pregnancy and
continuing through maternity. Stella explained it to me on one occasion
thus:

The mother endures pain and suffering in pregnancy and childbirth – but all that
pain vanishes on seeing the child. God could not be with us all, so an *Āmma*
[mother] was created to give us our experience of *aṉpu* [love] and *poṟumai* [patient
endurance]. While breast-feeding she will put up with all kinds of *patiyam* [dietary
restrictions – these are given by the Siddha medical ideas governing food and

bathing practices after birth and during pregnancy]. She does all this and more without *etirpārtal* [looking for returns]. This is the mother's way.

When questioning agricultural untouchable labourers, whose kinship system dictates both patrilocal and virilocal residence for the woman, why they nevertheless referred to their natal home as *tāy vīṭu*, or mother-home, a young teenage girl responded: 'Yes, our home will always be *tāy vīṭu*, just as our language is *tāy moḷi* [mother tongue]. When we are hurt we call out "*Āmma!*" not "*Āppa!*" [father]; when we sit we say "*Ām-matī!*" (colloq., said in relief). If we are hungry as children, is it not to our mothers that we go and ask for food?'

Such qualities which grow through pregnancy, birth and the physical acts of feeding and tending young infants were described to me as making women's hearts (*maṉacu*) soft, unlike men's hearts, which are like stone (*kal*). Trawick has, in her ethnographic work on Tamil Nadu, described the expression of these emotions in the maternal liquids of milk and tears which are also liquids of religious emotion in *bhakti* culture (1978, 1980, 1992).

Weeping is a crucial indication of subjective transformations indicating, for example, the acquisition of humility, remorse, the experience of love specific to separation (*viraha* (Skt)), the melting of egoism. These are also the kinds of transformations that are said to characterize the subjective transformation of woman into mother. My own apparent grief over my fieldwork separation from my daughter brought me a good deal of sympathetic acceptance – I was demonstrating that I was (despite appearances) still a Tamil *tāy* or mother. The weeping and pain of the woman in childbirth is but one of the many steps in this process of undergoing transformations in which hard egoism melts into the liquids of love. Maternal milk is likewise seen as an emanation of emotion, suffusing the mother's body at the very sound of her child's cry, endowing the child with far more than biological nourishment.

As mentioned earlier, such interpretations converge with the Catholic cult of the Virgin and the Mater Dolorosa (see Kristeva 1986). The convergence is particularly acute in women's invocations of the goddess during birth. The intimate way in which birthing women in the coastal community call upon the Catholic goddess, Mātā or Mother (Mary), to witness their pain and to help them in their anguish is exactly replicated by the call of their Hindu agricultural labouring counterparts. Vellachi, a woman from such a Hindu community of untouchable labourers in Chengleput District of Tamil Nadu, and now about sixty years old, related to me one of her particularly difficult birth experiences and her desperate invocation of Muthu Mari Āmman, the Hindu goddess: 'The pains were so bad that I abused Her. I said, "Don't you have eyes and ears to see and hear what I am going through? Aren't you a woman too? If you want to take me, take me, but don't give me this pain!" I lit a *karpuram* [camphor] to her, and the baby came.'

The treatment of birthing women in the hospital environment there-fore violates not only Mukkuvar women's perception of themselves as a proud and independent caste – instead positioning them as dirty and polluted – but it also profoundly violates a regionally widespread vision of femininity, and the maternal. It introduces a jarring and (to the women) inexplicable note, into the emotional, religiously informed experience of femininity at the very moment where it is most profoundly acquired and expressed, both by the birthing mother and by the midwife, the female kin and neighbours who gather to support her.

Conclusion

The use of women's bodies as markers of boundaries between communi-ties, nations, religions and ethnicities is now a widely documented and discussed issue – necessarily so, given the violence which currently forces such issues on our attention with such urgency. I have turned our atten-tion in this chapter, however, on to a war which has no name, partly because it is a struggle not necessarily between but *within* communities that are defined along the various identities of caste, ethnicity, religion or class. Within these communities, a struggle goes on between educated and uneducated segments. But an even more profound struggle occurs within the subjectivities of individuals.

We may trace some elements of this war to its founding moments in the colonial constitution of modernity and of tradition, which initiated for the colonized a relentless process of internalizing the colonial scrutinizing gaze. Native elites thus embarked upon an inextinguishable cycle of reform and intervention in the name either of the modern and the progressive – or, equally, in the name of the restitution of tradition (Nandy 1983; Panikkar 1995). The centrality of reconstituting 'woman' in this dialectic between colonialism and nationalism is by now well established for the Indian subcontinent. A volume of essays on colonial-ism by Indian feminists derives its title, *Recasting Women*, from the text of a nineteenth-century male social reformer, Koylaschander Bose, in which he declares that '[s]he must be refined, reorganized, recast, regenerated' (1846, cited in Sangari and Vaid 1989: page facing Introduction).

It is not difficult to perceive the strong set of continuities which trans-mit the peculiarly colonial mixture of power and reform along the chain of various prototypical reformist dyads: colonial administrators, doctors and missionaries (men and women) reforming the natives; 'native' husbands educating wives; middle-class men in general reforming women; middle-class men *and* women reforming the labouring classes and castes. The reforming priests of Kanyakumari partake of this longer tradition. The reformist texts of the Catholic priests examined here reveal a direct discursive continuity with the texts of nineteenth-century male social reformers, sharing the aporias of male enlightenment subjectivity in addressing women's sexual and maternal embodiment. The seemingly stable opposition between modernity and tradition with which the project of reform embarks in the colonies founders precisely on the very object which is meant to secure its efficacy, namely, the female body.

Today, the contradictions and power relations of such projects are in no simple sense confined to elites or outsiders. They reach right into the fishing community, for example, reorienting the perspective of many of the younger generation of girls, particularly where they have been directly trained by the priests, nuns and non-government organizations.

I have discussed subaltern cultural experiences of maternity and birth as a site of considerable tension for women who have to mediate between discourses. An older treatment of these issues occurs in the anthropology of medicine (Landy 1977; Leslie 1976), where the existence of competing meanings and strategies is perceived as a benign 'pluralism' of medical options and choices, reflective of an older folk tradition of syncretism and eclecticism:'From this perspective, the presence of plural medical philosophies is a reflection of a generally pluralized conception of the Universe. There are many gods, many roads to Heaven, many scriptures, many intellectual traditions, and many kinds of people' (Beals 1976:186).

The choices between this plurality of options are perceived as governed by the 'pragmatism' of concerns over illness and, more generally, the pragmatism of non-elite concerns:

The old woman, once her religious resistance had been modified, rather automatically moved to the position that henceforth both religious rites and scientific medicine would be utilized in dealing with Balaka Ram's illness. There was no notion on her part that one thing must be rejected on behalf of the other. The underlying dictum always seems to be: Try anything that is available and culturally legitimate. (Gould 1977:501).

Similarly, in the study of popular religion, Mandelbaum (1966) characterizes a specifically 'pragmatic' complex in religion which is especially peopled by non-elites such as the lower castes and women. For Mandelbaum, the childless woman exemplifies the pragmatic subaltern, indifferent to questions of meaning or power, alive only to practical efficacy: 'A childless woman generally tries every conceivable supernatural resource in her anxious attempts to bear a child' (1966:176). She pays scant attention to the divisions of caste, or of dualities of high and low gods.

Such accounts of pluralism in non-elite culture are not wrong in any simple sense. I could certainly give an account of Mukkuvar women's attempts to seek fertility and the preservation of children and familial health, of pregnancy and maternity, in a manner which would fit quite comfortably with such prevailing assumptions. After all, women certainly do move between prayers and offerings to the shrines of Jesus, Mātā and the saints, attendance at clinics for prenatal checks and inoculatory safeguards and the application of Siddha medical principles in the preparation of home remedies, all with the greatest of ease. However, the fact that people are willing to move between discursive frameworks cannot allow us to erase the centrality of the power relations that make these discourses co-exist in an unequal space.

Nor can we afford to treat the subject who moves between the discourses as someone who is constituted entirely outside these discourses. In the language of medical pluralism and pragmatism, non-elite members of postcolonial societies make choices between curative strategies on the basis of socio-economic status (Beals 1976; Gould 1977), they create 'hierarchies of resort for curative practices' (Romanucci-Ross 1977) according to their degree of acculturation, and assign complementary functions to 'scientific' and 'folk' medicine on the basis of illness typologies which they create for themselves (Landy 1977:469–74). Non-elite postcolonial subjects seem to enjoy a subjectivity that remains untouched by the formative capacity of discourses even as they exercise 'choice' in a neutral and untroubled fashion. To rest the argument at this point is to erase the enormous tensions that are created for the women in rural south India by the requirement that they mediate between discourses that actually construct female embodiment, femininity and the female subject in quite different ways. Each discourse makes an effort to induct, or, to use Althusser's term, to 'interpellate' the subject who is moving between these frameworks.

The tensions flow not only from their competing claims on female subjectivity, but from the fact that the discourses are of uneven historical depth and exercise unequal claims on female subjectivity. It would be fair to say that, despite fairly prolonged exposure to biomedical facilities as well as more recent inroads from projects of enlightenment in the name of science, women still derive their fundamental ideas of femininity and maternity from more archaic religious and regional cultural sources. While my account of contemporary cultural politics takes inspiration from contemporary 'postcolonial theory' particularly as developed for India (Chatterjee 1986; Guha 1983; Sangari and Vaid 1989), I have found it necessary to depart from a tendency in 'colonial discourse theory', both literary (Said 1978) and historical (e.g. Arnold 1989), to exhaust itself in the exegesis of the intricacies of the colonial *mentalité*. Such an account threatens to collapse the workings of power with the arrival of the colonizer, once more placing the complexities of the European at the centre of the historical stage. By contrast, I have argued that dominant discourses of modernity have an extremely uneven purchase on maternal subjectivity. Religion, both Hindu and Christian, informs the practices and subjectivity of women and men in ways that are not captured by most contemporary discourses on 'postcolonialism', even when the postcolonial is imagined as hybrid, multiple and unstable. The work of Homi Bhabha (1994), for instance, argues for a radical version of hybridity without his methodology requiring of him any significant insights either into his own experience as an Indian or into the cultural framework of the colonized. By contrast, in her powerful ethnography of women's death rituals in Greece, Seremetakis (1991) argues for a version of hybridity which requires the reader to recognize that 'death and gender possess their own historicity' (1991:11), allowing communication between the symbolic categories of archaic and classical Greece and contemporary Greece. My analysis of maternity and gender in Tamil Nadu suggests the fruitfulness of adopting a similarly long-term perspective in a culture which has comparable historical depths.

It is not only symbolic systems which diachronically link the experiences of maternity across the divide of modernity in Tamil Nadu. I have also pointed to ways in which, from the perspective of fisherwomen, contemporary forms of discrimination and oppression fuse with older ones, often indistinguishably. Women previously discriminated and oppressed because they were poor and low caste are additionally the targets of reform because they are 'traditional' in their modes of child care, hygiene and even in the very way in which they give birth. From their perspective, the older forms of hierarchical discourse are simply mapped on to newer versions, with high-caste intolerance of 'impurity', 'pollution' and lack of learning being transposed onto the idiom of hygiene, rationality and scientificity.

I have suggested also (without doing justice to the argument) that the project of reform as it is enunciated today is not only an emanation of colonization but also bears certain important continuities with much older precolonial forms of attention to the subaltern. In the religion of *bhakti* we find important antecedents to the postcolonial national preoccupation with the non-elite, one in which non-elite status becomes the site of redemption and change.

Such traditions have by now come to inform the very self-perception and practice of subaltern women today, sustaining the kind of criticisms they offer if actually consulted on their perceptions and opinions. Despite the combined weight of opprobrium attached to them by virtue of their gender, their caste and perceived 'backwardness', they retain the ability to deliver clear-eyed and starkly critical perceptions of the violence and suffering they have to endure even as they give birth. Given the way in which earlier religious discourses have entered into their bodily experiences, women are not simply moving between discourses in the sense of making mental choices. Rather, women are required to mediate, in the most dramatically embodied aspects of femininity (pregnancy, birth, maternity), the contradictions of female subalternity in the postcolonial period.

NOTES

1 I have followed the system of transliteration from Tamil to English spellings which is now commonly adopted, namely the spellings in the *Tamil Lexicon* authorized by the University of Madras, 1982. Sanskrit words, such as *dharma*, are indicated as (Skt) in brackets the first time they occur, and are left to their conventional spellings, rather than re-spelled in Tamil.

2 In future work I plan to devote attention to the discourses of the various village girls and women who have been affected by such programmes, ranging from those directly employed by the KSSS to the families of these girls, to the women who have been the object of interventions.

3 Dr Kandiah helped me to translate the book in Sydney in 1992, and I gratefully acknowledge his contribution.

4 See the collected papers by Indian feminists on the theme of the Ideology of Motherhood in India, in a special issue of the *Economic and Political Weekly* 25(42&43), 20–7 October 1990.

5 Other articles in this volume edited by Phoenix, Woollett and Lloyd explore the wide-ranging psychological definitions of deviance and pathology in maternity. The volume covers a wide range of habituses that are considered pathological. Given the narrow confines of an ideal which celebrates maternity only within marriage and a family and which enshrines mothers who do not work outside the home, the range of maternities productive of pathologies is necessarily all-encompassing.

6 The regional mobilization around the theme of language is comparatively recent and has absorbed many ingredients of colonialist discourse, such as the Tamils' description of themselves and their language as 'Dravidian' (as opposed to 'Aryan', here equated with the northerner).

  However, the celebration of language as a sacral entity, and an identification of region with this language, is very old in Tamil culture. See for example descriptions in the twelfth-century Tamil version of the Ramayana by Kampan, which celebrates the glories of 'speaking the sweet, eternal Tamil' and describes the sacred origins of the language as a gift from the god Siva to the sage Agastya, and in turn to the people:

Rising to great heights
by study of the four Vedas
and by examining poetic and ordinary
speech as they should be considered,
like the radiant god whose axe
glitters, whose red eye burns
from his lovely forehead, who gave the sage
the language, Agastya gave men Tamil. (Kampan, trans. Hart 1988:69)

7 For a detailed exposition of the annually celebrated transformation of the fierce Tamil warrior goddess Minakshi into the consort of Siva see Harman's *The Sacred Marriage of a Hindu Goddess*, 1989.

8 See Pandian 1992 for a more detailed analysis of the MGR film genre and its relationship to regional politics.

9 Parts of this section are published in an earlier version (see Ram 1994).

REFERENCES

Abraham, A. 1985 Subsistence credit: survival strategies among traditional fishermen. *Economic and Political Weekly* 20(6):247–52.

Acheson, J. 1981 Anthropology of fishing. *Annual Review of Anthropology* 10:275–316.

Alexander, P. 1982 *Sri Lankan Fishermen: Rural Capitalism and Peasant Society*. Monographs on South Asia, No. 7. Canberra: The Australian National University.

Alphonse, T. 1991 *Anpu Itayaṅkaḷ, Iṉpa Utayaṅkaḷ*. Trichinopoly: Holy Family College.

Arnold, D. 1989 (ed.) *Imperial Medicine and Indigenous Societies*. Delhi: Oxford University Press.

Beals, A. 1976 Strategies of resort to curers in south India. In C. Leslie (ed.) *Asian Medical Systems: A Comparative Study*. Berkeley: University of California Press, 184–200.

Bhabha, H. 1994 *The Location of Culture*. London: Routledge.

Chatterjee, P. 1986 *Nationalist Thought and the Colonial World: A Derivative Discourse?* London: Zed Books for the United Nations University.

Cole, S. 1991 *Women of the Praia: Work and Lives in a Portuguese Coastal Community*. Princeton: Princeton University Press.

Dirks, N. 1987 *The Hollow Crown: Ethnohistory of an Indian Kingdom*. Cambridge: Cambridge University Press.

Economic and Political Weekly 1990 Review of women's studies: *Ideology of Motherhood* Special Issue 25(42&43), 20–7 October.

Firth, R. 1943 *Housekeeping among Malay Peasants*. London: Lund, Humphries and Co.

Gould, H. 1977 Modern medicine and folk cognition in rural India. In D. Landy (ed.) *Culture, Disease and Healing: Studies in Medical Anthropology*. New York: Macmillan, 495–502.

Guha, R. 1983 *Elementary Aspects of Peasant Insurgency in Colonial India*. Delhi: Oxford University Press.

Hardgrave, R. 1969 *The Nadars of Tamilnad: The Political Culture of a Community in Change*. Berkeley: University of California Press.

Hardy, F. 1983 *Viraha-Bhakti: The Early History of Kṛṣṇa Devotion in South India*. Oxford: Oxford University Press.

Harman, W. 1989 *The Sacred Marriage of a Hindu Goddess*. Bloomington: Indiana University Press.

Irschick, E. 1986 *Tamil Revivalism in the 1930s*. Madras: Cre-A.

Jeffrey, R. 1992 *Politics, Women and Well-Being: How Kerala Became 'A Model'*. Basingstoke: Macmillan.

Kampan 1988[12th c.] *The Forest Book of the Ramayana of Kampan* (trans. G. Hart). Berkeley: University of California Press.

Kristeva, J. 1986 (French orig. 1977) Stabat mater. In J. Kristeva *The Kristeva Reader* (ed. T. Moi). Oxford: Basil Blackwell, 160–86.

Lakshmi, C.S. 1990 Mother, mother-community and mother-politics in Tamil Nadu. *Economic and Political Weekly* 25(42&43):WS72–WS83.

Landy, D. 1977 (ed.) *Culture, Disease, and Healing: Studies in Medical Anthropology*. New York and London: Macmillan.

Leslie, C. 1976 (ed.) *Asian Medical Systems: A Comparative Study*. Berkeley: University of California Press.

Mandelbaum, D. 1966 Transcendental and pragmatic aspects of religion. *American Anthropologist* 68:1174–91.

Mani, L. 1989 Contentious traditions: the debate on *sati* in colonial India. In K. Sangari and S. Vaid (eds.) *Recasting Women: Essays in Colonial History*. New Delhi: Kali for Women, 88–126.

Marshall, H. 1991 The social construction of motherhood: an analysis of childcare and parenting manuals. In A. Phoenix, A. Woollett and E. Lloyd (eds.) *Motherhood: Meanings, Practices and Ideologies*. London: Sage Publications, 66–85.

Martin, E. 1987 *The Woman in the Body: A Cultural Analysis of Reproduction*. Boston: Beacon Press.

Ministry of Health and Family Welfare 1991 *Health Information of India*. New Delhi: Ministry of Health and Family Welfare, Government of India.

1993 *National Family Health Survey 1992, Tamil Nadu*. New Delhi: Ministry of Health and Family Welfare, Government of India.

Nandy, A. 1983 *Intimate Enemy: Loss and Recovery of Self under Colonialism*. Delhi: Oxford University Press.

Pandian, J. 1982 The goddess Kannagi: a dominant symbol of south Indian Tamil society. In J. Preston (ed.) *Mother Worship: Theme and Variations*. Chapel Hill: University of North Carolina Press, 177–91.

Pandian, M.S.S. 1992 *The Image Trap: M.G. Ramachandran in Film and Politics*. New Delhi, London and Newbury Park: Sage Publications.

Panikkar, K.N. 1995 *Culture, Ideology, Hegemony: Intellectuals and Social Consciousness in Colonial India*. New Delhi: Tulika.

Pearson, M.N. 1987 *The Portuguese in India* (vol. I in Part 1 of *The New Cambridge History of India*). Cambridge: Cambridge University Press.

Prakash, Fr (Swami) J. 1991 *Pēya? Noyva?* Kanyakumari District, Tamil Nadu: Naalai Veliveedu Mullanganavilai.

Ram, K. 1991 *Mukkuvar Women: Gender, Hegemony and Capitalist Transformation in a South Indian Fishing Community*. Sydney: Allen and Unwin.

1994 Medical management and giving birth: responses of coastal women in

Tamil Nadu. *Motherhood, Fatherhood and Fertility. Reproductive Health Matters* Special Issue 4:20–6.

1995 Rationalism, cultural nationalism, and the reform of body politics: minority intellectuals of the Tamil Catholic community. *Contributions to Indian Sociology* (n.s.) 29 (1&2):291–318.

Romanucci-Ross, L. 1977 The hierarchy of resort in curative practices: the Admiralty Islands, Melanesia. In D. Landy (ed.) *Culture, Disease, and Healing: Studies in Medical Anthropology.* New York and London: Macmillan, 481–7.

Said, E. 1978 *Orientalism.* London: Routledge and Kegan Paul.

Sangari, K. and Vaid, S. 1989 (eds.) *Recasting Women: Essays in Colonial History.* New Delhi: Kali for Women.

Seremetakis, C.N. 1991 *The Last Word: Women, Death, and Divination in Inner Mani.* Chicago and London: University of Chicago Press.

Tamil Lexicon 1982 (6 vols. plus supplements, under the authorization of the University of Madras). Madras, India: University of Madras.

Trawick, M. 1978 The sacred spell and other conceptions of life in Tamil culture. PhD thesis, University of Chicago.

1980 On the meaning of *sakti* to women in Tamil Nadu. In S. Wadley (ed.) *The Powers of Tamil Women.* Foreign and Comparative Studies, South Asian Series No. 6. Syracuse, NY: Maxwell School of Citizenship and Public Affairs, Syracuse University, 1–34.

1992 *Notes on Love in a Tamil Family.* Berkeley: University of California Press.

5   The *dai* and the doctor: discourses on
     women's reproductive health in rural
     Bangladesh

Santi Rozario

Women in Western countries have been struggling for several decades
against what is now widely viewed as the unnecessary and excessive
medicalization of childbirth. The move to a less interventionist model for
childbirth has been a genuine gain for many women in the West (see
Martin 1987; Oakley 1986), but there is a real risk of mythologizing and
romanticizing the process of 'natural childbirth' and of projecting this
image on to a Third World context where it is not always appropriate.

World Health Organization (WHO) policy for some years has emphasized working through traditional birth attendants (TBAs) as the best
path to improving the appalling level of maternal and child mortality and
illness in much of the Third World (see pp. 166–7 below). Recently, some
doubts as to the universal appropriateness of this strategy have begun to
surface (e.g. Scheepers 1991 for Yemen; Stephens 1992 for Andhra
Pradesh). My own material on childbirth in rural Bangladesh[1] suggests
that we need to examine the concept of the TBA in more critical detail. It
is too easy, perhaps, to counterpose the midwife to the doctor, seeing the
former as a repository of traditional wisdom and the latter as a projection
of patriarchal intervention. In practice, both may have serious deficiencies in terms of delivering effective health care, and their effectiveness
may be further compromised by the cultural and material situation within
which they work. In this chapter we will see that neither the village
midwife (the *dai*)[2] nor the village doctor are really in a position to care
effectively for birthing women.

Childbirth in rural Bangladesh

Introduction

To begin with, I present a general description of childbirth in rural
Bangladesh, based on my own research and that of previous authors.[3] I

144

will argue that the way in which childbirth is managed in Bangladeshi village society, whether Hindu, Muslim or Christian, is distinctive and characteristic. The pattern varies little between Hindus, Muslims and Christians. Typical features of this Bangladeshi pattern include the low status and lack of expertise of TBAs (*dai* or *dhoruni*), the lack of significant antenatal or postnatal care for the mother and the heavy emphasis on birth pollution and vulnerability to spirits (*bhut*). This pattern is essentially the same as that described in some Indian studies (Jeffery *et al.* 1989; Stephens 1992), but it contrasts markedly with the way in which childbirth is managed among many other Third World societies.[4]

The two examples I present in this introductory section show most of the characteristic features of the Bangladeshi pattern of childbirth. In the first case – from one of the studies (Bhatia *et al.* 1980) carried out in Matlab in Comilla District by the International Centre for Diarrhoeal Disease Research, Bangladesh (ICDDR,B) – a *dai* (TBA) was present, while in the second – from Blanchet (1984) – there was no *dai*. The absence of a *dai* is by no means unusual, especially in poorer families. The two examples also demonstrate the emphasis on birth pollution and danger of attack by *bhut* (evil spirits).

Tasmina

Bhatia *et al.* (1980) relate the sequence of a delivery, in the Matlab area, which they regard as typical of a 'difficult' birth experience among local women:

A *dai*, aged sixty years, with no education, was called to deliver Tasmina's fifth child. As the *dai* waited for Tasmina's labour pain to increase, the mother-in-law went out and came back with some *pora pani* (sanctified water), which was given to Tasmina to drink. Labour pain increased, but the *dai* could not deliver the baby. So she dipped her left hand in some coconut oil and tried to widen the 'opening' of the vagina. It seemed the child's head was stuck. Tasmina spent the whole afternoon, the night and the half of next day in unbearable pain. During this time more *pora pani* (sanctified water) and a *tabij* (amulet) were brought from a *kabiraj* (folk-healer).[5] Some homoeopathic medicines were used, petals of flowers from Mecca were brought from a *fakir* (another type of folk-healer),[6] soaked in water and fed to Tasmina, but Tasmina was still 'wild with discomfort'. Tasmina implored the *dai* to 'cut open her belly with a knife' as she felt her insides were being torn apart. Her breathing started decreasing and all the members of the household became extremely concerned, some began to cry. They stopped working and prayed to Allah. Finally Tasmina's baby was delivered with great difficulty by the *dai* with the help of Tasmina's sister-in-law. After this, Tasmina's hair was dipped into kerosene oil and forced into her throat to induce vomiting and speed up the release of the placenta. After delivering the child and cutting the cord with a razor blade the *dai* washed her hands and cut her nails. She had not washed her hands before the delivery. (My summary, after Bhatia *et al.* 1980)

Tasmina's case is a good example of the *dai*'s helplessness in difficult labour. While through years of experience they gain sufficient knowledge about women's anatomy to tackle an uncomplicated birth, they are completely helpless in complicated cases. The *dai* could do nothing for Tasmina but wait, while the family members kept bringing in *pora pani*, *tabij*, homoeopathic medicines and prayed. The use of *pora pani* and *tabij* is very common and is linked to the fear of evil spirits, discussed in detail below. Nobody seemed to be concerned about the issue of hygiene. The *dai* thoroughly washed her hands and cut her nails after the delivery, not before. This is because birth is seen as such a polluting event that it is perceived to be useless to clean one's hands before, rather than after, the delivery.

The question of taking Tasmina to a suitable health centre never arose. Tasmina's family's class background is unclear from the above description. Rural women generally give birth at home, although it is not uncommon for a rich family to take a birthing mother to a health centre if delivery is perceived to be a complicated one. However, as we will see, the relationship between the villagers and modern medicine is more complex than the question of wealth alone.

Zori

My other example is taken from Blanchet (1984), who conducted her fieldwork in Jamalpur, in northern Bangladesh:

Blanchet was present at the first delivery of a seventeen-year-old Muslim girl, Zori. Zori was brought to her father's house, where the kitchen was used as the delivery room (*atur ghor*). Her guardians called for a *dai*, but she refused to come, as she had not been paid for past services. As Zori had been in pain for several hours, her mother and other female relatives began to panic. They kept feeding Zori *pora pani* to protect her from spirit attack. As time went on Zori began to look very tired and desperate, saying 'I want to die.' As the delivery became imminent it became evident that none of the other women present was prepared to tackle the birth. Instead, they asked Blanchet herself to be the *dhoruni* (i.e. to catch the baby). Blanchet asked for soap in order to wash her hands, but the women told her that 'it (was) not *before*, but *after*' (1984:84) that she should use soap. According to Blanchet, the birth was without complication, but throughout the birthing process the other women refrained from coming in contact with the birth substances. For instance, when the baby was delivered by Blanchet, she was advised to place it on the cold earth of the floor, as none of the women was willing to hold it.

Zori's mother lit a fire promptly after the birth. Then, in order to release the placenta, two women 'applied pressure to Zori's abdomen with their feet and tried to make her vomit by pushing her hair down her throat' (1984:85). As none of these techniques worked immediately, they tried various other methods including feeding Zori some more *pora pani*. As soon as the placenta was ejected (within 15 minutes of the birth), 'Zori's mother in a great haste placed a new amulet around the baby's neck' (1984:85). Blanchet reports on how after she placed the placenta on a piece of banana stem 'there were angry comments as to who would clean up. Up till then only I and the parturient mother had come in direct contact with the polluting substances of birth' [1984:85]. (My summary, after Blanchet 1984:83–6)

In these two accounts we see numerous typical features of childbirth in rural Bangladesh: lack of hygiene, lack of knowledge about birth, lack of medical services, lack of money, use of *pora pani* and *tabij*, and fear of pollution and *bhut*. These are confirmed by other studies (Aziz and Maloney 1985; M. Islam 1980; S. Islam 1981, 1989) as well as by my own research.

The fieldwork on childbirth described in this chapter was carried out in late 1991 and early 1992 in the Rupganj Subdistrict, which is located in Dhaka District, three hours by road from the city of Dhaka. The area was well known to me from my previous doctoral fieldwork (Rozario 1992), and my family originates from a nearby community, so that despite the brevity of the fieldwork period I was able to carry out useful research. My initial aim was to examine the impact of modern medicine and contraception, and the significance of local concepts of purity, on women's reproductive health. My data consist mostly of interviews with *dai*, family planning workers, folk-healers, biomedical (allopathic) and homoeopathic doctors, pregnant women and mothers with small children. Although I was unable to witness an actual birth on this occasion, the material I collected was entirely consistent with the two examples presented above.

Rupganj is similar to many rural areas in its lack of access to modern hospital facilities (the nearest hospital is two to three hours away) and in the evidently low level of expertise of local biomedical and homoeopathic doctors. It is, however, unusual in one respect: Rupganj is one of the few areas of Bangladesh with a substantial Christian (Roman Catholic) population. Consequently, my sample included Christian as well as Hindu and Muslim mothers and *dai*. In addition, the area has a number of dispensaries operated by local biomedically-trained Catholic nuns, who provide some health advice for pregnant mothers. I shall return to these dispensaries later, since they have a significant positive impact on childbirth practices in Rupganj.

The examples from Matlab (Tasmina) and Jamalpur (Zori) suggest, however, that the pattern of childbirth in rural Bangladesh is far from satisfactory. This is undoubtedly equally true for the Rupganj area. By contrast with patterns of indigenous midwifery elsewhere in the Third

World,[7] the level of expertise of Rupganj *dai* appears to be low, and they give no antenatal and little postnatal care. Although Rupganj people, like rural Bangladeshi villagers in general, place great emphasis on the birth of children (especially male children), giving birth for Rupganj women is a dangerous experience, with high infant mortality and a real risk of the mother's death. This situation is not improved by the complex of ideas concerning pollution, *bhut* and nutrition, which I shall look at in more detail shortly. These ideas and practices ensure that women before, during and immediately after childbirth are poorly fed, deprived of human contact and frequently terrified of attacks by evil spirits.

We should, nevertheless, beware of simply accepting the biomedical critique of Bangladeshi birth practices, as given in the Matlab studies, for example, at face value. This critique sees the *dai*, and traditional birth practices in general, as the problem. The solution is seen as the medicalization of birth on the conventional Western model, with the replacement of the *dai* by biomedically-trained birth attendants as an interim step. In reality, the situation is more complex than this, as the limited success of the biomedical solution even in the trial area of Matlab indicates. Matlab has been the focus of an extensive maternal health development effort since the late 1970s, but even the centre's own figures suggest that there has been little real improvement for local women giving birth (Bhatia 1989; Fauveau and Chakraborty 1988:3; Koenig *et al.* 1988).

The limited success of the biomedical solution derives, in my opinion, from its failure to give sufficient recognition to the perspectives and actual situation of the villagers themselves, both the women giving birth and their families, and the *dai*.

In the remainder of this chapter I will first examine local ideas about pollution, *bhut* and nutrition and then look in more detail at the villagers' perspectives on childbirth practices, followed by the perspective of the *dai*. After that I will look at the biomedical critiques of village childbirth practices in some detail. This will make it possible to arrive at an overall picture of childbirth practices in Rupganj and other rural areas of Bangladesh. Finally, I will present an evaluation of the situation and an examination of the prospects for change.

Pollution, *bhut*, confinement and nutrition

We have already encountered the notions of pollution and *bhut* in the two brief case studies given above. Pollution is, of course, a major issue in the sociology of South Asian societies, being particularly associated in contemporary debates with Louis Dumont's classic analysis of Hindu caste society as structured around ideas of purity and pollution (Dumont

1972). I do not want to enter here into the controversy on how fully Dumontian analysis applies to Hindu caste society in India (Berreman 1971; Heesterman 1971; Kantowsky 1971; Madan 1971; Marglin 1977; Reichle 1985; van der Veer 1985). In any case, caste in the Dumontian formulation has only a limited relevance in the predominantly Muslim society of Bangladesh. Bangladeshi village society is not, at least from the Muslim or Christian perspectives, divided into named endogamous groups ranked according to criteria of purity and separated by explicit restrictions on the sharing of food. A good case could nevertheless be made for notions similar to caste being present at a covert level. Commensality, let alone intermarriage, between low- and high-status groups is rare, and physical contact with low-status groups is undoubtedly seen by high-status groups as inappropriate and to be avoided. The *dai*, it should be noted, virtually all belong to these low-status groups.

In this context, it makes sense to ask how far the *dai*'s role is related to a covert underlying framework of ideas about pollution. In the north Indian context, Jeffery *et al.* argue that the *dai*'s function is centrally concerned with the removal of pollution: '[I]t is inappropriate to regard the *dai* as an expert midwife in the contemporary Western sense. Even in the absence of medically trained personnel, the *dai* does not have overriding control over the management of deliveries. Nor is she a sisterly and supportive equal. Rather, she is a low status menial necessary for removing defilement' (1989:108). They also note that '[c]hildbirth pollution is the most severe pollution of all, far greater than menstruation, sexual intercourse, defaecation or death. Consequently, touching the amniotic sac, placenta and umbilical cord . . . and delivering the baby, cutting the cord and cleaning up the blood are considered the most disgusting of tasks' (1989:106).

We may ask how far these ideas are present in Bangladesh as well. Some factors certainly suggest this, and I would regard the removal of pollution as at least one of the major functions of the *dai*, as suggested by the washing of hands after the birthing of both Tasmina and Zori. More significantly, in the case of Zori, it is evident that the women were concerned about the *dai*'s absence not because they needed her expertise, but because none of them were willing to take on the pollution involved in delivering the baby. Blanchet herself, after delivering the baby, had to undergo purification before being admitted back into the household where she was living. Katy Gardner, who did extensive anthropological fieldwork in Talukpur (Sylhet District), also noted that 'a woman who has given birth is seen as dangerously polluted in rural Bangladesh. If her dirt or blood contaminates the place where the family wash or clean their food . . . , great sickness is thought to ensue' (1991:26). Naseem Hussain

(1992), working in a village close to the Dhaka metropolitan region, again mentions childbirth pollution. All this is despite the high value placed on the birth of children (particularly sons) in rural Bangladesh.[8]

Contact with the birthing substances and especially the cutting of the umbilical cord are perceived to be so polluting that these tasks are even today reserved for a *dai*. If a *dai* cannot be obtained, the birthing woman may be made to cut the cord herself (Rozario 1995) (see Plates 4 and 5). An elderly Christian woman reported that in the past her parents had waited for hours, on one occasion for two days, for a *dai* to arrive to cut the umbilical cord. Meanwhile the baby lay on the floor and nobody would touch it.

The practice of waiting for the *dai* to arrive to cut the umbilical cord has no connection to the expertise of the *dai*, but is related entirely to the perceived pollution associated with cutting the cord. A twenty-year-old Hindu woman commented to me about the *dai* who would be called to 'catch' the baby and cut the cord: 'They are a separate *jati* [subcaste], there are no other *jati* below them.'

As I have already noted, Bangladeshi *dai*, whether explicitly seen as belonging to a separate *jati* or not, are almost uniformly of low status, so that it is appropriate for them to take on the pollution of birth. They are also typically so poor that they are prepared to take on this 'most disgusting of tasks'. Gardner (1991) also comments on the poor background and low status of *dai* in Talukpur (Sylhet District). Nevertheless, the *dai* does provide assistance and some expertise at the time of birth, and – as we will see later – *dai* regard themselves as delivering babies rather than merely removing birth pollution.

Besides the restrictions observed by the *dai*, several other features of rural Bangladeshi childbirth practices relate directly to pollution. For Muslim and Christian families, birth takes place in the kitchen or in a partitioned-off area of the main room so as to restrict pollution. Hindu families, as described below, will, if possible, build a separate hut for the delivery. The woman giving birth wears an old sari, since the clothes she wears will be polluted and will normally be given away to a beggar or the *dai*. It is for reasons of pollution, too, that the birth usually takes place on the mud floor with a bare minimum of bedding for the woman to lie on, even in houses where she would normally sleep on a bed.

Pollution and fear of *bhut* (evil spirits) are closely related concepts. The use of *pora pani* (sanctified water), as in the two examples given, serves to protect mother and child against *bhut*, as does the *tabij* (amulet) tied around the baby's neck immediately after birth, as in the case of Zori's baby. Belief in evil spirits (also referred to as *bhut-pret* or *jin*) is widespread and certain illnesses are consistently explained by referring to evil spirits ('bad air') in Bangladesh (Aziz and Maloney 1985; Blanchet 1984; M. Islam 1980; S. Islam 1981, 1989; Mahtab 1989; Maloney *et al.* 1981; Rozario 1992). Women are more vulnerable to evil spirits than men. In particular, unmarried women, new brides, pregnant and postnatal women are said to be very vulnerable to the attack of *bhut*. Hence they must try to avoid the *nazar* (that is, evil or greedy eye) of the *bhut* at all times. The times when the malevolent spirits are most active are high noon, sunset and midnight. Thus postnatal women, who are most vulnerable, must refrain from going out of the delivery room or hut at those times. In fact they must remain confined in their delivery room except for coming out to relieve themselves or perhaps to have a bath. This confinement lasts for a set number of days, which varies according to religion, class and lineage as well as the structure of the family, that is, whether it is nuclear, joint or extended.

Hindus are said to be strictest in this regard: postnatal Hindu women are supposed to be confined for thirty days, although in practice poor Hindu women in nuclear families may find it difficult to follow and leave their delivery hut much earlier, sometimes after eight days, sometimes after fifteen days. It is not uncommon for Hindu husbands to cook the meals during this time in the absence of other female members in the family. If they can afford it, Hindus must build a separate hut for birthing mothers. The hut is usually built inside the yard rather than behind the main housing complex where the *bhut* hang around in the big trees. To avoid the *bhut* at all costs, some Hindus will dig a hole near the delivery hut, so that women do not have to go behind the house to have a bath. An earthen pot will be used or a hole dug inside the hut for urinating and defecating, so that women do not have to come out during the inauspicious hours. The outside of the delivery hut is plastered with cow-dung and surrounded with thorny branches of trees, so that *bhut* cannot go inside. In the rainy season villagers usually place large strips of plastic over the hut to prevent rain water dripping inside.

On average, Muslims are said to be confined in the delivery room for five days in the case of a female child and six to eight days in the case of a male child. In addition to other purification rituals (to be discussed below) their confinement comes to an end with the shaving of the infant's hair. Christian women's postnatal confinement generally comes to an end with the baptism of the baby, which usually takes place after about fifteen days. Apparently, baptism used to take place between three to six days after the birth in the recent past. Muslims and Christians do not build separate huts for delivery, but they should ideally give birth in a separate room. However, this is not possible in most cases; so some people use the kitchen for this purpose, while others use one side of the

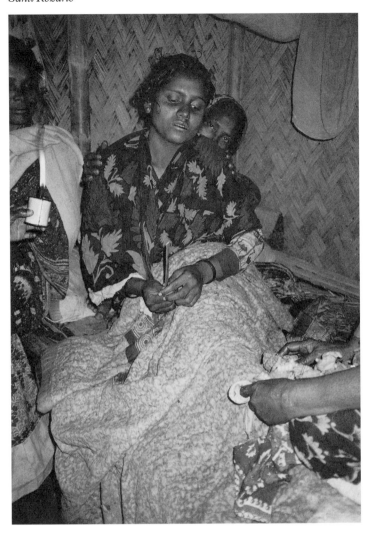

4 A birthing mother is being helped to sit up after the birth of her baby
and after the placenta has been ejected. She is holding a bamboo slit,
which she will use to cut the umbilical cord. The cutting of the cord is
perceived as so polluting that those *dai* who presently attend the birth
do not usually cut it, unless they are handsomely paid as compensation. Thus, in most families the birthing mother does this.

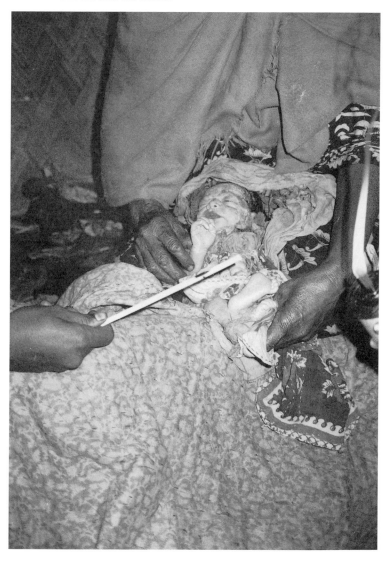

5 The birthing mother is cutting the umbilical cord while the *dai* holds
it to facilitate the cutting. The lamp is being held up by a sister-in-law
of the birthing mother. (This and photo opposite taken during
subsequent fieldwork in southern Bangladesh in January 1995.)

main room by partitioning it with a wooden bed if available. Whatever the number of days and the degree of rigidity, all women regardless of class and religious background practise confinement and all perform certain rituals as they leave the delivery room. The literal meaning of the words *atur* and *chodi*, which are used to refer to the delivery hut or room (*atur ghor, chodi ghor*) are 'sickness, distress' (*atur*) and 'infection, pollution' (*chodi*). Village women refer to the rituals that accompany the conclusion of confinement as *chodi tula* (removal of infection or pollution). *Chodi tula* rituals also take various forms. But every woman at least cleans and plasters the mud floor of the room or hut, washes bedding and personal clothes, as well as washes herself thoroughly. Confinement has as much to do with the danger from *bhut* as with the danger of pollution, which if allowed to get out of control, may harm both environment and people.

In addition to their confinement for a certain period of time, women have to follow certain food restrictions during pregnancy and the postnatal period. It is believed that the *nari* (umbilicus) of the baby remains 'raw' (*kacha*) for some months and therefore the breastfeeding mother should be careful about what she eats. North Indian women are also reported to follow food restrictions during this time (Jeffery *et al.* 1989). A typical diet for postnatal Rupganj women during the five to seven days after birth is puffed rice or *chira* (flattened rice) with tea in the morning, some rice with mashed potato and/or black cumin powder for lunch, flattened rice or dry bread with tea for the evening meal. After a week or so they can start eating some curries without spices. However, for up to three months they should avoid various types of seafood – two varieties of fish (*puti* and *booal*) and prawns – as well as beef, some avoiding beef for eighteen months. Prawns are believed to dry out the mother's milk. Such food taboos, linked either to the threat of *bhut* or of other physical illness, mean that postnatal women are deprived of nutritious food for long periods, affecting their and their infants' health adversely. Most of these women have had very little protein in their food intake during their childhood or during pregnancy, so that postnatal food taboos aggravate an already existing protein deficiency.

The elaborate precautions taken in relation to pollution and *bhut* contrast with the lack of precautions to avoid infection and the frequent unwillingness to seek biomedical aid. It is not that Bangladeshi villagers are unconcerned about the risk to the mother or her child. My interviews confirmed that the family's fear that they may lose the mother and/or the baby is very real. However, the dangers to the woman's life and the newborn baby's life are seen to derive from pollution and from the potential attack of the *bhut*. Thus miscarriages, menstrual complications, extended labour pain, stillbirth, haemorrhage, postnatal diarrhoea, infants' diarrhoea and tetanus are explained by evil spirits. The *bhut* is the symbolic representation of all the dangers of birth.

I now look at the family's perspective on the birthing process in more detail.

The family's perspective

I speak of the family's perspective rather than that of the birthing woman because, in practice, the birthing woman's perspective is not central in making decisions about her health.

To understand the vulnerability of rural Muslim women in Bangladesh, we have to realize that these women are still essentially dependants of men both in structural and cultural terms. The predominance of poverty in rural Bangladesh may mean lack of education and of employment for the vast majority of the population, but this situation is much worse for women. Moreover, although Muslim women have limited legal rights to property, their dependency relations with men and the cultural ideologies of honour and shame usually prevent them from exercising these rights. The institution of *parda* (*purdah*) – restrictions on female mobility, including veiling in some cases – is explained by reference to Islam. However, it is integrally linked to Bengali and Hindu ideologies of purity and pollution, the combination of which affects women's educational, economic and gender status. While, as I have suggested above, the caste system in its entirety is not present among Bengali Muslims or Christians, the concepts of purity and pollution regarding women are very much present. Although older women do exercise some power and make some important decisions in domestic affairs, young women are extremely restricted in this regard. Young women in nuclear families may fare better in this regard, but most women keep their opinion to themselves for fear of being labelled 'shameless', or 'forward', which is not a desirable quality for an honourable woman. Under the circumstances it is not difficult to understand the lack of decision-making power of birthing women in rural Bangladesh.

In practice, it is men and/or older women in the family who make decisions about the health care of birthing women. To understand the decisions which they make, we need to look in more detail both at indigenous concepts of illness and other cultural factors and also the practical options that are available to Bangladeshi villagers.

Indigenous concepts of illness and other cultural factors

We have seen how most of the illnesses related to childbirth are linked to pollution and *bhut*. Precautions against *bhut* are therefore seen as central to protecting the mother and newly born child from illness. Confining the mother to the delivery room after birth, and ensuring that she observes the food taboos strictly, are therefore important first lines of defence. As we have seen, it is likely that the food restrictions in particular make the mother's physiological condition worse by reducing the consumption of nutritious food at this critical period. It appears village women are becoming increasingly aware that it is important to have nutritious food during the postnatal period. However, as a young Christian woman told me, it is difficult not to follow the restrictions regarding food, because when babies become ill, young mothers are blamed for not being able to 'control their greed for food'. Whether staying with in-laws or with her own parents during the postnatal period, a woman will be under the surveillance of her mother-in-law or mother in this regard. In any case it is clear that these young women are not yet convinced that eating prohibited food is not going to be harmful for themselves or their babies.

Other minor precautions may be taken to protect the birthing mother and the baby from *bhut*. In Rupganj, women place a piece of iron or a burnt stick under the pillow of the new baby to deter the attention of *bhut*. To ward off the evil spirits the village women in Matlab place an old knife, old shoe or a broomstick under the mat of the birthing woman (Bhatia *et al*. 1980:7).

When, in Rupganj, despite these precautions the mother or child falls ill, families seek assistance from folk-healers (*kabiraj*, *fakir*). Most of the *dai* in Rupganj also practise as folk-healers to some extent, but serious health problems are usually referred to other more highly regarded folk-healers, who are usually male. When patients suffering from illnesses such as *sutika* (postnatal diarrhoea) or eclampsia (associated with *bhut*) are taken to a folk-healer, the healer will follow certain rituals to rid the patient of the evil influences of *bhut* and then also give an amulet to be used as a future protection against the attention of *bhut*.

Hindu women in Rupganj, in addition to calling on the services of the folk-healer, can also offer *puja* (worship) to a Hindu deity, such as Kali, for protection against attack from the evil spirits. Alternatively, they will often make a vow that if everything goes well, a big *puja* accompanied by a feast will be held in honour of the deity. Compared to Hindus, Muslims in Rupganj do not have access to such a recourse to get supernatural beings to act as their protector. Christians occupy an intermediate position. They do not make any offerings to supernatural beings, but do call upon the assistance of St Anthony. Like the Hindus, they also make vows regarding the health or general well-being of a child, or any member of the family (see Rozario 1992 for details). It would appear from this comparison that Hindus are in the best position in their dealings with the *bhut* in that they, like the Muslims and Christians, have access to folk-healers as well as to other deities as their protector. By appealing to St Anthony, Christians also appear to be able to reduce their anxiety about their health to a certain extent. In this regard Muslim women seem most vulnerable.

While Hindu and Christian women in Rupganj enjoy a recourse to supernatural help not available to Muslim women, it may be noted that women in many other Muslim societies do have such recourse. Two examples out of many are the well-known *zar* cult, practised by Egyptian and Sudanese women (Boddy 1989; Constantinides 1978) and the cults of saints in Morocco (Dwyer 1978). These practices do appear to have some parallels elsewhere in Bangladesh, but they were absent in Rupganj.[9]

In other respects, the situation of women in Bangladesh is undoubtedly disadvantaged in comparison with women in some other Muslim countries. We can contrast, for example, Laderman's (1983) study of childbirth practices among Malays, who are also Muslims. It is clear from Laderman's material that Malay birthing women are much more able to control the circumstances in which they give birth than are their Bangladeshi counterparts. In Malaysia the birthing mother's wishes and emotions are respected and every effort is made to make her comfortable. In one case witnessed by Laderman, a Malay birthing mother asked her relations to call in a male *bomoh* (folk-healer) whom she knew well. Laderman (1983:161) reports that Asmah, the birthing mother, rested her head on the *bomoh*'s lap and 'she put her arms around his back with every contraction'. Later on Asmah asked the *bomoh* to massage her abdomen. Malay women obey rules of feminine modesty similar to those of Muslim women in Bangladesh, but an incident like this would be difficult to imagine in Rupganj. In fact, Laderman contrasts favourably the degree of control exercised by Malay women with that of women in the United States: 'American women are delivered by obstetricians; Malay women give birth' (1983:173).

Moreover, Asmah's midwife was trained, confident and carried a delivery kit which contained everything starting from soap and Panadol to urethral catheter and forceps. Although Asmah's midwife was government-trained, Laderman points out that traditional midwives are also very competent and villagers in fact prefer the traditional midwife, who is said to be more readily available. There are some similarities in the birthing practices and beliefs between rural Malay women and rural Bangladeshi women, for example the influence of spirits, loosening the mother's hair and clothes, and opening up windows and doors in difficult labour. However, Malay women enjoy a higher status than north Indian and Bangladeshi Muslim women, and this is reflected in the status of their respective midwives and the relationships between the midwives and birthing mothers. This has implications for the quality of treatment and attention the birthing women receive in these countries.

Why are medical services underutilized?
It is also not very difficult to see the significance of the ideologies of *parda*, honour (*izzat* (*ijjat*)) and shame, purity and pollution in the family's choice of action in relation to women's health problems. Shamima Islam (1981) points out that owing to the norm of *parda*, bed-utilization rate was only 30 per cent at the *thana* (subdistrict) health complex staffed essentially by male doctors. Thus she argues that the maternal and child health (MCH) facilities, while inadequate for all rural women, were also underutilized (S. Islam 1981, 1989). Shamima Islam again relates a story in which despite the grave danger to mother and child, a pregnant woman's mother resisted all attempts to send her to an urban hospital 'where violation of *purdah* was inevitable' (S. Islam 1989:234). Islam observed 'it took four complete days' work on that woman to save her life as well as the family's *ijjat*', but the baby had to be sacrificed. Similarly Blanchet also argues that 'shame, an important component of *purdah*, as it is understood by Bengali village women, often explains why birth specialists or even relatives are excluded from attending the delivery of a child' (1984:27).

A number of village doctors in Rupganj (homoeopathic and allopathic) told me that Muslim female patients usually do not speak to them directly. The husband or father of the patient usually explains the problem to the doctor. Ideologies of purity and shame are so important in determining the status of a woman that the medical personnel do not even address a woman directly. Most families do not want male doctors to be at the actual scene of the delivery due to the notions of *parda*. In any case, most doctors would also rather not handle the polluted deliveries of illiterate village women. So they usually attend these cases alongside a *dai*, who does the actual delivery even when the doctor is present.

While families try to maintain the modesty and purity of their young women by keeping them away from male doctors and outside hospitals, the only option they are left with is the village *dai*. Women do not have to be concerned about their modesty in front of the *dai* who is local and familiar.

How villagers see biomedicine and contraception
It would be wrong to suggest that Rupganj villagers are opposed to biomedicine. However, lack of appropriate knowledge leads village families to accept certain services provided by biomedicine and ignore others. Unfortunately, the ones most acceptable to villagers seem to be 'injections' and 'saline'.[10] In any kind of emergency, for example difficult labour, families who can afford it will readily call for a doctor to give an injection or saline. These are perceived as miraculous agents of cure parallel to, but more powerful than, the remedies provided by the folk-

healers. The doctors (who are usually uncertified) happily go along with perpetuating this situation. On the other hand, as we have seen from the two case studies of birth, families take little or no notice of the rules of hygiene, a vital aspect of biomedical practice. This can be linked to the fact that families continue to link illnesses to *bhut* and to pollution derived from menstruation, birth-substances etc., rather than to unhygienic practices.

I could suggest that the problem is one of women locked within a 'traditional' worldview which prevents them from making use of modern facilities. There is some truth in this, but it would be a mistake to see the women as passive victims in this situation. For example, the use of contraceptive measures by large numbers of rural women is an instance of how women are prepared to exercise agency. While it is important for women to give birth to many children, especially boys, women are also aware of the danger to their health associated with giving birth. In the absence of a situation in which they can deliver healthy babies under safe conditions, a big percentage of rural women have now opted for contraception in order to reduce the number of births.

When I did my fieldwork in Rupganj in 1983–4, only a handful of Muslim women were using any form of contraceptives. When asked about the use of contraceptives, even women with up to eight children would say that either it was against God's (Allah's) wish or that 'children are God's gift and God will feed them', or that their husbands did not want them to use contraceptives because they feared repercussions from the Muslim *samaj* (community).[11] However, in early 1992 about 70 per cent of those women who have at least three to four children resorted to some form of contraceptive measures.[12] Moreover, many of them discussed this issue quite freely. This change has to be attributed to a combination of factors: aggressive campaigning on the part of the Bangladeshi government and non-governmental organizations, plus cheaper and much more easily available contraceptives compared to a decade earlier.[13] Radio talks and newspaper articles by *moulvis* (Muslim religious leaders) supporting contraceptives obviously made a great difference.[14] Most of all, as the option became a real possibility, women began to realize that if they could not make birth a safe event, then their best bet would be to reduce the number of births by taking contraceptives. Many women interviewed take contraceptives against the wishes of their mothers-in-law and husbands, often without their knowledge. Often a husband will be against the use of contraception by his wife because he only has daughters, or has only one or two sons. Opting for contraception can be seen as an attempt on the part of women to take some control over their bodies being used as a carrier of sons, bodies which have no other value of their own and can thus be endangered continually. This also clearly shows that given the option women are not of necessity opposed to modern reproductive technology.

Practical factors

We have examined the implication of different cultural values and ideologies for the kind of measures families take in dealing with women's health. At the same time we should take note of the many practical factors which are of equal importance to families in their decisions regarding women's health.

Poverty is the most glaring problem faced by most Rupganj families in this regard. Even when there is a hospital not too far away from the village, the cost involved is almost always beyond the means of an average rural family. There are said to be some government-subsidized hospitals based at the subdistrict level. However, even these are far too expensive for rural families. For example, during a check-up session at a local Catholic dispensary at which I was present, a woman was advised by a nun (who was a trained midwife) to go to a hospital for her delivery. She said, 'We are very poor; my husband does not have a job. We cannot afford to go to a hospital.' When the government-subsidized hospital (three hours away by train) was suggested, the woman said, 'Their so-called low charge (Tk500 – A$20.00) is still too much for us.' Apparently this woman's first delivery had also been complicated, the *dai* having torn the umbilical cord and the woman being taken to a clinic at the last moment.

In addition to the dire problem with money, the distance of the health centres and hospitals from the village dissuades many rural families. As families do not think about taking a patient to a hospital except in emergencies, the distance becomes a critical problem. In the case of a complicated labour, for instance, often it is too late by the time the birthing mother is finally taken to a hospital. Once a rural family arrive at the hospital, they do not usually get immediate attention either. It is well known that village people are treated as second-class citizens everywhere (courts, various other government institutions), and a hospital is no different, except here one is dealing with life and death. The kind of insulting and arrogant behaviour reported by Jeffery *et al.* (1989:110) and by Ram (this volume: Chapter 4) for Indian urban hospitals dealing with village women is entirely typical for Bangladesh as well.[15]

From all this we can see that while birthing women have little or no say on their own health matters, those with the decision-making power are also rather constrained both in cultural and material terms. The dependence on *dai* can largely be explained by this situation.

The *dai*'s perspective

Who are the *dai* in Rupganj? They are usually very poor, elderly, with no formal education or training, and often widowed. While some middle-class women may engage in the task of delivering babies, they usually do this only for their close relatives and do not leave their household or hamlet to deliver babies for other women. The poor background and low status of *dai* are also emphasized in the work of Blanchet (1984) and Gardner (1991) for elsewhere in Bangladesh. Although she does not explicitly say so, it is also clear from Shamima Islam's (1989) accounts of Bangladeshi birth attendants that they are always from lower classes and may or may not receive a cash payment for their services.

I have already cited above Jeffery *et al.*'s description of the *dai* in north India as 'a low status menial necessary for removing defilement' (1989:108) and I have suggested that similar ideas are very much part of the Bangladeshi village context. But how do the *dai* see themselves and their role? Most of the *dai* interviewed saw their role as helping out families who ask for their assistance in delivery. Many of them, however, expressed their grievances about the fact that families do not show recognition of their services sufficiently – for example they do not always buy the *dai* a sari, or anything else, to show gratitude for their assistance. But the *dai* claim that they continue to help out families in need: as one *dai* said, 'What can I do? I know the job, people call me, I cannot say no.'

Shamima Islam (1989:239) reports how some *dai* refrain from taking any remuneration, as they believe 'the road to heaven is a straight way to a person who helps delivering 101 babies without taking any remuneration'. However, in Shamima Islam's accounts these *dai* too were often presented with saris upon successful completion of deliveries. Thus, if the *dai* does not take any remuneration, it is perhaps not out of choice, but because *there is no remuneration* for this task, except sometimes in the form of a sari or other fabric. We have seen in Zori's case how a *dai* was called but refused to come, because she had not been paid for earlier services. Thus, while I do not want to query the compassion of the *dai*, linked to her role is also a clear material interest, which can doubtless be explained by her poverty.

The issue of lack of remuneration of *dai* gains further significance when it is seen in the context of the other health services available in rural areas such as Rupganj. The relationship between the *dai* and the doctor (biomedical or homoeopathic and usually uncertified) is an important one. There is a clear distinction between the way a family treats a doctor on the one hand and a *dai* on the other. In the villages, *dai*, who are poor and are accorded low status, are nevertheless recognized as experienced women whose presence is desirable at a birth. Within the limited options available to rural families, it is not surprising that a *dai* is often perceived as the only person who can help. After all, unless there are complications, delivering babies is a relatively simple task for *dai*, who have sufficient knowledge of female anatomy.

However, when complications arise, a *dai* will usually advise the family to call a doctor or to take the birthing woman to a hospital. She does this (i) because she feels unable to tackle the situation; and perhaps more importantly (ii) because she does not want to be responsible for any mishap or to ruin her reputation by being involved in a problem-delivery which may lead to the death of the birthing mother and/or the baby. In such a situation, if a family can afford it, a doctor (usually uncertified) will generally be called. Usually he simply gives an injection or administers a packet of saline and waits outside. Sometimes, he simply watches the *dai* deliver the baby, without making any physical contact with the birthing mother or the baby. At other times, the baby may be killed as a result of the doctor's attempts to deliver it by force. Whatever the case, and even if the mother or the baby dies, the doctor, who is almost always male, has to be paid a very substantial amount (anything between Tk500 to Tk1500 (A\$20 to A\$60). The *dai*, on the other hand, receives little or no recognition for her services, even if it was her who actually delivered the baby. This situation understandably creates a tension between the *dai* and the doctors. In the event of an accident, a family can blame and challenge a *dai*, but with a doctor they accept the accident as something that was beyond human control.

While for some health problems the family may have the utmost faith in doctors compared to *dai*, the *dai*'s perception of the doctor's knowledge is not as positive. The following stories help illustrate the conflicting interests of the *dai* and the doctors concerning deliveries.

Gaynoda, a poor Hindu *dai*, in her mid-forties, related to me a case in which she believed the doctor was responsible for the death of the baby. In this case, when she was called by the guardians she felt the pain of the birthing mother was not linked to labour, but to something eaten by her the day before. Gaynoda told the guardians that it was a 'false alarm.' Nevertheless, they called a doctor, who gave an injection to increase the labour pain and bring on the birth. 'The mother was in great pain, but there was no sign of the baby. Finally, with great difficulty the baby was delivered, but died instantly.' In Gaynoda's opinion the baby was not due for some time yet, but the doctor forced the baby out, and so caused its death. It is difficult to be sure who was correct in this case. The doctor referred to was not a certified one, nor was Gaynoda a trained midwife. In fact Gaynoda said that the way she decides whether or not the baby is due is by pulling out a certain plant. 'If the plant comes up with the root, then the baby is ready to be delivered; if the plant breaks somewhere in-between, then the baby is not due'. By following this method Gaynoda apparently successfully predicted in another case that the pain felt by the birthing mother was not labour pain. She said, 'I delivered that baby after eight days'. In another case Gaynoda attended, the birthing mother had been in labour for three days, but the doctor said the baby was not due for another week. Apparently two other elderly *dai* also said the baby was not due for some time yet. But Gaynoda said that she delivered the baby in two hours. 'The mother's head was hot and I knew the baby was due.'[16]

Gaynoda said she delivers about five to six babies each year and so far has had no major problems. She told me, however, that once she delivered a breech baby of her sister-in-law: 'The baby's legs were down and head up. With great difficulty I together with Niat Ali's mother delivered the baby, but it died almost instantly. The mother and the baby were both very dry.' There were in fact several other incidents of the death of breech babies related to me by other *dai* (trained and untrained). Although it is difficult to make any conclusive judgement about Gaynoda's expertise, it is clear that she has considerable experience with delivering babies and that she is generally successful. Yet I could not help feeling that she takes on a fair number of risks which have the potential to result in disaster.

I asked several *dai* why they thought that the families called them instead of a doctor. The reply usually was because doctors are very expensive. 'A *dai* is merely given a sari, if anything, and maybe a meal of chicken curry.' Another Muslim *dai* added that the doctors 'do not understand women's problems – where the pain is, why the pain, what the position of the baby is'. A number of *dai* also related stories of doctors who were called in emergency cases, but were unable to save the situation. Often the story took the form of the doctor coming to the birth and asking the woman's guardian 'do you want the tree or the fruit?' Usually the guardians agree to save 'the tree', meaning the mother. The doctor then proceeds to save the mother by 'bringing the baby out bit by bit'. Another *dai* told me of a case where a local doctor was called and tried to deliver the baby by force, with the result that the mother died. Apparently the umbilical cord was torn.

These stories make it clear that *dai*, who are always there when called by families to deliver babies but receive little or no recognition for their services, are very resentful of the doctors, who are paid large sums of money, whether they succeed in saving the mother and the baby or not.

We have seen earlier that most health problems of women are seen to be somehow linked to the threat or actual attack of evil spirits. This is especially true with complications in delivery. Thus, whether Hindu, Muslim or Christian, all the *dai* interviewed were wary about the danger posed by the *bhut* and took whatever precautions they could in order to avoid any danger. For example, Gaynoda said that in order to deter the *bhut* from entering the delivery hut she follows the following ritual as soon as she arrives at a delivery: she draws a line with a bent knife on the ground around the hut to keep the evil spirits away from it. Sometimes she also obtains a 2.5-foot long root of a certain plant and places it on the roof of the delivery hut. At other times she mixes turmeric powder with mustard seeds and spreads this around the hut. On questioning, Gaynoda said she utters some *mantra* as she administers these herbal medicines.

Christian *dai* in Rupganj recognize the existence of the *bhut* but do not deal with *bhut* themselves. Instead they refer women to the folk-healers for attention. On the whole, Christians try to dissociate themselves from having dealings with the *bhut*, as this is against the church teachings. It appears Muslim *dai* are also not comfortable in dealing with *bhut*. For example, an elderly Muslim midwife who was both poor and widowed revealed that she used herbal medicines when there were problems with delivery, and also to treat female patients suffering from *sutika*, postnatal diarrhoea, skinny children, crying babies, etc. However, she said she did not administer anything to tackle the problem of *bhut*. Both Muslims and Christians, like Hindus, resort to the treatment from the *kabiraj* for illness believed to be caused by *bhut*.

What I found alarming was that most Rupganj *dai*, despite their lack of training, were prepared to persist with very complicated cases as long as the guardians agreed that they were not to be blamed for any 'accidents'.[17] For example, when I asked one *dai* what she does in a complicated case, she said that she tried to do it herself. 'I only referred one case to the medical hospital – the baby died anyway.' She added 'I have also de-livered breech babies, although these are difficult. If the mother has courage, we can deliver.' Another *dai* told me that she uses the root of a plant to correct the position of the baby inside the mother's womb. If the delivery looks like a really difficult one, the *dai* looks for a rare plant, the root of which has to be collected when she is absolutely naked.

The case of another poor *dai* shows the kind of risks some *dai* are prepared to take:

For Pishima, delivering babies was one of the many ways in which she was trying to supplement her family's income. Yet she was being paid very little or nothing. She learnt to deliver babies from watching the *dai* delivering her first child and now has been practising for nearly thirty years. Pishima said her very first delivery was a bastard child. Because the whole community turned against the mother of the bastard child, no *dai* dared to come near the woman, but Pishima came forward and delivered the baby who died after about six days.

When asking Pishima whether she had come across any difficult deliveries, she related a case in which the baby was already dead in the abdomen. She thought that she had delivered at least eighty-seven babies. Not everyone gave her a sari, most people gave her only a blouse piece and sometimes Tk20 (A$0.75) as a compensation for not buying her a sari, which would cost a minimum of Tk100 (A$4). Pishima also practises as a *kabiraj*, in which capacity she supplies *milon guta* (a kind of love potion). She said she is also an experienced abortionist: 'The poor who cannot afford the big doctors come to me, I can abort babies even at nine months[!].' She then told me the story of how at the request of a landlord she aborted a nine-month-old baby for a housemaid in Dhaka.

Pishima said that she learnt how to perform abortions in a dream. She said, 'My own monthly period had stopped for a while when I had a dream about how I could regularize my period. I administered this treatment upon myself and within half an hour it worked. Since then I started to practise abortion.' However, Pishima says she no longer performs abortions, as the church members (since the popularity of the Charismatic Movement among Christians in Bangladesh) warned her that it was a sin to kill.

Like Pishima, other *dai* I interviewed were also very poor. Attending births is one of the few ways these women earn their livelihood. Unfortunately, poverty also means lack of education, which has implications for the health of women they assist in delivering. My interview with Shandha Rani, another poor Hindu *dai* in her forties, revealed that lack of hygiene and knowledge is still a major problem. Shandha too said she learnt to deliver by herself and had not received any formal training. She cannot read or write and has been practising as a *dai* for about twelve years; she is also an expert in delivering calves. Shandha does nine or ten deliveries a year. Recently a nun (a trained midwife) from the nearby dispensary advised her to either boil or burn the blade before cutting the umbilical cord.

It is evident from the *dai*'s accounts that they do all they can to assist a birthing woman during labour. However, their involvement only starts when they are called at the onset of the labour pain and finishes after the baby is delivered. *Dai* are not called beforehand to check a pregnant woman. Nor do they give any postnatal care, although almost all *dai* also practise some folk-healing. One could perhaps argue that given the lack of training of the *dai*, they would be of little or no help during pregnancy or the postnatal period in any case. The low status of the *dai* may also partially explain why their presence is restricted to the actual time of birth. Nevertheless, it is the *dai*, who are familiar and cheap, to whom most families resort for childbirth delivery. Only in emergency cases will they have to make a decision whether or not to call a doctor. This decision in turn is not made in a vacuum, as families must consider their material circumstances as well as other cultural constraints such as *parda* and *izzat*. We have seen that the *dai* do not fare very well in this scenario. For the reasons explained above, they may warn a birthing woman's guardians of a complicated labour and advise them to call doctors or even to take her to a hospital. However, in the process, they risk losing what little payment they would otherwise receive. Families hit by sudden large medical expenses are likely to feel that the only saving that they can make is by not recognizing the role played by the *dai*.

The biomedical remedy

Maternal health in Bangladeshi villages has received less attention than might be supposed, given the extensive aid effort directed at Bangladesh since the early 1970s. This is undoubtedly connected to the tendency of international agencies to conceptualize Bangladesh's problems primarily in terms of overpopulation. While there was a massive investment in the promotion of contraception and family planning in Bangladesh, the issue of women's health was not taken so seriously.

This began to change after the WHO started to develop strategies throughout the Third World to address the high maternal and infant mortality rates still prevailing in large parts of South Asia, Africa and Latin America. A key element of the WHO's approach, which was developed in a series of meetings from 1973 onwards (Stephens 1992:811), was to work where possible through TBAs. The idea was to upgrade the expertise of TBAs by giving them basic biomedical training (e.g. elements of hygiene, how to recognize birth complications, etc.) and equipment. According to the report of a WHO meeting in 1978, the 'major aim of developing traditional birth attendants (TBAs) [is] to incorporate them as a resource in the overall strategy of orienting all health programmes to the needs of the people' (WHO 1978).

Following this WHO recommendation the ICDDR,B added MCH services to their existing family planning (FP) service in rural villages, initially in the Matlab area, and gradually in the rest of the country (Anon. 1988). Yet Germain, who spent several years with Ford Foundation in Bangladesh, cited in 1987 that priority continued to be given to 'reducing the birthrate as rapidly as possible' and 'relatively less attention and fewer resources' were given to MCH services in Bangladesh (1987:20).

I have already implied that the developing biomedical analysis of childbirth problems in Bangladesh tended to view the *dai* as a problem rather than as a solution. Given the material I have presented in the previous section on the *dai*, this is hardly surprising. According to the reports of researchers from ICDDR,B the *dai* in the Matlab area, like those in Rupganj, were usually elderly, illiterate, widowed or divorced, and occupied a low status in society (Bhatia *et al.* 1980; Croley *et al.* 1966; Fauveau and Chakraborty 1988; Rahman *et al.* 1978). ICDDR,B workers initially decided that they were better off bypassing the *dai* altogether. Thus Bhatia *et al.* noted that 'as there appeared to be no way to improve effectively the TBAs' methods and practices we sought a compromise solution as an experimental project leaving the *dai*s outside a formal training program and using the younger, better-educated Female Village Workers (FVWs) as intermediaries (1980:11)'. The FVWs were to impart their knowledge to the pregnant women and to 'educate' the *dai*, but they were not intended to replace the *dai*. By late 1980s FVWs had been redesignated CHWs (community health workers) and were supposed to visit rural households to provide family planning and MCH services. However, Fauveau and Chakraborty (1988), who interviewed eighty CHWs, found that half of the CHWs had never seen a birth. Of 3,300 births in Matlab in 1985 only 89 were attended by CHWs. Lack of experience and training and the young age of the CHWs seem to be why they were rarely asked to attend deliveries. Of the 89 births attended by CHWs, 36 involved severe problems. The cases included '9 prolonged labors, 10 abnormal presentations, 2 eclampsias, 8 twin births and 7 severe haemorrhages' (1988:6). Sixteen of these cases resulted in the death of the newborn, and one in the death of the mother.

Fauveau and Chakraborty's account suggests that the CHWs had little success in educating Matlab *dai* to conform more closely with biomedical norms, despite the large number of health projects concentrated in the area. Thus, after cutting the umbilical cord with a razor blade or bamboo sliver, the *dai* continue to dress the proximal extremity with a mixture of burnt earth and cow-dung, with consequent risk of infection. Fauveau and Chakraborty also note that the *dai* do not usually examine to see if the cervix is fully dilated before asking the women to push, and often practise internal massage of the cervix through the vagina (as in Tasmina's case above). Both practices, according to Fauveau and Chakraborty, may have a negative effect on dilation by causing cervical oedema, which contributes to 'obstructed labour'.

Leaving the *dai* out of the picture has therefore had limited success. Subsequently, a National Dai Training Programme was introduced, which 'aims to train one traditional birth attendant (TBA) from each of the villages' (S. Islam 1989:234). By early 1992, however, within the villages of Rupganj, where I did my fieldwork, I came across only one trained *dai* who said she was trained at the *thana* (subdistrict) health centre in 1991. She said her training lasted only four days and consisted simply of a few lectures by some medical personnel. She was still waiting for a delivery kit and did not seem to be any more confident than other untrained *dai* in the area. Thus this programme's success has also been extremely limited.[18]

WHO researchers have recently reported that 'risk of maternal death can be reduced if fully-trained and supervised midwives are posted in villages and supported by reliable referral facilities' (WHO 1992a:8). However, as WHO, UNICEF and UNFPA (United Nations Population Fund) also point out, 'trained TBAs cannot be expected to reduce overall mortality and morbidity rates when poverty, illiteracy, and discrimination – the underlying causes of these problems – are not addressed (WHO 1992b:7). In the Bangladeshi context D'Souza found that 'families with more than 3 acres of land have very few deaths from birth-associated conditions' (1985:38). Moreover, my own research also shows that in an emergency situation the poor do not have a choice. When a *dai* says the case is complex and she is unable to tackle it, the family is compelled to tell her to persist, the end result being often disastrous.

As we have seen from the accounts of the *dai*, the local partially trained allopathic doctor can do very little when the *dai* gives up. When a doctor is called, his services consist of either giving an injection and/or waiting beside the *dai* when she delivers. He does not touch or examine the woman, unless he gets the consent of the family to deliver the baby by force. Delivering a baby by use of surgical equipment before it is due, or before the mother is fully dilated, often leads to the death of the birthing mother and/or the baby. In emergencies, however, this is the only help families have access to, provided they have money. In any case, it seems those with money get little relief from the presence of these 'doctors'. Hospitals and clinics with suitable surgical facilities are a several-hours trip away from the village. Thus it is usually too late if a family does make the effort of taking its birthing woman to a hospital in an emergency situation. However, we have seen that the rural families do not necessarily receive immediate or good treatment upon arrival at a hospital. Thus, the way things are, more access to biomedicine is not necessarily going to improve women's health.

Analysis and discussion

By now, we can begin to see the elements of the problem as a whole. The biomedical approach is, within its own terms, probably correct in seeing hygiene, nutrition and lack of expertise on the part of the midwife as major issues. We can see, however, that they are not easy to address. The problem is not the *dai*'s illiteracy and lack of education as such, since these could be in principle remedied. It is rather that the whole pattern of how childbirth is managed in Bangladesh defines the *dai* as a low-status and menial participant in the process of birth, because of her role in dealing with birth pollution. In these circumstances, women with eight to ten years of schooling are unlikely to take on the role of *dai*, and the potential for substantial upgrading of the *dai* into trained TBAs is very limited.

I suggested that the Bangladeshi pattern of childbirth which I have discussed in the beginning of this chapter is a regional one, which can be found throughout Bangladesh and is probably typical of most of South Asia. It contrasts strongly with, for example, the patterns of childbirth management described by Laderman (1983) for peninsular Malaysia or by Kitzinger (1978) for Jamaica. In both cases, TBAs have high status in the community and are extensively involved in caring for the mother before and after the actual birth. In both of these cases, upgrading the expertise of the TBAs has proved a relatively successful strategy.

This South Asian pattern is closely connected with the general logic of South Asian caste society and the hierarchy of traditional occupations within it. This logic continues to shape values throughout the subcontinent despite its official non-existence in Islamic Bangladesh and Pakistan and its formal abolition in India. Such exceptions to the South Asian pattern as I have come across generally refer to populations marginal in various ways to caste society. Thus Ram (this volume: Chapter 4, and personal communication) reports both a higher status for midwives and no concern with birth pollution among the Mukkuvar. However, this is a low-caste Christian fishing community which tends to distance itself from dominant values in other respects also, and would seem to be an exceptional case. As Ram notes, birth in south India is generally polluting, and middle and upper castes use low-caste midwives to remove pollution in the same way as we have seen in Bangladesh and north India. Ram's analysis of the Mukkuvar might be compared to that of Gisele Krauskopff (1989), working among the 'tribal' Tharu of Dang in southern Nepal, again somewhat outside South Asian caste society proper. Here, again, midwives have relatively high status, at least within the Tharu community itself, and their work involves both antenatal and postnatal care (1989:159).

In the case of Haggis' 'Bible women' from Travancore (Haggis, this volume) conversion to Christianity allows lower-caste and poor women to move outside the caste system, adopt a novel occupation and so transform their status by moving up the ladder of class. By contrast, Bangladeshi *dai*, whether they are Hindu, Muslim or Christian, have a traditional occupation whose low status is defined by its polluting character (see the section on 'Pollution, *bhut*, confinement and nutrition' p. 148 above). Becoming a *dai* is not an avenue for upward mobility. If anything, it is a bar to it, trapping the women who take on this way of living at the bottom of the class structure and status hierarchy. Elsewhere I have referred to this situation as a 'low-status trap'.

This is evident in the way in which, because of her low status and poor background, the opinion of a *dai*, even if she is trained, is given no value. *Dai* are laughed at if they suggest new ideas and are ridiculed if they bring their delivery kit to a birth (Rozario 1995:100).

The South Asian regional pattern of childbirth management clearly requires further research. We also need to devise strategies to deal with maternal health which somehow recognize and cope with this pattern. An important issue here is the lack of payment to *dai* for their services, either by village families or the government, which I argued earlier helps to maintain the vicious circle of low status within which the *dai* are trapped. If *dai* received a respectable salary in local terms, I believe that the job would become much more attractive and its status would gradually improve. This in turn would attract younger, educated women into this profession, as has happened with nursing.

As long as the *dai* are the poorest women in the community, exploited for little or no payment through the ideology of *sowab* (spiritual merit), there is unlikely to be any change to their status even with the limited training they receive (Rozario 1995:110). In addition, their low status makes it impossible for them to use any new insights and knowledge they gain through their training, since the village women would have no confidence in their new knowledge.

At present, the most effective biomedical intervention in Rupganj comes not from the *dai*, trained or untrained, nor from the local biomedical and allopathic practitioners or the CHWs, but from the dispensaries run by Catholic nuns which I have already mentioned. There are a number of these dispensaries in the villages of Rupganj. Within the existing biomedical scenario this set-up seemed to be most effective. There is at least one fully trained midwife in each dispensary. She conducts regular check-ups for women during pregnancy and if called by families also attends deliveries, except at night-time. If the midwife perceives complications during her check-up, she advises the woman to consider going to a hospital for the delivery. She also advises women about the kinds of food they should eat and supplies iron and calcium tablets for a small fee. I observed the midwife nun's interaction with village women during the check-up sessions at one of these clinics and felt that she had very good rapport with the village women. The nuns are usually local and often know the pregnant women or their families. Unlike the allopathic doctors, they do not maintain physical distance from the women.

While the nuns serve everyone regardless of religious background, the dispensaries are adjacent to Catholic missions and there are only a few in the whole country. That there are several of these dispensaries is because this region has a relatively heavier concentration of Christians.[19] Even then, there is only one dispensary for about fifteen villages. Thus only a limited number of women benefit from this set-up, because it takes several hours walking for women from distant villages to get to the dispensary. In any case, the dispensaries do not have any trained doctors or surgical facilities and thus their help is also limited in emergency situations. Moreover, as mentioned earlier, not every family can afford even the small fee charged by the dispensaries.

The Catholic dispensaries are exceptional for a number of reasons. Most of the nuns working there are local in origin, and able to communicate easily with local women from all religious communities. In this they contrast with the CHWs who mostly tend to come from outside the village and, in any case, are viewed by villagers as young and inexperienced. At the same time, the somewhat anomalous status of the Christian nuns places them outside the concerns with purity and pollution underlying Bangladeshi rural society. Like Hindu *sadhu*s (mendicants), they have in a sense rejected ordinary life, and can deal with birth pollution without sharing in the low status of the *dai*. Through the church, they have some access to education, health training and medical equipment. In fact, the high status of the education provided by the Catholic school system is generally recognized and no doubt helps to raise the esteem in which the dispensaries are held.[20]

The relative success of the Catholic dispensaries suggests that the villagers are open to the use of biomedicine, provided that it can be delivered at the village level in a relevant and appropriate form. At this stage, however, the health authorities in Bangladesh have little scope to do anything of the kind. Given the choice between cheap and familiar *dai* and folk-healers and expensive, inaccessible and hostile biomedical facilities, most rural Bangladeshi birthing women and their families have little choice but to continue relying on the *dai* and folk-healers, with their access to biomedicine limited to calling in the poorly trained local 'doctors' in those emergencies which the *dai* admits she is unable to handle.

NOTES

1 This chapter derives from some preliminary research on the question of childbirth and women's health in several villages in Rupganj (Dhaka District), the area of rural Bangladesh where I did my previous fieldwork (Rozario 1992).

2 *Dai* is the most common term used for TBAs in Bangladesh and north India. *Dhoruni*, literal translation being 'the one who catches the baby', is an alternative term for *dai* used in some regions of Bangladesh. *Dhatri*, which is the more literary translation of the English term 'midwife', is never used by villagers, although Shamima Islam (1989) notes that the term is used to refer to 'better-off women who have education and perform this function only in very select houses'.

3 While my own material is limited in some respects, since I could only spend around five weeks in the field, it is consistent with previous studies elsewhere in Bangladesh, in particular the work of Therese Blanchet (1984), the writings of Shamima Islam (1981, 1989) and the series of studies carried out by the ICDDR,B (including Bhatia 1989; Bhatia *et al.* 1980; D'Souza 1985; Fauveau and Chakraborty 1988; Fauveau *et al.* 1991; Koenig *et al.* 1988). I should make it clear that I do not consider this previous research to be all of equal value. Only Blanchet's study is based on substantial anthropological fieldwork at village level (in Jamalpur District). The various studies undertaken by the ICDDR,B in Matlab (Comilla District) have an obvious bias towards the medical viewpoint and are often based on very limited data, such as material derived indirectly from Female Village Workers (FVWs) and Community Health Workers (CHWs). However, this body of research in Bangladesh, for all its deficiencies, provides a relatively consistent picture of the general nature of childbirth in rural Bangladesh.

4 Compare, for example, the Muslim villagers in Malaya described by Laderman (1983) or Kitzinger's (1978) study of Jamaican villagers in the Caribbean. In both cases, the status of midwives is considerably higher, and their care of birthing women is more thorough and extensive.

5 *Kabiraj* is the term most commonly used to refer to folk-healer. While their specialty is in herbal medicine, they also deal with evil spirits. Thus, villagers will consistently seek assistance from *kabiraj* for illnesses they believe are linked to *bhut*. Homoeopathic and allopathic doctors are thought to be of no use with illnesses caused by *bhut*.

6 Villagers also seek assistance from *fakir* for various illnesses, including those caused by *bhut*. *Fakir* in this context refers not to beggars (the usual meaning of the term in Bengali), but to Muslim ascetics, who are perceived to possess great spiritual power owing to their religious fervour. Like *kabiraj*, *fakir* also give out *tabij* and *pora pani* to deal with *bhut*, but they do very little in the way of herbal medicine.

7 Such as the Malay and Jamaican studies cited earlier.

8 In connection with the recent literature on 'auspiciousness' as a value distinct from purity and pollution (see Carman and Marglin 1985; Madan 1991; Marglin 1985; Parry 1991; Samanta 1992), there are several Bengali terms that may be translated as 'auspicious' and which apply in some contexts to married women (*shubha, kalyan, mangala, lokkhi* (Lakshmi), etc.). The birth of children might certainly be regarded as 'auspicious' in several of these senses. However, I do not see any evidence for 'auspiciousness' in the context of birth as a positive value countering the negative attitudes to birth pollution.

9 Hussain (1992), working in another village close to the Dhaka metropolitan centre, speaks of women visiting the shrines *(mazar)* of dead Muslim saints and also consulting living Muslim holy men *(pir)*.

10 Katrina Anderson, an Australian medical doctor who recently spent several months working with birthing mothers in a Catholic dispensary in rural Bangladesh, suggests that this is because of the dramatic effectiveness of intravenous fluid treatment in cases of diarrhoea and dehydration: 'People are used to seeing a patient going from death's door due to dehydration to almost perfectly well within a few hours when IV fluids are given. Hence they expect the same miraculous cure for childbirth' (Anderson pers. comm.).

11 Sufian (1984) also points out that at the time acceptance rate of family planning services was very low despite intensive effort put into the National Family Planning Programme.

12 A WHO Newsletter reports that in the Matlab area of Bangladesh 'contraceptive prevalence rose from 8% in 1975, . . . to almost 40% in mid 1984' (WHO 1991:8).

13 However, there are still many problems associated with the use of contraceptives. In rural areas most family planning programmes involve handing out pills (not on a regular basis), sometimes giving information to clients that they could opt for the IUD, bimonthly injections or other methods. However, these latter methods require women to travel miles on foot, and sometimes to pay a set fee, which discourages them. Even if women were interested in trying different methods, there is hardly any possibility for follow-up medical servi-

ces in case of side-effects or problems. Thus it is not difficult to understand why rural women were often dubious about the use of contraceptives. This also perhaps explains why most women in Rupganj preferred the ligation operation. For detailed information on the popularity of sterilization in Bangladesh as a whole refer to Pillsbury (1990).

14 Women told me that these days *moulvis* (Muslim religious leaders) say on radio that every form of contraception except for the operation of ligation is acceptable in Islam, e.g. pills, injections, copper T (IUD). This, of course, coincides with the fact that in Bangladesh, family planning is now being promoted as a tenet of Islam.

15 Elsewhere (Rozario 1995:101) I discussed the mistreatment of and lack of treatment for patients by government hospital staff, including the MB (Bachelor of Medicine) doctor, in charge of a maternity ward in a small-town hospital in southern Bangladesh. For instance in my diary for one day I wrote that it took the MB doctor

> about 10 to 12 minutes, no more, to go around 26 patients. His rounds consisted of merely making a hand gesture to the attending nurse with a few words like 'discharge this one', or 'let her be for another day', or taking an old bandage off Caesarian patients and putting on a new one, throwing the old one on the floor. There was hardly any interaction with the patients. Sometimes patients would call to him as he turned away, but he simply continued to the next patient. A few patients I spoke to before the doctor arrived had many questions they wanted to ask the doctor, but they could not. The women were overwhelmed, clearly feeling out of place.

The nursing staff were not much better. The whole ward was littered with old bandages or other throw-away items, the toilets were very unclean, and often did not have any water. The doctors' and nurses' knowledge of hygiene and cleanliness was nowhere reflected. Indeed I was told that if a patient's guardians pay a large sum of money to the doctor and the nurses, they usually keep an eye on the patient. Otherwise there is no guarantee that the patient is going to be attended to when needed. The doctor usually did not handle the normal delivery, which was done by the ward nursing midwife. The doctor mainly looked after the surgical patients, whose family in turn would have to pay enormous amounts of money for this service to the doctor, in addition to all the other bribes they needed to pay to numerous other people (nurses, *ayas*, guards, etc.). It is important to note that none of these monies are levied by the hospital officially, as it is supposed to be free.

16 Gaynoda uses various other techniques in dealing with difficult labour. She said to bring on labour pain, a root of a special tree is tied to the left thigh and taken off as soon as the mother delivers, 'otherwise the whole of the mother's inside will come out with the baby', since the root is thought to be so potent. Alternatively, the woman in labour is sometimes given basil leaves to sniff or the root of a young tamarind tree is placed in her mouth in order to bring on her labour pains.

17 Blanchet (1991) notes that in Nasirnagar (Brahmanbaria District) the guardians of birthing women often ask the *dai* to persist in difficult labour in order to avoid the huge bills from doctors or to avoid the dishonour of having to send a birthing woman to a hospital.

18 Stephens (1992), working in urban Andhra Pradesh, also argues that training the *dai* has had very limited success.
19 While less than half a per cent of Bangladeshi population is Christian, Rupganj has approximately 20 per cent Christians.
20 The nuns also have or had a role in training *dai*. Several *dai* said that they had been trained by the local Catholic dispensary nuns many years ago.

REFERENCES

Anon. 1988 The relationship between MCH service development and contraceptive use: evidence from Matlab, Bangladesh. MCH-FP Extension Project Briefing Paper No. 9. Dhaka: International Centre for Diarrhoeal Disease Research, Bangladesh.
Aziz, K.M.A. and Maloney, C. 1985 *Life Stages, Gender and Fertility in Bangladesh*. Monograph No. 3. Dhaka: International Centre for Diarrhoeal Disease Research, Bangladesh.
Berreman, G.D. 1971 The Brahmannical view of caste. *Contributions to Indian Sociology* (n.s.) 5:16–23.
Bhatia, S. 1989 Patterns and causes of neonatal and postneonatal mortality in rural Bangladesh. *Studies in Family Planning* 20(3):136–46.
Bhatia, S., Chakraborty, J. and Faruque, A.S.G. 1980 *Indigenous Birth Practices in Rural Bangladesh and their Implications for a Maternal and Child Health Programme*. Dhaka: International Centre for Diarrhoeal Disease Research, Bangladesh.
Blanchet, T. 1984 *Women, Pollution and Marginality: Meanings and Rituals of Birth in Rural Bangladesh*. Dhaka: University Press.
——— 1991 *Maternal Health in Rural Bangladesh: An Anthropological Study on Maternal Nutrition and Birth Practices in Nasirnagar, Bangladesh*. Dhaka: Save the Children (USA).
Boddy, J. 1989 *Wombs and Alien Spirits*. Madison: University of Wisconsin Press.
Carman, J.B. and Marglin, F.A. (eds.) 1985 *Purity and Auspiciousness in Indian Society. Journal of Developing Societies* Special Issue 1(1).
Constantinides, P. 1978 Women's spirit possession and urban adaptation in the Muslim northern Sudan. In P. Caplan and J.M. Bujra (eds.) *Women United, Women Divided: Cross-Cultural Perspectives on Female Solidarity*. London: Tavistock Publications, 185–205.
Croley, H.T., Haider, S.Z., Begum, S. and Gustafson, M.C. 1966 Characteristics and utilization of midwives in a selected rural area of East Pakistan. *Demography* 3(2):578–80.
D'Souza, S. 1985 *Mortality Case Study, Matlab, Bangladesh*. Dhaka: International Centre for Diarrhoeal Disease Research, Bangladesh.
Dumont, L. 1972 *Homo Hierarchicus: The Caste System and its Implications*. London: Paladin.
Dwyer, D.H. 1978 Women, Sufism, and decision-making in Moroccan Islam. In L. Beck and N. Keddie (eds.) *Women in the Muslim World*. Cambridge, MA: Harvard University Press, 585–98.
Fauveau, V. and Chakraborty, J. 1988 Maternity care in Matlab: present status and possible interventions (Matlab MCH-FP Project). Special Publication

No. 26. Dhaka: International Centre for Diarrhoeal Disease Research, Bangladesh.

Fauveau, V., Stewart, K., Khan, S.A. and Chakraborty, J. 1991 Effect on mortality of community-based maternity-care programme in rural Bangladesh. *The Lancet* 338(8776):1183–6.

Gardner, K. 1991 *Songs at the River's Edge: Stories from a Bangladeshi Village*. Calcutta: Rupa and Co.

Germain, A. 1987 Reproductive health and dignity: choices by Third World women. Technical paper prepared for International Conference on Better Health for Women and Children through Family Planning, Nairobi, Kenya, 5–9 October 1987. New York: The Population Council.

Heesterman, J.C. 1971 Priesthood and the Brahman. *Contributions to Indian Sociology* 5:43–7.

Hussain, N. 1992 Women in a Bangladesh village: sources of female autonomy. PhD thesis, Macquarie University, Sydney.

Islam, M. 1980 *Folk Medicine and Rural Women in Bangladesh*. Dhaka: Women for Women Research Group.

Islam, S. 1981 *Indigenous Abortion Practitioners in Rural Bangladesh*. Dhaka: Women for Women Research Group.

Islam, S. 1989 The socio-cultural context of childbirth in rural Bangladesh. In M. Krishnaraj and K. Chanana (eds.) *Gender and the Household Domain: Social and Cultural Dimensions*. New Delhi: Sage Publications, 233–54.

Jeffery, P., Jeffery, R. and Lyon, A. 1989 *Labour Pains and Labour Power: Women and Childbearing in India*. London and New Jersey: Zed Books.

Kantowsky, D. 1971 The problem of sponsored change. *Contributions to Indian Sociology* 5:47–50.

Kitzinger, S. 1978 *Women as Mothers*. London: Fontana/Collins.

Koenig, M.A., Fauveau, V., Chowdhury, A.I., Chakraborty, J. and Khan, M.A. 1988 Maternal mortality in Matlab, Bangladesh: 1976–85. *Studies in Family Planning* 19(2):69–80.

Krauskopff, G. 1989 *Maîtres et possédés: les rites et l'ordre social chez les Tharu (Népal)*. Paris: CNRS.

Laderman, C. 1983 *Wives and Midwives: Childbirth and Nutrition in Rural Malaysia*. Berkeley: University of California Press.

Madan, T.N. 1971 Introduction. On the nature of caste in India: a review symposium on Louis Dumont's *Homo Hierarchicus*. *Contributions to Indian Sociology* (n.s.) 5:1–13.

1991 Auspiciousness and purity: some reconsiderations. *Contributions to Indian Sociology* (n.s.) 25(2):287–94.

Mahtab, N. 1989 The household–state interface: health education and nutrition of rural women in Bangladesh. In M. Krishnaraj and K. Chanana (eds.) *Gender and the Household Domain: Social and Cultural Dimensions*. New Delhi: Sage Publications, 209–32.

Maloney, C., Aziz, K.M.A. and Sarker, P.C. 1981 *Beliefs and Fertility in Bangladesh*. Monograph No. 2. Dhaka: International Centre for Diarrhoeal Disease Research, Bangladesh.

Marglin, F.A. 1977 Power, purity and pollution: aspects of the caste system reconsidered. *Contributions to Indian Sociology* (n.s.) 2(2):245–70.

1985 *Wives of the God-King: The Rituals of the Devadasis of Puri*. Delhi: Oxford University Press.

Martin, E. 1987 *The Woman in the Body: A Cultural Analysis of Reproduction*. Boston: Beacon Press.

Oakley, A. 1986 *The Captured Womb: A History of the Medical Care of Pregnant Women* (paperback). Oxford and New York: Basil Blackwell.

Parry, J. 1991 The Hindu lexicographer? A note on auspiciousness and purity. *Contributions to Indian Sociology* (n.s.) 25(2): 267–86.

Pillsbury, B. 1990 The politics of family planning: sterilization and human rights in Bangladesh. In W.P. Handwerker (ed.) *Births and Power: Social Change and the Politics of Reproduction*. Boulder, San Francisco and London: Westview Press, 165–96.

Rahman, M., Osteria, T., Chakraborty, J., Huber, D.H. and Mosley, W.H. 1978 A study of the field worker performance in the Matlab contraceptive distribution project. CRL Working Paper No. 5. Dhaka: Cholera Research Laboratory.

Reichle, V. 1985 Holism versus individualism: Dumont's concepts of hierarchy and egalitarianism as structural principles. *Contributions to Indian Sociology* (n.s.) 19(2):331–40.

Rozario, S. 1992 *Purity and Communal Boundaries: Women and Social Change in a Bangladeshi Village*. Sydney: Allen and Unwin.

1995 *Dai* and midwives: the renegotiation of the status of birth attendants in contemporary Bangladesh. In J. Hatcher and C. Vlassoff (eds.) *The Female Client and the Health-Care Provider*. Ottawa: International Development Research Centre, 91–112.

Samanta, S. 1992 *Maṅgalmayīmā, sumarigalī, maṅgal*: Bengali perceptions of the divine feminine, motherhood and 'auspiciousness'. *Contributions to Indian Sociology* (n.s.) 26(1):51–75.

Scheepers, L.M. 1991 Jidda: the traditional midwife of Yemen? *Social Science and Medicine* 33(8):959–62.

Stephens, C. 1992 Training urban traditional birth attendants: balancing international policy and local reality. *Social Science and Medicine* 35(6):811–17.

Sufian, A.J.M. 1984 The effects of infant and child mortality on fertility in Bangladesh. PhD thesis, Michigan State University.

van der Veer, P. 1985 Brahmans: their purity and their poverty on the changing values of Brahman priests in Ayodhya. *Contributions to Indian Sociology* (n.s.) 19(2):303–21.

WHO (World Health Organization) 1978 The promotion and development of traditional medicine: report of a WHO meeting. Technical Report Series No. 622. Geneva: WHO.

1991 *Safe Motherhood: Newsletter of Worldwide Activity in Maternal Health* 7 (November 1991–February 1992). Geneva: WHO.

1992a *Safe Motherhood: Newsletter of Worldwide Activity in Maternal Health* 8 (March 1992–July 1992). Geneva: WHO.

1992b *Safe Motherhood: Newsletter of Worldwide Activity in Maternal Health* 10 (November 1992–February 1993). Geneva: WHO.

6 Other mothers: maternal 'insouciance' and the depopulation debate in Fiji and Vanuatu, 1890–1930

Margaret Jolly

There is no State womb, there are no State breasts, there is no real substitute for the beauty of individual motherhood.   (Saleeby 1909:32)

See that heathen mother stand
Where the sacred current flows
With her own maternal hands
Mid the wave her babe she throws
Send, Oh send, the bible there,
Lets its precept reach the heart;
She may then her children spare –
Act the tender mothers's heart. (cited in Forbes 1986:WS-2)

It is impossible to convince a tough old hag that her method of child-rearing is wrong. She considers herself a living witness to its excellence.
(Durrad in Rivers 1922:15).

Introduction

Maternity has often been proclaimed as a source of sameness and identification between women – we are all born of mothers, and although some of us cannot or do not become mothers, our being in a woman's body is often identified with its procreative potential. The identification of woman with the maternal has been implicated in many Western theories which purport to explain woman's essential condition – either our alleged universal subordination (Chodorow 1978; de Beauvoir 1972 (1949); Ortner 1974; Rosaldo and Lamphere 1974) or to explain and celebrate our difference from men (Gilligan 1982; Irigaray 1985; Kristeva 1980; Trebilcot 1983).

Although maternity will, I imagine, continue to be a powerful factor in and a potent metaphor of women's identity and unity, what I consider here is rather how maternity has *divided* women – how class, race and nation have constituted us as 'other mothers'. In the connections created by colonial processes and subsequent patterns of global development

177

some mothers have been cast as heartless or hopeless, while others have been glorified. In early twentieth-century Britain, working-class mothers were in a series of government and medical reports singled out as a major cause of British population problems, racial degeneration and imperial decline. In this same period, in several British colonies in the Pacific, mothers were similarly singled out as a major cause of depopulation, portrayed as the dead heart of the dying race. But, although similar forms of surveillance and intervention were devised to police maternal 'incompetence' or 'insouciance' and to instruct women to be better mothers, ambivalence about promoting the fertility of colonized peoples, and the weakness of some colonial states, meant such projects were uncertain in their forms and uneven in their effects.[1] But in both projects of maternalism,[2] some women, because of their class or racial background, were privileged not just as idealized models of maternity but as active instructors or educators of 'other mothers'.

It is important not to overestimate the effects of such interventions, nor to see working-class or colonized women as being passive recipients of such advice. Very often such instructions were ignored or forcefully spurned. There is always a gap between an idealized image of maternity and the bloody lived experience of giving birth and mothering a child (cf. Kristeva 1980). And this gap is probably greatest in those class and colonial contexts where idealizations of The Mother have been promoted by legislative and moral interventions in the lives of actual mothers. But, although such discourses did not establish hegemony, they did impinge on the maternal experience of working-class and colonized women by creating an intimate contest about how to mother and by constituting customary maternal practices as recalcitrant tradition.

Motherhood in imperial Britain and beyond

In an influential paper Davin (1978) has argued that in early twentieth-century Britain there was a novel reconstruction of motherhood in terms of the perpetuation of the Anglo-Saxon race and the expansion of the British Empire. In nineteenth-century Britain there had been a resurgent celebration of the value of motherhood as part of the idealization of domesticity in the evangelical Christianity of the emergent middle classes (e.g. Davidoff and Hall 1987). But this was not then wedded to a national concern about declining fertility. Rather, the prevalent approaches tended towards a Malthusian view of population – that overpopulation was a threat to finite resources and that natural catastrophes such as wars and famines were necessary evils to keep populations in check. Thus, there were strong arguments against interventions to increase population, as 'unnatural' or courting disaster. Although there were many projects to 'improve' working-class mothers, these were focused more on the arduousness and morality of women's industrial work, on the associated risks of licentiousness and alcoholism and the way in which both their work and leisure regimes compromised Christian ideals of the home. But from the early twentieth century increasingly such projects of maternalist improvement were linked to the threats of population decline, racial degeneration and imperial collapse.

From 1900 onwards there was a succession of governmental enquiries, medical reports and voluntary efforts dedicated to understanding and redressing the causes of the declining birth rate and the persisting high levels of infant mortality. This was consistently seen not just as a matter of personal tragedy for the mothers concerned, but a matter of national and imperial emergency. The new language employed was that of population as a national asset, as human capital and as imperial armoury. To quote the eminently quotable Saleeby, author of *Parenthood and Race Culture* and *Woman and Womanhood*: 'The history of nations is determined not on the battle fields but in the nursery, and the battalions which give lasting victory are the battalions of babies' (cited in Davin 1978:29). The battalions of baby boys at least were conceived as fighting on future battlefields for Britain. The Boer War had prompted concern about the flat-chested, flat-footed, rheumatic and rotten teethed amongst Britain's prospective soldiers – one third of potential recruits were rejected (Davin 1978:11, 15). Morbidity was often cast as a lack of virility – the expansion of the British race as a form of phallic extension, its retreat a matter of emasculation.[3] The threat was not just the Boers in South Africa, but the rival imperial extensions of France, of Germany, of the United States and of Japan where some suggested there was no danger of 'race suicide', because mothers were not 'shirking from maternity' (Davin 1978:17).[4]

National and imperial concerns about British population had effects on women of all classes. Middle-class women were prevailed upon not to 'shirk' their maternal duty to race and class, and to refrain from using birth control. There were a range of state policies and voluntary associations and projects directed to them, from proposals about the endowment of motherhood through to doctors' refusals to give contraception to middle- and upper-class women. Although many eugenicists had reservations about preventive medicine and state intervention as interfering with natural selection and thus leading to degeneracy, they propagandized, particularly amongst the middle and upper classes, to encourage breeding on the part of those in 'eugenic marriages' – those of superior stock.[5] The 'fathers' of British eugenics, Pearson and Galton concurred with Herbert Spencer's earlier verdict that 'the penalty to be paid for race predominance was the subjection of woman' (cited in Davin 1978:20). The 'new woman' of the middle classes was admitted to be a more interesting companion for man, but maligned as engaged in the frivolity of 'frills, dances and flirtations' rather than the serious business of being 'mother of the race'. And for those numerous middle-class women who could not find husbands in this period, it was advocated that they go to the colonies to marry and breed, or else be surrogate virgin mothers at home or abroad, involved in the important business of nursing or teaching (Davin 1978; Forbes 1986:WS7).

Whereas women of 'superior stock' were encouraged to breed or in other ways contribute to mothering the nation, the maternity of working-class women was perceived as a problem. Some eugenicists espoused the curbing of their fertility – arguing that the growth of an urban proletariat threatened the British Empire as much as it had the ancient imperium of Rome. But many concerned with declining birth rates promoted the fertility of *all* classes, given the need not only for populating the globe with gentlemen administrators and officers, but with white settlers. The decline in fertility rates and the persisting high rates of infant mortality amongst the working classes were for them of urgent concern. Infant mortality in England and Wales in 1899 was 163/1,000, a disturbing increase over the rates of the 1880s. This meant a loss of about 120,000 lives per annum. The rate was highest in those regions which were most densely populated and poorest (Davin 1978:10).

Numerous reports addressed this national problem. Several levels of the state were involved in attempts to document, explain and improve this appalling anomaly in an otherwise improving health profile. Moreover a range of voluntary societies was formed to deal with the problems of public health and domestic hygiene.[6] Though voluntary, these organizations were very influential and often overlapped with state authorities, both in personnel and concerns. In the litany of reports and conferences, a number of factors were adduced: sheer poverty and its effects in poor nutrition, inadequate and overcrowded housing, poor heating and ventilation, maternal fatigue through overwork, exposure to the elements and infectious diseases. In many reports and conferences the broader public health questions and the environmental indices of poverty were implicated, but, as Davin shows, these were ultimately discounted or de-emphasized in favour of the view that decreased fertility and persistent infant mortality was the result of 'bad mothering' (1978:27). It was presumably much harder and less politically feasible to get landlords to improve their slum dwellings and local authorities to replace middens and ash privies with water-borne sewage than to blame working-class mothers for the problem. Several aspects of working-class maternity were attacked: insanitary procedures at birthing itself, careless infant feeding practices, sharing adult food with children, exposure of children to the elements and infection, leaving children with minders, and simply careless or undisciplined mothering.

Schemes of surveillance, intervention and education were devised to improve these alleged maternal malpractices: health visitors, child welfare laws, municipal milk depots, competitions for bonny babies. Voluntary societies promoting public health and domestic hygiene intensified their efforts with working-class women and schools such as St Pancras School for Mothers in London were opened. These projects for maternal improvement varied from the censorious intrusions of health visitors through to the more tolerant and humane education of schools like St Pancras. But there was a constant insofar as all forms of surveillance and instruction typically relied on 'the lady', the upper- or middle-class woman, assuming responsibility for helping working-class mothers improve.[7] This created not only a class-based hierarchy of mothering, which was endorsed by the state, but also resentment and resistance on the part of working-class mothers. Witness Somerset Maugham's depiction of the district visitor in his novel *Of Human Bondage*, an interior view probably derived from his days as a medical student in the poor households of Lambeth:

The district visitor excited their bitter hatred. She came in without so much as a 'by your leave' or 'with your leave' . . . she poked her nose into corners, and if she didn't say the place was dirty you could see what she thought right enough, 'an' it's all very well for them 'as servants, but I'd like to see what she'd make of 'er room if she 'ad four children, and 'ad to see to the cooking, and mend their clothes, and wash 'em'. (Cited in Davin 1978:37)

Although Davin situates this class-based maternalism in the context of imperial expansion, she does not consider how similar projects of maternalism were at this time undertaken in the colonies themselves. Such class-based maternalism within Britain was transformed into a racially-based maternalism in a number of British colonies. Lenore Manderson has already considered the evidence from colonial Malaya from the early twentieth century (1982, 1987, 1989 and this volume). She suggests that from around 1900 there was a new concern with biological reproduction as the necessary precondition for a growing and healthy labour force (1989:86). High rates of infant mortality, much higher than in Britain,[8] were a cause for concern on the part of colonial administrators and from around 1905 a series of official reports and enquiries ensued (1989:89). As in Britain a range of environmental factors were highlighted – lack of sanitation facilities, potable water, ventilation, light and overcrowded houses – as well as factors more directly related to mothering – maternal and child nutrition and child-rearing practices. Although some administrators stressed the environmental causes, those local officials with some responsibility for them were more inclined to favour explanations in terms of 'the native ignorance' of local mothers (Manderson 1989:89; cf. Hull 1989).[9]

Depopulation in the Pacific: blaming bad mothers again?

Here I consider a parallel process in two of Britain's Pacific colonies – Fiji and Vanuatu (previously New Hebrides/Nouvelles Hébrides) – which Britain conjointly administered with France from 1906 (see Maps 3 and 4). Throughout the Pacific there was a simultaneous concern with population, but although it echoed that within the metropolis, it had rather different reverberations. Moreover, despite some parallels with colonial Malaya, my research so far suggests that the desire to reduce indigenous infant mortality and restore population growth was a more ambiguous and contested policy. Many white traders and settlers were dubious about it, rather seeing the solution to their labour problems in importing 'Asiatic labour'.[10] Moreover, whereas the Fijian race and culture was perceived by the British colonial state to be worth preservation, in Vanuatu there was a far less sympathetic attitude to indigenous peoples and the Condominium government was both divided and weak (Jolly 1992). State-sponsored surveillance and education of indigenous mothers was thus attempted far more vigorously in Fiji than in Vanuatu where such concerns remained those of the missions until very late in the colonial period (cf. Denoon 1989).

Moreover, widespread concern about high infant mortality and the character of indigenous mothering was here not so closely linked to ensuring a healthy and growing labour force, but more a part of a broader shift to a governmentality concerned with 'population', with census-taking, health and sanitary interventions, coupled with rhetorical justifications of colonial state rule as 'improvement'. In the Pacific at least a renewed concern about bad mothering emerges as part of the late nineteenth- and early twentieth-century discourse about depopulation or, as it was then expressed, the 'decrease of the native population' (*The Report of the Commission Appointed to Inquire into the Decrease of the Native Population* 1893–1896 (hereafter Decrease Report); Pitt-Rivers 1927; Rivers 1922; Roberts 1927; Speiser 1990(1923)). I have written elsewhere in some detail about how this emerged as a topic of concern for administrators, missionaries, medical officers, ethnologists, and how it was conceived and explained (Jolly n.d.a). Both indigenous and exogenous factors were taken into account for the phenomenon of the 'dying race' – and their relative weighting much debated. Some laid stress on indigenous causes – on pre-existing diseases, on practices of abortion, infanticide or widow strangulation, on protracted periods of sexual abstinence, on the propensity for feuding and cannibalism. Thus, the Reverend Gunn (a missionary resident on Futuna, Vanuatu) pronounced that 'decrease of the population had its birth in the heathenism of the people' (Gunn 1914:262). Others insisted that heathen practices had not had a cata- strophic effect until the impact of whites – that they had brought new diseases which had spread as epidemics, that labour recruiting had gener- ated new forms of sexual abstinence, as well as taken a toll in male lives, that guns had increased the mortal effects of warfare, and that new clothes, new foods and especially new alcoholic beverages had proved hazardous to local health. But often those who stressed the salience of exogenous factors were less concerned with the external influences in themselves – for example the devastation of new diseases, like measles, whooping cough and influenzas – and more how Pacific peoples respon- ded. Thus Beatrice Grimshaw asked apropos the depopulation of Tahiti and the entire Pacific:

Why? Old island residents will tell you that, even if every disease brought by the white man were rooted out to-morrow, the native would still diminish in numb- ers. He has done so in islands where the effects of European diseases were comparatively slight. He does so in New Zealand, where the Maori (the supposed ancestor of most of the island peoples) is petted, cherished, and doctored to an amazing extent by the ruling race, and yet persists in dying out, although he is not effected by consumption or other evils to any serious extent. There are un- doubtedly other causes, and perhaps among them not the least is the fact that, for most Pacific races, life, with the coming of civilisation, has greatly lost its savour. (1907:25)

The academic texts of Rivers (1922), Speiser (1990 (1923)), Pitt-Rivers (1927) and Roberts (1927) transformed such popular ruminations into anthropological and psychological theories. Although most of these writers stress the centrality of introduced rather than pre-existing causes, they also tend ultimately to find the deeper explanation within the bodies and more especially the minds of Pacific peoples. All these authors in various ways privilege the despair and demoralization wrought by colo- nialism seeing this as the underlying or deeper cause. Rivers (1922) constitutes colonization as akin to the trench warfare of World War I[11] in Europe – as inducing a psychological malaise in its victims, which results in a lack of interest in living and especially a profound pessimism about the future.[12] This malaise clusters around two gendered symptoms – that of emasculation and that of maternal 'insouciance' (or 'carelessness', a

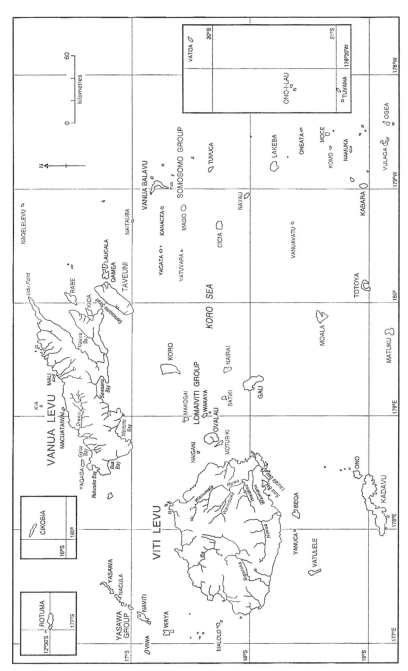

Map 3 Fiji

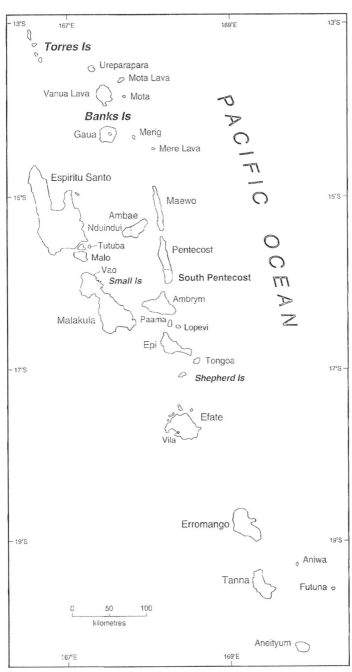

Map 4 Vanuatu

term beloved by these colonizing men). The propensity to die out is typically associated with a loss of virility in men, expressed both as a fact about their bodies and their activities. The problem was patent in the male psychological response to pacification and colonization – the masculine arts of warfare and cannibalism had disappeared, but had not been replaced by equally invigorating activities. The British Governor of Fiji from 1904, Im Thurn (1922), and the anthropologist Rivers both pondered the effects of the suppression of headhunting in the Western Solomons. The second observed that this had been 'not only an interesting sport but his one means of proving his manhood and gaining his wife . . . It was indeed a changed world in which the islander found himself and one in which he had little desire to stay' (Rivers 1922:xvi).

In Rivers' formulation, the decrease in population on Vella Lavella and Eddystone Island (Simbo) in the Western Solomons was, paradoxically, linked to the abolition of headhunting, which had been not just the focus of masculine virility but also central to the activity of building houses and canoes and propitiating ancestors (see Dureau, this volume). He speculated whether this loss of interest could be redressed by substituting porcine for human sacrifice: 'the head of a pig for that of a human being' (1922:108).

The Sydney University historian Stephen Roberts reconciled indigenous with exogenous influences by suggesting that degeneration had set in centuries before European arrival; he found evidence for 'the stultification of the last six hundred years' (Roberts 1927:16).[13] He contrasted the heroic age of voyaging and migration with the enervated races which Pacific people had become. He posited both a climatic and a genetic cause for this degeneration,[14] 'the race denied the health-giving process of selection and of struggle was giving way' (Roberts 1927:60). He suggested that because 'natives luxuriated in enervating tropical islands, where life was too easy and nature too bountiful' (1927:60) and because there had been no recent migrations to invigorate the stock, the 'race' had become lazy and degenerate. Such loss of virility and general lassitude he adduced to explain the horrific devastations of epidemics. Thus, as in Grimshaw's popular accounts, it was not so much the new scourges themselves – tuberculosis, influenza, leprosy, smallpox – but the indigenous response to them which proved fatal (Roberts 1927:74ff).

It has been seen that the evil of depopulation is due primarily to psychological causes, and so any remedy to be effective, must cope with the peculiar gap in native life – the gap between old and new which gives rise to morbidity in the native mind. Medical and sanitary remedies and everything which touches the native's body alone, merely skim the surface. It is not only a question of bodily health. If the work affects the body alone, without inducing a corresponding healthy activity in the mind . . . then it cannot suffice. (Roberts 1927:129).

Whereas Im Thurn and Rivers had espoused inventing new rites of masculinity to compensate for those lost, Roberts (1927) espoused indirect rule. He maintained that a form of 'native government' was needed to engage men to 'invoke mental activity and healthy rivalry, and pride of existence' (1927:129). He observed that in those places where governments had established firm foundations and undertaken educational and economic programmes native psychology had improved and the population had started to increase again.

But alongside this malaise of emasculated male inactivity these men imputed the parallel malaise of maternal indifference and despondency. Women were alleged to be resisting being mothers – this was perceived as their pathological response to colonization. Women's loss of desire for life was to these men palpable in maternal rejection – abortion, infanticide, neglect. The relation between these twin symptoms of emasculation and maternal rejection is evoked in this statement from the German ethnologist Felix Speiser based on research in Vanuatu in 1911–12 (1990(1923):50). He quotes a woman from Port Olry in Santo: 'Why should we go on having children? Since the white man came they all die.'[15] Speiser interprets this not as a statement about the spread of epidemic diseases (which it most probably was), but rather as a statement about the spread of despair and demoralization. His gloss of her statement is: 'the race is being repressed by the whites and is dying out visibly' (1990(1923):50).

Anthropologists such as Speiser and Rivers and historians such as Roberts debated with missionaries and colonial officials about how and why Pacific women were bad mothers. Pitt-Rivers (1927) alone maintained that high infant mortality and bad mothering was not implicated in depopulation. For the most part these gentlemen agreed that it was, and rather differed as to whether these were innate characteristics of Pacific mothers or responses to the colonial context. Bad mothering was patent to them in the desire for abortion or infanticide, insanitary procedures at birthing, inappropriate infant feeding, failure to protect the child from the weather or infectious diseases, and in general a lack of interest in disciplined nurture. This is a similar catalogue of abuses imputed to working-class mothers in England, but the arguments about causes were significantly recast in the colonial context. Moreover, schemes for surveillance and intervention entailed even more profound tensions than in Britain between a eugenicist celebration of the decline of an 'inferior stock', the demands of labour and the state's desire to demonstrate its power over population.

The bad mothers of the Pacific: from missionary lament to state surveillance

It is not hard to find disparaging assessments of Pacific mothers on the part of European men. One of the most notorious is that of Charles Abel, of the Kwato mission, who proclaimed, 'I know of no animal, except perhaps the duck, which is more careless in attending to its young than the average Papuan mother' (1934:50–1). These kinds of disparaging laments had been part of missionary discourses for decades – justifying as they did missionary interventions in general and in particular attempts at remoulding mothering (see Grimshaw 1989; Jolly 1991; Langmore 1989; Young 1989). But what I want to ponder here is how these denigrations assumed a novel significance with the new science of population and eugenics, and a potential new force with the threat of increased surveillance and intervention by the colonial state.

As earlier intimated, Rivers, Speiser and Roberts oscillate between seeing indigenous women as innately indifferent to maternity and as having become so because of the demoralizing effects of colonization. Contraception, abortion and infanticide, they all agreed, were practised precolonially. Apropos contraception, Speiser thought that the mechanical means of contraception used could not have been too effective and the long periods of sexual abstinence and of breast-feeding more consequential, and most likely explained the 'sterility' of women reported by early travellers (1990(1923):40). Contraception and sexual abstinence, he considered, had persisted but not increased since contact.

On the other hand, he believed that although the induction of abortion was 'always known', and thus 'the vice was not a novelty imported by the whites', it had become more common (Speiser 1990(1923):40). He attributed the following motives to the aborting woman: 'desire for an easy life, her disinclination to be burdened with many children, and also her wish to disappoint a brutal husband' (Speiser 1990(1923):40). He reported that men did not approve of the practice and alluded to a case in north Pentecost where a husband almost beat his wife to death for practising abortion. Still he considered that the desire for children on the part of both men and women had declined and abortion increased: 'demoralization caused by the whites has led to a more frequent practice of abortion' (Speiser 1990(1923):40).[16]

Infanticide on the other hand, he posited, had likely decreased because of missionary intervention. Certainly missionaries had a vital interest in ending the practice, and thus a tendency to hyperbolic rhetoric about it; the missionary Durrad, writing in Rivers' collection, proclaimed that in the old days infanticide was very prevalent and there was 'open throwing of an unwelcome baby to the sharks' (1922:14). Speiser disputed this suggesting that although twins, females and late-born children were more commonly killed, infanticide was never very common and that 'in general the natives love children' (1990(1923):41). He agreed that infants might be killed where the mother was overworked (1990(1923):33) (which in Vanuatu at least seemed to admit a wide range of cases). Speiser maintained that, like abortion, infanticide was often condemned by men and that it had virtually disappeared among the Christian population.[17] He cited the case of Banmatmat in north Pentecost where in 1910 there were only two babies to twenty marriages, but where 'the local missionary brought his influence to bear, and during the next 2 years, 17 children were born, 14 of them surviving' (1990(1923):40). Quite how the missionary brought his influence to bear is not clear – presumably by inveigling against killing babies, but also perhaps by advocating sanitary improvements and encouraging more conjugal intimacies (see Jolly and Macintyre 1989).

Roberts related local birth-control practices to the 'ill-nurture of the people in general', an ill-nurture which in his view caused an abnormal infantile mortality,[18] and combined with 'the artificial restrictions of births to bring about a decline in the population' (1927:61). He attested that

abortion and infanticide were prevalent everywhere. The early missionaries in Tahiti estimated that two thirds of all children were either strangled or pierced with bamboo sticks at birth. John Williams, in the thirties, casually asked three women about their children and unconcernedly, they confessed to having killed nineteen infants between them (sic). And Ellis in Tahiti met two women who had murdered thirteen of their babies. Only in Tonga, the Gilberts and in the early days in New Zealand were children really cared for; in the other groups, if they were not killed, they simply had to look after themselves. Even in the present century the insouciance of Fijian mothers presents a grave problem, and this was much worse in savage times when there were no spurs to make the mothers take any care at all. (1927:61–2)

The 'spurs to make the mothers care' I will discuss below. Let me now review some other complaints these men had about indigenous mothering, complaints about birthing, infant feeding and forms of maternal nurture. Most of these writers (with the important exception of Pitt-Rivers) attest to high rates of infant mortality and suggest that this derived both from the poor nutrition of the pregnant woman and bad birthing practices, especially the lack of hygiene in delivery and cutting the umbilicus.

Durrad insisted, however, that in those cases where a pregnancy went full term, rates of mortality for infants and mothers were low. Indeed, he contended that apart from first pregnancies, deaths in childbirth were few (Durrad 1922:15). But, he maintained, newborn infants often died because of inadequate nurture. Echoing the laments of the Presbyterian missionaries on Aneityum seventy years earlier,[19] Durrad claimed that maternal practices were a hazard to infant health. As well as undue exposure to heat, cold, rain and smoke he alleged that infants suffered from dyspepsia and digestive trauma due to early supplementary feeding.

> The method of feeding new born children is crude and stupid. The mother's milk is supplemented from the earliest moment with chewed taro or yam. This practice is followed in spite of all entreaties, suggestions, upbraidings and advice on the part of the European missionaries . . . It is impossible to convince a tough old hag that her method of child-rearing is wrong. She considers herself a living witness to its excellence. (1922:15–16)

Speiser echoed this verdict – proclaiming the hazards of injudicious early infant feeding. But he also recognized the hazards to the birth rate in prolonged suckling, which he thought not only inhibited ovulation but caused sterility (1990(1923):41). He also noted that surrogate maternal milk was available to other children if they were in need, or simply crying and needing solace.

Indeed, Speiser alone among these authors attested to the strength of mother love in Vanuatu (see Plate 6):

> The mother's love is naturally more ardent than that of the father. A mother is never separated from her new-born child; she first carries it in her arms and then in a mat on her back. Mothers are often seen caressing their children; they do not kiss them but rather snuffle over them and lick them. (1990(1923):69)[20]

He noted that the death of an older child could send mothers into a 'veritable melancholia' (1990(1923):69). This attestation to mother love (even if naturalized, rendered as animalistic, 'snuffling' and licking) is in marked contrast with the more common accusation of maternal callousness, which most other writers saw as both inherent in Pacific mothers and amplified by the colonial experience.

Demoralization was alleged to have affected women in part through attenuating their already weak maternal desires, but also through a new sexual licentiousness. The negative correlation between maternal and sexual desire is attested to by Speiser and Roberts. Thus Speiser posited: 'The woman is no longer under the eye of her united relatives, leads a life as sexually untramelled as that of the men, and the fruit of her promiscuity is all the less desirable in that it impedes her freedom and detracts from her enjoyment' (1990[1923]:50).[21]

Roberts thought that in both Polynesia and Melanesia the disintegration of custom had given way to 'personal desire and licence' (1927:81). He seems to have concurred with the view of the Fiji Decrease Report of

6 Contemporary, collective mother love, persisting despite colonial
admonitions. Young mothers breast-feeding in Bunlap, south
Pentecost, Vanuatu – a baby snatches greedily at another mother's
breast.

1896 that early marriages were a 'preventative of vice', and simultaneously a remedy for depopulation.

This link between women simultaneously rejecting maternity and em-
bracing sexuality is most obviously developed in that singular text on Fiji
on which Roberts relied so heavily – the Decrease Report (1896).[22] This
had a series of detailed recommendations as to how to redress depopulation. I concentrate on the representation of Fijian women's maternity and
sexuality in this report and then consider how women were intimately
implicated in many of the recommendations and ensuing regulations
about how to redress depopulation. There were, as we shall see, several
'spurs' suggested to make mothers care.

Maternal 'insouciance' and 'spurs to make mothers care': the Fiji Decrease Report[23]

This report is singular for several reasons. First, the sheer extent of the
submissions to the Commission is extraordinary, as is the range of the
Commissioners' analysis. The lengthy report influenced a host of later
scholars and administrators, most of whom concurred with its conclusions.

Even those who did not, like Pitt-Rivers (1927), had perforce to deal with its analyses and recommendations. Secondly, unlike many colonial reports it was distinctive in that many of its recommendations were implemented in some form, if not universally through enacting Native Regulations then through the regulations of provincial councils, set up by the British administration. Thirdly, it is distinctive in that in its pages we hear not just the voices of European men – missionaries, colonial officials and anthropologists – but some indigenous voices, albeit the testimony primarily of high-ranking Fijian men. They, like the European men discussed above, adduced a wide range of causes for depopulation.[24] But they too privileged the maternal and sexual behaviour of women as a crucial source of the problem.

In his appraisal of the report Macnaught concludes:

> If the respondents agreed on one thing, it was that Fijian mothers were bad mothers – a 'race of blunted sensibilities' claimed one official: 'I have lived among natives during the past 23 years and have never seen any particular affection shown by a child to its mother.' A Wesleyan missionary contributed the story of a mother with a frail child living in his compound at Vuna Point, Taveuni. He asked her to come twice a day to his house for fresh cow's milk, yet 'although her child was dying of starvation, she found it irksome to apply for milk. Her maternal affection failed under the strain of walking 110 yards twice a day . . . she is but a type of most Fijian mothers of delicate children.' (1982:14)

The stress on reforming bad mothering was reflected in the recommendations of the Commission. A range of remedies were proposed. These included a more efficient administration and political legislature, 'subversion of the communal system', creation of incentives to industry, more disciplined and steady work and the encouragement of more 'robust games'. More direct interventions in health proposed included the concentration of villages and establishment of model villages, the improvement of sanitation and inculcation of sanitary principles (see Thomas 1990) and attempts to restrict the spread of yaws.

The rest of the recommendations related directly to women as maternal and sexual beings. These included some tough measures – inquests into infant deaths and more effective deterrents against abortion. The Commissioners also recommended improving 'infant dietary', encouraging the use of cow's or goat's milk, and circulating instructions in nursing. Mothers themselves were not totally neglected insofar as the Commissioners also suggested better care of pregnant, lying-in and suckling women, and indeed advocated a general improvement in women's 'status'. Child care in later years was addressed by provisions for the prevention of neglect of children and the institution of village creches. Early marriages were to be facilitated and rewards instituted for large families. A slightly confused picture emerges about what the Commissioners themselves thought of the alleged sexual licence of the 'new women' of Fiji, arguments to restrain miscegenation and 'prevalent immorality' jostled with proposals to relax the existing laws against fornication and adultery. Finally in this reform of the maternal and sexual being of the Fijian woman, the European woman is called upon to engage in 'hygienic missions'.

These were the pious plans of colonizing men, but the strength of the colonial state in Fiji, and especially its heavy reliance on the local authority of chiefly men, did result in some draconian and pervasive interventions. Women were subject to inquests into the deaths of their babies, even if they miscarried or were stillborn, and were often accused of procuring abortions (see Lukere n.d.a).[25] Given that the rate of infant deaths was extremely high – in 1893 27.17 per cent of infants died in their first month and 44.17 per cent died in their first year – a huge number of Fijian women were liable to such inquests. Both these inquests and those into alleged abortions were conducted locally. The rationale for this is obvious from an extensive correspondence in the colonial records discussing what legal measures should be used against abortion (CSO 2320/1895). Here it was stated that 'abortion is a common offence in the provinces, far commoner than the ordinary Europeans have any conception of'. But against the view that this should be a matter for the Supreme Court in Suva it was argued that such cases needed to be dealt with by provincial courts or councils or, as it happened, native stipendiary magistrates. '[I]t would be quite out of the question to think of bringing all such cases to Suva . . . it is a difficult offence to prove. It is full of intricate native technicalities and the interpretation is often extremely difficult more especially when native midwives are permitted to express what they know' (CSO 2320/1895). The recalcitrance of indigenous ideas of conception and of controls over fertility by mothers and midwives is broadly hinted at here. More detailed evidence of particular inquests reveals a pervasive presumption of maternal guilt, coupled with insinuations of husband's neglect or violence and the collusion of indigenous midwives, whom on occasion the colonial state 'permitted to express what they know'! But, as Lukere (n.d.a) attests, presumptions of maternal guilt or neglect were hard to sustain in the face of overwhelming evidence that exotic, infectious diseases were to blame.[26]

Not only were mothers and midwives thus cast as secretive and recalcitrant, but the power which men had in reproductive matters was probably thereby amplified by the colonial state.[27] Fathers rather than mothers were, under a regulation of 1897, rewarded for having more than five living children with a tax remission and having their name published in the Fijian language newspaper *Na Mata*. On the other hand, childlessness was publicly denounced. A couple of cases from the island of Kadavu suggest extreme attempts to exert reproductive power by local chiefs. Thus the *Buli* (district chief) of Sanima prosecuted several married couples before the native magistrate on the grounds of abortion – the sole evidence being that they were childless. The charges were dismissed, but all these women subsequently bore children. Also on Kadavu, in 1911 the *Buli* of Nakasaleka ordered thirteen childless women to conceive, and all of them did so within two years. The *Roko Tui* (government provincial head) of Bua in 1898 obliged the colonial government with the following statistics on married women in his province: 12 per cent were childless because they were barren or knew how to prevent conception, 17 per cent had aborted, 46 per cent had had children but neglected them until death, and 25 per cent had 'healthy families'. So, although colonial state and indigenous chiefs were engaged in novel legislations over their reproductive lives, some women at least were still evading or resisting such controls (Macnaught 1982:14–15). And, as Lukere attests (n.d.a), even when inquests were held and women accused, it was extremely difficult to prove wilful abortion or neglect, and prosecutions were thus rare. Still, despite lack of enthusiasm on the part of some white and Fijian officials, these inquests persisted till 1948.

After birthing, Fijian women were subject to novel inspections of their maternal nurture. It is recorded in the resolutions of the minutes of the provincial council meeting of Colo East in 1899 that 'mothers shall not chew food for their children, but pound as formerly was the custom in many districts'. The Commissions' recommendations about protecting the health of pregnant women and all women of reproductive age often led to attempts to restrict women's work. In the same meeting of the provincial council of Colo East, it was resolved that 'women of all conditions are not to fish at night under the pain of *Talaidredre* [the punitive clauses of the Native Regulations] and that pregnant women be forbidden to fish either by day or by night.' [28] Similar edicts were pronounced in the several provincial councils of Fiji for several decades, although the effects they had are hard to gauge. Thus it was noted in the minutes of the provincial council of Colo West in 1926 that in the interests of the better care of infants and mothers the following resolutions were taken:

That no woman shall do any digging or carrying of firewood or heavy loads during the period of her pregnancy and for six months after the birth of her child.

That the husband of any pregnant woman shall give notice to the Native Medical Practitioner one month before the expected date of the child and shall report to the Native Medical Practitioner any subsequent illness of the child during its first year. [29]

At this same meeting some concessions were also made to fathers – by exempting them from the demands of communal labour, for three months after the birth of a child.

The demands of enforced communal labour on women were often a subject of contention. Colonial state sanitation regulations required all indigenous Fijians to assist in the weeding of villages and towns. Women were exempted from this work in the eastern provinces quite early, but not until much later in the west. At a meeting of the Colo West provincial council in 1928 it was noted that 'Colo West was one of the few remaining provinces where the women help to weed the towns', and it was resolved in future to exempt women from this work. The object of the resolution 'of course is to safeguard the health of women and their unborn children'.[30] The 'of course' is rather suspect, since earlier discussions of exempting women from weeding work had rather linked this to questions of sexual morality. Thus five years earlier, in 1923, the provincial council of Colo West had resolved *not* to exempt women from weeding in the following terms:

The object of the resolution is to inhibit the long absence from their villages of women and girls, which is possible when a penalty lies only after 60 days absence. It is said that the morals of the women suffer as a result of their absenting themselves from the restraining influences of their villages . . . there is much to be said in favour of the exercise of some women who continually desert their domestic duties for the pleasures of cosmopolitan towns; but it is to the Missions rather than to the Government that one should look for amelioration.[31]

This passage is extremely interesting – suggesting as it does a tension between the way in which communal work might be seen to prejudice women's maternal energies while releasing them from such duties was tantamount to releasing their sexual energies for acts of cosmopolitan pleasure. This was a view often espoused by those Fijian men of high rank who had been appointed *Buli*. The penalties referred to in this passage are those instituted in 1912 (Regulation 4, Section 77), whereby women could be fined for being absent from their villages for more than sixty days. The mobility of Fijian women was clearly a matter of some con- testation – with the indigenous appointees of the colonial state often wanting to restrict this more than the British colonial officials thought proper for government. The British author of these minutes clearly thought it more the work of missions to dedicate women to their 'domes- tic duties'. Elsewhere, British colonial officials were enjoined to prevent women leaving their husbands and running away to Suva or other towns. In the minutes of the provincial council meeting of Colo East in 1925, *Buli* Waima asked that all the old regulations regarding women be re-enacted and that the regulations be extended to apply to married women. The official noted that these regulations already applied to married women. In the same meeting *Buli* Lutu suggested that all *Buli* be asked to have all women not in employment in Suva returned to their districts. The British official commented: 'There is very strong feeling over these matters and the people think they should be given assistance. I endeavoured to explain to them that times were changing.'[32]

Times were perhaps changing insofar as government officials were less inclined to enact regulations which were clearly in the service of protecting Fijian women's sexual virtue rather than their maternal potential, although the missions were vigorous in promoting both. But there was also a change in that, alongside the coercive measures of colonial government, there was an increasing stress on education and persuasion, in which both government and missions were involved. White women were implicated in this, not just as models of idealized maternity but also as active educators in maternity. Claudia Knapman notes how the pervasive presumption that white women knew more about childbirth and child care was seemingly confirmed by the 1896 report, and that '[t]he European response was to supplement the emphasis on example with more direct teaching of European child rearing practices to Fijian women' (1986:20–1). The grim birthing experiences of many white women in the colonies and the high rates of infant and maternal mortality amongst them should not have inspired such feelings of maternal superiority. This is graphically documented by Knapman. But despite the grim reality of miscarriages, lonely, unassisted and complicated births, postpartum disease and death, and the lack of reliable contraceptive techniques, white women in Fiji presumed that they had superior knowledge and practice of mothering, and that Fijian women had nothing to teach them (1986:20, but see 28).

Rather, they presumed to be the teachers, even if they were not mothers. This was especially clear in the work of the Hygiene Mission and later in mission education. Thus, Laura Spence accompanied her husband Frank, a Provincial Inspector, through Cakaudrove and Bua, on a hygienic mission in 1899–90. Macnaught (1982) recounts how this 'energetic lady' in one month in 1900 inspected 299 houses, burnt 665 dirty mats and treated 60 cases of ringworm.[33] Central to her mission was instructing local women, whom she saw as 'densely stupid', in infant care (1982:18). Catholic missionary women were also drawn into such endeavours. Although the Methodists resolutely refused,[34] Catholic nuns, like Sister Stanislas, ventured into remote areas like Wailevu or Namosi, on clean-up campaigns,[35] an intrinsic part of which was to show mothers how to care for their children. An enthusiastic Fijian supporter applauded: '[T]he Sisters are the enemies of dirt, they are the enemies of all foetid atmospheres, they are kindly, they are loving, they are anxious to assist us' (cited in Macnaught 1982:19). One wonders how celibate, childless sisters could be viewed as credible teachers by Fijian mothers. Their efforts were shortlived. Partly because of conflicts with both Methodists (who joined the mission belatedly with their own unmarried 'sisters') and the colonial government (about how they conducted their campaign), the Hygiene Mission petered out around 1903. But there was also resistance, evasion and ridicule on the part of Fijians – chiefs, men in general and especially the women they were trying to instruct.

Later, the Catholic sisters continued their concern to improve maternal nurture by devoting themselves to education in their own establishments. And it was this strategy that the Methodists preferred and had already adopted. Segregated schooling had long been part of Catholic education, but from 1899 the Methodists also established specialist girls' schools, such as Matalevo, where regimes of cleanliness and discipline were central. Although it had problems with food supplies, its own sanitation arrangements and indeed with local acceptance, schools such as this were central in educating Fijian women and, from 1908, those who went on to train as native obstetric nurses (NONs). Although beset with early difficulties, this programme persisted and was central to later transformations of Fijian birthing and mothering.

Ironically, despite white women's denigration of the mothering of both Fijian and Indian women, the latter were in the twentieth century increasingly employed as nurses or nannies by white families. In the nineteenth century, more affluent settler families had poor Irish, Welsh or English nurses or nannies. But increasingly Fijian, Indian and Solomon Island women and girls replaced them. This does not, however, suggest a novel trust of local mothering skills, since they were carefully instructed in the 'right', namely British, forms of child care, and the white mothers still retained close scrutiny over food preparation and the health care of their children (Knapman 1986:31–4).

Debates about maternal 'insouciance' and attempts to reform mothering worked out rather differently in Vanuatu. Although mothers here too had been equally singled out as a cause of depopulation, the colonial state did little in the early twentieth century to remould indigenous maternity. Despite the new rhetoric of population and the threat of state power to redress depopulation, missions remained the crucial agencies in European attempts to improve mothering and provide for maternal and child health. In part this is a reflection of a weak and divided colonial state (see Jolly 1992). In part it also reflects a more ambiguous attitude to the indigenous population on the part of white settlers and the state.

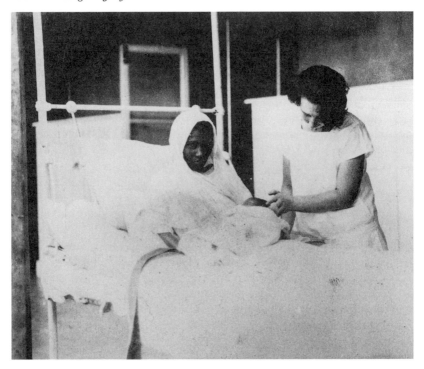

7 Doctor and patient, Ba Hospital, Fiji, *c.* 1926. Dr Doreen Hensley
worked at the Methodist Mission Hospital at Ba from 1926 to 1929,
where she is shown tending an Indian mother and baby.

Elsewhere I have suggested that there was a profoundly different colonial policy about land – that whereas in Fiji customary relation to land was
ratified and chiefly authority over it enhanced (see Macnaught 1982), in
Vanuatu it was not (Jolly 1992). For some this reflected a view that Fijian
culture, unlike the cultures of Vanuatu, was worth preserving. This
preservationist view was less apparent amongst colonial administrators in
Vanuatu, and even less so among those white settlers who were trying to
establish profitable plantations and trading stores. They were constantly
beset by the problems in securing a local labour force, but also expectantly
hoped that they might be able to repopulate these islands vacated by the
'dying race'. The solution, finally envisaged by the majority who were
French planters, was not to rely on the strength and health of local
labourers, but rather to import labour from Indochina, which they did
from 1923. In Fiji, some white settlers entertained rather similar expectations about the indigenous population 'dying out' (Knapman 1986:28).

But it was the colonial state as much as settler interests here which initiated the importation of indentured Indian labour from 1879. Thus, although there was a strong state concern and draconian measures introduced to arrest the decrease of the Fijian population, this cannot be understood primarily in terms of ensuring a labour supply. Indeed, in the same period the colonial state was instituting these population policies it was also inhibiting the rights of British settlers to recruit local Fijians as labourers and closely controlling the intersection of Fijian custom and commerce.

Conclusion

Although the productive and the reproductive aspects of empire intersected, they were not always consonant. Thus, the debate about depopulation in the Pacific has to be understood in its own terms as a new discursive and legislative force in the lives of Fijians, and to a lesser extent ni-Vanuatu. Although many reasons for the decline in population were countenanced and the reasons for it hotly debated, there was no doubt undue blame attributed to the 'heartless and hopeless' mothers of Fiji and Vanuatu. The 'improving' measures introduced by the colonial state in Fiji and by missionaries in both colonies in many cases did sometimes enhance the health of infants and mothers (see Plate 7). But such improvements also entailed a dynamic of blaming mothers for aspects of life for which they could not have been responsible – preeminently the devastating effects of exotic infectious diseases, like measles, influenza and dysentery. In Fiji it led to increased surveillance, not just of women's maternal lives but their sexual lives as well. It promoted a racist denigration of the indigenous mother and a glorification of the white mother.

But how far did this colonial rhetoric about mothering impinge on the indigenous women of Fiji and Vanuatu? Can we see this as mere racist and masculinist rhetoric which had little meaning or effects on the lives of actual mothers? But we must also ask how can we imagine or reconstruct the actualities, the 'experiences' of mothers in the past? We have a few, distantiated depictions by outsiders from the early colonial period (see above). We do not have oral traditions or documentary materials which would afford insights into 'being a mother'. Thus my analysis here perforce deconstructs those masculinist, colonialist discourses which rendered indigenous women 'other mothers'. But although the subjectivities of ancestral mothers are unknown and perhaps unknowable, we might speculate on the basis of later histories and contemporary ethnographies, including my own in south Pentecost, Vanuatu (Jolly 1994), the surveys of both Osteria (1984) and Walter and Bourdy (1986) for Vanuatu, and the archival work of Lukere for Fiji (n.d.a).

Being a mother no doubt differed greatly between the Pacific and Europe one hundred years ago. These differences were not just in the sites and the postures of birthing but in the meaning and value given to being a mother. In the ancestral cultures of Vanuatu and Fiji women were typically sequestered at birth – either in a house set apart for menstruation and parturition or in their own houses, with men and children absent. They typically assumed active rather than prone postures, crouching, squatting or bracing themselves against a tree or a rope to deliver. In some islands of both archipelagos women birthed alone, but, more commonly, they were assisted by close female kin and/or midwives, e.g. the *bui ni gone* of Fiji (Lukere n.d.a) or the *loas po isin* of south Pentecost (Jolly 1994:145–7). Midwives intervened if the presentation was wrong or the labour proceeded too slowly – using both massage and herbal preparations to facilitate birth. They cut the cord with a bamboo knife, ensured the afterbirth was delivered and then buried the placenta in the ground to secure attachment to place. These 'wise women' would offer assistance if the mother desired to abort or to kill her child. Babies were often fed premasticated tubers before the milk started flowing, but then were usually breast-fed for two to three years during which time mothers (and often fathers) refrained from sex. All adult women were expected to be mothers and those who were infertile adopted children from sisters or other close kin. Although being a mother was crucial to adult identity, mothers were not solely or even primarily responsible for the nurture and care of their children. Fathers, aunts and uncles, grandparents and elder siblings all nurtured.

These were the stark contours of ancestral maternities. The features to which the colonists objected are patent – the 'dirt' and danger of indigenous parturition in thatched houses on earthern floors; the active postures of birthing; the all-female, seemingly clandestine nature of birthing and of family planning; the power of 'wise women'; the early feeding of solids; the denial of conjugal intimacies during breast-feeding. All these aspects of indigenous maternities were strange, perhaps even threatening. Moreover the diffuse collective responsibility for children no doubt suggested to them that the love of mothers was deficient and undisciplined. These stark corporeal and social facts were part of the cultural contest of colonialism, contests of philosophies and of theories of social reproduction, as much as of power. European colonists of this period – missionaries and colonial officials, men and women – were alike committed to a new model of the bourgeois family, with the domesticated woman, the mother, at its moral and religious core (see Jolly and Macintyre 1989). In proselytizing this new ideal of the nuclear family and individuated person in relation to economy and society, the greater control of men and the state over both birthing and mothering was thereby promoted.

The ancestral cultures of the Pacific not only vaunted collectivity over individuals or families but were based on very different notions of person-hood and of human reproduction (cf. Strathern 1988). Human fertility was intimately connected with natural fertility and both were thought to be secured through ancestral power, its efficacy unleashed through the rituals of the chiefly or the high-ranking. Fertility was not uncontrolled fecundity, but rather subject to human ritual control in cycles of sexual continence. Just as parents should refrain from sex for two to three years to ensure the health and growth of their infant, so gardeners and agricultural priests had to be sexually continent at certain periods to ensure a bountiful harvest (see Jolly n.d.b). Women were sequestered at birth in Fiji and Vanuatu not so much because they were polluted, but rather because they were then dangerously proximate to the power of the ancestors (Hanson 1982; Keesing 1989). The wise women who assisted mothers were not just midwives but, rather, female priests or healers who had a more general capacity to heal, to divine and to secure ancestral blessings.

But although women were secluded and set apart at birth and although mothers and midwives were influential in decisions about abortion and infanticide, we should not create a feminist romance about women's control over reproduction, another sacred 'separate sphere', pertaining to a Pacific past (cf. Dureau, this volume). Men also had powers to control reproduction as fathers, as brothers and as members and leaders of larger kinship collectivities, of clans and lineages. And despite the variety of indigenous concepts of conception and theories of kinship in these two island groups, women's corporeal and spiritual place as mothers was usually eclipsed by the corporeal/spiritual claims of paternity.

We might then ponder, as Dureau has done for the Solomons (1994 and this volume), how maternities changed in the colonial period, and how this impinged on the respective powers of men and women. The combined effects of pacification, of missionary ideals, of introduced diseases and Western medicine all played a part, alongside those interven-tions of the colonial state in the name of 'population' I have privileged here. But we should not presume, despite the force of their promulgation (in Fiji at least) that any of these Western models and colonial interven-tions had immediate or automatic effect. For Fiji, it is clear that the invasive inquests into infant death failed to find much evidence of ma-ternal guilt, and that few mothers or midwives were prosecuted. The draconian regulations restricting women's work and movements often went unheeded. Early attempts to introduce cattle to substitute for women both as 'beasts of burden' and as sources of milk were ridiculed, not least by women themselves. The rhetorical campaigns waged in the Fijian newspaper *Na Mata* were ineffectual, since few women could read.[36] The efforts of white women to reform by persuasion were resisted, ignored or satirically subverted. And yet, contemporary birthing and mothering practices in Fiji (and in Vanuatu) do attest to some profound transformations initiated in the colonial period.[37]

Arguably in both places it was the influence of missionary education rather than the efforts of state coercion which was crucial. But, importantly, these only started to take real effect when women themselves were persuaded of the differences between the 'darkness' of past practice and the 'enlightenment' of the new ways. Central to this internalization of Christian and colonial values was the education of women as wives, mothers and especially nurses. In Fiji, in the early stages this entailed a conflict between older indigenous midwives[38] and those younger Fijian women who were trained as native obstetric nurses (NONs). Thus the colonial contest between traditional and introduced medicines became a contest between generations of indigenous women. But the older women were not so easily discredited, and as the NONs themselves aged and gained experience, they also accommodated more to the knowledge and the techniques of the indigenous midwives. Lukere (n.d.a) thus suggests that the NONs far more than male native medical practitioners effected the merging and blurring of traditional and colonial medicines in Fiji. There has been, in Fiji at least, as much an indigenizing of scientific medicine as an appropriation of traditional techniques by nurses.

This is not to deny the hierarchical language which was applied to birthing and mothering. Reproducing persons, as much as reproducing cultures, became saturated with the dichotomous tropes of recalcitrant darkness and accommodating enlightenment (see also Ram, this volume: Chapter 4). Such language persisted long after the concern about depopulation had passed, and into the postcolonial period when control of a burgeoning population was urged (see Underhill-Sem 1994). Fijian women, like most Pacific Christians, contrast the past 'time of darkness' with their being 'in the light' today. But just as Fijian women long defied the colonial hierarchizing of them as 'bad mothers' and white women as 'good mothers', they today embrace 'traditional' and 'modern' forms as equally their own. Women in independent Pacific states, in Fiji and in Vanuatu today typically portray themselves not as 'bad mothers', but as very good ones, perhaps even better than the white women they witness and hear about (see Dureau, this volume).

NOTES

1 This was not true of some settler states where the assaults on indigenous mothering included not only surveillance, rhetoric and instruction but actual physical removal. In Australia up until the 1960s many Aboriginal children, and especially those classified as 'half-castes', were forcibly removed from their mothers into the care of mission homes, institutional schools and white foster families (Huggins 1993).

2 Maternalism was a term devised by Saleeby and others to describe their eugenic approach to mothering. It opposed state policies which threatened to substitute for the biological mother. I am here using maternalism in a different sense, consonant with feminist theories of white women's place in colonialism or critical theories of colonizing discourses within Western feminism (e.g. Jolly 1993; Ramusack 1990). It could legitimately be applied to understandings of middle-class women's relation to working-class women in the period under discussion. Crucial to my meaning of the term is not just the presumption of remoulding the mothering of other women, but the assumption of the locus of the mother on the part of the powerful woman (a locus which situates the less powerful woman as daughter rather than sister).

3 Apropos the Boer War recruitment, Davin quotes from Major General Maurice, who combined the metaphoric links between semen and milk:

Whatever steps are taken . . . whether you raise the standard of the Army either in numbers or physique seem to me only like more careful methods of extracting cream from milk. The more carefully you skim the milk, the more poor is the residue of the skimmed milk. I think it is safe to say that no nation was ever yet for a very long time great and free when the army put into the field no longer represented its own virility and manhood. (Cited in Davin 1978:15)

4 It should be noted that this fear about the declining birth rate leading to race suicide was as much a cause of concern in the colony of Australia as in Britain itself (see Bacchi 1980 and De Lepervanche 1989; see also Gordon 1975 on America). And although Britons may have constructed German mothers as not shirking from maternity, there was in fact a parallel concern in early twentieth-century Germany about the declining birth rate (Usborne 1992:1–30). Usborne makes the useful contrast between pronatalists, neo-Malthusians and the eugenicists (or proponents of racial hygiene) in the debates in Germany (a classification which might equally apply in Britain). See also Stepan (1991) for a fascinating consideration of the different trajectory of eugenics in Latin America.

5 In one statement of an ideal eugenic marriage it was envisaged that the couple should be able to produce certified records of ancestry dating back three or four generations which showed the absence of 'nervous prostration, sick headaches, neurasthenia, hysteria, melancholia, St Vitus dance, epilepsy, syphilis, alcoholism, pauperism, criminality, prostitution . . . insanity, . . . deafness, colour blindness and other indications of defectiveness and degeneracy' (Charles Hadden 1904, cited in Davin 1978:20, 59).

6 Davin lists the following: the Institute of Hygiene (1903), the Infants' Health Society (1904), the National League for Physical Education and Improvement

(1905), the Food Education Society (1908), the National League of Health, Maternity and Child Welfare (1905), the Eugenics Education Society (1908) and the Women's League of Service for Motherhood (1910). The membership of such societies, Davin (1978) tells us, was both 'ladies and gentlemen', but most of the work was done by the ladies.

7 Manderson (this volume) suggests that preference was given for home visitors to be of 'similar class and background' to mothers, but this is at variance with Davin's claims.

8 The rates in colonial Malaya in the early twentieth century ranged between 250 and 500 per 1,000 with an extreme of 760 per 1,000 reported in Kuala Lumpur in one week in 1921 (Manderson 1989:88).

9 Reducing high rates of infant mortality was thus a prime concern of new colonial projects of maternal and child health in Malaya. In the first instance this was through European nurses and the European lady medical officers. Training of indigenous midwives was instituted (in Singapore) in 1910 and of mothercraft nurses in the same year. Maternal and infant welfare clinics were established and forms of inspection of local mothers promoted – either through their attending such clinics or their being visited at home, by the figure of surveillance familiar from Britain – the health visitor (Manderson 1989:92). She might be a midwife or a nurse – she was perforce a European. Manderson observes that Malay, Chinese and Tamil women were all implicated in the official representations of unclean, incompetent and sometimes wilfully neglectful mothers (1989 and this volume).

10 Beatrice Grimshaw, journalist, novelist and propagandist for such settler interests, proclaimed in 1905: 'The brown races are everywhere dying out with fearful rapidity, in another generation or two they will be extinct, leaving all their fertile lands to be worked by the energetic white races, assisted by Indian or Chinese labour' (*Sydney Morning Herald*, 2 Dec. 1905:6).

11 Rivers is an ancestral figure in the genealogies of both anthropology and psychology. He both researched and treated the victims of 'shell shock' in World War I. A superb recent trilogy by Pat Barker (1992, 1994, 1995) offers a compelling portrait of Rivers in this period and, though fictional, it is derived from intimate knowledge of Rivers' life and work. The last book in the trilogy, *The Ghost Road* (1995) (awarded the Booker Prize that year), moves between the trenches in Europe, the hospitals in England and Scotland and the islands of the Solomons. There are intriguing convergences and divergences between Rivers' views of masculinity and warfare in Europe and the Solomons. He diagnoses the depression and malaise of his patients as due not just to witnessing the shocking carnage of the war but also due to the enforced inactivity of the trenches inducing what he sees as 'feminized' passivity or emasculation.

12 This is expressed by Beatrice Grimshaw at several points in her travel writing. Here is another observation apropos Tahitian depopulation and the Pacific in general:

They are quite happy and uncomplaining, and manage to have a reasonably good time in a quiet way, but they *will* die out, and nobody can prevent them. You see, they are rather bored, and when you are bored, the answer to the

question, 'Is life worth living?' is, at the least debatable – to a Pacific islander
. . . *mutatis mutandis,* it applies to nearly all the island races. It is not only the
Tahitian who looks back with wistful eyes to the faded sunset of the bad old
times, with all their savage gaudiness of scarlet blood and golden licence, and
languishes in the chill pale dawn of the white man's civilization. It is the whole
Pacific world, more or less. (Grimshaw 1905:33 (emphasis in the original))

Felix Speiser expressed similar ideas about demoralization in the language of
scientific racism suggesting that the 'decay of the native culture' meant

the gradual debasement of the natives' intellectual heritage such as is caused
by the intercourse between the two races. The inferiority of its own culture is
inevitably recognised by a weaker race in its confrontation with a stronger one,
and the greater the difference between the two cultures and the longer the
superior one neglects to absorb the inferior one into itself or to replace its lost
intellectual heritage by another, the more rapidly the weaker race is de-
moralized. (Speiser 1990 (1923):48–9)

13 Both Roberts and Pitt-Rivers disputed what the latter called the 'innate native
     degeneracy theory'. Pitt-Rivers observed that there was little evidence of a
     pre-European decline in population and that this theory 'absolves Europeans
     of any greater crime than of having accelerated by their advent the inevitable
     extinction of "this decadent people"' (1927:276). I should note, although
     these two books were published by the same publisher in the same year,
     Roberts slightly before Pitt-Rivers, that they do not address each other, apart
     from Pitt-Rivers' concluding note which states that it 'would be impossible to
     notice this book at this late hour' and that he welcomes it as a scholarly
     restatement of those popular delusions and fallacies which his own book
     exposes and refutes (1927:276).
14 This is obvious in this statement by Roberts:

     Primarily, there was a general racial decline, an indefinable *malaise* of the stock
     itself. Since the thirteenth century, that time of migrations throughout the
     Orient when the Khmers were ejected from Cambodia and when the Poly-
     nesians spread from Samoa and Tahiti to the farthest confines of the Pacific,
     the conditions of life had changed. The voyage-urge was removed, and the
     natives luxuriated in enervating tropical islands where life was too easy and
     nature too bountiful. (Roberts 1927:60 (emphasis in the original))

15 Compare Rivers' assertion that 'The people say to themselves "Why should
     we bring children into the world only to work for the white man?"' (1922:104).
16 The low birth rate he attributes not only to contraception, abortion and
     infanticide but to other features of pre-colonial sexual economy – the way in
     which women were monopolized by older, less virile men, the sterility in
     women ensuing from being 'used' for sexual purposes at a very early age, and
     women's strength being overtaxed in general.
17 He similarly discounts the effects of widow strangulation – noting that it was
     only ever widespread on Aneityum, and to a lesser extent Aniwa and Tanna in

the south, and that it had been reduced to a 'harmless cause' (Speiser 1990 (1923):41; see Jolly 1991).

18 The stress which Roberts and others placed on infant mortality as a key factor in depopulation was disputed by Pitt-Rivers, who claimed that he had 'definitively shown' that it 'had nothing to do with it' (1927:277, see also 76–85). He was far more critical than Roberts and others of Fiji's Decrease Report of 1896 and thought its analyses and recommendations out of date. See Jolly (n.d.a) for a more detailed appraisal of Pitt-Rivers.

19 For example Charlotte Geddie lamented that mothers gave their babies 'all kinds of trash' rather than just maternal milk (cited in Jolly 1991:40). Missionary and state warnings against early infant feeding induced one of the few changes in maternal behaviour which was early and pervasive throughout Vanuatu. For example, even in the traditionalist communities of south Pentecost where I worked in the early 1970s, women told me that their grandmothers had given up feeding infants pre-masticated taro because of the advice of Christian converts returning from plantations in Queensland in the early part of this century (Jolly 1994:146).

20 Fathers, he thought, were more tender and indulgent with their sons.

21 It is interesting to situate Speiser's perceptions of changes in sexual morality in Vanuatu in relation to debates going on in Germany about the 'new woman', whose sexual promiscuity was also alleged to be antagonistic to maternal sentiments and the cause of increased abortions (see Usborne 1992:156ff and plates).

22 A range of indigenous marriage practices were also seen, especially by Speiser, to inhibit rates of reproduction. In particular he linked early marriage and maternity to polygamy and gerontocratic control. He posited that women were rendered prematurely sterile by sexual activity and parturition at too early an age. He thought the birth rate was also reduced by the fact that women were forced into marriage with old men – who often had several wives. This meant that women's reproductive potential was not fully realized, since the more virile and fertile men had no sexual or reproductive partners, except for periods of occasional licence. Speiser suggested that complementing gerontocratic polygamy was a pattern of ritualized 'general freedom' when the wives of polygamists 'became the common property of the young men of the village' (Speiser 1922:34). Thus polygamy generated a kind of polyandry. I quote:

Prostitution assumed rather the form of hospitality and guests were openly and as a rule freely provided with women by their hosts, who being in a position to make feasts, usually had the majority of the women. So it has followed that the short age of women among the ordinary men through polygamy and other causes led to polyandric conditions – for polygamists lent their women as rewards for services rendered, and to retain the good will of the young men. (1922:35)

23 The Commission was initiated in 1893 when government officials sent 'circulars to everyone of note or of long residence' asking for submissions as to reasons for the decrease in population. This included many Europeans, but

excluded most Fijians except high-ranking men. The report of the Commission was published in 1896.

24 Thus Basil Thomson, who served on the Commission suggested that the report portrayed Fijians collectively as 'cankered through and through with monogamy, in-breeding, unchivalry, communism and dirt; individually by insouciance, foreign disease, kava-drinking and excessive smoking' (cited in Macnaught 1982:14).

25 Victoria Lukere is presently completing a doctoral thesis which examines the character of the Decrease Report and its consequences for indigenous mothers in both coercive and persuasive projects. This is a far more detailed and subtle analysis than I can offer here. An overview of her material is available in Lukere (n.d.b).

26 This is precisely what is emerging in the recent work of Lukere. These inquests were held in the case of infant deaths, stillbirths and miscarriages. Although by far the majority of these deaths were ultimately ascribed to infections with exotic diseases and their effects on both child and mother, there was a pervasive presumption of maternal guilt. Lukere demonstrates through translations of several such inquests how mothers were invited to implicate themselves and others to blame them. But, significantly, there were also frequently insinuations about the failure of the husband to provide or being violent or of pregnant women having to carry heavy loads (n.d.a). A regulation had been passed in 1885 preventing women from carrying heavy loads, but this was habitually ignored. Whereas the colonial government claimed this caused stillbirths or miscarriages, women by contrast often asserted that staying inside plaiting mats was the cause of difficulties on birthing (see Lukere n.d.a).

27 Again I am indebted to Lukere here. The Decrease Report spoke of a 'freemasonry among women which conceals the practice [of abortion] not only from the police but from their husbands and fathers' (1896:121). The indigenous sphere of reproduction was probably primarily under female control, although men no doubt had some investments in it as husbands and fathers, members of descent groups and chiefs. Perhaps their main involvement was through restraint and celibacy – especially in the postpartum period. If this was not adhered to the baby was thought to be at risk of death, from a particular illness, *dabe*. As Lukere also stresses, birthing was sacralized in Fijian tradition, and midwives were seen as channelling spiritual power from the ancestors/gods to the living. Thus, arguably, 'midwives' were as much priestesses as healers.

28 This derives from a meeting of the provincial council at Naibita Nailega on 26–27 April 1899. Women here, as in much of the precolonial Pacific, gave their infants pre-masticated food. But it appears that in parts of Fiji this was sometimes complemented by *yaqona* (kava), a component of infant diet which was no doubt even more alarming to colonial administrators. It should be noted that attempts by Brewster and others to introduce cow's milk and feeding bottles were singularly ineffective, women refused to use them (Lukere n.d.a) in contrast to Malaya (Manderson, this volume).

29 This was at the provincial council meeting of Colo West, 3–5 November 1926, held at Taqaqe, Korolevuiwai.

30 This was recorded as a resolution of the provincial council meeting of 28 September 1928 at Lawaqa.
31 This is from the minutes of the provincial council meeting of 21 November 1923, held at Tubairata, Mavua.
32 From the minutes of the meeting of the provincial council of Colo East held on 17 September 1925 at Korovatu.
33 Lukere (n.d.a) stresses how all of this was unpaid work, rendered as the wife of a government employee.
34 The Methodists refused to get involved in this. Both Catholics and Methodists were approached in 1898, but the latter were unenthusiastic and pessimistic. Bishop Vidal, by contrast, placed the entire resources of the Marist mission at the government's disposal, fourteen Europeans and twenty-four Fijian sisters. As Lukere suggests (n.d.a), this readiness was probably partly due to the novelty of having official favour and, especially when the Methodists demurred, an attempt at Catholic expansion at the latter's expense. The Hygiene Mission thus became in Lukere's view 'a religious war'.
35 Macnaught reports a delightful instance of colonial inversion, whereby the *Roko* (government-appointed head of a province) of Serua, engaged in his own clean-up campaign at the sisters' own mission station while they were away in the hills. He had all the mats inside the church pulled out, pronounced filthy and burnt on the spot (1982:20). Burning precious mats was hardly a way of gaining the confidence and support of Fijian women, or men for that matter. Lukere (n.d.a) also reports an incident of young men in Nailaga harassing both white and Fijian sisters, including lifting up their *sulus* in front of the latter and farting.
36 Lukere suggests that even high-ranking women and men found it hard to read or write, and that the readership of this newspaper, like other official publications, was restricted to a tiny elite of male officials.
37 A number of indigenous practices have almost ceased: not suckling until a few days after birth, feeding the infant pre-masticated taro, long postpartum sex taboos. But indigenous forms of contraception – both herbal and physical – are used alongside the pill, the IUD and Depo-Provera. In Vanuatu home births still predominate over births in clinics and hospitals, except in cases of difficult presentation or first births. Breast-feeding is both routine and prolonged. Arguably the greatest effects are in the intensity and concentration of maternal nurture.
38 I am here referring to *bui ni gone,* those 'wise women' who were in fact often more than midwives. Some specialized in certain techniques of contraception, abortion or birthing, but they might also be experts in herbal cures for other complaints, in bonesetting, incisions, massage and manipulation – including the internal manipulation of male organs (Lukere n.d.a).

REFERENCES

Abel, R.W. 1934 *Charles W. Abel of Kwato: Forty Years in Dark Papua.* New York: Fleming H. Revell Co.
Bacchi, C. 1980 Evolution, eugenics and women. In E. Windschuttle (ed.) *Women, Class and History.* Melbourne: Fontana/Collins, 132–56.

Barker, P. 1992 *Regeneration.* Harmondsworth: Penguin Books.

1994 *The Eye in the Door.* Harmondsworth: Penguin Books.

1995 *The Ghost Road.* Harmondsworth: Penguin Books.

Beauvoir, S. de 1972(1949) *The Second Sex* (trans. and ed. H.M. Parshley). Harmondsworth: Penguin Books.

Chodorow, N. 1978 *The Reproduction of Mothering: Psychoanalysis and the Sociology of Gender.* Berkeley: University of California Press.

Davidoff, L. and Hall, C. 1987 *Family Fortunes: Men and Women of the English Middle Class, 1780–1850.* London: Hutchinson.

Davin, A. 1978 Imperialism and motherhood. *History Workshop* 5:9–65.

Decrease Report 1896 *Report of the Commission Appointed to Inquire into the Decrease of the Native Population.* Suva: Government Printer.

De Lepervanche, M. 1989 Woman, nation and the state in Australia. In N. Yuval-Davis and F. Anthias (eds.) *Woman–Nation–State.* London: Macmillan, 36–57.

Denoon, D. 1989 Medical care and gender in Papua New Guinea. In M. Jolly and M. Macintyre (eds.) *Family and Gender in the Pacific: Domestic Contradictions and the Colonial Impact.* Cambridge: Cambridge University Press, 95–107.

Dureau, C. 1994 Mixed blessings: Christianity and history in women's lives on Simbo, Western Solomon Islands. PhD thesis, Macquarie University, Sydney.

Durrad, W.J. 1922 The depopulation of Melanesia. In W.H.R. Rivers (ed.) *Essays on the Depopulation of Melanesia.* Cambridge: Cambridge University Press, 3–24.

Forbes, G. 1986 In search of the 'pure heathen': missionary women in nineteenth century India. *Economic and Political Weekly* 21(17):WS2–WS8.

Gilligan, C. 1982 *In a Different Voice.* Harvard: Harvard University Press.

Gordon, L. 1975 Race suicide and the feminist response. *Hecate* 1(2):40–53.

Grimshaw, B. 1905 Life in the New Hebrides. *Sydney Morning Herald,* 25 November 1905–6 January 1906.

1907 *In the Strange South Seas.* London: Hutchinson and Co.

Grimshaw, P. 1989 *Paths of Duty: American Missionary Wives in Nineteenth Century Hawaii.* Honolulu: University of Hawaii Press.

Gunn, W. Rev. 1914 *The Gospel in Futuna.* London: Hodder and Stoughton.

Hanson, F.A. 1982 Female pollution in Polynesia? *Journal of the Polynesian Society* 91(3):335–81.

Huggins, J. 1993 Pretty deadly *tidda* business. In S. Gunew and A. Yeatman (eds.) *Feminism and the Politics of Difference.* Sydney: Allen and Unwin, 61–72.

Hull, T.H. 1989 The hygiene program in the Netherlands East Indies: roots of primary health care in Indonesia. In P. Cohen and J. Purcal (eds.) *The Political Economy of Primary Health Care in Southeast Asia.* Canberra: Australian Development Studies Network and ASEAN Training Centre for Primary Health Care Development, 140–8.

Im Thurn, Sir Everard F. 1922 Preface. In W.H.R. Rivers (ed.) *Essays on the Depopulation of Melanesia.* Cambridge: Cambridge University Press.

Irigaray, L. 1985 *This Sex Which Is Not One* (trans. C. Porter with C. Burke). Ithaca, NY: Cornell University Press.

Jolly, M. 1991 'To save the girls for brighter and better lives': Presbyterian missions and women in the south of Vanuatu, 1848–1870. *Journal of Pacific History* 26(1):27–48.

1992 Custom and the way of the land: past and present in Vanuatu and Fiji. In M. Jolly and N. Thomas (eds.) *The Politics of Tradition in the Pacific*. Oceania Special Issue 62(4):330–54.

1993 Colonizing women: the maternal body and empire. In S. Gunew and A. Yeatman (eds.) *Feminism and the Politics of Difference*. Sydney: Allen and Unwin, 103–27.

1994 *Women of the Place:* Kastom, *Colonialism and Gender in Vanuatu*. Reading and Chur: Harwood Academic Publishers.

n.d.a *Engendering Colonialism: European Visions of Women in Vanuatu* (typescript).

n.d.b Damming the rivers of milk? Fertility, sexuality and celibacy in Vanuatu, Fiji and Amazonia. Paper for Wenner Gren Symposium No. 21, Amazonia and Melanesia: Gender and Anthropological Comparison, 7–15 September 1996, Mijas, Spain.

Jolly, M. and Macintyre, M. 1989 (eds.) *Family and Gender in the Pacific: Domestic Contradictions and the Colonial Impact*. Cambridge: Cambridge University Press.

Keesing, R.M. 1989 Sins of a mission: Christian life as Kwaio traditionalist ideology. In M. Jolly and M. Macintyre (eds.) *Family and Gender in the Pacific: Domestic Contradictions and the Colonial Impact*. Cambridge: Cambridge University Press, 193–212.

Knapman, C. 1986 *White Women in Fiji 1835–1930: The Ruin of Empire?* Sydney: Allen and Unwin.

Kristeva, J. 1980 Motherhood according to Giovanni Bellini. In J. Kristeva *Desire in Language: A Semiotic Approach to Literature and Art* (trans. T. Gora, A. Jardine and L.S. Roudiez, ed. L.S. Roudiez). New York: Columbia University Press, 237–70.

Langmore, D. 1989 *Missionary Lives: Papua 1874–1914*. Pacific Islands Monograph Series, No. 6. Honolulu: University of Hawaii Press.

Lukere, V. n.d.a Mothers of the Taukei. PhD thesis in preparation. The Australian National University, Canberra.

n.d.b Fijian women and the decrease of the race. Paper under consideration by a journal.

Macnaught, T. 1982 *The Fijian Colonial Experience: A Study of the Neotraditional Order under British Colonial Rule Prior to World War II*. Pacific Research Monograph No. 7. Canberra: The Australian National University.

Manderson, L. 1982 Bottle feeding and ideology in colonial Malaya: the production of change. *International Journal of Health Services* 12(4):597–616.

1987 Blame, responsibility and remedial action: death, disease and the infant in early twentieth century Malaya. In N. Owen (ed.) *Death and Disease in Southeast Asia: Explorations in Social, Medical and Demographic History*. Singapore: Oxford University Press for the Asian Studies Association of Australia, 257–82.

1989 Political economy and the politics of gender: maternal and child health in colonial Malaya. In P. Cohen and J. Purcal (eds.) *The Political Economy of Primary Health Care in Southeast Asia.* Canberra: Australian Development Studies Network and ASEAN Training Centre for Primary Health Care Development, 79–100.

Ortner, S. 1974 Is female to male as nature is to culture? In M. Rosaldo and L. Lamphere (eds.) *Woman, Culture and Society.* Stanford: Stanford University Press, 67–88.

Osteria, T.S. 1984 *Report on the Maternal and Child Health Survey of Vanuatu.* Port Vila: Ministry of Health, Government of the Republic of Vanuatu.

Pitt-Rivers, G.H.L.F. 1927 *The Clash of Culture and the Contact of Races.* London: George Routledge and Sons.

Ramusack, B.N. 1990 Cultural missionaries, maternal imperialists, feminist allies: British women activists in India, 1865–1945. *Women's Studies International Forum* 13(4): 309–21.

Rivers, W.H.R. 1922 (ed.) *Essays on the Depopulation of Melanesia.* Cambridge: Cambridge University Press.

Roberts, S.H. 1927 *Population Problems of the Pacific.* London: Routledge and Sons.

Rosaldo, M. and Lamphere, L. 1974 (eds.) *Woman, Culture and Society.* Stanford: Stanford University Press.

Saleeby, C.W. 1909 *Parenthood and Race Culture.* London: Cassell.

Speiser, F. 1922 Decadence and preservation in the New Hebrides. In W.H.R. Rivers (ed.) *Essays on the Depopulation of Melanesia.* Cambridge: Cambridge University Press, 25–61.

  1990[1923] *The Ethnology of Vanuatu: An Early Twentieth Century Study.* Bathurst, Australia: Crawford House.

Stepan, N.L. 1991 *'The Hour of Eugenics': Race, Gender and Nation in Latin America.* Ithaca and London: Cornell University Press.

Strathern, M. 1988 *The Gender of the Gift: Problems with Women and Problems with Society in Melanesia.* Berkeley and Los Angeles: University of California Press.

Thomas, N. 1990 Sanitation and seeing: the creation of state power in early Colonial Fiji. *Comparative Studies in Society and History* 32:149–70.

Trebilcot, J. 1983 (ed.) *Mothering: Essays in Feminist Theory.* Totowa, NJ: Rowman and Allenheld.

Underhill-Sem, Y. 1994 Blame it all on population: perceptions, statistics and reality in the population debate in the Pacific. In 'A. Emberson-Bain (ed.) *Sustainable Development or Malignant Growth? Perspectives of Pacific Island Women.* Suva: Marama Publications, 1–15.

Usborne, C. 1992 *The Politics of the Body in Weimar Germany.* London: Macmillan.

Walter, A. and Bourdy, G. 1986 Pregnancy and confinement in Vanuatu – methodological notes and preliminary results. Anthropology Work Paper No. 6, April (mimeo). Port Vila: ORSTOM.

Young, M. 1989 'Suffer the children': Wesleyans in the D'Entrecasteaux. In M. Jolly and M. Macintyre (eds.) *Family and Gender in the Pacific: Domestic Contradictions and the Colonial Impact.* Cambridge: Cambridge University Press, 108–34.

Unpublished sources (consulted in Government Archives, Suva, Fiji)
CSO 2320/1895.
Minutes of the provincial council meeting at Naibita Nailega, 26–7 April 1899.
Minutes of the provincial council meeting at Tubairata, Mavua, 21 November 1923.
Minutes of the provincial council meeting of Colo East at Korovatu, 17 September 1925.
Minutes of the provincial council meeting of Colo West at Taqaqe, 3–5 November 1926.
Minutes of the provincial council meeting at Lawaqa, 28 September 1928.

Just add water: remaking women through childbirth, Anganen, Southern Highlands, Papua New Guinea

Leanne Merrett-Balkos

Introduction

The first Catholic mission health sisters of the Capuchin Order from Switzerland arrived at Det, in the Southern Highlands Province of Papua New Guinea, in 1969 following the establishment of the mission in 1964. One of the women originally posted there was still present at the mission in 1988 and she recalled some of the events from that period of early interaction with the Anganen. In the establishment of the aid post, the sisters focused primarily on the health of birthing women and their children. With this goal in mind, the sisters encouraged women from nearby villages to give birth at the aid post, then built of corrugated iron with a dirt floor. The sister with whom I spoke related accounts of trekking into the hills surrounding Det and walking women who were late in their pregnancy to the aid post. Sometimes the women went into labour en route, leaving the sisters with no option but to light a fire and set up a makeshift camp in the bush until after the birth.

Through the birth records kept at the centre I discovered the second birth there was in 1970 by a woman living at Kamberi. This was the same area in which I lived in the late 1980s and, as it turned out, I knew both the woman who gave birth and her daughter. In that same year, the sisters assisted with a further fifty-five deliveries, both in the bush and at the aid post. This suggests a remarkable intervention rate by the sisters in birthing practices. The factors facilitating this relatively high rate of intervention are difficult to discern, but there appear to be at least two dominant ones: the acceptance of the sisters' power and authority by Anganen women; and the influence of women's perception of colonization. One might ask what choice women had, but, equally, I might ask why Anganen men did not intervene.

The initial establishment of the health centre was marked by a radical and unprecedented protest at the aid post. Accounts by both mission sisters and Anganen women who were present on this particular occasion suggest that it signalled a disruption to the relationship between the sisters (embodying colonial and mission power) and the colonized Anganen women. This was, moreover, an act of protest at a time when the language barrier between whites and the Anganen was vast. Early in 1970 several hundred angry Anganen women sat down in and around the aid post. A local man who worked at the mission was found to translate from Pidgin to Anganen. He explained that the women wanted placentas taken from mothers who had given birth at the aid post to be returned to them. The sisters had, by this time, already disposed of the afterbirth and, for health reasons, would not agree to give birthing women their placentas in the future. Eventually a compromise was reached: the sisters and protesting women agreed that a few inches of umbilical cord would be retained by new mothers.

This incident raises the question: why was the placenta so important to Anganen women – so important that its loss prompted a mass protest? As the following discussion reveals, the afterbirth is pivotal to the construction of women's identity, including awareness of their location in the world. It also raises other questions regarding Anganen women's experience of colonial and mission influences.

The Anganen were renowned by patrol and administration officers as difficult. The Anganen threatened and attacked several patrols during the 1950s (Nihill 1986). Although the region was 'pacified' and derestricted in 1964, there was another significant incidence of violence between the Anganen in 1965–6, which resulted in the arrest and imprisonment of men in Mendi following a forced march from the area in leg chains. This incident is still prominent in the memories of older women who recounted great fear for themselves and the lives of their men. Anganen women were then sent to work on the construction of the road which had previously been undertaken by the arrested men. So they, too, received a form of punishment for the outbreak of hostilities.

Following these events a permanent administration and patrol post was established at nearby Poroma, and from this period on the Anganen had much closer contact with colonial agents. Women in particular had direct experience of whites through the establishment of the Capuchin mission at Det, where many were brought to work in the mission gardens in the early 1970s. Through the mission both Anganen men and women came to associate whites with wealth and saw a potential increase of wealth for themselves. Both the notion and the expectation of 'development' were fostered.

In the early years of contact and interaction with whites, Anganen women experienced the power of both colonialism and the Catholic mission. It may well be that with this cognizance of external power to bring harm and/or wealth the women had little choice but to go to the aid post with the sisters to give birth. The mission sisters exerted considerable influence with their personal commitment to improving maternal and child health and ability to communicate despite lacking a common language. The rapid increase in the number of Anganen women who attended the health post to give birth is testament to this.

In the relatively brief period since the late 1960s, Anganen women have been part of rapid social change including an overland road connection to Mendi to the north-east, the introduction of coffee cultivation in individual plots, increasing cash income, Anganen *bisnis* (TP) activities like trade stores and public motor vehicles (PMV in Tok Pisin), the mission, videos and the advent of national politics. Change has been particularly evident in health care for women and children, and especially birthing practices. Anganen women have largely ceased bearing children in the isolation of the 'mother house', *engi and*, located at their husbands' place. The majority of women now give birth at the mission health centre attended by sisters trained in Western biomedical practices. During 1987/8 virtually all pregnant women living within easy walking distance of Det (up to two hours) came to give birth at the health centre. Women whose parturition is expected to be difficult are transported from more distant and isolated areas by four-wheel drive or helicopter loaned by the oil exploration company at nearby Poroma (part of an agreement to provide assistance in medical emergencies).

These changes have important implications for the cultural conceptions held by Anganen women as well as the processes of identity construction. To address this issue I adopt my female informants' notion of time expressed in Pidgin as the disjunction between *bipo* (TP) (before) and *nau* (TP) (now, or the period since) the arrival of whites. For Anganen women perceive their way of living as punctuated by the arrival of whites, and especially the establishment of the mission in 1964. Women talk of 'before' and 'now' – the entire period since the coming of whites – as distinct periods, pointing out the differences in values and practice. Yet they also recognize similarities between these two phases. There are, of course, inconsistencies between the views expressed by women of different generations about the qualitative or moral value of practices undertaken 'before' and 'after' the coming of whites, for example in coffee cultivation or work for cash income (see Merrett 1992).

Older women with adult children and grandchildren of their own commonly emphasize the positive value of work done in the time *bipo* (TP): this work was harder and, for them at least, of greater value than work done since. Work which is not so 'hard', that is, made easier by steel implements such as shovels and cutting tools, is seen to devalue the women who undertake it. Younger women do not dispute this view, but neither do they choose to confirm it. Their silence is, however, accompanied by a respect for their husbands' mother and older women in general.

Essential to this discussion of generational difference is a consideration of the paradigms and metaphors which shape women's knowledge of the world. This enables a consideration of the significance of some changes following colonization in the epistemology of Anganen women. This is more than a review of 'before' and 'after' and a comparison of the intrusiveness or not of colonial power relations on an indigenous people: it is a vignette of Anganen epistemology in the complex processes of changing gender relations with mission contact and colonization. Thus, while I focus on women's accounts of birthing practices undertaken 'before' their use of the health centre, I use this as the theoretical basis for an analysis of the meanings women articulate about birthing at the health centre in the contemporary context. Finally I return to the implications of changing practice for the understandings held by women and their construction of identity.

Self, identity and birth

I take a phenomenological approach to the construction of identity, assuming a universal experience of self in the world and processes underlying the development of cultural meanings. But Melanesian 'personhood' (Strathern 1988)[1] is predicated on kinship relations into which a person is born. Identity is thus constructed and enacted throughout a person's life, and in death, through the actions of others. Exchanges of wealth in Anganen, as with other Highland groups, both express and give substance to relations with others. From this perspective each person is both partible and has 'multiple authors' (Biersack 1991; Jolly 1992; Strathern 1988).

Identity, and knowledge of the world, is an ongoing struggle attained through metaphoric processes. Two points are central to my argument: first, the fundamental connection between the experience of birth for women and the construction of self; and second, the particular notion that the neonate is not yet constituted as a person. The child has a limited human identity, although the neonate is regarded as existent in corporeal terms.

I draw on the work of Fernandez, who talks of the 'primordial human condition' as one of 'inchoateness' (1986:11, 223, 263). The quest is to 'predicate' some identity upon 'others' and 'self' (1986:11) where predication comprises the location of self in the world with reference to objects and others. This process is essentially the same for children as it is for birthing women. For example, Anganen women's identity is overwhelmingly predicated on conceptions of mothering – although this is undergoing some change with the involvement of women in cash-generating activities. Thus, through predications such as 'women are like sweet potato runners' and 'women are the road', or links between groups of men in marriage, some of the qualities of the predicative source are conveyed to the subject. The subject about whom the predication is made moves from a lesser known to a better known realm of experience.[2]

Anganen women's 'everyday' identity is premised on such metaphors as 'women are like sweet potato runners' and 'women are the road', that is, women are identified with objects appropriate to their gender and thus are constituted as 'Anganen' women. So, sweet potatoes and women both have a flexible attachment to place and are 'replanted' between communities (Merrett 1992). If this is the quotidian form of female identity, what occurs during birth? I argue there is a disjuncture caused by birthing which requires the repredication of women's identity, and constructs a dualistic notion of gender at a much more fundamental level.

As Anganen women tell it, during the process of birth they experience a loss of identity and become disoriented from the world. This disorientation is addressed through the articulation of bodily exuviae as symbols – the placenta and umbilical cord. Through cutting, handling and burying the afterbirth, women reinternalize the two gendered modes of being which constitute the dualistic structure of the social order, they gain awareness of their place in the world in relation to men, the gendered other.

But to explicate this I need to locate the Anganen.

The Anganen

The Anganen are located in the Lai and Nembi valley of the Southern Highlands Province of Papua New Guinea. They reside in small villages scattered throughout named territories associated with agnatic clans. Descendants of several clans reside in one territory and may act as a territorial group. The Anganen are largely shifting horticulturalists – growing sweet potato, bananas, green leaf vegetables, sugar-cane, beans and so on – and pig rearers, although coffee has become increasingly important as a cash crop in recent years. The activities, interests and to some extent values of women and men are clearly gendered, with women relocating at marriage to cultivate gardens at their husbands' place (see Plates 8 and 9). Men are active in the heavier productive tasks and

8 Anganen women working in a sweet potato garden.

9 *Yasolu* (ceremonial pig-kill and exchange) – woman tending pig.

political exchanges of wealth. These exchanges locate men in the social world and articulate the fabric of a particular kind of Anganen social relationship, notably the connection between members of different clans and territorial groups. Women do not publicly participate in political or exchange affairs and can be said to be located 'in between' individual men and groups (M. Strathern 1972). In essence, women are not the same kind of clan members as men and are characterized by a different form of personhood. Thus, personhood is gendered.

Since the 1960s the Anganen have experienced changes in gender relations. In particular the cultivation of coffee in individually held plots and consequent access to cash has effected changes, as has Anganen participation at the mission church. Men have become active in what is colloquially known as *bisnis* (TP), such as running local stores, selling coffee to travelling buyers and running public motor vehicles. Wage labour on tea and coffee plantations elsewhere in the Highlands or even labour work on the coast is also regarded as *bisnis* (TP). Men's involvement has, to some extent, transformed the significance of their involvement in exchange activities, especially *moka* (TP) (the ceremonial exchange of wealth including pigs and pearlshells) (Nihill 1986, 1991). But there has been another dimension to such changes in gendered activity. In 1988 some women were planting peanuts with the specific intention of roadside sale. Women have gained direct access to small amounts of cash through the sale of vegetables at the market or roadside and, they believe, to the powers of Jesus and Mary.

The outcome of these changing gender relations in 1988 included the increasing shift of men into activities for cash income (although the interpretation of the significance of these activities deserves separate attention, see Nihill 1991), while women have become more involved in the mission and express the desire to gain access to the beneficence of Mary. This situation has generated a complex set of relations in which men and women are renegotiating their relations in the context of both existing Anganen paradigms and those of colonialism. But the fundamental metaphors/paradigms of Anganen gender are reproduced. Indeed, it is precisely these metaphors/paradigms of meaning and action that provide the plan and propel Anganen actions and constructions of meaning into the future as it becomes the present.

The act of birth: severing the umbilical cord and planting the placenta

In the past, when birth was imminent, women secluded themselves in an *engi and*, literally 'mother house', away from the main settlement. These houses were built by women and used by those married into a particular *lain* (TP) or subclan. 'Mother houses' were located on the lower slopes on the high ridges on which settlements were built – primarily for defence positions in times of dispute. Women say these houses were also located in the scrubby regrowth of gardens left in fallow rather than currently cultivated sites or uncleared bushland.

Except in cases of extreme distress, where the life of the child and/or mother appeared threatened, women experienced and managed delivery in isolation. In such cases women, preferably of the same line as the birthing mother and married into the residential group, came to the birthing woman's assistance. Precisely how or when it was determined that assistance during birth was required is not known, but it is generally accepted that the woman would 'sing out'. Whether this was an intentional request for aid or an indication of suffering is unclear.

The only preparation a woman made for the birth of her child was the placement of bamboo tubes of water and a bamboo knife in the 'mother house'. Following delivery, the umbilical cord was tied with string made of bush fibres and cut with sharpened bamboo after it had ceased to pulsate. Women washed themselves and their infants in water they themselves had carried and, later, when sufficiently recovered, 'planted' the placenta and attached cord.

The *nu,* or placenta, was wrapped in fresh banana leaves and fastened with vine. The bundle was either placed in the highest crook of a nearby tree, preferably a casuarina, which the women could reach, or was buried in the ground. In both cases the *nu* had to be 'planted' in the child's father's clan ground. The *nu* of a child inadvertently born at the mother's natal place was wrapped in banana leaves and carried to the child's father's place for 'planting'. While some women suggested that the placental 'base-place' of children of either sex is planted in this way, one elderly woman claimed only male children's *nu* should be placed in trees.

In the contemporary context of mission health care, women no longer give birth in *engi and* nor plant their child's *nu* in trees. Nevertheless, the overall significance of the practice persists. Newborn infants and their mothers spend from three to seven days at the health centre where mothers are fed rice, tinned fish and vegetables from mission supplies and gardens. Soon after parturition each mother is given a small section of umbilical cord (about two to three inches), which they keep with them at all times until returning home. On one occasion I visited a young neighbour in hospital after she bore her first child. The young woman proudly produced a section of her son's umbilical cord for me to see from its newspaper wrapping.

When she leaves the health centre every mother takes with her a piece of umbilical cord and secretes it in or near her residence. This practice arose after Anganen women demanded the afterbirth be returned to them by the sisters when the first women came to the health centre to give birth. After some disputation the Anganen women agreed to take a portion of umbilical cord in its stead and, through this action, condensed the significance of the entire afterbirth into a short piece of umbilical cord.

One possible reason the women accepted a portion of the cord as a substitute in this way is that, following parturition, the placenta is considered rotting rubbish. It is foul-smelling, full of blood and decays relatively quickly. The cord, however, dries out and will keep for many years. Several young mothers living at Kamberi revealed – to the consternation and distress of an old woman who feared sorcery may be worked through the knowledge – that they hid their children's umbilical cord in the thatching of their house. Other women, they claimed, buried the cord in the ground near their residence.

From the sisters' perspective, they agreed to return a section of the umbilical cord, partly because it could be washed and hygiene was, and continues to be, a high priority for the mission sisters. The fact that the sisters did negotiate on the issue of birthing demonstrates something else, however. In spite of the prevailing colonial power relations the Capuchin sisters have shown a high degree of consideration and respect for local *kastom* (TP). For their part Anganen women, like their male counterparts, are skilful negotiators, and this played a role in the outcome of this interaction.

Gender and the afterbirth

Femaleness, mediation, roads and mongol

The umbilical cord is also known as the 'road' or *polu* (TP) between mother and child. The road indicates more than a path for physical transportation however, it is also the metaphor for relatedness. Most importantly, married women are the connection between *mbetinu*, affinally related men. In the context of birth the umbilical cord is thus more than a path for physical connection.

Vital substance, *ip* (*gris* (TP)), flows from the mother to the unborn child along this path and the cord is the source of life for an infant. The Anganen recognize the importance of this link by specifying the cord should never be cut before it stops pulsating or while it has life. The *ip* which flows from mother to child comprises the food a woman eats, but it also conveys aspects of identity to the unborn.[3] While a woman may primarily eat food grown on her husband's clan land, the child consumes *ip* transformed by the mother and then conveyed through the umbilical cord. For the child there is a duality of transformation and transmission of substance and identity.

An infant relies totally on his or her mother for life and, until the cord is cut and tied, remains physically attached to his or her mother. This connection is known as *ronga*, meaning to 'bind' or 'fasten'. After delivery, the corporeal form of this link remains through direct consumption of mother's substance as breast 'milk'. During this period women are careful to take actions that will encourage the infant's spirit (*remo*) not to wander, especially during sleep. Likewise special kinds of leaves are placed in the base of a child's net-bag to entice the spirit to stay as well as to promote growth in the child. Net-bags themselves are considered to have growth-promoting and protective qualities for the children they carry, with a single net-bag for each infant. They are part of the way in which women continue to convey their nurturance to their children. The embodiment of women's essence in both the bush string and net-bags which they construct is discussed elsewhere (Merrett 1992).[4]

Before birth a child 'eats' woman's procreative substance, or *waluma* and *ip* transformed from ingested food.[5] Following birth a child continues to consume his or her mother's *ip* in the form of breast milk. After the first months of subsisting only on breast milk and once they begin to move about, children eat their mothers' *ip* transmitted through hard work (*kele*) and embodied in the products of that work such as sweet potato. In particular, a neonate remains a single entity with the mother until he or she begins to eat solid food and the fontanelle closes over. Likewise, children consume the products of men's hard work, but, at this time of a child's growth, women do not attribute any significance to this complementary consumption of nurture. Mothers consider themselves the archetypical nourishers and growers of children.

In contrast to these assertions by women, Anganen men place considerable significance on feeding children 'male' food. Fathers are generally held to feed children their first solid food in the form of mashed banana. This food is gendered male and has some significance for the joint 'taming' (*kumupi*), of children by their parents (pers. comm. Nihill). There is a complementarity between women's role in nurturing infants and men's role in taming children, which is partly expressed through conceptions about the appropriate gendered feeding of children as they grow.

The severance and tying of the umbilical cord is the initial act which eventually culminates in an infant being acknowledged as a person in his or her own right. After the natal 'road' is sealed and cut, the bond between mother and child remains – regardless of the distance between them. This 'road' is not limited by space or time. At death, for instance, it is the 'road' of *mongol* which links a person with their deceased natal kin and is recognized through mortuary compensation payments.

Notably, it is in the act of cutting the cord that the multivocality of *mongol* emerges. An important example of this concerns the severance of the umbilical cord, which is known as *pheti*. In kinship terms, *pheti* also refers to a woman's male affines. Men in this category include a woman's husband, husband's brothers and husband's clan brothers. As the cord is the corporeal embodiment of the relationship between a child and his or her mother, and therefore at the structural level of mother's brother and maternal clan, the cutting and tying of this 'road' indicates the tension between maternal and paternal kinship relations.

Specifically, in a social system structured by male clan solidarity and co-residence it is a woman's husband and his clan brothers who separate her from her natal kin at marriage. A woman's *pheti* separate and 'cut' her off from daily contact with her natal kin. The category of male affines (*pheti*) comes to represent the separation that women experience with marriage. From the perspective of a man's wife, the consequences of a social structure founded on patrilineality, male solidarity and virilocality are located in the specific kinship category of husband and husband's brothers. At birth, it is the same category of male affines with whom a newborn child is associated by patrilineality and clanship. In this context *pheti*, as a category of men, distances a child from his or her maternal kin and clan. This separation is a structural replication which resonates with women's experience of the distancing of themselves from their natal kin at marriage.

It is perhaps more than coincidence that birth, particularly *mongol* severance and fastening, is also the time when a child's spirit (*remo*) is bound to his or her physical presence. In contrast to the animating force of *wesa*, which is gained during pregnancy, *remo* is fastened to a child at birth. *Remo* is associated with personal and clan identity and it is this 'essence' which lingers near the living after death. The time of *mongol* fastening is also the time when a child gains identity with his or her father's clan. While the Anganen do not explicitly identify the assumption of *remo* with the acquisition of paternal clan identity, there is a logical association between the two. In addition, when the cord is cut and the child is distanced from maternal kin and clan, a woman's *pheti*, who are also a child's clansmen, gain a significant claim to that child as the source of his or her being. What women did not assert, however, was that children born at the mission acquire some form of Christian spirit at the time of birth in the same way it is held that infants gain the *remo* of their fathers' line. This would appear to be an unresolved issue in the minds of women, but there is certainly the potential for greater influence by the mission and hence attribution of postcolonial powers in this situation.

There are other implications of this conception of birthing transposed into the setting of the mission. In particular, younger women generally assert that children born at the mission are more likely to desire Western goods. There is certainly some association with these children and the assumption of Western values and potentially, or so women hope, the wealth which whites seem to access so readily. In addition, women believe the Christian spirit Mary protects both the birthing mother and the neonate during this dangerous period. There is a dual conception of protection by powerful external spirits and of potential access to wealth items, including well-being (cf. Read 1966).

While men are more likely to perceive *bisnis* (TP) as the way to access the wealth of whites, women have for the most part aligned themselves with the mission. A large part of this tendency is tied to the influence exerted by mission sisters, who hold impressive sway over both sexes in everyday as well as life-threatening situations. It is perhaps also significant that the sisters have such influence over both the Anganen and their enemies, whoever these may be at the time, given the complex political relations which permeate the region. There have also been noticeable improvements in the morbidity and mortality of Anganen women and children, which is directly attributed to the combined power of the sisters' ministrations and their associated Christian spirits. It must be said, however, that younger women do have a pragmatic approach to their involvement with the mission. They perceive benefits for themselves and their children, which they seek to access. Men, they say, can look after themselves. In this regard, women's conception of Christian spirits is much more a transposition of notions held about traditional Anganen spirits than any 'conversion' to Catholicism.

Maleness, 'base-place', trees and nu

Territoriality is central to male notions of being in the world. There is a close connection between Anganen notions of the land and the time of *bipo tru* (TP), or of the ancestors. The spirits of dead kinsmen are believed to be located on and in their territorial ground and to have a continuing influence on both the fertility and growth of the land and the well-being, including prosperity, of those currently living. While this is the traditional view of the relationship between the living, the ancestors and place, and is certainly significant in the strong desire to be buried on one's ground even

now, there are complications introduced by migration. Women are consistently placed in an invidious position, some claiming their spirits return
to their fathers' place, others saying they stay with their husband at their
territorial place. Some enterprising women quite reasonably suggest the
spirits of women have a choice and that they remain where they are most
wanted.

Place is equally significant for birth. In pre-mission times a woman
would ensure she gave birth at her husband's place – to give birth at her
father's place would be a flagrant disregard for the marriage and an
indication that the woman sought to return to her father and brothers. It
would seem that, in conjunction with traditional practices and views on
the placement of the placenta and the high priority Anganen women give
to the retaining and location of at least part of the afterbirth, territory is an
important marker in birth as well.

In the present as well as prior to the advent of the mission, once the
umbilical cord has been cut, the placenta is outside a woman's body and
is no longer the child's source of life. At this stage *nu* is regarded as
dangerous, polluting waste. Full of unshed and congealed menstrual
substance, the placenta is regarded as *remi*, 'rotten', foul-smelling and
decaying rubbish. The placenta also has positive connotations, however,
since it is the uterine 'base-place' of a child. Every placenta is unique to
the child, whose life it supports, and is said to belong to the child rather
than the mother. This strong identification between child and his or her
'base-place' gives special significance to the disposal of *nu*. The placenta
carries or gives life to and nourishes a child. The menstrual substance of a
woman is different every time it emerges, and every *nu* formed from that
substance gives rise to a different child. In this logic, a placenta is
identified with the child, and not the child's mother.

Following birth, a mother's actions towards the placenta have meaning
beyond the disposal of body leavings. As a uterine 'base-place', *nu* has the
same characteristics as clan and clan land, which are likewise the 'base' of
clan members. The significance of the bond (*ronga*) between a child and
its physiological, uterine source is infused with the meaning of the bond
between clan members, clan land and clan as a socio-political group. In a
similar way, relations with significance for the reproduction of groups and
clans are fused with the specific, visible connection between mother,
placenta and child. Tree or ground burial of the placenta is the action
which effects this fusion of meaning such that a mother's actions enact
both these dimensions and enliven the meanings of clanship, the ground
and territoriality. The fundamental relations constitutive of Anganen
groupness is reaffirmed through precisely those persons rendered ambiguous by those relations, that is, women themselves.

Deconstituting and reconstituting women

My argument here is grounded in the construct of women's identity, posited through metaphors. Being women involved in sweet potato gardening and pig rearing contributes to the construction of and provides a domain of experience in which women's identity as mothers shapes a larger ontological view of a human lifespan (see Merrett 1992 for a more detailed exploration of this process).

For Anganen women childbirth is both similar to the work of growing sweet potato and pigs, and unique in itself. This uniqueness lies partly in birth as the archetypal generative act and partly in woman's experience of producing an entity from her own body. In sweet potato cultivation and pig rearing women's actions in *kele* (labour) are directed towards the object of her attention; in birth women's *kele* is upon herself. Rather than a subject acting towards an object, woman is simultaneously subject and object. The significance of this will become apparent in the following discussion.

Childbirth, or *rabo*, is the most painful and difficult form of *kele*. While some women locate the pain of birth deep inside the pelvic region, others do not give it a specific location, indicating instead its diffusion throughout the body. The construction of childbirth pain as internal, diffuse and encompassing corresponds to women's comments about losing awareness and will, or *kone*, during labour. Women say the pain of birth is so intense they 'lose all thought or awareness of who or where they are'. In particular, women say they 'forget' their kin, and if they stood in front of them would not know their faces. After giving birth women become disoriented; in particular, they are unaware if it is day or night, hot or cold, or how long they have been in the house of birth.

Women in childbirth lose awareness of not just their place in the world of space and time, but of their place in social relationships. In essence, women lose awareness of their mode of being. During the extraordinary experience of childbirth women temporarily transcend or stand outside of their existing social relationships and the larger social order. It is appropriate, therefore, that birthing women are physically located outside of everyday social space. In the past, *engi and* ('mother house') were located on cleared but uncultivated land, the transitional region between everyday living space on mountain ridges, cultivated gardens and uncultivated bush. With the advent of the mission health centre, birthing women are still positioned beyond the daily living space of Anganen women and men – in this case, within the auspices of Westerners, their knowledge and spirits.

During this period of pain and loss of awareness, a woman is extremely vulnerable, particularly to the loss of spirit from her body. In addition, the nexus of social relations which uniquely identify and locate a woman are, from the perspective of the birthing women, dissolved. Her integration into collective, social life is, for the duration of this experience, annulled and must be reconstructed following birth. In this sense, women's apparent externality to the constraining principles of social structure at the time of birth is a potential threat to that structure. The usual order of social life must be restored, identity and structural location reconstituted. This reconstitution of structure and women's place in it is effected through the manipulation of *nu* and *mongol* together with their meanings and the potential awareness of being this generates.

Likewise, it is only after the primary principles of social organization have been reconstituted within woman herself that women's exegesis becomes meaningful. Without the principles of clanship and affinal exchange women's interstitiality would either not exist, or would be constructed differently. Women's awareness and experience of their being rests on their prior incorporation into a particular form of social order. Thus, it is only in the context of male groups based on clan land, fraternity and affinal exchange that women's particular construction of being becomes meaningful. It is women's handling of the afterbirth which articulates and re-establishes the significance of Anganen social order.

After giving birth a mother plants the *nu* in the ground, or places it wrapped in banana leaves in the branches of a nearby tree, where it can be eaten by birds. Women's actions in severing the umbilical cord and planting the *nu* with attached cord articulates a complex set of meanings which reconstitute the social order and mode of being for women. In a negative sense the reconstruction of women's ontology also affirms the ontology of men in relation to each other. At the same time women internalize these meanings, and relational ontologies, thereby reconstituting Anganen social order and the duality of gendered modes of being within themselves. Women's actions in handling the afterbirth, concrete representations of multiple meanings and relations between the sexes, articulate and unify these meanings into a single experience.

In some contexts *nu* literally means 'collectivity', for example in *amenu*, namely a collection of *ame* (brothers) and *mbetinu* (men related as affines). In this discussion I focus on the association of *nu* with collectivity, fraternity, 'base-place' and maleness. Correspondingly, *mongol* is associated with the concept of 'road' or connectedness, and in this sense condenses the link between *mbetinu* (woman's husband and woman's father/brother), the location of women as mother and mediator, as well as the road along which wealth flows. *Nu* and *mongol* have at least two different kinds of associations: *nu* represents the fundamental relationships of Anganen social organization, that is *amenu* and *mbetinu*, where *amenu* denotes relatedness between brothers – and is fundamental to the construction of clan solidarity – and *mbetinu* the relationship between men of different *amenu*. *Nu* and *mongol* also represent the duality of these two kinds of relationships. In addition, the duality of gendered modes of being, or the ontology of women and men, is represented in the pairing of *nu* with *mongol*, since *nu* and 'base-place' have male connotations, while *mongol* and 'road' have female connotations. Women's practice of handling the afterbirth articulates the meanings condensed in the afterbirth. Through this practice women reconstruct not only the form of womanhood but their orientation towards the world, especially with regards to the mode of being for men.

As symbolic practice women's manipulation of the placenta and the attached cord is more than a representation of the complementary relation between gendered modes of being. Each individual woman's actions reconstitute and facilitate her reassimilation of the social order. By locating the Anganen social order in the afterbirth, corporeal matter born of woman herself, it is rendered self-evident and 'immutable'.

Women's reconstitution and internalization of the social order also raises the issue of subject–object relations in Anganen. The relation between 'invisible realities', of subjective ideas and the 'material world' (Godelier 1986:229) may be reformulated as the relation between subject and object mediated by symbolic practice. In birth, women objectify the social order and then internalize that order, thereby reconstituting themselves with reference to that order. There is a double movement at this moment between subject (woman) and object (afterbirth). The placenta and umbilical cord move from inside to outside a woman's body, a division recognized and marked by the boundary on the skin, while manipulation of *nu* and *mongol* – together with the meanings these objects condense – are internalized by woman through movement in the reverse direction from outside-object to inside-subject.[6]

The movement between object and subject confers identity on Anganen women and refers to the articulation of meanings through concrete referents or symbols, as in the case of women's manipulation of the afterbirth. Manipulation of the afterbirth structures and reconstitutes women's awareness of dual modes of being in the world. This invests women with the origins of being within themselves – a powerful concept which, to my knowledge, is not overtly expressed elsewhere.

Metaphor, experience and interpretation

Women's reflexivity about their manipulation of the afterbirth and association with other domains of experience comes through comments about *nu* and *mongol*. *Nu* as a generic term for collectivity is likened to net-bags, which are also generically known as *nu*. It is *nu* which is the 'base-place' or source of a child. *Mongol*, in contrast, is known as the 'road' between mother and child. While women do not explicitly associate the afterbirth with aspects of other domains of practice, the meanings articulated by women about *nu* and *mongol* correspond with associations emergent elsewhere. *Nu*, like trees, are associated with collectivity, fraternity, clan solidarity, maleness, territoriality and endurance through time, while sweet potato runners, like *mongol*, are associated with the notion of 'road', connectedness, mediation, transitivity, replantability and femaleness. It is through these correspondences that the different domains of women's practice and experience are brought together and rendered coherent in relation to each other.

On one occasion an elderly woman with adult children and several grandchildren remarked on the planting of the afterbirth, and her comments indicate the potential for reflection about childbirth through *nonope*, an indigenous genre of verbal metaphor. In a discussion about planting the placenta, this old woman remarked that only the afterbirth of boys should be planted in trees. When I enquired about the reason for this she replied: 'A boy child's *nu* is planted in a tree so that he can grow into a big/strong man and one day collect many birds' eggs.'

The old woman would not give any further explanation, expecting – as indeed it is the object of *nonope* – her audience of a young unmarried woman and myself to find our own meaning in the expression. The younger woman could not provide an interpretation of these remarks and instructed me to disregard them, claiming the old woman 'did not make sense'. While in this particular instance and at this particular moment reflection was not generated (since the younger woman did not understand the tale), this genre of verbal aphorism has similarities with women's use of metaphor elsewhere.

The remark was intended to prompt reflection and 'edification' for the listeners,[7] through puzzlement, in a manner comparable to the use of riddles by the Fang of West Africa (Fernandez 1986:171–87).[8] To understand the old woman's remark the listener must move beyond the spoken 'text' to its 'cultural context', including the immediate circumstances in which the response was made as well as the cultural context from which the significance of that remark is drawn (1986:181). The old woman's comment emerged in the context of a discussion about childbirth, specifically in reply to my query concerning why the placenta of male infants were 'planted' in trees. Based on my understanding of Anganen epistemology, its primary location in metaphor and daily practice, the reply was intended for didactic purposes, for both myself and my unmarried, female research assistant.

In the wider cultural context, the remark condenses and conjugates key dimensions of Anganen sociality. Planting a child's placenta is linked with a child's territorial and clan origins and, in particular, the comment focuses on males for whom fraternity, clanship and territoriality are fundamental to their mode of being in and orientation towards the world. There are two sets of relations articulated in this *nonope* which relate specifically the notions of maleness:

birds' eggs – tree
and
boy/man – pearlshell – clan continuity/territoriality

The old woman's remark involves only some of these elements: the boy who grows/transforms into a man; birds' eggs; and tree. If the significance of these elements is explored, it becomes apparent that trees are associated with collectivity, brotherhood, clan continuity and territoriality. This brings together the third pair in these two sets of relations. In *inji*, or fictional stories, men transform into birds (cf. LeRoy 1985), while male dancers at *sing sing* (TP) events are decorated and likened to birds of paradise (Nihill 1986, 1988). Among Anganen speakers birds are also thought to live collectively in groups like people. The Wola to the northwest of Anganen also liken birds to men (Sillitoe 1988).

The reproductivity of birds through eggs also corresponds with Anganen notions of men's actions in exchange as reproductive of social relations. Birds produce eggs and this connection between source and product is analogous to men's view of themselves as the source of pearlshells through exchange. In other parts of the Highlands eggs are metaphorical of crescent-shaped pearlshells (Clark 1991). Wagner (1986) provides some insightful remarks concerning these associations for the Daribi near Mount Karimui. He represents Daribi notions of the connection between human reproduction, kinship and the circulation of objects (pearlshells) in exchange as these are encapsulated in the reproductive cycle of birds. In the imagination of Daribi speakers, birds' eggs and pearlshells metaphorize human reproduction and sociality. Thus: 'Pearlshells . . . embody the relativizing of the life process: they and the considerations and debts they entail restrict, channel, and redistribute the flow of relationships like a sort of escape mechanism. Immortal themselves, they flow unendingly among clans and backwards against the relationships that constitute those clans' (1986:56). The two kinds of reproduction embodied in birds' eggs and pearlshell circulation move in different directions:

The eggs of human beings are immortal – they move externally and opposite to the flow of human reproduction, causing it without ever hatching, whereas birds produce their 'pearlshells' out of their own bodies, only to see them destroyed in production of offspring. People reproduce against the flow of their immortal *ge* [egg/pearlshell]: birds reproduce by moving through their mortal *ge*. (1986:58)

Likewise, the medium of reproduction is both external to the body and generated by it. Indeed, the dynamic of Daribi associations concerning these two entities may lie precisely in the tension between bodily reproduction on the one hand and, on the other, reproduction through the circulation of objects. At this level, these associations also metaphorize women's mode of reproduction in the physical acts of pregnancy and birth, together with men's mode of reproducing social groups through exchange – a set of associations which apply equally well to both Daribi and Anganen peoples. Pearlshells and birds' eggs, therefore, are not only closely connected by people in several Highland societies, but the flow and similarities of these entities stand for key processes of human reproduction and sociality.

In the present discussion the old woman's comments indicate that only male children's placenta should be placed in trees, since only boys are transformed into men, and only men, usually, engage in exchange to 'collect' pearlshells. Several sets of associations are brought into conjunction by the use of *nonope* in this instance, associations which are affirmed through their emergence in other domains of women's experience. Thus:

Mongol	:	*Nu*
Sweet potato runner	:	Tree
Mode of being for women	:	Mode of being for men
Production	:	Exchange

In this particular use of *nonope* not all of these elements are explicitly presented for reflection. Those that are made explicit include:

Mongol	:	*Nu*
—	:	Tree
—	:	Mode of being for men
—	:	Exchange

The reflection generated through this form of verbal metaphor is, therefore, primarily about the mode of being for men, although it is founded on the duality of gendered modes of being in the world and the whole they constitute. Women's reflexivity is oriented towards the other rather than womanhood. Edification about the other is also, to a degree, edification about what woman is not. Indeed, womanhood can only be constituted and reflected upon after the mode of being for men and the principles of social organization, such as fraternity, clan continuity, territoriality, virilocality and exchange, have been established, since it is interstitiality and, relative to men, their lack of incorporation into clans, which is essential to female ontology.

The particular construction of being for women is only significant in the context of the prior constitution of a social order based on male groupness and exchange. It is in the articulation of meanings such as this that there is significant potential for change to be manifest, that is, in Anganen interpretations of birth at the mission. But up until the time I left the New Guinea Highlands, this did not appear to have yet occurred.

Conclusion

At the beginning of this discussion I referred to some of the changes women have experienced since the coming of whites, especially the mission health sisters. The *mongol* and *nu* are still gender-associated, but through removal and burial of most of the afterbirth at the mission they also embody the quality of women's interaction with Westerners. Women who experience the disorientation of birth, therefore, gain an awareness of their place in the world in relation to Westerners, the cultural other, as well as Anganen men, the gendered other. At this point, I raise some of the implications of these changes for the construction of women's identity.

The previous discussion assumes there is a degree of continuity of meaning, or structures of interpretation, between childbearing practice prior to the arrival of the sisters and those of the period when this ethnographic material was gathered. That is, the metaphoric processes of constructing identity have remained unchanged, while the content of those processes have expanded to include Anganen women's experiences of and with Europeans. For example, when the sisters 'took' the afterbirth of women, they removed an entity central to the construction of identity and, for birthing women, the Anganen social order. There is a strong indication of the perceived power not just of whites, but of white mission sisters, which surely must have come into play at the time. This act was in itself a powerful demonstration of the superior strength of Europeans and the mission over the Anganen and their spirits.

By protesting against the loss of their placentas, women regained part of the afterbirth for those who would bear children at the mission health centre in the future. The afterbirth, however, was already laden with the significance of gender relations in which women were 'tamed' by men through marriage. On one hand, the cord came to condense the significance of the entire afterbirth and the Anganen social order; on the other, women received the feminine part of the afterbirth, while the masculine part was located at the mission. This separation of the placenta and umbilical cord was a product of circumstance, but it corresponds with and affirms Anganen perceptions of being 'tamed' by Europeans. The umbilical cord and placenta retain their earlier significance, but in the context of birth at the mission and intervention by the sisters other dimensions are added to these meanings.

Thus far I have addressed only the implications of these activities for Anganen women. My focus has been on exploring the symbolic constructs of Anganen women centred on the experience of birth. There are, of course, implications for children born at the health centre, which I have only touched on in this chapter. For example, there seems to be an emergent connection between children born at the mission and women's strong desire for their offspring to eat Western food, wear Western-style clothes, attend church and school to learn Western ways. It may be that children born at the health centre, and whose placentae are buried there, are perceived to be more closely aligned with Europeans than others. These children have a 'base-place' at the mission as well as their fathers' place. But what significance will, or does this already, have for children now reaching their late teens and early twenties?

Another aspect not explored in this chapter is the mass protest by Anganen women at the mission in 1970, clearly a collective action in the early days of contact with Europeans. Mission influence on Anganen behaviour and cultural values at this time was slight and, therefore, collective action by women was a cultural possibility enabled by indigenous circumstances, in conjunction with outside provocation.

What is the significance of this? Potentially, the significance is enormous. Sexton (1984, 1986) has provided some insight into one form of collective action by Simbu women in the *wok meri* (TP) movement. The majority of existing Highlands literature in the region takes a perspective based on men's experience (Josephides 1983, 1985; Lederman 1986; Nihill 1986). In essence, the distinction between men as exchangers and women as producers (M. Strathern 1972) has been replicated in the ethnographic accounts and theoretical analyses undertaken in Melanesia. There are, however, the beginnings of alternative perspectives on women's role in cultural reproduction in the later works of Strathern (1988), Weiner's (1976) work in the Trobriands and Lederman's (1980, 1986, 1989) work on women's participation in *moka* (TP) wealth exchange.

In the context of existing ethnographies, the collective action demonstrated by Anganen women is clearly a rich area for investigation. Strathern's (1988) discussion of same-sex and cross-sex relations, individual and collective forms is a base from which to proceed. For Anganen women there is same-sex collective action in other domains as well, for example in net-bag and grass-skirt prestations at the time of marriage (Merrett 1992). Cross-sex transactions, on the other hand, are always 'singular' or 'individual'[9] in nature.

Taking existing theoretical and ethnographic research further, there may well be a continuum of cultural forms similar to that explored in relation to modes of production, in types of exchange and ceremonial activity across Melanesia (Feil 1987; Lindenbaum 1984). The distinction drawn between bodily and non-bodily forms of wealth/substance used in transactions is particularly interesting here. Godelier's work with the Baruya (1986), for example, hints at this (cf. Lindenbaum 1984) with the exchange of breast milk among women, while for the Simbu, *wok meri* (TP) demonstrates a kind of ritualized 'banking' exchange and reproduction of social groups by women. Closer to the Anganen, Lederman (1980, 1986, 1989) discusses Mendi women's participation in *moka* (TP) wealth exchange, while for Anganen women, there are transactions of *gris* (TP) embodied in material objects such as net-bags and grass skirts.[10] As noted earlier, a few elderly Anganen women have recently become involved in *moka* (TP), but this is a response to improving communication and transport networks within the region.

A secondary aspect of such changes has been the indigenous use of metaphor (*nonope*) to generate reflexivity and understanding. While a postmodernist perspective entails awareness of the need to let others speak for themselves, and of the inherent difficulties in this, Anganen women employ a practice of encouraging reflexivity by letting others *hear* and find their own meanings within existing cultural parameters. Anganen culture is thus dynamic, realized in particular moments or contexts (cf. Wagner 1972, 1981, 1986). In this sense, the process of eliciting reflexivity and interpretation within Anganen culture has an immediate reality recognized by Anganen women, but the interpretations generated are more fluid. This chapter represents my interpretation of these meanings and their dynamic processes of articulation.

NOTES

1 The second dimension of Strathern's exploration of agency (1988) is the development of the differentials in power relations between persons involved in social action. She proposes both men and women may be 'passive' or 'active' depending on the situation. In this regard I differ from Strathern. While I acknowledge the significance of addressing the debate about inequity and dominance in gender relations as these have come to prominence in the literature (Josephides 1983, 1985 and even earlier by Weiner 1976), I regard the lines of discussion to be misdirected. Based on my experience with the Anganen there is potential for persons to occupy different positions of power in different situations, but these are almost entirely within same-sex relations (the recent involvement of a few elderly, postmenopausal women in *moka* (TP) exchange with men is the exception). Rather, it is a matter of exploring the character of difference and its relation to notions of power. The option I have taken is indeed to let Anganen women 'speak for themselves' while recognizing

the inherent limitations of such an approach (cf. Bourdieu 1977; Clifford 1988; Clifford and Marcus 1986; Rabinow 1977).

2 This is a substantially different perspective to that utilized by MacKenzie (1991) who deals with the metonymical association between women and objects of their action, i.e. net-bags. From my theoretical position net-bags, together with other objects of women's (and men's) attention, are both metonymical to and used metaphorically by the Anganen themselves.

3 In this sense Anganen notions of substance and its significance for social relations is consistent with other ethnographic work in the Highlands (LiPuma 1988; Meigs 1984; A. Strathern 1972, 1973; Weiner 1982), although the twist I have provided is to focus on women's notions of substance transference which is somewhat unusual.

4 MacKenzie (1991) also provides a good overview of the significance of net-bags and their distribution through mainland Papua New Guinea.

5 *Waluma* refers to fertile substance which is specific to the womb, while *ip* is generic fertile substance which is located in the earth and food.

6 Munn (1970) discusses a comparable movement between subject and object in the construction of the meaning of identity for the Pitjantjatjara people of Central Australia. Ritual mediates subject–object relations. For the Pitjantjatjara, however, the subject–object relation includes ancestral beings, the landscape and a second subject in the form of later descendants. The living gain aspects of identity and learn a 'mode of experiencing the world' (Munn 1970:157–8) from ritual practice undertaken near aspects of the external world, that is, the landscape which ultimately derives from the ancestors. In a comparable way, Anganen women condense subject–object relations into themselves and the afterbirth such that woman and her product are simultaneously subject and object. But see Strathern (1988) for a critique of the subject–object distinction in relation to Melanesian persons.

7 In my earlier work (Merrett 1992) I elaborate on the theoretical significance of indigenous use of metaphor as a means of eliciting meanings at some length. Suffice to say here that the Anganen have inherent mechanisms for generating reflexivity which are entirely consistent with a postmodernist approach – that is, while as an anthropologist I am keen to let the other speak, the Anganen encourage the other in their own society to *hear* for themselves.

8 I cite Fernandez at length on this point, since the resemblance between cult sermons among the Fang and Anganen women's use of *nonope* is striking:

> As will be seen (the sermons themselves are not explained to the congregation), the interpretation of these midnight sermons *requires reference to experience otherwise acquired in Fang culture.* As in a riddle, the images of these sermons send us elsewhere to obtain our answers. They are rich in images which must, however, be contextualized by extension into various domains of Fang culture. The interpretive task is, therefore, to move back and forth between text and context . . . there is here a much greater obligation to contextualize in order to find meaning due to the lack of expository or didactic aids. (1986:181 (emphasis mine))

While upon initial reading this passage may be taken as referring to the interpretative act of the analyst, it also describes the interpretative task undertaken by Fang, and Anganen, themselves in their quest for meaning and understanding. It is this second aspect to which Fernandez himself attends. Thus, he argues this process of interpretation through contextualization in wider cultural experiences 'revitalizes' the meanings of that experience (1986:181).

9 I use the term individual cautiously, fully aware of the difficulty in transferring European concepts to other cultural contexts and refer instead to a notion of 'self' rather than 'collective' interest (Strathern 1981). Compare Strathern's concept of 'dividual' (1988:13).

10 This may represent a midway point between body and non-body produced wealth given the openness of boundaries regarding the self and influence on others. For example, through the damage sorcerers and others can do to a person by acting on body leavings such as hair or fingernails, the operation of *kone*, 'bad thoughts', and the influence external substances can have on the growth of infants. Again, Anganen women have a particularly strong notion of the importance of *gris* (TP), its transmission through 'work' and the consumption of food grown in their gardens.

REFERENCES

Biersack, A. 1991 Thinking difference: a review of Marilyn Strathern's *The Gender of the Gift: Problems with Women and Problems with Society in Melanesia*. *Oceania* 62(2):147–54.
Bourdieu, P. 1977 Afterword. In P. Rabinow *Reflections on Fieldwork in Morocco*. Berkeley: University of California Press, 163–7.
Clark, J. 1991 Pearlshell symbolism in Highlands Papua New Guinea, with particular reference to the Wiru people of Southern Highlands Province. *Oceania* 61(4):309–39.
Clifford, J. 1988 *The Predicament of Culture: Twentieth-Century Ethnography, Literature and Art*. Cambridge: Harvard University Press.
Clifford, J. and Marcus, G. 1986 (eds.) *Writing Culture: The Poetics and Politics of Ethnography*. Berkeley: University of California Press.
Feil, D. 1987 *The Evolution of Highland Papua New Guinea Societies*. Cambridge: Cambridge University Press.
Fernandez, J.W. 1986 *Persuasions and Performances: The Play of Tropes in Culture*. Bloomington: Indiana University Press.
Godelier, M. 1986 *The Making of Great Men: Male Power and Domination among the New Guinea Baruya* (trans. R. Swyer). Cambridge: Cambridge University Press.
Jolly, M. 1992 Partible persons and multiple authors: review of M. Strathern's *The Gender of the Gift*. *Pacific Studies* 15(1):137–49.
Josephides, L. 1983 Equal but different? The ontology of gender among Kewa. *Oceania* 53(3):291–307.
    1985 *The Production of Inequality: Gender and Exchange among the Kewa*. London: Tavistock Publications.
Lederman, R. 1980 Who speaks here? Formality and the politics of gender in Mendi, Highland Papua New Guinea. *Journal of the Polynesian Society* 89(4):479–98.

1986 *What Gifts Engender: Social Relations and Politics in Mendi, Highland Papua New Guinea.* Cambridge and New York: Cambridge University Press.

1989 Contested order: gender and society in the southern New Guinea Highlands. *American Ethnologist* 16(2):230–47.

LeRoy, J. 1985 *Fabricated World: An Interpretation of Kewa Tales.* Vancouver: University of British Colombia Press.

Lindenbaum, S. 1984 Variations on a sociosexual theme in Melanesia. In G.H. Herdt (ed.) *Ritualized Homosexuality in Melanesia.* Berkeley: University of California Press, 337–61.

LiPuma, E. 1988 *The Gift of Kinship: Structure and Practice in Maring Social Organization.* Cambridge: Cambridge University Press.

MacKenzie, M.A. 1991 *Androgynous Objects: String Bags and Gender in Central New Guinea.* Chur: Harwood Academic Publishers.

Meigs, A.S. 1984 *Food, Sex, and Pollution: A New Guinea Religion.* New Brunswick, NJ: Rutgers University Press.

Merrett, L. 1992 New women: discursive and non-discursive processes in the construction of Anganen womanhood. PhD thesis, The University of Adelaide.

Munn, N.D. 1970 The transformation of subjects into objects in Walbiri and Pitjantjatjara myth. In R.M. Berndt (ed.) *Australian Aboriginal Anthropology: Modern Studies in the Social Anthropology of the Australian Aborigines.* Nedlands, WA: University of Western Australia Press for the Australian Institute of Aboriginal Affairs, 141–63.

Nihill, M. 1986 Roads of presence: exchange and social relatedness in Anganen social structure. PhD thesis, The University of Adelaide.

1988 'Worlds at war with themselves': notions of the antisociety in Anganen ceremonial exchange. *Oceania* 58(4):255–74.

1991 Money and '*moka*': men, women and change in Anganen mortuary exchange. *Journal of the Polynesian Society* 100(1):45–69.

Rabinow, P. 1977 *Reflections on Fieldwork in Morocco.* Berkeley: University of California Press.

Read, K.E. 1966 *The High Valley.* London: George Allen and Unwin.

Sexton, L. 1984 Pigs, pearlshells and 'women's work': collective response to change in Highland Papua New Guinea. In D. O'Brien and S. Tiffany (eds.) *Rethinking Women's Roles: Perspectives from the Pacific.* Berkeley: University of California Press, 120–52.

1986 *Mothers of Money, Daughters of Coffee: The Wok Meri Movement.* Ann Arbor, MI: UMI Research Press.

Sillitoe, P. 1988 From head-dresses to head-messages: the art of self-decoration in the Highlands of Papua New Guinea. *Man* 23(2):298–318.

Strathern, A. 1972 *One Father, One Blood: Descent and Group Structure among the Melpa People.* Canberra: Australian National University Press.

1973 Kinship, descent and locality: some New Guinea examples. In J. Goody (ed.) *The Character of Kinship.* Cambridge: Cambridge University Press, 21–33.

Strathern, M. 1972 *Women in Between: Female Roles in a Male World: Mount Hagen, New Guinea.* London and New York: Seminar Press.

1981 Self-interest and the social good: some implications of Hagen gender imagery. In S. Ortner and H. Whitehead (eds.) *Sexual Meanings: The Cultural Construction of Gender and Sexuality*. New York: Cambridge University Press, 166–91.

1988 *The Gender of the Gift: Problems with Women and Problems with Society in Melanesia*. Berkeley and Los Angeles: University of California Press.

Wagner, R. 1972 Habu*: The Innovation of Meaning in Daribi Religion*. Chicago: University of Chicago Press.

1981 *The Invention of Culture* (rev. and exp. 2nd edn). Chicago: University of Chicago Press.

1986 *Symbols that Stand for Themselves*. Chicago: University of Chicago Press.

Weiner, A.B. 1976 *Women of Value, Men of Renown: New Perspectives in Trobriand Exchange*. Austin: University of Texas Press.

Weiner, J. 1982 Substance, siblingship and exchange: aspects of social structure in New Guinea. *Social Analysis* 2:3–34.

8 From sisters to wives: changing contexts of maternity on Simbo, Western Solomon Islands

Christine Dureau

Introduction

Maternity is more than a simple dyadic relationship, for it necessarily reflects, and is constituted by, other social relations. This chapter explores the changing contexts of maternity during the twentieth century on Simbo, Solomon Islands (see Map 5). At the turn of the century, women experienced maternity within an ethos dominated by ancestor veneration of which, for present purposes, headhunting was a major feature. In this situation, the single most important gendered relationship was that between classificatory opposite-sex siblings (*luluna*). Women were viewed primarily as sisters rather than wives. Today, *luluna* relationships remain significant, albeit in new ways, but Christian marriage is held to be the most important adult gender relationship. Maternity ideally occurs within marriage, as always – the critical difference now is that a woman's husband is seen as having control over her and their children. These alterations in kinship relations were precipitated by local responses to colonial and postcolonial practices, in particular those associated with Christian conversion.

The transformation of the contexts within which maternity occurs means that its significance for women has varied historically. Women today, as Christian wives and mothers in an environment of high (albeit declining) fertility rates, consider themselves unduly burdened (Dureau 1993, n.d.a). By contrast, pre-Christian women exercised autonomy in their modes of fertility limitation. However, they experienced problems with low rates of fecundity and child survival. Infractions of reproductive norms were punished by violent reprisals at the hands of *luluna*.

This chapter follows a historical sequence. I start with an account of pre-Christian kinship and its relationship to maternity, derived from the considerable body of material on pre-Christian Simbo. The

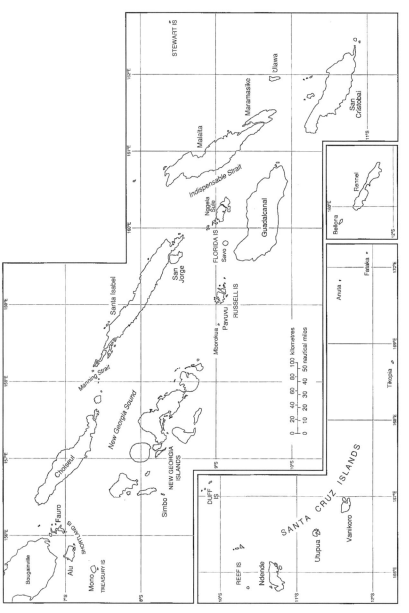

Map 5   The Solomon Islands, showing location of Simbo in the west

anthropologists A.M. Hocart and W.H.R. Rivers conducted ethnographic research directed at pre-pacification practices on the island, and
others in the vicinity, in 1908. Although their research did not deal
directly with maternity, information can be gleaned, in particular from
Hocart's works. I also make extensive use of anecdotal, biographical and
autobiographical oral accounts by Tinoni Simbo.[1] These different sources present problems of perspective. Hocart, for example, was concerned
with the reconstruction of an 'authentic' pre-pacification society and,
true to his time, concentrated on male informants working within Euro-
pean-defined public spaces. His work almost automatically denigrates
women's activities – women chiefs, 'of course', had nothing to do with
warfare and were probably no more than overseers of the cooking for
feasts (n.d.a); parents who accepted gifts from their daughters' suitors
were selling the girls into 'prostitution' (1931, n.d.c); and so on. In
Rivers' published corpus, women are even less visible, except in the form
of highly abstracted kinship categories.

The oral accounts which I gathered, too, are hardly disinterested:
reminiscences on Simbo are inevitably commentaries on the contemporary state of sociality as people juxtapose the past and present. Not that local
pasts are necessarily blatantly created in order to confront contemporary
issues, but the particularities of what is remembered and disremembered,
and by whom, are clearly related to the politics of everyday life in the here
and now. On Simbo it is not a case of which sex may remember or evoke the
past or present. Rather, processes of remembrance revolve around questions of what seems to be germane at any given moment and of what can
conceivably be retrieved or is held to be irretrievably 'lost'. Thus, for
example, women and men depict their ancestors' conjugal relationships in
ways which draw pointed contrasts with the most contentious issues
within contemporary marriages. Even when they concur as to the general
characteristics of ancestral marriages, as they frequently do, their interpretations and the particular features they highlight are often contested or
opposed with alternative propositions.

Nor can my own positioning be separated from the kinds of ethnography I write or the interpretations I make. I approached Simbo as a mother
of a small child at an age (early thirties) when most women on the island
already had several children; as a white woman from a society (Australia)
locally regarded as both powerful and wealthy; as a wife in what clearly
was a troubled marriage (and later as divorced woman); and as an avowed
feminist. These characteristics at least were immediately manifest and
undoubtedly inflected not only the kinds of dialogues in which I engaged,
but the particular people with whom I interacted, the kinds of knowledge
they (and I) proffered, the questions we asked of each other and the issues

I pursued. This is exemplified by my status as the mother of a single small child: women of all ages perceived this as reflecting Australian women's ready access to contraceptives and my own autonomy in doing so. This in turn prompted many women and girls to seek advice on, information about, or direct assistance in acquiring, them. Similar perceptions also prompted many women to talk about sexuality, marriage and parenthood. But it was perhaps my own interest in reproduction and feminist issues that allowed me to be seduced into the numerous discussions of women's reproductive, sexual and conjugal lives which were attendant upon these discourses of contraception.

And it is undoubtedly a difference of perspective which leads Scheffler (1962:155 n8) to characterize Simbo women as 'troublesome' and me to perceive them as resilient and indomitable. The partiality of texts – by Hocart and Rivers, by Tinoni Simbo and by myself – can thus be only imperfectly addressed, although comparison of the various sources reduces the ambiguity lent by the particularity of each. But my intention is not to give a comprehensive view of 'traditional' Simbo society, if ever there was such a thing, but to evoke an impression of some aspects of social life in the years immediately following the 'pacification' of 1899–1900 and, again, in the early 1990s. First, I sketch the post-pacification period and analyse contemporary kinship and maternity. I contrast contemporary Simbo women's and my own interpretations of historical transformations in mothering. Finally, I review some of the broader anthropological literature on transformations of kinship relations and suggest that the historical ethnographic material poses problems for any simplistic or universalistic adjudications about women's reproductive lives in relation to men.

Background[2]

Simbo is a small rugged volcanic island (less than four square miles in area), and the westernmost of the New Georgia Group of islands in the Western Province of the Solomon Islands. Gizo, the Province capital is about twenty miles distant – or two and a half hours by 15–horsepower canoe. The major staples are sweet potato, cassava, rice and tinned fish. Megapode eggs and a variety of fish and crustaceans augment the diet when seas and seasons allow. Domesticated pigs are eaten, in small quantities, only on celebratory occasions. Tinoni Simbo speak an Austronesian language and are culturally related to the peoples of the North Solomons Province of Papua New Guinea. The population varies from about 1,400 to 2,000, depending upon the season. This variation reflects the number of people living in urban or development areas, or married into other islands.

Simbo has had some 200 years recorded contact with Europeans. For the first hundred years this was characterized by trade with passing ships in which regional primary products, food and water, and later copra, were exchanged initially for iron and steel goods, and later for a larger variety of manufactured products (Bennett 1987; Hocart n.d.d; Jackson 1978). These introduced articles contributed to an expansion of headhunting throughout the nineteenth century. By the 1850s, New Georgian head-hunting was infamous within European discourse, an infamy that re-vealed at least as much about European preoccupations as it did of New Georgian values. In the late nineteenth century there were increasing numbers of white settlers in the West and when the British Solomon Islands Protectorate (BSIP) was proclaimed in 1893, one of the Adminis-tration's first concerns was to eradicate the practice in order to protect European interests. This was swiftly and decisively achieved between 1899 and 1900 (Bennett 1987).

Following pacification, the New Zealand-based Methodist Mission sent Fijian and Samoan missionaries to Simbo in 1903. Simbo people rapidly converted to Christianity and by the 1930s the ancestral shrines were entirely abandoned, although they have never lost their reputation as loci of supernatural power. The missionary presence continued, vir-tually unbroken, until the establishment of the United Church of Papua New Guinea and the Solomon Islands (UC) in 1968.[3] Ministers are now all members of the indigenous church, most of them from the Western Solomons. From its beginning the Methodist Mission introduced pri-mary school education and simple medical services for adherents. There has been a school on the island ever since and a professionally staffed clinic for many years.

Although New Georgians were resistant to labour migration before pacification, many now leave the island for short-term employment and others have made permanent careers in urban and development centres. Incorporation within a monetary economy permeates kin relations. Money is a constant concern for everyone – for payment of taxes, school fees, contributions to church and lineage, purchase of food when the gardens run short and other consumer items. Everyone engages in cash-generating activities – temporary labour migration, selling pandanus mats in urban centres, harvesting fruit and excess produce for sale, and manu-facturing copra. Such production is undertaken by individuals, who retain the profits of their labour. Married couples, however, pursue their goals and their interests in a joint fashion.

Mothers and sisters, *c.* 1900–10

The pre-Christian patterns of kinship and maternity I depict are those pertaining around 1900. This is not a static traditional picture, for the previous 130 years of intercourse with Europeans had already witnessed shifts in kinship relations, which were no doubt also changing before European contact. In this period, as well as being subject to kinship, women were actually or potentially victims of warfare, captives (ultimately absorbed into local society), ritual 'prostitutes', 'chiefs' (*banara*) or traders. These statuses are virtually ignored in this chapter, focused as it is on mothers and sisters.

While headhunting was only one manifestation of the ancestral veneration which pervaded social life, its scale during the nineteenth century had profound consequences for local kinship and demography. Families were small both because of high infant mortality rates (Bennett 1987) and cultural practices which, either by design or coincidence, resulted in lower fertility rates – men slept in men's houses whilst preparing for bonito and headhunting expeditions, children were ideally suckled for about four years, and women used contraceptives and abortifacients and practised infanticide in order to maintain an ideal of two dependent children per woman. It is difficult to assess the relative contribution of these practices, or their significance for particular women. Although the deliberate restriction of fertility rates in order to maximize mobility in warfare situations has been noted in several Papua New Guinea societies (McDowell 1988:238), it is easy to overstate the degree of volition reflected in low rates of reproduction.

Infant mortality rates were high and endemic yaws and malaria-induced anaemia made many women miscarry repeatedly. The tendency to leave those who died without issue out of genealogical reckonings makes generalization unreliable, but the limited data I do have suggest that for many, if not most, women it was a struggle simply to achieve the ideal of two live able-bodied children.[4] It is likely, then, that fertility control was practised by those relatively few women troubled by excessive numbers of healthy progeny and by unmarried girls and adulterers against whom the penalties for pregnancy were heavy (see below). Whatever the relative weight of the various restraints on fertility, around 1900 most women did, indeed, successfully raise only about two children to adulthood.

The vulnerability of young children presumably imparted great value to them, but there were undoubtedly other factors involved in determining the desirability of children. Parenthood today is unambiguously regarded as a necessary concomitant of adulthood and I presume this to have been the case in the past. McDowell's (1988) assessment of the value of children in rural Papua New Guinea notes the pervasiveness of the conceptual linkage between security in old age and relations of reciprocity between parents and offspring. This is certainly the case on Simbo today and in retrospective accounts of parenthood in the past. Although such accounts are inflected with nostalgia for a time seen as epitomizing the golden kinship ideal of reciprocity, similar themes are reflected in accounts of ancestor veneration, which are tinged, rather, with disapproval. In these accounts people are depicted as caring for their direct ancestors out of 'love' for the 'love' they had previously received. Women and men needed descendants in order to become ancestors, and the person with no descendants was foredoomed to early obscurity because there was no one to sustain them through sacrifices at ancestral shrines. There are two local words for 'childless' persons. *Egoro*, those who have never had offspring, are regarded as inadequate or unfulfilled. *Lumu*, those whose children had[5] all predeceased them, were figures of tragedy, for – despite their nurturance – their children had not survived to sustain them in old age and death.

The needs that children may have fulfilled does not necessarily explain imperatives for having them. Such motivations, like the emotional ties between parent and child in the past, can hardly be explained retrospectively. The pathos of *lumu*, however, makes it clear that children were highly valued, possibly more than at present. Christianity ensures adherents of post-mortem endurance, whereas previously only descendants could do so.

Social and kinship norms are easier to delineate. Cognatic descent and inheritance meant that authority over offspring belonged to both the fathers' and mothers' sides. Young children followed the mother in times of divorce, older children followed either parent or moved between the two. Divorce was frequent and remarriage swift. Genealogical records suggest a typical pattern of several divorces prior to permanent marriage. Authority over individuals lay with those of senior generations, the semi-hereditary leaders (*banara*) and, for women, their classificatory brothers (*luluna*). *Banara* were also entitled to formal 'respect' (*pamana*), as were a woman's *luluna*. This relationship between *luluna* was the most important relationship between women and men and will be considered at some length here.

Everyone was expected to 'follow' the desires of parents and older kin. The authority of such people was informed by their 'love' for their juniors. The latter in turn submitted out of obligation to those who had nurtured them. A similar relationship pertained between the living and the ancestors. *Luluna* relationships were removed from this nexus of love and benign authority by an explicitly hierarchical secular relationship structured around the concept of *pamana* ('shame/respect') and by a mystical relationship between female sexuality and male warriorhood. These were linked to rigid expectations of opposite-sex sibling avoidance and to the public control of female corporeality.

Pamana (literally 'in/via mouth') is an intrinsically hierarchical relation in which the one who gives overt respect to another feels shame in regard to that person. It is directly linked to the power of the important person/s and cannot be reciprocated. In the case of siblings, female *pamana* was linked to 'fear' of their *luluna*'s violent strength. It was a consequence of the requirements of opposite-sex sibling avoidance in a situation in which men were legitimately able to physically chastise their *luluna*.

Avoidance was achieved through formal female restraint in the vicinity of their *luluna* and *pamana* was manifested in verbal respect to them. No woman might go into any part, including the open verandah, of her *luluna*'s house. She must always walk behind and if forced to pass in front of *luluna*, must stoop or crawl and not step over their legs. Physical touch was taboo. She must not eat her *luluna*'s betel-nut or use any of their personal possessions. Finally, it was absolutely forbidden to mention any part of her *luluna*'s head or to use a variety of words associated with eating, sexuality or elimination in their presence or when speaking of them. These restrictions approximated the society's general respect codes. There is significant overlap, for example, between *luluna* restrictions and the constraint which everyone showed to *banara*. Thus, although women had diffuse mystical powers over their *luluna*, they were none the less subordinate, much as ordinary people were to *banara*.[6]

Avoidance extended beyond the formal realm, depicted above, to absolute injunctions against men being aware of their *luluna*'s corporeality. Any such awareness aroused their anger – to glimpse a woman's genitals, to know she was going to urinate or defecate, that she was menstruating, or that she had a lover – anything that brought her physical functions to their notice were sufficient to enrage *luluna*. Female containment, then, consisted not simply of appropriate decorum but of the denial, insofar as their *luluna* were concerned, of a bodily existence. Even the acknowledgement of a girl's marriage, revealed after the initial event, required payment of compensation to her *luluna* because it tacitly acknowledged her sexuality.

The social regulation of female sexuality and maternity was tied to these respect and avoidance requirements by its cosmological connection to male warrior safety. When a person died, their soul had to reach Sondo in the Shortland Islands in order to become an ancestor. They could reach this place only through the ritual interventions of their living descendants, which were not observed for anyone who had died an untoward death. Such persons became malicious spirits (*tomate*) in the bush. This included warriors killed in battle, who became *tomate maza* ('spirit/s [of] beheaded person/s'). The death of warriors was attributed to corporeal transgressions by their *luluna*. Inappropriate sexuality, such as adultery or premarital pregnancy, exemplified such wrongdoing.

The prohibition of premarital pregnancy did not reflect norms of sexual restraint, but was rather a reflection of the significance of sexual discretion (see also Nash 1981:121). Boys and girls engaged in sexual activity before marriage (Hocart n.d.c), but such sexuality was regulated through a system of gifts flowing from a girl's suitors to her parents (Hocart n.d.c, n.d.d). This practice is glossed 'prostitution' by Hocart and the missionary Waterhouse (1949), but I would argue that it is more analogous to the flow of gifts attached to the various stages of marriage. In particular, the wealth received by parents was probably directed towards containment of *luluna* outrage when news of sexual relationships became public. Parental acceptance of wealth, like *luluna* acceptance of compensation from parents, legitimated a woman's relationships. It was involvements outside this realm which were both socially illegitimate and cosmically dangerous to *luluna* – clandestine premarital relationships, adultery, relationships opposed by parents, and so on. All women were potentially dangerous to their *luluna*, a danger they were responsible for containing (cf. Faithorn 1975; Keesing 1985; Kerns 1983).

In all of this, while there were undoubtedly reciprocal spheres of power – women influencing their *luluna*'s safety and men having power of violent chastisement of their *luluna* – the relationship was overtly unequal. Maternity occurred within this context of male *luluna* material power and supernatural vulnerability. While the restrictions on men being aware of their *luluna*'s corporeality prevented their directing women's sexual and marital activities, they effectively acted as enforcers, punishing infractions of normative rules against extra-marital maternity and inappropriate sexuality.

If women ensured supernatural protection of *luluna*, men were obliged to protect their *luluna* and their children from hardship – they must prevent affines from mistreating a woman, provide for her and her children in times of crop failure, widowhood or divorce and, as warriors, they contributed to their general safety. Any aggrieved woman could appeal to her *luluna*.[7] Cognatic descent and shifting postmarital residence also meant that men retained an interest in their *luluna*'s children and may have lived in close proximity to them for many years. This probably helped strengthen the supportive bonds which were the obverse of *luluna* antagonism.

While women were explicitly subordinate to *luluna*, marriage was ideally an egalitarian relationship. Leaving aside the gifts flowing between suitors, parents and probably *luluna*, mentioned above, there were at least two ceremonial stages of marriage (*tari pipiro* and *tari binola*), in both of which the partners' equivalence was stressed. *Tari pipiro* was the surreptitious establishment of the marriage.[8] Late at night, the boy and his parents crept to the girl's house, where she bade him enter. His family gave her parents a small amount of shell money to acknowledge the mother's provision of breast milk and the father's climbing for green coconuts to give his lactating wife. The two sides then exchanged and consumed baskets of betel-nut, after which the boy's family returned home, leaving him for one night at the girl's house. Male and female inside a house together was, and remains, the definitive proclamation of marriage. The following day small amounts of compensation were distributed to her *luluna* to 'straighten' the relationship and avert their wrath. The newly established couple then went to the man's house for a single night before moving to whichever place they would subsequently remain.

The marriage was later confirmed by *tari binola*, in which equal amounts of shell money, pudding and cooked pigs were exchanged between the two sides.[9] This celebration also involved a contest between both sides of the marriage in which clam-shell money was laid on opposing mats, each person having control of their own pieces. The dual objects of the contest were to exchange one's own money for another of equivalent size and value from the opposite side and, importantly, to ensure that not all pieces were matched, that is that certain pieces remained with those who had brought them. I would interpret this requirement again as a clear symbolic statement of the equality and retention of the lineage rights of each party.

Marriage was essential to the birth of children, and unmarried pregnant women were killed by their *luluna*.[10] It is here that I see indigenous abortifacients, contraceptives and infanticide as having been relevant (see Dureau n.d.a for a discussion of the efficacy of indigenous fertility control). Even allowing for late menarche and low fertility rates in pre-pacification Simbo, the simultaneous norms of premarital sexuality and postmarital childbearing are antithetical, unless the connection between coitus and conception can be broken. Hocart (n.d.c) notes that the child of an unmarried mother was regarded disapprovingly on Roviana (the only case he cites) in 1908 when men were only recently constrained from killing their *luluna*, and that unmarried girls were treated contraceptively.

The legitimately conceived infants of married women were born in the forest and for several months afterwards the woman and her child remained in a succession of locations there. Birth was a time of great danger, for it attracted the spirits which sought to consume mother and child. A woman gave birth sitting on a stone in a clearing surrounded by female kin who fearfully encircled her in order to keep away the spirits. One of them knelt to receive the infant on a mat of banana leaves. Female genitalia were, and are, regarded as repulsive by women, and others were unwilling to help with the birth, although one of them might do so out of 'love' (see also Rozario, this volume). Afterwards, the woman was led into the forest where she dug a hole and buried the placenta and bloody leaves before going into the hut, previously prepared by her husband, where she remained under the care of her cognatic and affinal kin.

Birth in the forest and the subsequent isolation there presumably precluded notions of women bearing children under male control and would certainly have provided ample scope for infanticide which, although it is impossible to quantify, undoubtedly occurred, according to autobiographical accounts. This does not mean that birth was an entirely female responsibility: the husband's interests in the child were demonstrated by his provision of successive huts. Further, the bilineal connection of children was manifested in the alternation of care and sustenance of mother and child by matri-kin and patri-kin while they remained in the forest. The mutual affinal responsibility for children – and perhaps also a degree of antagonism – was reflected in a secret female ceremonial contest. On moving into a postnatal hut (*savo*), a sapling with slippery sap was cut down and the bark removed. The child's matrilateral and patrilateral female kin then lined up on opposite ends and had a tug-of-war to see who would nurture the mother and child on the following day – the winner assumed this task.

The breadth of the child's connections continued to be expressed throughout childhood. The first birthday was a celebratory occasion when both parents feasted the child's cognatic kin. In an environment of high infant and child mortality, thriving children reflected ancestral approval of the parents' good living and this was a time of thanks that the first dangerous year had passed. According to oral histories, children were suckled for approximately four years[11] and in that time remained close to the mother's hamlet; thereafter they might remain there or live for variable periods with other kin. Fosterage was common, a practice which increased, rather than shifted, an individual's circle of kindred: household boundaries were in any case not rigid and fosterage or adoption was simply a manifestation of their porous quality. These movements between households further cemented cognatic ties (cf. Scheffler 1962).

This equality vis-à-vis children was reflected generally in marriage. In direct contrast to the punctilious female discretion demanded by *luluna* relationships, marital relationships were ideally characterized by openness on all matters. This was based upon the asserted equality between spouses (reflected in the marriage exchanges). Men and women owned wealth independently and women had control over the distribution of all household foodstuffs. Fertility control was regarded as women's business, an attitude reinforced or caused by the secrecy enjoined by *luluna* relations. This conjugal autonomy of economics and fertility, combined with men's obligations to protect their *luluna*, meant that most of the potential bases for men's domination of their wives were lacking (see Schoeffel 1977, 1978).

The difference between a woman's conjugal and sibling relationships is aptly illustrated by the consequences of female adultery. The husband of an adulterous woman could cast her out or return to his own place. Her *luluna*, in contrast, would be justified in executing her and casting aside her body, unless she was able to take refuge with her mother's or father's classificatory siblings until *luluna* compensation was arranged.[12] While her husband and his kin might petition the *banara* to punish her, this formality of procedure was in contrast to the passionate slaying by *luluna*. A more usual course was to divorce or for her kin to arrange a formal feast and prestation of money to the husband under the auspices of the *banara*, thus re-establishing the marriage.

These conjugal and sibling relations, together with the constraints on fertility mentioned earlier, framed maternity prior to 1900. The powers of male *luluna* enjoined premarital contraception, and certainly restricted birth to within those marriages sanctioned by senior kin. Conversely, the power of men to protect their *luluna* from abusive husbands or affines, coupled with the ease of divorce, cognatic descent and independent control of wealth deprived husbands of untoward powers over their wives. Maternity was constrained by male authority relationships associated with the sexual constraint imposed upon women by *luluna* relationships, rather than by conjugal relationships. Birth and child care were bilineal responsibilities, and healthy infants, in the hands of the ancestors, reflected the blessings wrought by righteous living.

Wives and mothers in 1990

In 1903, three years after headhunting was abruptly suppressed by the British Protectorate forces, the first Samoan and Fijian missionary families arrived. The island had had intensifying connection with Europeans for more than a century and in that period the various political and economic forces generated by contact had influenced Simbo social practice. But throughout that time, local people had remained apparently autonomous: exchange had been on their terms, they had disregarded the occasional, poorly directed and often impotent retaliatory missions of the

Fiji-based British administration (e.g. WPHC 1886), and their growing enmeshment in the world economy had not yet become apparent (Bennett 1987; Jackson 1978). Pacification was both unexpected and calamitous: the disdained Europeans, previously subject to local pressures, had abruptly eliminated a way of life. Into this state of indigenous disintegration, the first missionaries arrived and, largely because of the disorientation wrought by 'pacification', people almost immediately began adopting Christian practices (Dureau n.d.b; Rivers 1922; see Jolly, this volume: Chapter 6, for an evaluation of Rivers).

The advent of the Christian mission ushered in momentous changes in kin relations. Here I consider missionary interventions in sexual morality, maternal health practices and family relationships and the ways in which these articulated with local understandings to shape contemporary motherhood. In particular, I focus on an increasing tendency towards a nucleated family[13] in which conjugal relationships are dominated by conflict over the extent to which husbands control women as wives and as mothers. I then briefly consider how the parallel relative decline of *luluna* relationships has affected maternity through the enhancement of husband's authority and through creating new occasions of extra-marital birth. The outcomes of these shifts in male power leave women with somewhat more sexual autonomy but continuing lack of control over their own fertility and maternity. Economic forces reinforce the centrality of marital relationships and, coupled with husband's jealousies, contribute to contemporary patterns of adoption.

Mission enterprises had much in common with Protectorate and settler interests, notwithstanding the frequent conflict between the various parties (Thomas 1992). Their preaching on sexuality, for example, coincided with later Administration attempts to regulate sexual morality. Protectorate health and sanitation goals were also congruent with early missionary exertions to make people adopt floored and roomed houses. However, by and large it was the missions who instigated, supervised and enforced the economic and kinship transformations which occurred on the island (see also Macintyre 1989; White 1990). Jolly and Macintyre (1989:6–7) argue that the particular significance of mission influence in Pacific colonial history was ensured by the continuity of their presence and fluency in local languages, their emphases on local engagement and their roles as 'self-conscious agents of change'. Thomas (1992) also points to the low level of Administrative supervision in the Western Solomons. Certainly those changes on Simbo came earlier, and perhaps more comprehensively, for being in missionary hands. In the process mission hegemony was consolidated. Tensions between local practices and the various ideological, political and economic forces for social change have subsequently been negotiated through local interpretations and mediations of biblical texts and Methodist Mission (and later UC) teachings.

This is apparent in the mission's emphasis on health. No doubt at some point medical treatments would have become available to islanders through the Administration, but resources were initially reserved for Europeans (see also Denoon 1989). The European medical care of Solomon islanders was left to missions which, as in Papua New Guinea, often focused on maternal health (Bennett 1987; Denoon 1989). This included medicalizing childbirth. For some years women continued birthing in the woods, but by about 1930 continued missionary castigation of the wrongs of continuing to submit to spirits, coupled with the residence of mission-trained indigenous nurses, had seen the building of birth huts on the outskirts of most villages and, eventually, the movement of all births to the local clinic building. This was more than a shift in locale: it was accompanied by a steady weakening of the fears of mystical hazards of birth and the development of ideas that intervention by trained personnel could resolve most obstetric crises.

It is important to be aware of the underlying premises of this view of birth as less dangerous. Missionaries did not challenge the reality of spirits so much as allegiance to the old cosmological system. The Christian faith was presented as stronger than the old pagan practice which was held to entail the placation of devils. Thus, for them and Tinoni Simbo alike, spirits were omnipresent (see also Macintyre 1989). The test of faith lay – and lies – in perceiving that Christianity weakened those forces. The obstetric safety associated with clinic births, then, has been seen as a product of Christian power and faith rather than inherent in Western medical practice, a perception that continues despite the formal modern separation of faith and health along church and state lines. The fiendish spirits which sought parturient women are weakened 'because [the] church is strong now'. There is also an implicit understanding that ancestral forces may harmonize with Christianity. Thus, even if not all birthing problems are perceived as caused by women's sexual duplicity, such wrongdoing nevertheless remains subject to supernatural sanction.

The interplay is demonstrated by the case of Nenisi,[14] a woman of about twenty, who was married in church to a man from nearby Ranongga. When she ran away with another man, claiming her husband had mistreated her, her parents refused to effect a customary divorce, claiming they were fearful of violating a Christian marriage. She eventually returned pregnant, suffered a prolonged labour and was reportedly close to death. Her mother, attending her with the registered nurse, desperately sent for the minister, who came and chastised Nenisi on the grounds that her situation was consequential to her adultery. He then stroked her and prayed for her,[15] whereupon the birth was quickly effected and the woman and her baby completely recovered. This case was held as irrefutable evidence that Nenisi's adultery was being punished, as it always had been, with the death of the woman and that only the greater power of the Christian god had been sufficient to defeat that mystical force.

As was the case with reformations of childbirth, missionary reform of indigenous fertility control was ultimately endorsed by the administration and, later, government (O'Collins 1978, 1979). Opposition to infanticide, in particular, corresponded with official concerns, but mission attitudes regarding female autonomy in fertility restriction and co-residence of spouses would also have been compatible with the values informing both the Protectorate Administration and European settlers (see Jolly, this volume: Chapter 6; Manderson, this volume).

On Simbo these issues were entangled, not merely with the cultural values and legislations of the prevailing colonial power, but with the particular religious doctrine of Methodist missionaries. Of crucial significance here was not merely the opposition to all indigenous fertility controls on the grounds that they were immoral, promoted promiscuity and involved pagan invocations, but the fact that this coincided with an equally new emphasis on women's submission to their husbands. Marriage has subsequently become the central field of adjudication and contestation about maternity, notwithstanding the dramatic increase in extra-marital maternity, which I consider below. There is a widespread sentiment that children should be born within marriage and, less unanimously, that they should be raised under the authority of the woman's husband.

It is not clear to what extent such values were directly espoused by missionaries and to what extent they were outcomes of Simbo engagement with missionary pronouncements on marital relations. Indigenous peoples have frequently reformulated the mission doctrines they have adopted (Barker 1990; Burt 1983; Comaroff 1985; Harwood 1971; Oboler 1985; Wolf 1958). On Simbo there was little of the resistance to colonial and/or mission hegemony which often accompanies conversion (Dureau n.d.b; cf. Barker 1990). None the less, Methodism was not simply imposed. People today ascribe all changed practices and values to mission teachings, but men's resistance to the church's attempts to disown models of subordination of wives (see below) indicates that people are not passive recipients of foreign lore.

Nineteenth- and early twentieth-century European middle-class missionary social values did stress male authority. Miller (1985:66) argues that Protestant American and European Mission boards also saw nuclear families, regarded as emblematic of Western culture and civilization, as the most effective means of imparting Christian models. Missionary households were to be both exemplary of Christian conjugality and the foundation for female and male missionaries' intervention in indigenous domesticity. Missionaries on Simbo were thus all married couples jointly charged with reforming local sociality. However, the Methodist missionaries to Simbo were South Sea islanders from Fiji, Samoa and Tonga where indigenous ideas about marriage and gender relations differed from those of Europeans. Gailey (1980:318, *passim*) points out that, in Tonga at least, traditional female submission to husbands involved '[s]imple deference', rather than 'structural and economic dependency' as in Europe. Schoeffel (1977, 1978) similarly notes that Samoan men's authority as husbands was limited.

South Sea islander missionary ideas regarding Christian marriage were a product of dialogue between European missionaries and their converts in their own homelands. Thus, their ideal of marriage may have been one tempered by pre-Christian indigenous understandings of deference rather than dependence. We must also consider local receipt of missionary messages, for local people necessarily interpreted exotic ideas in their own terms. On Simbo deference has always indicated both status and power differentials. Benign authority is incumbent upon all power holders, but is secondary to the exercise of power and the subject person's submission to that power. In all cases, open or covert non-compliance justifies the outrage of the power holder. *Banara*, the epitome of pre-Christian authority, must be peaceful persons, concerned first and foremost with communal welfare. They were concerned, however, only with the good of those who properly acceded to their will and paid due homage. The same can now be said of church ministers, who have largely displaced *banara* in the new order (see also White 1990). Indeed, the Christian god also exhibits similar expectations: thus the loving 'Papa God', to whom all can turn for solace, can become the vengeful 'Chief on High' (*Banara pana Ulu*) who metes out punishment to sinners. In the case of siblings, men's care of their *luluna* was dependent upon the latter's unquestioned respect and restraint.

It was inevitable, then, that missionary messages about women's deference to their husbands would be interpreted as an argument that men were to exercise power over their wives. The basis of marital relationships has subsequently been transformed from equality to hierarchy. While both parties retain rights in their cognatic descent groups, a husband's authority has increased markedly. Thus, in the ideal contemporary marriage, a husband is required to be a benign dictator only when his wife both acknowledges his higher status and is obedient. A man is deemed, by appeal to St Paul's letter to the Ephesians (especially Eph. 5:22–5),[16] to possess his wife, a relationship in which she does not have reciprocal rights. A man's rights in his wife's body evinces his authority: her labour, her sexual fidelity and control of her fecundity are areas within which a woman's obedience are deemed reflected.

These modulations are mirrored in modifications to *tari binola* and in the evolution of attitudes toward wives' bodies. Some time after Simbo people began to accept the notion of husbands' authority, the symbolic assertions of equality in marriage exchange began to wane and the formal exchange of exactly equivalent pieces of shell money was discontinued. Although the man's side has always paid an amount of separate wealth, additional to that exchanged between the two sides, Hocart, Rivers and Scheffler (Scheffler 1962) all maintain that it bought membership for the children of the marriage in the father's lineages.[17] This may be counter-posed to the nascent modern notion that the wife is purchased. Thus, at one wedding a woman named Hilida gave three particularly beautiful pieces of clam-shell money at her son's marriage. This was widely inter-preted as imposing heavy affinal obligations on Lava, her son's wife. A common remark was that 'Lava will have to work very hard now, because Hilida really paid heavily for her!' While this reflects an emergent pre-sumption of wife purchase, control over the woman is regarded as vested in her husband.

Paralleling the shift to husbands' authority is a stress on their corporeal control of their wives. This is remarkably akin to the emphasis on female corporeality in *luluna* relationships. Thus, the most significant index of a woman's submission to her husband is her sexual continence. Men do not perceive adultery in terms of discarded affection or betrayal of procreative rights.[18] What enrages them, they say, is that the woman has shamed them. One cuckolded man said: 'If she committed adultery and no one knows, that's something. But they know and I just feel no good about that. She shamed me for good.'

Anxiety about women's fidelity seems to impel many men to consist-ently assert their authority verbally and through control of their wives' activities and absences from home. This concept of husbands as overseers of female corporeality justifies the physical chastisement typical of many marriages, just as it did *luluna* violence. Women and men now endorse the idea that there are appropriate degrees of, and occasions for, violence within marriage. A woman, struck with an 'acceptable' degree of viol-ence, and for 'acceptable' reasons, is hit because she was failing in her responsibilities to her husband and he is correct in bringing her to good order.[19]

Women individually maintain that violent acts against themselves are manifestations of jealousy. However, if men are anxious about women's sexual fidelity, they phrase their demands about women 'remaining quiet' in terms of children's welfare. A woman should remain home and look after the family's children, they say. In retrospectively explaining an act of violence, a man invariably attributed it to the fact that his wife was not taking adequate care of their children and it was his responsibility to ensure that she did, or that the woman had shown insufficient respect by nagging or failing to have food ready when he expected it. (The two are often linked by the statement that he came home to eat and found the children hungry.) Whatever actually precipitates such violence, both women's denials of its *particular* legitimacy and men's justifications accept the premise that women's responsibility for child care is indicated by being a responsible spouse.

None the less, there is a range of interpretations of ideal conjugal behaviour. Everyone agrees that women should respect their husbands and obey their wishes. What varies is the stress on different values, and interpretations as to what constitutes respect, obedience and appropriate chastisement. This is reflected, within kinship practice, in disjunctions between church and community values and in incompatible male and female definitions of appropriate behaviours.

A prominent theme in local church pronouncements on marriage, made primarily through sermons and minister's speeches on important occasions, is that of the husband's benign authority over his wife and, more markedly, of her obligations of obedience to his wishes, obligations particularly focused on her parenting under his supervision. Although services are led by members of the community, there are none the less notable disjunctions between their church commentaries on family life and community perceptions of family relationships. Thus, while church readings and sermons stress a husband's love, expressed through authority, community appeals to that biblically sanctioned authority are expressed in the divergent terms of controlling female bodies.

Local church statements also differ markedly from what might be designated official church views. The UC now formally upholds the equality of husband and wife, stressing a partnership of mutual enablement. This distinction corresponds to men's and women's disparate interpretations of obedience and benign authority. Women define obedience in terms of fulfilling their traditional female obligations – preparing food to have available for men when desired, respecting affines and so on. They are, in other words, willing to follow what they see as the legitimate wills of their husbands. They regard as illegitimate other rights claimed by men – rights to determine access to family planning services, to force them to remain in the household, to refuse to care for children, and so on. A constant theme of women's comments when discussing, both publicly and privately, their participation in non-domestic affairs was men's refusal to commit themselves to child care and family planning and/or their (sometimes violent) anger at finding their wives absent from home. Men counter-claim unqualified power over wives. In their interpretations, the requirements of benign dictatorship are negated by women's flouting of what men see as their obligations towards them. They argue that injunctions to be loving towards wives are contingent upon prior female submission to their authority. They respond with anger to women's accusations, indicating a strong tension between men's and women's interpretations of Christian life.

Each cite church authority – women by reference to contemporary church injunctions and to the former Bishop's repeated pronouncements on marital equality, and men by direct reference to popular biblical passages which some claim to invalidate the church's current urging. Men's arguments, supported by the tenor of pronouncements by consecutive local ministers, might be seen as receiving more reinforcement, given that women's authorities – the church hierarchy in Roviana – rarely give local support to their arguments. However, women also sanction their position by recourse to claims about local *kastom* ('tradition' in Solomon Islands Pidgin), according to which men are supposed to follow their wives' requests because of love and to concede female household autonomy.

This is a complex situation but, to oversimplify, men ultimately concede some validity to the view that the arbitrary use of force against their wives is against *kastom*[20] while simultaneously strongly arguing their rights vested in Christianity. This results in their complaining that women fail to fulfil the customary expectations of sexual faithfulness and adequate care of children, while in fact chastising them for contesting emergent conjugal norms.

This ongoing contention about husbands' and wives' powers pervades contemporary debates about fertility levels. Men generally agree that Simbo population growth must be drastically reduced if land is not to be continually degraded. However, this is a general not a personal concern. Thus, elsewhere I have considered a father of eight children recommending the exile of couples with many children and, simultaneously, denouncing women's perceived propensity to illicitly seek contraception (Dureau n.d.a). This apparent inconsistency derives from the dissent about rights over wives' bodies.

Men do not seek large numbers of children per se, for paternity also places demands on them for increased labour and money and visibly threatens contracting natural resources. Rather, it is by circumventing women's expressed goals of restricting fertility that they exert control over their wives' bodies. There is a strong notion that female reproductive freedom facilitates licentiousness. The conflict between ideals of fertility restraint and restraint of wives is reflected in women's frequent complaints that even when their husbands do agree to contraceptive techniques, such as the rhythm method or withdrawal, they object to women's particular requests for co-operation. The rhetoric of these objections is principally phrased in terms of accusations that the wife has a lover.

Both women and men argue that men's reluctance to allow their wives free access to family planning services are related to sexual mores. Women ascribe this to unjustifiable sexual jealousy, men to female sexual duplicity. Although missionaries have long reinforced the latter view, it is important not to unquestioningly ascribe it entirely to Christian influences. Adultery has long been a focus of Simbo norms and Hocart (n.d.c) reports the violent responses of both women and men to the partners in their spouse's adultery just five years after the mission's establishment. McDowell (1988) also notes the pre-contact masculine conflation of contraception and promiscuity in Papua New Guinea. The point is, rather, that the transformations wrought in Christian marriage provide an innovative legitimating framework for many men's opposition to these purported consequences of female contraceptive usage. This, combined with women's alienation from the available methods, results in many more children than women desire (Dureau 1993). Some men allow their wives virtually full autonomy, some are habitually violent, most fall somewhere between the two extremes, and most women protest about husbands, child care and restricted autonomy.

The growing commitment to views of the safety of Christian birthing enables women to hold that their health is subject to human agency. Thus, although they still maintain that adulterous conception can result in a parturient woman's death, it is also held that many or frequent births are debilitating and may affect mortality. This perception partly informs women's resentment of repeated births imposed by their husbands' insistence on following their own mission-promoted views of conjugal rights (Dureau 1993). (Ironically, while women blame their husbands' adherence to early mission doctrines about marital relations for their high birth rates, this excess fecundity may also have been enhanced by their own adherence to missionary injunctions against prolonged breast-feeding.) They complain not only about the numbers of children but about the added work this entails and the proportion of that work which they assume (Dureau 1993). Men, on the other hand, lament what they regard as their wives' 'constant anger' and lack of respect, although they habit-

ually justify violence against their wives, or restraints on female autonomy, in terms of the women's responsibility to their children.

It is in this context that women bemoan *luluna* relationships. There is a
strong oral tradition that men were obliged to protect their *luluna* from
abuse, but women now lament that their *luluna* are afraid of the police.
Men certainly cite such forces in their refusal to intervene on their *luluna*'s
behalf, but while accounts by those Simbo men who have been gaoled for
violence are, indeed, graphic, it is a factor cited only in explaining their
non-protection of their *luluna*, and not in other cases of violent action.[21]

A more probable explanation for men's refusal to support their *luluna*
lies in the diminished significance of this relationship. It is not merely that
marriage has been transformed: the shift to Christian practice has seen an
increased emphasis on marriage as the dominant field of significant adult
gender relations. Women continue to respect their *luluna* verbally (although the physical marks of respect are much reduced) and to be
discreet in bodily matters, but husbands have ultimate authority over
women and offspring. The degree to which marriage has undermined the
primacy of sibling mutuality is illustrated by the case of Alesi, a thirty-
two-year-old woman with three children, estranged from her husband,
who had left her for another woman in Honiara.

About six months after their separation he began sending her money 'for the
children'. Shortly afterwards he sought a reconciliation and paid a large compensation to her parents. She said she would return because of her concerns about
maintaining her children. Two of her natal brothers, working in Honiara, sent
word to her that they opposed the reconciliation and that they would provide for
her children. She rejected their offer because: 'It's all right that they say they will
look after us, but I have to think about my children. We need money to look after
children. Now they say they'll care for my children, but you wait for the time when I
need money for my children and they need it for their children. Their wives won't
prevent them giving money to my children? Of course they will think of their own
children first and their wives will see that they always have something to think of for
their children. It's all right to be angry with him, but I have to think of my children,
because my brothers will have plenty of their own children to think of.'

Irrespective of her motivation (and a number of people expressed doubts
about that), the idiom was regarded as legitimate and her brothers'
interpretation of the resumed marriage as an illicit liaison received little
support from her other *luluna* or the wider community.

This case implicitly suggests that inequitable marriage relationships
might derive from women's acknowledged need of husbands' economic
support to sustain increased numbers of children. Redistribution has
diminished as nuclear families have been privileged as the site of primary
obligation and responsibility, but there is not necessarily a causal relation-

ship between nuclear family formation and private disbursement. Rather, economic dependence on spouses may be interpreted as arising from the obliteration of local leadership. In the past, redistribution was associated with the sponsorship of client relationships, which underlay *banara*'s power (Hocart n.d.a). Ownership of wealth was always individual and the emphasis on reciprocal generosity between close kin was probably simply strengthened when the site and context for public redistribution disappeared with the abolition of local political forces, which Hocart noted to be well advanced by 1908. In that context, retention of wealth within the household (always the site of production) was one possible outcome, ultimately enhanced by missionary promotion of nuclear family ties.

Production has remained largely individualistic. Women and men co-operate in making gardens, but women control the distribution of household food products. Other items belong to the person who laboured over them. Thus, if a woman sends a bucket of oranges to market in Gizo, she retains the profit. When women say they need to marry men to help provide for their children, then, they mean that they need to enter into a co-operative relationship with a man to optimize their well-being and that of their children. Both men and women have access to land, and while men usually make copra, women can and do so. Women are also more likely to market garden surpluses, although men may do so; women can also make regular sums from the sale of mats, an avenue closed to men. Women's slight dependence on men for cash is more than offset by men's dependence on women for garden produce. Both are reduced in their circumstances, if forced to live unmarried. An unmarried woman with several children is short of cash to buy kerosene, clothing, betel-nut, rice and tinned foods, and their diet is a monotonous round of sweet potato. Likewise, a man with no wife has no one to whom he can give his fish, unless he lives with another family, where he is only ambivalently welcome. He drifts from household to household, usually with no garden, a figure of amusement or pity.

Such men are regarded as inadequate. Although marriage is seen to confer adulthood on women and men, a woman's not marrying can be partially offset by the birth of children. This is reflected in attitudes to former polio victims, who are regarded as inappropriate marital partners. All women who are former polio victims have extra-marital children, virtually all such men have none. There is a notable difference in attitudes towards the two: the women cannot marry because of their physical inadequacies, but have demonstrated a social adequacy through being mothers. Male polio victims, on the other hand, are depicted as burdensome or vaguely amusing persons because they cannot establish relations with either spouses or offspring. [22]

The account of Alesi also demonstrates the degree to which *luluna* relationships now pose problems of conflicting demands by spouses and siblings for both men and women. It is not simply the emphasis on nuclear families that has diminished *luluna* relations. Pacification undermined rationales for male *luluna* powers, particularly because women's corporeality is no longer associated with *tomate maza*. It also eliminated execution by *luluna*. Although it is important not to understate the degree to which their coercive powers continue to constrain women's lives, there has been a marked decline in the effective powers of *luluna*. Women now generally manage their lives via public modesty, surreptitious independence in their sexual lives and, when necessary, taking refuge with senior kin while their mothers or mothers' sisters arrange compensation for their *luluna*. If men continue to demand respect from their *luluna*, to assault them, or receive compensation, for corporeal transgressions, women express resentment at the demands imposed by these relationships. They describe the violence of such men as 'unfitting' and say that they are 'afraid' of them, rather than *pamana*. To such women, *luluna* relationships are dictated by unyielding *kastom*, rather than by cultural logic.

The decline of *luluna* has paralleled a surge in premarital pregnancy and births. Thus, most households now support at least one child of an unmarried daughter. However, *luluna*'s diminished retaliatory power only partially explains this phenomenon. The availability of contraceptives has shifted simultaneously. Hocart (n.d.c) reports that unmarried women regularly undertook contraceptive treatments, an option now available only to married couples (O'Collins 1978, 1979). If *luluna* can no longer intimidate women into marital maternity, the simultaneous shift in contraceptive technology and availability now compels many to unwanted extra-marital maternity.

Macintyre's analysis (n.d.) of deliberate extra-marital maternity on Tubetube raises the question of whether Simbo women might regard this as a means of avoiding the endemic conflicts of marriage. However, only one unmarried mother (of two small children) expressed such sentiments to me. Most women who become pregnant want to marry the father, and in cases where this does not occur it is usually because of parental opposition, structural impossibility or resistance on the part of the man. In any case, women feel that they need husbands to help with the gardening and cash-generating work associated with children and most eventually marry.

If women with premarital children ultimately marry, there is a strong stress upon the attainment of biological parenthood within marriage. Although fosterage of children is common, it preferably enhances, rather than replaces, biological parenthood and is, further, ideally the offspring of close kin. While men may accept children from former relationships, there is a strong feeling that only exceptional men can unjealously do so. Marriage can thus entail emotional distress for a woman whose children are likely to be adopted by her parents. This was explained by one woman who consistently complained about her child-care burden, but had insisted on keeping her daughter's two sons from previous relationships when the daughter went to live virilocally after five years uxorilocal residence.

I kept them because when men look at their wives' children by other men they are jealous. I have seen Edi at my house for five years and he treats them well. He has made gardens for them and brought them rice and given them fish. Not once have I seen him hit them or be angry with them. But who knows what is in his thinking? Who knows what he does when we cannot see him? So I thought to myself, 'I must keep those two boys with me.'

This is not an arrangement regarded with equanimity by women. Another couple, who had also insisted on maintaining their daughter's three children when she remarried and lived virilocally, told me:

Pula? She cried! She cried and cried for her children. Start in the morning until come the night, she cried! She wanted to stop us but we were firm. For months she would come down here every day [from her marital home] and she cried bitterly to take her children, but we stopped her. She's quiet now but she continues to think of them.

Parents who insist upon the adoption of their daughter's children are not exclusively concerned with male jealousy, however. As Schulte (1984) demonstrates, maternity, like other affective relationships, cannot be seen as entirely disinterested. The emotional as much as the pragmatic aspects of such relationships are structured by constraining socio-economic factors. On Simbo, too, parenthood is shaped by both emotional and strategic considerations which have changed considerably over ninety years of economic and domestic transformations. With the increasing stress on conjugal relations and the parallel emphasis on household economy centred around the nuclear family, redistribution to kin has declined markedly. Parents in particular say that their offspring do not support them in the way they sustained their own parents (cf. McDowell 1988). In this context, fostered children may become both the eventual minders of their elderly foster parents and a focus of their parents' and grandparents' relationships. It is not insignificant, then, that both of the mothers of the above-mentioned fostered children visited their parents daily, helped with their gardening and shared the produce of their marital enterprises with them. Another woman who repeatedly sought to foster her unmarried teacher-daughter's infant pointed out that her daughter could not 'forget/neglect' her if she and her husband supported the child.

Older people's insistence on fostering their daughter's children, then, may be seen as both a response to diminishing intergenerational nurturance arising from accumulation within the conjugal unit and an attempt to vitiate the sexual jealousies of contemporary marriage.

Mothers as sisters, wives as mothers

This chapter deals with the contexts of maternity, but shifting contexts inflect motherhood differently. Contemporary maternity is characterized by higher fertility rates, problems with access to and acceptability of fertility control, increasing costs of children, female perceptions of children as burdensome and increased animosity between spouses (Dureau 1993, n.d.a). I have interpreted most of these developments as arising out of the privileging of marital relationships by the Christian missions and churches in the Western Solomons.

But there are other factors at work. One might point to the pressures of a money economy in imposing additional labour demands on mothers: the costs of clothing and education, for example, impose incessant monetary anxieties. Higher fertility rates stem as much from declining mortality as from loss of indigenous contraceptives and abortifacients. Public surveillance of maternity by local clinics also contributes to this as much as private surveillance by husbands. The clinics do so both directly, through their authoritative role in overseeing women's and children's health and indirectly, through enhancing husbands' awareness of their wives' reproductive condition by bringing such issues into the public space of the local clinic. Thus, the shifting of birth from the site of the supernatural vulnerability and pragmatic dangers of self-delivery in the forest to the local clinic enabled, first, mission and, later, state medical officers to supervise women, both prenatally and postnatally.

In general, men's interests as husbands dovetail with the pressures exerted by those other forces. Thus, if mortality has fallen, it is husbands who impede the use of contraceptives which would allow married women to pursue parallel declines in birth rates. Likewise, state administration of family planning (FP) and maternal and child health (MCH) services reinforce men's control over their wives' fertility in its insistent stress on sexuality as a marital practice – reflected in the restriction of contraceptive services to married couples – and on child welfare as an exclusively female concern. If modernization has problematized maternity, then, it has done so within the framework of state- and church-sponsored legitimation of a more patriarchal form of marriage (Sarei 1974). It is here that I situate the experiential account of maternity I have recorded elsewhere (Dureau 1993). Simbo women complain frequently that they have too many children, citing the physical decline this inflicts upon them, the labour imposed by their many children and the behaviour of both children and husbands.

It is impossible to quantify male coercion in reproductive practices, either now or in the past, but women are now subject to two forms of male regulation of their reproductive bodies: to husbands who assert their *rights* in women's bodies and to *luluna* who still maintain some of their disciplinary powers. Although the stress on marital relationships runs counter to men's interests as *luluna*, male *luluna* effectively reinforce the coercive power of husbands through their continuing violent reactions to awareness of female corporeality. This was repeatedly demonstrated when women initiated conversations with me about how to use Western contraception in their own situations – a concern that saw many seeking instruction in the rhythm method or asking for small calendars which would enable them to contracept secretly. Again and again, sitting with a small group of women, I, oblivious to everyone else's sudden silence, would be hushed as some man approached or passed nearby, and when he had gone I would be told that he was *luluna* to at least one of the women present.

Maternity was hardly unproblematic in the pre-Christian world, either. If it was not perceived as a burden, it was permeated by anxieties about the safety of birth, the well-being of children and the coercive power of *luluna*, which confined women to birth within marriage and compelled them to use fertility limitation measures towards that end. There are no records of the expressed attitudes of such women to their offspring and I am reluctant to impute particular emotions. However, even today their descendants who bemoan their maternal obligations clearly respond with deep affection to their own and others' children – calling them, feeding them and carrying them, soothing their upsets and belittling or pitying the childless.[23] I imagine, then, that pre-Christian maternity, involving as it did continuing visible dangers of warfare and disease for children, meant that women were often either anxious or mourning. In such circumstances, the imperative upon unmarried women to abort their embryos or kill their neonates in order to avert *luluna* vengeance was presumably acquiesced to with resignation at best.

Simbo women depict pre-Christian maternity and the transformations of family relationships in different terms. Where I interpret their grandmothers' maternity as formed by difficult circumstances and threatening tragedy, they stress their forebears' freedom from child care. They argue that women were skilled in the use of now forgotten contraceptives and abortifacients; that men were 'good people', incapable of mistreating their spouses. There is an ambivalence here, however. The pre-Christian past is simultaneously presented as a homogeneous *totoso kame rane* ('time one day') and the people *kame rane* as people living in the 'darkness'. There is a constant tension in Simbo oppositions of paganism and Christianity between the state of sin of their ancestors and their reputation as good people: 'I can't say properly. They were people of the Darkness, people of sin; but they were good people then, not like people now.'

This ambivalence also informs women's interpretations of the relationship of their marital practices to the maternal hardships they now describe. They champion Christian marriage[24] for having eclipsed their ancestors' unbridled sexuality, but deprecate husbands' 'unfairness' in their sexual and disciplinary demands. This 'unfairness' is opposed to proper Christian and *kastom*-ary conjugality, as I noted earlier. Marital conflict over maternity is thus not assessed in terms of historical transformation, but of moral illegitimacy in both Christianity and *kastom*. Of course, neither Christianity nor the privileging of marital relationships necessarily cause the maternal difficulties prevailing on Simbo. These, Simbo women's interpretations remind us, are merely the particular ways in which maternity is currently embodied and negotiated.

Conclusions: kinship, social change and gender relations

The shifting context of mothering in the face of prolonged engagement with outsiders is not unique to Simbo. There is little doubt that European imperialism has transformed women's lives globally (Etienne and Leacock 1980; Moore 1988). Of particular interest to maternity is the widespread trend towards the increasing nucleation of families (Leacock 1981; Moore 1988), a development rooted in changing economic, political and ideological forces (Gailey 1980; Leacock 1981; Oboler 1985).

On Simbo, Christianity has provided the principal framework for these changes, although they cannot be isolated from a long history of local aspirations to appropriate a range of exotic goods and practices. The Christian face of such developments is common in the Solomons (Keesing 1989), in the Pacific (Gailey 1980; Jolly and Macintyre 1989; Macintyre 1989), and elsewhere (Leacock 1981; Mann 1985; Oboler 1985). As in other places, the development of the Christian nuclear family on Simbo has been associated with what women see as a loss of their traditional autonomy. The nature of these changes seems to vary depending upon indigenous social categories, norms and values, and the particular conversion and colonial experiences. Thus Oboler (1985) argues that Nandi men in Kenya have manipulated Christian ideology in order to appropriate women's traditional wealth as it has become commercially valuable. This is quite distinct from Simbo where the contested issue has been that of men's power over, versus women's autonomy in, female reproductive bodies. Yet, in both places women have resisted by asserting that their traditional rights have Christian validity.

The degree, effect and efficacy of such resistance is highly variable even within the Pacific, and colonial repercussions have not afflicted women homogeneously. Thus, Linnekin (1990) argues that the position of elite Hawaiian women was enhanced by early colonial experiences, while Ralston (1989) maintains that ordinary women suffered under the same circumstances. Gailey (1980) argues that Tongan women were disadvantaged by analogous processes; however, Schoeffel (1977, 1978) maintains that local kinship structures constrained Christian transformations of gender relations in Samoa. Finally, Weiner (1980) sees Trobriand women as having negated colonial pressures by maintaining traditional sibling relations. Etienne and Leacock (1980) suggest, however, that where women appear not to be adversely affected by colonialism, or to have benefited from it, such conditions can only be temporary, that the progressive effect must be one of cumulative disadvantage to women.

The history of gender transformations on Simbo suggests that such adjudications are overly simplistic and that the combined effects are equivocal.[25] Etienne and Leacock's analysis depends on depicting women as victims of exogenous forces. Rather than seeing local responses to these forces as dialectically generated consequences of engagement, such analyses teleologically construct indigenous sociality as inevitably overwhelmed by colonial forces: particular local responses cannot have distinct outcomes, only variant forms of an unprecedented gender inequity. Although kinship relations have undoubtedly been significantly reconfigured in the face of local engagements with outsiders' insistent stresses on women as wives, the extent, shape and significance of these revisions have been highly variable. Simbo mothers have been progressively transformed from sisters to wives, but the shift has had particular local ramifications. Here, the salient transformation has been one from subordinate sisters and autonomous wives to one of reluctant wives and marginal sisters. Significantly, the enforcement of wifehood in Tonga, Samoa and Simbo has seen women deprived of particular rights in regard to children: in Tonga and Samoa women's influence as father's sisters has weakened with declining recognition of matrilateral principles. On Simbo, the losses have not related so much to corporate as to corporeal freedoms. That is, because marital constraints are vindicated in terms of husbands' perceptions of women's obligations towards children, women's autonomy in fertility control techniques and child raising has been eroded.

Sacks (1979), who is concerned with linking changing kinship and productive relations, suggests that in situations in which sibling relationships predominate, the status of women is greater. She uses sisterhood as a metaphor for equality, arguing that where sibling relations are privileged, sexual equality prevails. The determinacy she grants them suggests that sibling relationships are innately equitable and marriage relationships inequitable. Indeed, much work on Pacific sibling relations would tend to support her argument. I have already pointed out Gailey's and Schoeffel's papers which evoke the power, autonomy and prestige of Tongan and Samoan women, respectively, in their early contact roles as sisters. Weiner (1977, 1980) also demonstrates the complementarity of brothers and sisters and the centrality of this relation in contradistinction to that of husband and wife.

The transformation on Simbo raises doubts, not about the thesis that colonial forces have colluded to transform women into wives, but about that which explicitly equates relations of sisterhood with equality (and the associated argument which sees the elaboration of wifehood as necessarily correlated with a lessening of women's status and powers). Women on Simbo have certainly been, as Sacks (1979:7) maintains, transformed from sisters to wives, but the transformation has not been complete; nor has it been from one of equality to inequality, so much as from one mode of inequality to another. As Hendrix and Hossain insist, although Sacks creatively raises the question of how women's position varies according to their status as siblings or spouses, '[w]e also need to conceive and to develop multidimensional measures of sexual inequality in each of these relations' (1988:452).

It is thus with greater subtlety and with less teleological certainty that changes in Simbo motherhood must be viewed. While it is undoubtedly true that motherhood has become an often burdensome role, increasingly under the purview of husbands, it is important not to romanticize the lives of pre-contact women (Grimshaw 1989). If women have lost or surrendered much of their autonomy in matters of fertility, and if they now lament the size of their families and the jealousy of their husbands, they have gained a relative assurance of their children's and their own survival through the transformed epidemiology that was a parallel outcome of missionary endeavours in the region. If *luluna* force, including the possibility of annihilation, was more violent, it was more intermittent than that of contemporary husbands who are able to exert consistent pressure on women. Women may have been freed somewhat from their *luluna*'s tyranny, but they remain subordinate and what power their *luluna* do exercise, no longer tied to pre-Christian rationales, is experienced as arbitrary and unjustifiable. The greater freedoms of premarital maternity are ultimately negated by husband's reputed jealousies of the children of other men, jealousies which, time and again, see those children move from the maternal to the grand-maternal household. These ambivalences and tensions could be depicted indefinitely, but the problems of adjudicating questions of improvement or worsening could hardly be resolved, neither by anthropologists nor by contemporary Simbo women who themselves alternately idealize and vilify the past. If women today look back wistfully to times of limited fertility, they disregard the uncertainties entailed in the maternal and infant death rates of the past and the mystical terrors which birth entailed. Nor do they yearn for the reinstigation of *luluna* powers of life and death, even while they bemoan their disinclination to ameliorate the violence and increased dependency entailed in marriage.

Sacks points out that '[w]omen have borne children and taken on the social relations of motherhood everywhere. The biological process is the same . . . but motherhood is not' (1979:93). We might add a temporal dimension to this claim: for Simbo women the meanings, values and experiences of motherhood today are radically dissimilar to those of one hundred and two hundred years ago. The terrain of 'being a mother' has shifted in the wake of 'reformed' kinship relations precipitated by European contact, pacification and Christianization. When women were sisters, sibling gender hierarchy facilitated women's pragmatic autonomy in fertility control, but involved a punitive male authority which absolutely dictated motherhood within marriage, in lineage interests. As they have 'become' wives, first and foremost, their maternity has been progressively subjected to the control and adjudication of husbands.

NOTES

1 Literally 'people [of] Simbo'.
2 The fieldwork on which this chapter is based was carried out between April 1990–May 1991 and December 1991–April 1992, in all but one Simbo community.
3 This remains the majority church. There are also small communities of Christian Fellowship Church (CFC), Seventh-Day Adventist (SDA) and South Seas Evangelical Church (SSEC) adherents.
4 Yaws and polio left many physically disabled and it is almost certain that such children were not regarded as fulfilling the ideal. Certainly today such people are regarded as less than adequate. Some indication of the difficulty of raising children to adulthood is suggested by Bennett's claim that 40 per cent of children died of malaria alone. Other potential causes of childhood death included tuberculosis, smallpox and any of the various European-induced epidemics of measles and influenza which followed the ships (Bennett 1987). The Western Solomons were racked by successive epidemics in the last years of the nineteenth century (Jackson 1978), which typically killed the very young and the very old disproportionately. Blackwood's (1935) data on Bougainville

and Buka is also evocative. In a similar epidemiological environment of indigenous and introduced diseases before the adoption of Western medicine, she mentions the history of eleven polygynous marriages: of thirty-one children born to these marriages, sixteen died in childhood or infancy and one woman died in childbirth. Elsewhere she mentions that miscarriage was frequent. Lancaster and King (1985:15) maintain that about 50 per cent mortality of infants and children is usual for such 'simple economies'.

5 I deliberately use the past tense here. There are no *lumu* on contemporary Simbo.

6 There is a further parallel between *luluna* and *banara*. Hocart (n.d.b) reports that adultery was thought to result in the death of *banara*. There was no such opinion when I did my own fieldwork eighty years later, presumably because of the decline of the *banara*.

7 A further asymmetrical element in *luluna* relations concerned the extent to which obligations were felt. Women were susceptible to the ire of *luluna* to the extent of second (and sometimes third) cousins. However, it was usually only natal or adoptive *luluna* who had lived in close proximity who intervened on behalf of aggrieved women, except in cases of exceptional hardship.

8 Hocart (n.d.d) describes this as enabling cohabitation without marriage, but it was a stage of all marriages.

9 I do not know how frequently this was performed. Presently it occurs in about 50 per cent of marriages.

10 In such cases, women were executed by decapitation and became *tomate maza*, the same fate which befell men beheaded in battle. This implies some kind of equation or relation between male warriors and reproductive females. It is possible that it reflects views of men and women as linked respectively to death and life, or as both generative in some way. However, the idea certainly was not explicit at the time of my fieldwork. In another context, Scheffler (1962) doubts that theoretical death penalties for other infractions of *luluna* relationships were ever exacted. I would suggest that the severity of contemporary *luluna* violence undermines such assertions. In particular, a notably vicious response to an incest violation in 1992, while it did not result in death, saw a woman and her lover kicked in the head, throat, abdomen and kidneys, a beating entailing considerable risk of fatality. In times past when every man walked around with an axe over his shoulder, swift decapitation would have been quite feasible.

11 The only written source on this subject that I am aware of is the 1931 census report (WPHC 1931), which holds that children were suckled for about two years. The information is presented as a response by district officers to an ethnographic questionnaire circulated with the census. Against this, I place the claimed memories of geriatric women who recall their own mothers' extended suckling and can cite local missionaries' attempts to reduce the period.

12 Hocart (n.d.b) also suggests that her *luluna* might be killed, but is unclear about who might do so. I suspect that he may have misinterpreted the supernatural consequences of a woman's adultery as an intentional social act.

13 In saying this I do not suggest that a nuclear family form identical to the normative Western family of father, mother and children pertains on Simbo. I

mean to convey a contraction of kinship obligations and an increasing tendency to see the primary locus of identity, authority and responsibility as lying within the paternally headed single generation unit. In economic matters, there is an ongoing conflict here between extant values of generalized reciprocity between kin and neoteric notions that resources belong within that unit. There remains a general assumption that grandparents (in local idiom 'Old Mother' and 'Old Father') retain influence over, and interest in, children, and that parents' classificatory siblings (the child's classificatory parents) remain concerned with the child's well-being.

14 All names are pseudonyms.

15 Stroking and praying over invalids was a traditional healing technique (Hocart 1925).

16 'Wives, submit yourselves unto your own husbands as unto the Lord. For the husband is the head of the wife, even as Christ is head of the church; and he is the saviour of the body. Therefore as the church is subject unto Christ, so let wives be to their husbands in everything. Husbands, love your wives, even as Christ also loved the church, and gave himself for it.'

17 Which renders their term, 'brideprice', rather inappropriate.

18 Thus there are a number of cases on the island in which men who did not divorce their wives subsequent to adultery have accepted the children of the adulterous liaison.

19 This is not to say that marital violence never occurred, although older people are adamant that this was the case. I have a number of accounts of men who were never able to remain married because of their inability to refrain from beating their wives. The point is that it was illegitimate and women could evict their husbands or return to their own kin or call upon their *luluna* to avenge them. In such cases, men could only persuade their wives to return by paying them – and sometimes their parents – compensation.

20 A number of men claim, in fact, that wifely subordination is enshrined in *kastom*. These are primarily younger, educated men, or those middle-aged men who received considerable education or influence from the Methodist Mission.

21 When a woman, severely beaten and left with hearing defects by several of her *luluna* after she ran off with her mother's sister's son, defiantly spoke of pressing charges in the magistrate's court, many men retorted that the law has no rights of adjudication in customary matters. Alternatively, they may argue that, irrespective of legal sanctions, the obligations entailed in particular relationships must be fulfilled – this was the reasoning given by men who had defended their 'brothers' in brawls, for example.

22 The two who have children – one through marriage to a much older widow, the other through a youthful love affair – are often ridiculed.

23 The planned childlessness of my visiting sister was utterly disbelieved.

24 By this I do not mean marriage sanctified in church; I refer to marriage between Christian people in an avowedly Christian environment and assessed by the criteria of local Christianity.

25 Mann's (1985) analysis of religious changes in colonial Lagos has similar implications. She argues that women and men strategically negotiated their

shifting allegiances to Christianity and traditional religions in the face of progressive political and economic developments.

REFERENCES

Barker, J. 1990 Encounters with evil: Christianity and the response to sorcery among the Maisin of Papua New Guinea. *Oceania* 61:139–55.

Bennett, J.A. 1987 *Wealth of the Solomons: A History of a Pacific Archipelago, 1800–1978*, Pacific Islands Monograph Series, No. 3. Honolulu: University of Hawaii Press.

Blackwood, B. 1935 *Both Sides of Buka Passage*. Oxford: Clarendon.

Burt, B. 1983 The Remnant Church: a Christian sect in the Solomon Islands. *Oceania* 53(4):334–46.

Comaroff, J. 1985 *Body of Power, Spirit of Resistance: The Culture and History of a South African People*. Chicago: University of Chicago Press.

Denoon, D. 1989 Medical care and gender in Papua New Guinea. In M. Jolly and M. Macintyre (eds.) *Family and Gender in the Pacific: Domestic Contradictions and the Colonial Impact*. Cambridge: Cambridge University Press, 95–107.

Dureau, C. 1993 Nobody asked the mother: women and maternity on Simbo, western Solomon Islands. *Oceania* 64(1):18–35.

n.d.a Mutual goals and conflicting means: family planning on Simbo, western Solomon Islands. In M. Jolly and K. Ram (eds.) *Borders of Being: State, Fertility and Sexuality in Asia and the Pacific* (forthcoming).

n.d.b 'Time of light and cleanliness': pacification and Christian conversion on Simbo, Western Solomon Islands. *Social Analysis* (forthcoming).

Etienne, M. and Leacock, E. 1980 Introduction. In M. Etienne and E. Leacock (eds.) *Women and Colonization: Anthropological Perspectives*. New York: Praeger, 1–24.

Faithorn, E. 1975 The concept of pollution among the Kafe of the Papua New Guinea highlands. In R.R. Reiter (ed.) *Toward an Anthropology of Women*. New York: Monthly Review Press, 127–40.

Gailey, C.W. 1980 Putting down sisters and wives: Tongan women and colonization. In M. Etienne and E. Leacock (eds.) *Women and Colonization: Anthropological Perspectives*. New York: Praeger, 294–322.

Grimshaw, P. 1989 New England missionary wives, Hawaiian women and 'the cult of true womanhood'. In M. Jolly and M. Macintyre (eds.) *Family and Gender in the Pacific: Domestic Contradictions and the Colonial Impact*. Cambridge: Cambridge University Press, 19–44.

Harwood, F.K. 1971 The Christian Fellowship Church: a Melanesian revitalization movement. PhD thesis, University of Chicago.

Hendrix, L. and Hossain, Z. 1988 Women's status and mode of production: a cross-cultural test. *Signs* 13:437–53.

Hocart, A.M. 1925 Medicine and witchcraft in Eddystone of the Solomons. *Journal of the Royal Anthropological Institute* 55:229–70.

1931 Warfare in Eddystone of the Solomons. *Journal of the Royal Anthropological Institute* 61:301–24.

n.d.a Chieftainship. Hocart Collection: papers held by the Alexander Turnbull Library, Wellington, New Zealand.

n.d.b *Ranggoso molu*: the charm for determining sex. Hocart Collection: papers held by the Alexander Turnbull Library, Wellington, New Zealand.

n.d.c Relations between the sexes and marriage. Hocart Collection: papers held by the Alexander Turnbull Library, Wellington, New Zealand.

n.d.d Trade and money, Mandegusu. Hocart Collection: papers held by the Alexander Turnbull Library, Wellington, New Zealand.

Jackson, K. 1978 *Tie Hokara, Tie Vaka*, Black Man, White Man: a study of the New Georgia Group to 1925. PhD thesis, The Australian National University.

Jolly, M. and Macintyre, M. 1989 Introduction. In M. Jolly and M. Macintyre (eds.) *Family and Gender in the Pacific: Domestic Contradictions and the Colonial Impact*. Cambridge: Cambridge University Press, 1–18.

Keesing, R.M. 1985 Kwaio women speak: the micropolitics of autobiography in a Solomon Island society. *American Anthropologist* 87(1):27–39.

1989 Sins of a mission: Christian life as Kwaio traditionalist ideology. In M. Jolly and M. Macintyre (eds.) *Family and Gender in the Pacific: Domestic Contradictions and the Colonial Impact*. Cambridge: Cambridge University Press, 193–212.

Kerns, V. 1983 *Women and the Ancestors: Black Carib Kinship and Ritual*. Urbana: University of Illinois Press.

Lancaster, J.B. and King, B.J. 1985 An evolutionary perspective on menopause. In J. K. Brown and V. Kerns (eds.) *In Her Prime: A New View of Middle-Aged Women*. South Hadley, MA: Bergin and Garvey, 13–20.

Leacock, E.B. 1981 Montagnais women and the Jesuit program for colonization. In E.B. Leacock *Myths of Male Dominance: Collected Articles on Women Cross-Culturally*. New York: Monthly Review Press, 43–62.

Linnekin, J. 1990 *Sacred Queens and Women of Consequence: Rank, Gender and Colonialism in the Hawaiian Islands*. Ann Arbor: University of Michigan Press.

McDowell, N. 1988 Conclusions: continuity and change. In N. McDowell (ed.) *Reproductive Decision Making and the Value of Children in Rural Papua New Guinea*. IASER Monograph No. 27. Boroko: PNG Institute of Applied Social and Economic Research, 237–63.

Macintyre, M. 1989 Better homes and gardens. In M. Jolly and M. Macintyre (eds.) *Family and Gender in the Pacific: Domestic Contradictions and the Colonial Impact*. Cambridge: Cambridge University Press, 156–69.

n.d. Motherhood and marriage on Tubetube. Paper presented to Gender Relations Project Maternity Workshop, The Australian National University, Canberra, 13–15 July 1992.

Mann, K. 1985 *Marrying Well: Marriage, Status and Social Change among the Colonial Elite in Colonial Lagos*. Cambridge: Cambridge University Press.

Miller, C. 1985 Domesticity abroad: work and family in the Sandwich Island Mission, 1820–1840. In C. Miller (ed.) *Missions and Missionaries in the Pacific*. New York and Toronto: Edwin Mellen Press, 65–90.

Moore, H. 1988 *Feminism and Anthropology*. Cambridge: Polity Press.

Nash, J. 1981 Sex, money and the status of women in aboriginal South Bougainville. *American Ethnologist* 8:107–26.

O'Collins, M. 1978 Overview of social welfare and family planning programmes in the Solomon Islands. Report prepared for the UN Interregional Technical Meeting on social welfare aspects of family planning, mid-1978, Manila, Philippines.

    1979 Family planning programmes in Papua New Guinea and Solomon Islands. Paper for the 49th Congress of the Australian and New Zealand Association for the Advancement of Science, Auckland, New Zealand, 22–6 January 1979.

Oboler, R.S. 1985 *Women, Power and Economic Change: The Nandi of Kenya.* Stanford: Stanford University Press.

Ralston, C. 1989 Changes in the lives of ordinary women in early post-contact Hawaii. In M. Jolly and M. Macintyre (eds.) *Family and Gender in the Pacific: Domestic Contradictions and the Colonial Impact.* Cambridge: Cambridge University Press, 45–64.

Rivers, W.H.R. 1922 The psychological factor. In W.H.R. Rivers (ed.) *Essays on the Depopulation of Melanesia.* Cambridge: Cambridge University Press, 84–113.

Sacks, K. 1979 *Sisters and Wives: The Past and Future of Sexual Equality.* Westport: Greenwood Press.

Sarei, A.H. 1974 *Traditional Marriage and the Impact of Christianity on the Solos of Buka Island. New Guinea Research Bulletin*, No. 57. Port Moresby and Canberra: New Guinea Research Unit, The Australian National University.

Scheffler, H.W. 1962 Kindred and kin groups in Simbo social structure. *Ethnology* 1:135–57.

Schoeffel, P. 1977 The origin and development of women's associations in Western Samoa, 1830–1977. *Journal of Pacific Studies* 3:1–21.

    1978 Gender, status and power in Samoa. *Canberra Anthropology* 1(2):69–81.

Schulte, R. 1984 Infanticide in rural Bavaria in the nineteenth century. In H. Medick and D.W. Sabean (eds.) *Interest and Emotion: Essays on the Study of Family and Kinship.* Cambridge: Cambridge University Press, 77–102.

Thomas, N. 1992 Colonial conversions: difference, hierarchy and history in early twentieth-century evangelical propaganda. *Comparative Studies in Society and History* 34:366–89.

Waterhouse, J.H.L. 1949 *A Roviana and English Dictionary: With English–Roviana Index List of Natural History Objects and Appendix of Old Customs* (revised and enlarged by L.M. Jones). Sydney: Epworth.

Weiner, A. 1977 *Women of Value, Men of Renown: New Perspectives in Trobriand Exchange.* St. Lucia: University of Queensland Press.

    1980 Stability in banana leaves: colonization and women in Kiriwina, Trobriand Islands. In M. Etienne and E. Leacock (eds.) *Women and Colonization: Anthropological Perspectives.* New York: Praeger, 270–93.

White, G. 1990 *Identity through History: Living Stories in a Solomon Islands Society.* Cambridge: Cambridge University Press.

Wolf, E.R. 1958 The virgin of Guadalupe: a Mexican national symbol. *Journal of American Folklore* 71:34–9.

WPHC (Western Pacific High Commission) 1886 Australian Station: New Guinea and Solomon Islands correspondence respecting outrages by natives on British subjects . . . Case 8: Murder of Mr Childe, an English settler by natives of Narovo.

1931 Report on the Population Census of the British Solomon Islands Protectorate.

Epilogue *Maternal experience and feminist body politics: Asian and Pacific perspectives*

Kalpana Ram

The chapters in this volume stand heir to more than one genealogy in the way in which they approach the conceptualization of maternal embodiment. The first genealogy links the volume to anthropological conceptualizations of the relations between culture and bodily experience. This epilogue opens with reflections on anthropological traditions, presenting them not only as internally diverse and contested, but as a tradition capable of being recast into new forms of life. The second genealogy links the volume to controversies within feminism regarding the most appropriate ways in which to understand the construction of the female body within and through relations of power.

The two genealogies are not commensurate. Feminist theory has grown out of a fundamental ethical and political impulse rather than out of any notion of a 'pure' pursuit of knowledge, and withers where divorced from those impulses. Anthropology, for all the necessary departures of its practitioners from the halls of Western academia for life in very different cultures, and for all the internal complexities of anthropology as cultural critique, remains firmly located within the power/knowledge nexus of academic discourse.[1]

Anthropology and feminism are also not commensurate in respect of the part they play in shaping this epilogue. Without attempting to do justice to all the anthropological questions raised by this volume, I will endeavour to characterize the debates over just two key terms which are central to the anthropology of maternity: the body, and culture. Taking advantage of the prerogative of the epilogue writer to revisit the concerns of a volume, I have chosen to elaborate and in some ways *re*contextualize just one concern, albeit a central concern of the volume. I refer to the impulse, common to all contributors, to transform existing accounts of Asian and Pacific women – which may be said to describe only 'maternality-for-the-other' – and to replace them with an account of 'maternality-for-the-*mother*' (Edelstein 1992:29). I take this impulse to signify a quintessentially feminist set of imperatives. A recent review of feminist literature on motherhood and maternity by Ross (1995) finds a common preoccupation with representing 'the mother increasingly [as] a subject rather than a distant, looming object' (1995:413). If this is a concern which this volume shares with other feminist literature, then we may ask how contributors utilize their chosen focus on Asian and Pacific women's experiences in negotiating issues that have come up in feminist theory. Does the perspective on maternity from the 'periphery' rather than from the 'metropole' extend the debate in any specific way? I will examine these questions with reference to several conceptual controversies which underlie feminist but also any contemporary treatment of body politics.

Anthropological locations

Certain old but enduring concerns of anthropology – such as cultural variability, and the interpenetration of cultural meaning, language and symbolism, on the one hand, and the structures of physiological experiences, such as pregnancy, birth and feeding, on the other – regenerate themselves in this volume. They are recast, however, within a new and emergent framework. When contributors, such as Rozario, emphasize the power of pollution ideology to shape the rituals and practices of childbirth and birth attendance, or when Merrett-Balkos explains historically unprecedented actions by Anganen women (such as their reclamation of placentas from the mission hospital), by referring to the centrality of gender metaphors in language, ritual and kinship practices, they draw on well-established and powerful antecedents. These antecedents are provided in the Durkheimian tradition elaborated by Hertz (1973), Mauss (1973) and Dumont (1970), as well as in the British structuralist tradition of Leach (1958) and Douglas (1973). When Dureau opens her chapter with the assertion that '[m]aternity is more than a simple dyadic relationship, for it necessarily reflects, and is constituted by, other social relations' (this volume, p. 239), she in turn mobilizes, for her own purposes, an anthropological tradition of holism. This tradition posits that maternity, or indeed any important social relation, cannot be understood without conveying an ethnographic sense of the totality of practices, meanings and systemic transformations that constitute the whole.

However, this very tenet of holism should alert us to the way we understand apparent continuities in anthropological traditions. 'Tradition, heritage, and authenticity are all now terms proper to a landscape of heteroglossia and one of intense contestation', write the editors of a volume taking a fresh look at expressive traditions in South Asia (Appadurai *et al.* 1991:23). The same may be said, not of expressive, but of anthropological traditions. This volume's attention to symbolism and holism occurs in a context that reflects new and productive destabilizations of core assumptions occurring within the discipline itself. *Both* the key terms, entailed in an investigation of the cultural variability of the body, are under challenge. Just what anthropology means by 'the body' or for that matter, by 'culture' can no longer be taken for granted. In the face of a Foucauldian preparedness to regard the body as constructed entirely by the shifting regimes of knowledge and power, the thesis of cultural variability no longer seems quite so radical a means of contesting Western philosophical predelictions. Anthropology has been called upon to clarify what precisely is meant by the model of cultural difference. The calls to do so have come from diverse vantage points. From the perspective of scholarship and activism generated by gay and feminist movements in the United States, Carole Vance (1989, 1991) finds that many of the anthropological claims to view sexuality as 'constructed' lapse into or perhaps never depart from what is in fact a much milder version of constructionism, which she terms 'the cultural influence model'. In this model, numerous core assumptions of Western philosophy and culture regarding the biological basis of a phenomenon such as sexuality are retained in unexamined fashion:

although culture is thought to shape sexual expression and customs, the bedrock of sexuality is assumed – and often quite explicitly stated – to be universal and biologically determined; in the literature, it appears as 'sex drive' or 'impulse'. Although capable of being shaped, the drive is conceived of as powerful, moving toward expression after its awakening in puberty, sometimes exceeding social regulation, and taking a distinctively different form in men and women. (1991:878)

From another vantage point, that provided by the philosophical tradition of phenomenology, Jackson (1989) and Csordas (1994) formulate criticisms which share elements of Vance's dissatisfaction. Characterizing the earlier anthropology as one which studies the body 'as an object or theme of analysis, often the source of symbols taken up in the discourse of cultural domains such as religion and social structure' (Csordas 1994:4), Csordas, like Vance, finds problematic the tendency to reduce the body to the status of biological raw material on which culture operates (1994:8).

The term 'culture' has, by comparison, been a beneficiary of the overwhelming turn towards representation in social theory. Culture – newly transmuted into Foucault's 'discourse', Bourdieu's 'habitus', or into anthropological preoccupations with 'representations' – now enjoys a vastly expanded investiture of powers and a seemingly infinite capacity to (pre)determine experience. At stake is precisely the older anthropological appreciation of 'culture' as a systemic and integral whole. Such a vision can no longer be sustained once primacy and centrality have been accorded to relations of domination and subordination. The whole is irretrievably splintered by intersecting identities produced by class, race, gender and colonialism. While the newly fragmented vision of culture has posed critical questions for ethnographic representation (Clifford and Marcus 1986), the challenge has been taken up in a positive fashion in the emergence of new kinds of ethnographic interpretations. Cultural practices such as mourning rituals, genres of performativity such as oral poetry, songs – all along the province of traditional anthropological enquiry – now become the site of new ethnographic traditions that interpret them as so many spheres in which both subordination and resistance are played out (e.g. Abu-Lughod 1986; Appadurai *et al.* 1991; Raheja and Gold 1996; Seremetakis 1991).

The anthropology of maternity, despite the marginal status it has been allocated by masculinist presumptions according to Ginsburg and Rapp (1991:311), McClain (1982:37) and Jordan (1983:51), reflects the impact of these contestatory paradigms within the larger disciplinary field. The present volume, with the attention it pays to issues of colonialism, and of representation, as well as to class, gender and caste, aligns itself more closely with those recent authors who give primacy to the 'politics of reproduction' (Ginsburg and Rapp 1991; Greenhalgh 1995:17; Handwerker 1990) than with the ethnographic ambition of delivering a complete account of 'the biosocial production of childbirth in different cultural settings', as Jordan describes her aspirations in the pioneering *Birth in Four Cultures* (1983:i).

However, evaluations of shifts in intellectual paradigms are as vulnerable to the allure of teleologies of progress as are other kinds of historical writing. It is necessary, therefore, to remind ourselves that an appreciation of 'politics' is not unique to the present phase, and that various versions of 'anthropology as cultural critique' (Marcus and Fischer 1986) have been evident at every phase in the ethnography of birth.[2] In Spencer's compilation of cross-cultural data on 'primitive obstetrics' (1977(1949–50)), the very juxtaposition of the idea of 'primitives' with the idea of 'obstetrics' is used to disrupt the expectations born of modernization theory, that social complexity in 'primitive' communities will only reflect the stage of material development (Landy 1977:289). When American women take up the ethnographic concern with birth and maternity in other cultures, their interest is quite clearly fuelled by the growing crisis within the most highly developed version of medicalized childbirth to be found anywhere in the world. Mead and Newton (1967), obliged as they are, thanks to the overwhelming neglect of the topic, to cull scattered references to birthing practices and to organize them into comparative categories, nevertheless utilize the data as a reflexive device by which to locate American birth as one 'biosocial' system among others, and a historically changing one at that. Jordan (1983) not only utilizes the Yucatan birth system to reflect on the inadequacies of the obstetric model of birth, but reflects at length on the paradoxes of the historical moment in which this ethnographic documentation takes shape. The very practices under increasing scrutiny and criticism from women in Western countries are being confidently exported as an integral component of progress and development to the women of the 'Third World' (Jordan 1983:67ff).

Texts such as *Birth in Four Cultures* (Jordan 1983) are of particular interest, as they wind their way through successive editions, providing a kind of documentation of the shifts within the anthropology of maternity. Van Hollen (1994) makes this point in her review of a 'burgeoning' anthropology of birth. Birth is no longer reflective of 'largely uncontested cultural patterns'. Instead, there is a growing conceptualization of birth as 'an arena within which culture is produced, reproduced and resisted', of culture as situated historically 'within the context of particular political and economic relations' (1994:501). Such transitions, always uneven in their impact, produce particular tensions in the fourth edition of Jordan's ethnography (Jordan 1993).

This volume situates itself squarely in the framework of these contemporary concerns and preoccupations. However, it also deepens the challenges of this theoretical moment in very particular ways. It goes further than other treatments of maternity in challenging the 'leaden' identification of colonialism with 'History' (Prakash 1995:4). It does so by attempting to break down the powerful epistemic and political partitions that divide colonialism off from the postwar political economy of 'development'. The colonial shaping of reproduction (see Ginsburg and Rapp 1991:315–16 for an overview) has been treated in separation from ethnographies that document the contemporary inequalities of global reproductive politics (see, for example, Corea *et al.* 1987; Pillsbury 1990; Scheper-Hughes 1987). Yet the division between the colonial and the postcolonial must rank as one of the most contentious issues in the contemporary human sciences, for at stake is the negotiation of colonialism within scholarship itself. Prakash raises the objections in their strongest form:

This view is complicit with western domination but offers itself nonetheless as a clear lens through which we can understand colonialism. It sequesters colonialism tightly in the airless container of History, and casts postcoloniality as a new beginning, one in which certain old modes of domination may persist and acquire new forms of sustenance but one that marks the end of an era. To pry open the reading of colonialism from this prison-house of historicism requires more than the concept of neocolonialism. (1995:4–5)

Although no individual contributor has set herself this explicit task, the volume taken as a whole pushes ahead with the project of blurring the divisions between historical past and ethnographic present. It is this project in turn which provides the broader framework within which the anthropological past becomes a living resource for new forms of reflection and utilization. Returning for a moment to the example of Dureau's holism, it is clear that the canvas provided by this project is far larger than the holism informing previous ethnographies of birth. In Jordan, for example, the whole within which the 'parameters for birth location, admissible personnel, [and] support systems' (1983:79) are determined extends as far as the moral framework characteristic of any stable society (1983:69). For Dureau, maternity is to be located not only within kinship and the totality of gender relations, but is to be appraised with reference to the vast changes wrought by colonial practices.

Jolly has already shown how the rich empirical material offered to the readers of this volume sustains fresh reflections of a comparative nature on colonial critiques of mothers in Asia and the Pacific; as well as on the permutations of these discourses into present-day accommodations and resistances on the part of these societies (Jolly, this volume: Introduction). In this Epilogue, I will consider these and other issues within the framework of feminist theory.

Feminist controversies

(a) Universalism and difference

Historically, feminist concerns have described a universalizing trajectory. Feminists have been unable to contain or content themselves with catering only to the female self, or even to one group of women. The 'other woman' for them was simply any other woman located in any place or, indeed, any period of time. Western feminist theory and practice was geared to make ethical interventions on behalf of any woman: the 'Third World Woman' as much as the figure of the witch in preindustrial Europe.

The broad feminist ethical concern to do justice both to the commonality of women and to the differences between women has traditionally allocated a privileged place to the female body and, in particular, to a defence of the integrity of the female body. Powerful emotions of solidarity and sympathy, as well as anger at division and privilege, have surged wherever the violation of the female body has been encountered. Rape, cliterodectomy, the sexual abuse of the girl child, *sati*, dowry deaths and domestic violence – all these are issues which bring out in particularly powerful ways the tensions between constructing commonality and acknowledging differences between women.

Maternity and maternal embodiment partake of this more general feminist political investment in the female body. The female reproductive body can be considered one of the crucial sites on which constructions of sexual difference and feminine subjectivity have been erected, cutting across divisions of culture and power. Even for theorists who have thrown into doubt other bases for sexual difference the claims of the reproductive body retain their capacity to provide a lodging place for a notion of 'woman'. Kristeva asks at the start of her paper on the 'Stabat Mater':

> If it is not possible to say of a woman what she is (without running the risk of abolishing her difference), would it perhaps be different concerning the mother, since that is the only function of the other sex to which we can definitely attribute existence? (1986:161)

The terms of this universalism have come under severe scrutiny, and for good reasons. Its ethics and epistemology were severely vitiated by an inability to incorporate within their framework an attention to the relatively privileged social location of the theorizing feminist self (or even collectivity). The privileging of gender-based oppression – a necessary precondition for feminist endeavours – itself led to the obscuring of the complexities of class and racial oppression, which intersect with and radically redefine gender oppression.

Such absences left feminist language wide open to charges of replicating the very mechanisms through which earlier forms of Western universalism had exercised their hegemony over subject populations. Women whose social relations have been radically redefined by colonialism and postcolonial capitalism found themselves unrepresented, and indeed unrepresentable, within the language of 'second-wave' feminism. The groups mounting the challenge have been diverse, since the relations of colonialism have themselves had a differentiating impact on the location of women. Not only women within so-called Third World nations, but also black American, diasporic and immigrant women have had a significant contribution to make to critiques of race and colonialism within feminist theory.

Critiques of white feminism have been particularly powerfully articulated by American black women. Dealing specifically with the subject of black women's experiences of maternity, Collins writes:

White feminist work on motherhood has failed to produce an effective critique of elite white male analyses of Black motherhood. Grounded in a white, middle-class women's standpoint, white feminist analyses have been profoundly affected by the limitations that this angle of vision has on race . . . While white feminists have effectively confronted white male analyses of their own experiences as mothers, they rarely challenge controlling images such as the mammy, the matri-arch, and the welfare mother and therefore fail to include Black mothers 'still cleaning somebody else's house or . . . caring for somebody else's sick or elderly'. (1990:116)

Motherhood has become a booming field of feminist enquiry. According to Ross: 'The significance, power, richness, and scope of mothering and motherhood, in practice, in fantasy, in fiction, and in politics, has been discovered, and the small stream of 1970s and 1980s books about ma-ternity has widened in the 1990s; a torrent of notable contributions appeared just during the year this project sat on my desk' (1995:402).

Yet, despite the large field of books reviewed and cited in two separate essays by Ross (1995) and Adams (1995), the body of writing by Afro-American feminists remains the only sustained exception to the continu-ing dominance of white women's experiences. Far less has been pub-lished by Asian and Pacific women on the way in which their experiences have also been shaped by colonial relations.[3] Both Ross and Adams in turn note that black women do not seem to share white women's ambiva-lence about honouring mothers (Ross 1995:401) and, in the less chari-table words of Walters, exhibit none of the 'psychological whining' she perceives in white women's writings (cited in Adams 1995:418). Yet such differences find no explanatory framework, unless we understand the inadequacy of purely psychological and representational accounts of maternity for those women who have experienced power relations of race and colonization. As we document in this volume, European men and women have had the power not only to represent the Asian and Pacific (M)other but to actually enforce those representations through the insti-tutionalized apparatuses of Western religion, medicine and administra-tive policies, backed by the authority and violence of the colonial state. This volume has demonstrated that the concerns of the colonial state can be enormously varied when and if it chooses to intervene in the sphere of reproduction. If in colonial Malaya, the state was concerned with infant mortality in order to secure a labour force (Manderson, this volume), then Jolly (this volume: Chapter 6) details an alternative route taken by the state. In Fiji and Vanuatu, concern with infant mortality emerges in the midst of a broad concern with the perceptions of decline, demorali-ation and depopulation of what is assumed to be the province of the dying races of the Pacific. The precise division of labour between missions and the colonial state that is entailed in the propagation of medicine, science and civilization also varies from case to case. If in Malaya, it is the state which 'discovers' the child and attempts to supervise and control maternity (Manderson, this volume), then in Fiji and Vanuatu, Jolly describes a shift from an early phase of 'missionary lament' to a later one of 'state surveillance' (Jolly, this volume: Chapter 6). In India, the colonial state only begins to concern itself beyond the civil and military constituency at the close of the nineteenth century (Arnold 1989) – it is the medical missionaries who take '"Christ and surgery" to areas where the colonial state did not care to intervene' (Shetty 1994:192–3). Despite these significant variations, one feature remains constant: relations of economic and political domination enabled European women to 'visit' their colonial female subjects in order to dictate the pursuit of more enlightened beliefs, both religious (see Haggis and Dureau, this volume; Ram, this volume: Chapter 4) and medical (see Manderson and Merrett-Balkos, this volume).

In the South Asian region, colonialism not only conferred a measure of subjecthood on upper-class white women who could reconstitute themselves as 'lady missionaries' (Haggis, this volume), but it also created alliances across the colonial divide, alliances between the English and Indian upper-class women. Missionary endeavour may not always have succeeded in converting quite the right class quality of souls: conversions from the subaltern castes have always been normative for South Asia, whether it was the Nadar 'Bible women' who were converted to Protestantism in the nineteenth century (Haggis, this volume) or the Mukkuvar fishing communities who were converted to Catholicism in the sixteenth century (Ram 1991 and this volume: Chapter 4). However, significant foundations were also laid during the colonial period for equipping Indian middle-class women with the education and professional qualifications necessary to emulate the 'lady missionaries'. This laying of foundations is particularly striking in the case of medicine, a field closely allied in the colonies with the propagation of the Bible. In her study of colonial obstetrics and gynaecology in India, Shetty (1994) has examined the dramatic contrast between the recruitment of women into medical science in the metropole, and their recruitment in the colony. By the late nineteenth century, the barriers to the recruitment of women erected by male physicians in England and America were remarkably absent in India. Instead, there were consistent efforts to recruit a 'better class' of European, but, equally, of Indian women to become 'lady doctors' (Shetty 1994:195).

Such structures of power prefigure the emergence of contemporary postcolonial elites, particularly large and significant in Asia. It prefigures also the positioning of women within the middle classes which are burgeoning in places like Malaysia (see Stivens, this volume). Issues of differences and power relations which divide women and make some beneficiaries in the oppression of others, far from disappearing along with direct colonial rule, pose even more complex versions of difference for analysts to contend with. They must analyse interaction between discourses of Western modernity and caste and class relations (see Ram, this volume: Chapter 4, and Rozario, this volume). Other contributors, such as Stivens (this volume), take up the challenge of providing an understanding of particular forms taken by the temporal coincidence and mutual imbrication of 'tradition' and 'modernity' in Malaysia. Here, religious movements and pronatalism are paralleled by 'modernist' ideologies of child psychology and the commoditization of child care. Are these to be understood as parallel but unrelated phenomena, or is there a particular relationship between modernity and tradition which is quite specific to the global inequalities of cultural and economic transaction?

Colonial discourses of medicine, religion and science cannot be located as external – they are now even more widely espoused as part of modernity by men and women from the region. At the same time, these discourses introduce into the subjectivity of men and women profound divisions and splittings. Postponing discussion of these issues for the moment, it will be seen that the volume significantly aligns itself with the 'difference' end of the universalist/difference debate within feminism.

Having said this, it must be added that this volume can in no sense claim to be taking on the speaking-position of colonized women themselves. Most of the contributors are not Asian or Pacific women. But then, it is unlikely that there would even be a feminist enterprise if it were robbed entirely of the impulse to reach out to the other woman, who will necessarily never occupy a subject position of utter identity with the feminist subject. Of the two Asian women who write here, one is separated by privileges of caste and class from the women she writes about. The other comes as close as one can to writing about one's own community, but also feels the intellectual need to write comparatively about women from other religious groups. Both women are separated from their countries through migration and relocation in Australia. Critiques based on difference collapse through internal incoherence if interpreted to mean that relations of utter identity are the prerequisite for writing and speaking. What is important is that earlier claims to universalism should respond to and be shaped by the critiques of power and privilege within feminism and, more broadly, among women. One relevant response calls for reformulating the terms of the universalist ethical impulse.[4]

(b) Maternity as discourse and maternity as experience

The sympathy with which the claims of the maternal body have been treated by feminists has been highly variable. Earlier generations of feminism tended, in keeping with a broader inclination to mistrust the claims of the body, to regard maternity as a miring of female subjectivity. De Beauvoir, for instance, sees maternity as a dramatization and final seal in the general tendencies of female biology to drag down and ensnare the girl's budding aspirations (de Beauvoir 1972(1949)).[5] Several feminist commentators have remarked on the way in which feminism oriented itself towards the subject position of the angry daughter, rejecting not only mothers but the mother in themselves (Ruddick 1989:39; see also Braidotti 1989:96).

This is true not only of Western feminism but of other feminisms as well. The writings of Indian feminists which fill a special issue of one of India's journals of national intellectual importance, the *Economic and Political Weekly*, express their critical rage both as daughters neglected by mothers in favour of sons and as daughters of a culture dominated by the imagery of maternity even down to the symbolic mapping of its anti-colonial struggles (1990).

For contributors such as Stivens (this volume), there has been (despite exceptions of some significance), 'comparatively little interest in mothering as a social institution in the central texts of recent Western feminist theorizing' (Stivens, this volume, p. 53).

Nevertheless, we have witnessed, since the seventies, the gradual emergence of a position which tries to distinguish between maternity as an institution – an institution which has both disciplined and regulated women's subjectivity and aspirations – and maternity as experience. The same year, 1977, saw the publication of Rich's *Of Woman Born* in the United States and of Kristeva's *Stabat Mater*, both pleading in powerful terms for a reformulation of feminist attitudes to maternity and asking feminists to respect a distinction between oppressive ideologies of mothering and maternal experience. Rich expresses this in terms of distinguishing between what 'patriarchal thought' has made of female biology and a new vision of 'the corporeal ground of our intelligence' (Rich 1977:39). Maternal experience itself, according to both Kristeva and Rich, is not to be understood as inherently either romantic or oppressive, but rather as a complex mixture of pleasure and pain. Mothers, writes Kristeva, 'live on that border, crossroads beings, crucified beings' (Kristeva 1986:178).

Just how easily the distinction between experience and dominant (patriarchal) discourse can be maintained in actual analysis is another matter. For Rich, as for Anglophone feminism in general, the bringing of female experience into discourse, into language, is one of the primary goals of feminism itself. This orientation, aligned with a philosophical tradition that has a trusting attitude towards language and its relation to human experience, has allowed Anglophone feminism to generate significant reflections on maternal experience, as the work of Rich, and more recently, Ruddick (1989) exemplify.[6]

By contrast, although there is a similar urge in the work of Kristeva and Irigaray to create a discourse of the mother, such a desire must do battle with an equally, if not more powerful, philosophical legacy in France. The legacy pertinent here is the reformulation of theories of language by the psychoanalytical work of Lacan. In this reformulation, language becomes the medium for the passage of the human infant into the realm of symbolic human culture, which is not to be distinguished from the imposition of the Law of the Father (Ragland-Sullivan and Bracher 1991).

The tension between the feminist and the Lacanian formulations is writ large in the way Kristeva (1986) and Irigaray (1985) refer to maternity. On the one hand, there are numerous claims in their work to an excess of female embodied experience over and above discourse. These claims, usually expressed in metaphors of plurality, multiplicity, doublings, splittings and folds (see for example, Kristeva 1986:178; Irigaray 1985:239), are said to allow female pleasure, *jouissance*, to constantly seep outside and disrupt the confines of a singular, logocentric male language. On the other hand, there is an equally urgent need to insist that the symbolic order rests on the absolute alterity of Woman. The hysteric woman of psychoanalysis, 'stripped even of the words that are expected of her upon that stage invented to listen to her' (Irigaray 1985:239), becomes in many ways their dominant metaphor of woman in patriarchy. Maternal embodiment is that which exceeds male discourse, but, by virtue of the equation between male discourse and the symbolic order of culture, becomes that which cannot be represented. It follows from this logic that strategies of resistance cannot successfully seek to write maternal experience into language, but rather must take the path of textually disrupting language itself:

Given that, once again, the 'reasonable' words – to which in any case she has access only through mimicry – are powerless to translate all that pulses, clamors, and hangs lazily in the cryptic passages of hysterical suffering-latency. Then . . . turn everything upside down, inside out, back to front. *Rack it with radical convulsions* . . . Insist also and deliberately upon those *blanks* in discourse which recall her exclusion and which, by their *silent plasticity*, ensure the cohesion, the articulation, the coherent expansion of established forms. (Irigaray 1985:142 (emphasis in original))

The chapters in this volume steer a mid-way course between claiming the absolute unrepresentability of maternal experience within existing discourse and assuming, on the other hand, that maternal experiences, particularly those of Asian and Pacific women, are readily available for feminist or anthropological representation.

Such easy assumptions of representability cannot be sustained. There are profound social distances between the women writing and the women written about: distances of time, of culture, of language, and of class, as well as the great cleavage of colonialism itself.

Those contributors grappling with colonial archives confront, in a particularly acute sense, the colonized Asian or Pacific mother as 'blanks in discourse which recall her exclusion'. Empiricism, particularly in historiography, is necessarily thrown into crisis at such junctures (Manderson, this volume), even without the additional provocation of debates with French theory.

Further, as I have noted, the women who write here about colonialism are divided from their subjects by more than just textual barriers: such barriers mingle with political divisions of power. Thus Jolly (both here and elsewhere)[7] and Haggis seek to highlight rather than avoid awareness of the historical antecedents of their feminism in the 'missions of sisterhood' through which white women participated in the imposition of Western models of gender, femininity and maternity on to colonized women in Asian and Pacific countries. Such awareness does not result in any easy possibility of the writers' transcending their positioning as Western feminists. In Haggis' text the desire to do justice to the Indian woman is held up for critical scrutiny as a contemporary version of 'the white woman's burden': to emancipate the hitherto suppressed voice and agency of the Third World woman. The divided subjectivity of the European feminist concerned with colonialism is further qualified by the absence of the voice of the colonized woman in the textual evidence, to produce, at best, a deconstructive reading, and, at worst, a constant flirtation with the danger of 'continuing a colonizing discourse in reverse essentialist terms – the benevolent white woman softening the dominating agency of the European male's imperial ambitions' (Haggis, this volume, p. 83).

Those who write about the present have also to contend with the fact that the individual woman, whose views are sought by Western feminist perspectives, disappears into collectivities of kin, families, caste, and class. Nor do the problems posed by colonial discourse cease to exercise effects in the present. White missionaries, doctors, administrators, nurses are replaced by 'indigenous' counterparts without notably allowing the perspective of the maternal female subject to emerge.

The challenge for those writing in the present becomes that of understanding the interconnections between colonial and local forms of power. What are the new forms of articulation between European discourses of Christianity, science, medicine and the state and local formations of power? How do they come together in shaping the reproductive lives of women?

Within the collective groupings of class, kinship, caste and clan, women's unitary location cannot be assumed. Power relations between older and younger women, or between women of upper and lower caste, vie for feminist attention, rivalling the claims of feminism's more traditional focus of attention on relations between men and women. Feminist investment in the perspective of the birthing woman comes up against indigenous understandings of the event as a group endeavour, dominated by collective understandings, which Rozario (this volume) terms 'the family perspective'.

In a manner somewhat reminiscent of Irigaray's and Kristeva's views on language, Merrett-Balkos (this volume) reflects on the power of linguistic metaphors in Anganen culture both to posit women's identity and to socially incorporate the experience of childbirth that, as the women describe it, has the force of a phenomenological rupture. The women experience the pain of childbirth as dislocating their awareness not only of time, but of their place in social relationships. Given the salience, in that culture, of metaphors which construct women essentially as pathways or roads that connect kin groups, such experiences are threatening to the male-dominated social order, and great emphasis is therefore placed on the reintegration of the postpartum mother through specific injunctions regarding the handling of the afterbirth.

Unlike Kristeva and Irigaray, however, most of the contributors who work in 'the ethnographic present' do assume that language also makes available the resources with which women can articulate their experience and communicate it to one another, and even across significant barriers to the (sufficiently dedicated) feminist outsider/anthropologist. The move from maternity-for-the-other to maternity-for-the-mother is perceived as fraught with difficulties, but not as insuperable. The epistemological optimism is reflected in the relatively unproblematized utilization of women's voices, and women's opinions, complaints and reflections, which occurs in the second half of the volume. Their voices are not conceptualized as occurring 'outside' of, or at some extreme margin of culture and language. If we continue for a moment with Merrett-Balkos' handling of the subversive episode of birth, it is made clear that these 'experiences' are understood as threatening and confusing precisely within the symbolic apparatus of language. It is within language that women conceptualize the experience of birth and pain as 'disorienting' and 'disarticulating'.

Implicit in the various stances taken in the chapters on the relation between language and experience, and on the relation between anthropological feminist enquirer and the women about whom she writes, is a hopeful envisioning of the power/knowledge nexus, where power and knowledge are not seen as coinciding or as entirely mutually reinforcing one another. Insofar as all the chapters seek to highlight the operation of power in *constraining* various dimensions of maternal choice and subjectivity, they also take up a more emancipatory position in relation to knowledge and autonomy than would be permitted within a strictly poststructuralist perspective. In this respect, too, the chapters (for all the differences between them) steer a mid-way course between adopting Foucault's language of discourse and espousing the stance of emancipatory universalism. Perhaps, as Benhabib (1992) has cogently argued, the dilution of poststructuralism that occurs in this process is no accident, but is necessary if the enterprise is to cohere even minimally with feminism's aims and goals.

(c) Cultural difference and sexual difference

Given its focus on maternity, this volume has a contribution to make on debates concerning the relation between physiology, culture, language and the symbolic. Within feminism, such debates have not been strongly informed by anthropological and ethnographic endeavour. A few structurally inspired anthropologists such as Lévi-Strauss were incorporated very early via the structuralist and poststructuralist canons which began to inform feminist theory by the mid-seventies. Lévi-Strauss' theory on the exchange of women and the incest taboo found a ready niche, for example, in Mitchell's (1974) attempt to bring together a structuralist Marxist theory of ideology and a psychoanalytic theory of the unconscious. More remarkably, this solitary theory of kinship (and no other) continues to function as the centrepiece of the anthropological theory actually utilized in many otherwise avant garde feminist philosophical debates on body politics (see Butler 1990 for a recent example). When a feminist philosopher, like Braidotti, commends the treatment of the mother metaphor within feminist theory as '[o]ne of the most accurate ways of measuring the progress accomplished by feminist thought on biology and the female body' (1989:96), she is referring primarily to work done by philosophers such as Irigaray and Kristeva, not to the work of feminist ethnographers.

In part, as I have discussed earlier, the neglect has been earned by anthropology's slowness to clarify its own adjudication of several contending ways in which one might philosophically conceptualize the relation between physiology and culture. The contribution of this volume lies not so much in engaging in such philosophical clarification, but in making it clearer that such work cannot proceed on the basis of a mutual ignorance on the part of feminist philosophy and anthropology. Each has remained remarkably uninformed of the way in which the other has conceived of sexual and cultural difference respectively. The descriptions provided by our contributors regarding the cultural construction of the female body of reproduction reveal complex dimensions of symbolic inferiority and oppression within the societies they examine. Deepening our understanding of these dimensions will require the combined strengths and insights of both bodies of theory.

Through their analysis of maternal oppression, contributors such as Dureau and Rozario reflect critically on romantic assumptions within feminist anthropology and feminist theory more generally.

Dureau (this volume), utilizes her account of the symbolic construction of female corporeality in precolonial Simbo to criticize easy assumptions of reciprocity in male/female relations before colonialism. Her description of brother–sister relations in Simbo explicitly undermines the tendency among feminists to equate sisterhood (even with men) with egalitarianism, at the opposite pole to the subordination of a wife to her husband. Such tendencies, which have their corollary in politically romantic accounts of motherhood in the Pacific islands, are challenged by her account of the absolute suppression of the female body in the course of any communication between the woman and her most significant and dominant male other: her *luluna*, or brother. Birth in Simbo was attended not only by fear of the *luluna* in cases where the woman was pregnant outside of marriage, but by a more pervasive cultural distaste for female genitalia. Although women would accompany the birthing woman, it was more in order to ward off threatening spirits than to actually extend any form of assistance which required touching her. The birthing woman was therefore physically separated, not only from the locus of civilized culture, the hamlet, but also from her female kin.

Similarly negative views, this time of the polluted nature of the reproductive outflows of the female body, structure birth in South Asia. The problem is wider than gender. If the woman is regarded as polluted periodically by menstruation and birth, there are entire low-status groups whose occupation and (by extension) whose very ontology is constructed as polluted. Female pollution and the pollution of untouchable castes come together in Rozario's account (this volume) of the structuring of birth in rural Bangladesh. Neither the families of upper-caste women nor the male biomedical staff are prepared to handle the polluted effluents of birth – midwives, specifically recruited from a caste already bearing the stigma of pollution, are called in to take upon themselves the burden of accruing and removing pollution from higher-caste environs. The negative values of pollution in the society combine with Rozario's negative valuation of the beliefs in supernatural spirits to represent the pregnant, the birthing and the postpartum woman as weak, vulnerable and endangered.

If Dureau's account undermines romanticism concerning brother–sister relations as egalitarian, Rozario's account makes a significant contribution to questioning assumptions regarding that romantic figure of feminist theory, the midwife, as the wise and revered figure of preindustrial society. Although Rozario joins other feminists in seeking to distinguish between social constructions oppressive to the woman (here the midwife) and the voice and perspective of the midwife herself, she also perceives the midwife as herself in need of supplementation from Western biomedical training. There is a tension here between representing the interests of the woman as midwife and those of woman as birth-giver.

Merrett-Balkos and Ram, by contrast, tend to view the cultural and symbolic constructions of the female body as more ambiguous and heterogeneous in their implications for feminist analysis.

On the one hand Merrett-Balkos views the dominant metaphors for women and birth, as well as the actual practices by which afterbirth is handled, as operating to flatten out the potentially ambiguous meanings of the experience of childbirth for women. They serve to reintegrate women into their proper place, as links between groups, rather than permitting them to belong intrinsically either to the territory or to the child they have borne. On the other hand, Merrett-Balkos sees the metaphoric language as allowing a process of conceptual reflection on the part of women, especially those women whose life experiences are in tension with the dominant norm of woman as mother.

Ram's account is critical of certain aspects of the culture which shapes the reproductive experiences of a low-status group of women in south India. Her criticisms centre on the culture of caste which ensures that such women (who have no midwife of lower status to remove pollution) must endure the degrading treatment of upper-caste personnel if they venture to give birth outside their own community and in the context of clinics and hospitals. There is a merging of the idioms of pollution and hygiene, of caste and class power, to the accentuated detriment of poor low-caste women.

However, she perceives the religious traditions as plural, with some more sympathetic to and already more informed by feminine maternal subjectivity than others. In particular, notions of religious love and practices of goddess worship provide even the poorest of women with a language and symbolism with which to imagine and represent their experience of pain, suffering and maternal love. Equally, it is the representation of maternal experience as a dissolution of egoism which, in reciprocal fashion, provides the model for religious ethics in the popular *bhakti* tradition.

In this corpus of arguments there is rich material for reflecting further not only upon the plurality of cultural constructions of the female body but upon how we might go about negotiating the difficult terrain of evaluating and representing 'traditional' culture in relation to women's interests. Such reflections cannot proceed without an awareness that the terrain comes to us already shaped by the legacy of colonialism. As Stivens has demonstrated (this volume), non-Western cultures must constantly labour under the burden of proving themselves against the claims and evaluations of Western modernity, of which feminism is an integral component.

Equally, feminist philosophy's contemporary forms of theorizing on the female body needs to scrutinize its chosen terrain. Overriding the divergences of approach, there is a general assumption that the female body is constructed entirely within the premises of Western postenlightenment philosophy. Given the lack of reflection or curiosity about other traditions, the language of feminism continually replicates the universalist tones of the master discourse it aims to disrupt. Each of the key terms in psychoanalytic feminism's conceptualization of maternity – 'the maternal body', the Law of the Father, Culture – is troublingly singular in its conceptualization. Viewed from the perspective of women who have inhabited at least two cultures simultaneously since colonization, the lacunae in such conceptualizations are particularly dramatic. Few feminist philosophers who write about the female body write about religion, and even those who do, like Kristeva, 'share the contemporary intellectual consensus that the era of religion is past', as the editor of a volume dedicated to exploring her writings on religion puts it (Crownfield 1992:xvii). Certainly her thoughtful reflections on the Marian cult are framed by the assumption that the symbolic resources afforded to women by the cult have been superseded by the comparative symbolic void of enlightenment philosophy, only partially filled by the resources of psychoanalysis and potentially feminism itself. Yet colonialism has long since ensured that, whatever the status of the Virgin in the West, She and Christianity enjoy a flourishing status in Asia, the Pacific, Latin America and Africa.

The salience of religion in the region covered by this volume itself has

vast consequences for the way in which the dominant models of embodiment are conceived. As the various contributions to this volume make
clear, women's bodies are not everywhere constructed as deviations from
a central model that assumes a unitary and unified male subject. Instead,
religious constructions are necessarily committed to assuming a degree of
incompleteness on the part of the human subject. Typically accompanying this are assumptions of a permeability of bodily boundaries, of the
capacity of the human body to exist on a continuum with and to be open
to occupation and penetration by supernatural and metaphysical entities,
whether these be divine or malign. More physiologically-based systems of
belief, such as the Asian traditions of 'humoural' medicine (to use a
Western misnomer), also posit a complex set of interrelations between
foods, liquids and spices imbibed and states of bodily balance and imbal-
ance.

The female body of reproduction is therefore located within dominant
systems of meaning which already privilege plurality and permeability.
Unlike the conclusions reached by a feminism which bases itself exclusively on Western models of philosophy, it is not possible to assume for the
Asian and Pacific regions that male dominance operates under the exclus-
ive sign of 'logocentrism', nor that feminist subversion can proceed
confidently under the sign of internal doublings and multiplicity.

Through the work of psychoanalytic feminism, such terms as the
splitting of the maternal subject have become extensions of a universal
human ontology. In this view, pregnancy, birth, and even the ambivalent
mixture of maternal pleasure/pain, become exemplifications of a fundamental gap that already exists at the heart of human subjectivity, between
the chaotic drives (*Triebe* in Freud, the *semiotic* in Kristeva) and the
introjected unified image of the Other.[8]

The work on maternity in the colonial and postcolonial contexts gives
quite different, more directly political meanings to the language of split
maternal subjectivity. Here mothers must contend with and negotiate the
colonially derived splitting of culture into 'Tradition' and 'Modernity'.
The cleavages are not unconscious, but part of the explicit preoccupation
of people. Women mull over and constantly reflect upon the meanings of
bipo (TP) and *nau* (TP) (Merrett-Balkos, this volume), particularly in
societies where the historical depth of the colonial presence is shallow
enough to be contained in one lifetime. Women in Simbo exhibit such
profound ambivalence over mission evaluations of their ancestors that an
internal cleavage erupts even within the one sentence: 'They were people
of the Darkness, people of sin; but they were good people then, not like
people now.' Speech itself becomes problematic: 'I can't say properly'
(Dureau, this volume: p. 265). In other societies such as India, the

complexities of the colonial subject are old enough to have produced generations for whom modernity and its contradictory relation to local culture have long become part of a deep-rooted internal dilemma: how can India 'modernize' without losing that which is specifically 'Indian'? How can Indian women – locus of the most cherished features of 'Indian-ness' – be allowed to remain traditional, that is, sunk in superstition? On the other hand, how can they be educated to see the superiority of reason, science and modernity, without encouraging the emergence of the sexually active, emancipated 'Westernized woman'? (Ram, this volume: Chapter 4). In societies such as Malaysia (Stivens, this volume), modernity itself calls forth a 'story line' very different from the teleology of industrialization accompanied by modern mothering in urban nuclear families. Instead, religions such as Islam provide the terms necessary for a critique of modernity and its attendant social problems, while providing women with a framework for understanding and negotiating the complex and conflicting demands they are placed under.

As mothers, women may be conceived as the heartland of Tradition, alternately romanticized and denigrated. But as members of societies where sexual separation is a barrier to the 'modernizing' and 'enlightening' drive of colonial and postcolonial agencies, select groups of women must also be targeted to become the emissaries of reform and modernity. The volume documents successive intermediary figures who unwittingly become located at the intersection of contradictory discourses: the native woman missionary (Haggis, this volume), the midwife who must be retrained to give birth not only to babies but to a more modern approach to the body (Rozario, this volume).[9] The subjectivity of the women themselves is yet to receive sympathetic representation in the literature.

What the volume makes abundantly clear is that the perspective on body politics afforded by a location in the colonies and ex-colonies can breathe new life into theory. This perspective redefines the meaning of splitting and doubling in contemporary theories of the maternal body.[10] However, an example such as this does not fully convey the scope of this volume. Taken collectively, the complexities of maternal experience represented by our contributors make a significant addition to the ongoing reconceptualization of an even larger, more overarching theoretical category derived from European experience – modernity itself.

NOTES

1 Strathern's (1987) reflections on the tensions which this must generate for 'feminist anthropology' remain one of the more stimulating statements on the subject. The constraints on anthropology's capacity to move outside its frame-

works have been characterized with even greater severity by Val Daniel (1984). Daniel argues that anthropology and sociology are not only academic, but unmistakably a part of 'Western man's concerns and are constituted of Western cultural symbols', making efforts at constructing reciprocal ethnosociologies as recommended by Marriott and Inden (1977) for India, an 'anachronism' (Daniel 1984: 54–5).

2 This is not meant to convey the scope of a comprehensive review of the literature. But see Ginsburg and Rapp 1991; McClain 1982; Van Hollen 1994.

3 But see the collection of black women's writing on maternity, colonialism and issues of language in South Asia, Africa and the Caribbean, *Motherlands*, ed. Nasta (1991). See also Shetty (1994).

4 We are beginning to see more sober reformulations of universalism (Benhabib 1992) and, indeed, calls for 'post-humanist' concepts of the human (Mohanty 1989). See also Said's (1985) warnings against certain interpretations of his own critique of Orientalism to mean that only 'insiders' can speak for the group.

5 On this point there have been numerous reflections by recent feminist commentators. See, for instance, papers in Allen and Young (1989); Gatens (1991).

6 See also literary collections on maternal experience and mother–daughter experience such as *Close Company* (Park and Heaton 1987).

7 See for instance Jolly (1993).

8 In addition to Kristeva 1986, see also Young (1990).

9 On this issue, see also Saunders (1989). Through a comparison of Guatemalan and Malaysian evidence, Saunders argues that the midwife in WHO policy is largely viewed as a conduit for Western biomedical and obstetric practices.

10 See Guha (1983) and Bhabha (1985) for exploration of repetition and mimicry in the colonial context. See Butler (1990) for a contrasting picture of mimicry and body politics in the United States.

REFERENCES

Abu-Lughod, L. 1986 *Veiled Sentiments: Honor and Poetry in a Bedouin Society*. Berkeley: University of California Press.

Adams, A. 1995 Review essay: Maternal bonds: recent literature on mothering. *Signs* 20(2):414–27.

Allen, J. and Young, I.M. 1989 (eds.) *The Thinking Muse: Feminism and Modern French Philosophy*. Bloomington and Indianapolis: Indiana University Press.

Appadurai, A., Korom, F. and Mills, M. 1991 (eds.) *Gender, Genre, and Power in South Asian Expressive Traditions*. Philadelphia: University of Pennsylvania Press.

Arnold, D. 1989 (ed.) *Imperial Medicine and Indigenous Societies*. Delhi: Oxford University Press.

Beauvoir, S. de 1972 (1949) *The Second Sex* (trans. and ed. H.M. Parshley). Harmondsworth: Penguin Books.

Benhabib, S. 1992 *Situating the Self: Gender, Community and Postmodernism in Contemporary Ethics*. Cambridge: Polity Press.

Bhabha, H. 1985 Signs taken for wonders: questions of ambivalence and authority under a tree outside Delhi, May 1817. In H.L. Gates, Jr (ed.) *'Race', Writing and Difference*. Chicago and London: University of Chicago Press, 163–84.

Braidotti, R. 1989 The politics of ontological difference. In T. Brennan (ed.) *Between Feminism and Psychoanalysis*. London and New York: Routledge, 89–105.

Butler, J. 1990 *Gender Trouble: Feminism and the Subversion of Identity*. New York and London: Routledge.

Clifford, J. and Marcus, G. 1986 (eds.) *Writing Culture: The Poetics and Politics of Ethnography*. Berkeley: University of California Press.

Collins, P. 1990 *Black Feminist Thought: Knowledge, Consciousness, and the Politics of Empowerment*. London: Unwin Hyman.

Corea, G. *et al.* 1987 (eds.) *Man-Made Women: How New Reproductive Technologies Affect Women*. Bloomington: Indiana University Press.

Crownfield, D. 1992 Pre-text. In D. Crownfield (ed.) *Body/Text in Julia Kristeva: Religion, Women, and Psychoanalysis*. Albany: State University of New York, ix–xx.

Csordas, T. 1994 Introduction: the body as representation and being-in-the-world. In T. Csordas (ed.) *Embodiment and Experience: The Existential Ground of Culture and Self*. Cambridge: Cambridge University Press, 1–24.

Daniel, E.V. 1984 *Fluid Signs: Being a Person the Tamil Way*. Berkeley: University of California Press.

Douglas, M. 1973 *Natural Symbols: Explorations in Cosmology*. New York: Vintage.

Dumont, L. 1970 *Homo Hierarchicus: An Essay on the Caste System*. Chicago: University of Chicago Press.

Economic and Political Weekly 1990 Review of women's studies: *Ideology of Motherhood*. Special Issue 25(42&43), 20–7 October.

Edelstein, M. 1992 Metaphor, meta-narrative, and mater-narrative in Kristeva's 'Stabat Mater'. In D. Crownfield (ed.) *Body/Text in Julia Kristeva: Religion, Women, and Psychoanalysis*. Albany: State University of New York, 27–52.

Gatens, M. 1991 *Feminism and Philosophy: Perspectives on Difference and Equality*. Cambridge: Polity Press.

Ginsburg, F. and Rapp, R. 1991 The politics of reproduction. *Annual Review of Anthropology* 20:311–43.

Greenhalgh, S. 1995 Anthropology theorizes reproduction: integrating practice, political economic, and feminist perspectives. In S. Greenhalgh (ed.) *Situating Fertility: Anthropology and Demographic Inquiry*. Cambridge and New York: Cambridge University Press, 3–28.

Guha, R. 1983 *Elementary Aspects of Peasant Insurgency in Colonial India*. Delhi: Oxford University Press.

Handwerker, W.P. 1990 (ed.) *Births and Power: Social Change and the Politics of Reproduction*. Boulder, CO: Westview Press.

Hertz, R. 1973 The pre-eminence of the right hand: a study in religious polarity. In R. Needham (trans. and ed.) *Right and Left: Essays on Dual Symbolic Classification*. Chicago: University of Chicago Press, 3–31.

Irigaray, L. 1985 *Speculum of the Other Woman* (trans. G.C. Gill). Ithaca, NY:

Cornell University Press.

Jackson, M. 1989 *Paths Toward a Clearing: Radical Empiricism and Ethnographic Inquiry*. Bloomington: Indiana University Press.

Jolly, M. 1993 Colonizing women: the maternal body and empire. In S. Gunew and A. Yeatman (eds.) *Feminism and the Politics of Difference*. Sydney: Allen and Unwin, 103–27.

Jordan, B. 1983 *Birth in Four Cultures: A Crosscultural Investigation of Childbirth in Yucatan, Holland, Sweden and the United States* (3rd edn). Montreal: Eden Press.

1993 *Birth in Four Cultures: A Crosscultural Investigation of Childbirth in Yucatan, Holland, Sweden and the United States* (4th edn). Prospect Heights, IL: Waveland Press Inc.

Kristeva, J. 1986 (French orig. 1977) Stabat mater. In J. Kristeva *The Kristeva Reader* (ed. T. Moi). Oxford: Basil Blackwell, 160–86.

Landy, D. 1977 (ed.) *Culture, Disease and Healing: Studies in Medical Anthropology*. New York and London: Macmillan.

Leach, E. 1958 Magical hair. *Journal of the Royal Anthropological Institute* 88:147–64.

McClain, C.S. 1982 Toward a comparative framework for the study of childbirth: a review of the literature. In M. Kay (ed.) *Anthropology of Human Birth*. Philadelphia: F.A. Davis Company, 25–59.

Marcus, G. and Fischer, M. 1986 *Anthropology as Cultural Critique: An Experimental Moment in the Human Sciences*. Chicago: University of Chicago Press.

Marriott, M. and Inden, R. 1977 Towards an ethnosociology of South Asian caste systems. In K. David (ed.) *The New Wind: Changing Identities in South Asia*. The Hague: Mouton, 227–38.

Mauss, M. 1973 (French orig. 1935) Techniques of the body. *Economy and Society* 2:70–88.

Mead, M. and Newton, N. 1967 Cultural patterning of perinatal behavior. In S.A. Richardson and A.F. Guttmacher (eds.) *Childbearing: Its Social and Psychological Aspects*. Baltimore, MD: Williams and Wilkins, 142–244.

Mitchell, J. 1974 *Psychoanalysis and Feminism*. London: Allen Lane.

Mohanty, S.P. 1989 Us and them: on the philosophical bases of political criticism. *Yale Journal of Criticism* 2:1–31.

Nasta, S. 1991 (ed.) *Motherlands: Black Women's Writing from Africa, the Caribbean and South Asia*. London: The Women's Press.

Park, C. and Heaton, C. 1987 (eds.) *Close Company: Stories of Mothers and Daughters*. London: Virago Press.

Pillsbury, B. 1990 The politics of family planning: sterilization and human rights in Bangladesh. In W.P. Handwerker (ed.) *Births and Power: Social Change and the Politics of Reproduction*. Boulder, San Francisco and London: Westview Press, 165–96.

Prakash, G. 1995 Introduction: after colonialism. In G. Prakash (ed.) *After Colonialism: Imperial Histories and Postcolonial Displacements*. Princeton: Princeton University Press, 3–17.

Ragland-Sullivan, E. and Bracher, M. 1991 (eds.) *Lacan and the Subject of Language*. New York: Routledge.

Raheja, G. and Gold, A. (eds.) 1996 *Listen to the Heron's Words: Reimagining Gender and Kinship in North India*. Delhi: Oxford University Press.

Ram, K. 1991 *Mukkuvar Women: Gender, Hegemony and Capitalist Transformation in a South Indian Fishing Community*. Sydney: Allen and Unwin.

Rich, A. 1977 *Of Woman Born: Motherhood as Experience and Institution*. London: Virago Press.

Ross, E. 1995 Review essay: New thoughts on 'the oldest vocation': mothers and motherhood in recent feminist scholarship. *Signs* 20(2):397–413.

Ruddick, S. 1989 *Maternal Thinking: Towards a Politics of Peace*. London: The Women's Press.

Said, E. 1985 Orientalism reconsidered. *Race and Class* 27(2):1–15.

Saunders, P.-J. 1989 Midwives and modernization. A feminist analysis of the World Health Organization's suggestion that indigenous midwives be incorporated into primary health care programmes. BA (Hons) sub-thesis, The Australian National University, Canberra.

Scheper-Hughes, N. 1987 Culture, scarcity and maternal thinking: mother love and child death in northeast Brazil. In N. Scheper-Hughes (ed.) *Child Survival: Anthropological Perspectives on the Treatment and Maltreatment of Children*. Dordrecht: D. Reidel Publishing Company, 187–208.

Seremetakis, C.N. 1991 *The Last Word: Women, Death, and Divination in Inner Mani*. Chicago and London: University of Chicago Press.

Shetty, S. 1994 (Dis)locating gender space and medical discourse in colonial India. In C. Siegel and A. Kibbey (eds.) *Eroticism and Containment: Notes from the Flood Plain*. New York: New York University Press, 188–230.

Spencer, R. 1977 (1949–50) Embryology and obstetrics in preindustrial societies. In D. Landy (ed.) *Culture, Disease and Healing: Studies in Medical Anthropology*. New York: Macmillan Publishers, 289–99.

Strathern, M. 1987 An awkward relationship: the case of feminism and anthropology. *Signs* 12(2):276–92.

Vance, C.S. 1989 Social construction theory: problems in the history of sexuality. In D. Altman and contributors *Homosexuality, Which Homosexuality? International Conference on Gay and Lesbian Studies*. Amsterdam: Uitgeverij An Dekker/Schorer, 13–34.

1991 Anthropology rediscovers sexuality: a theoretical comment. *Social Science and Medicine* 33(8):875–84.

Van Hollen, C. 1994 Perspectives on the anthropology of birth. *Culture, Medicine and Psychiatry* 18:501–12.

Young, I.M. 1990 Pregnant embodiment: subjectivity and alienation. In I.M. Young *Throwing Like a Girl and Other Essays in Feminist Philosophy and Social Theory*. Bloomington: Indiana University Press.

Index

Abel, C., 188
abortion, 4, 8, 16, 19, 26, 33, 122, 164–5,
  183, 187, 188–9, 192–4, 200, 201,
  244, 263, 264
abstinence, *see* sexuality
Adams, A., 282
adoption, 58, 200, 249, 251, 262
adultery, *see* sexuality
affines, 221, 223, 227, 247, 249, 250, 255
agency, 1, 30, 72, 85, 87, 88–9, 90, 95, 98,
  106, 128–9, 133
'native agency', 10–11, 99, 100–2
Alphonse, T., 121–5
Althusser, L., 138
ancestors, 186, 201, 224, 239, 241, 243,
  244, 245, 249, 250, 265
Anganen (PNG), 14, 17, 18–19, 213ff
anthropology, 275–80, 289–90
Asad, T., 84–5
atur ghor, see birthing sites
auspiciousness and danger, 15, 131, 172n
  see also pollution
Australia, 114, 203n, 235n, 241–2

Bangladesh, 14–15, 144ff
Bayly, S., 110n
Beauvoir, S. de, 285
Benhabib, S., 289
Bhabha, H., 139
bhakti (Sanskrit, Hindu religious
  devotionalism) 134, 135, 139
bhut, see spirits
Bible women, 10–11, 82, 85, 90–107, 132,
  169, 283
  origin of, in London, 100–2
  Ranyard, E., 100–1
  see also missionaries
bidan, see midwives
bipo and *nau* (Tok Pisin, before and now),
  17–18, 20, 215–16, 224, 293
birth
  anthropology of, 278–9, 280

caste and, 129–31, 169
complications, 133, 146–7, 154, 160,
  162–5, 167, 168, 170, 173n, 220,
  252–3
hygiene, 131, 145–7, 154, 159, 165,
  166, 168, 181, 189, 221
loss of awareness during, 226
medicalization, 4, 15–16, 23n, 26, 34,
  37, 61, 115, 116–17, 118–19, 128–9,
  144, 148, 252
pain during, 132, 133–6, 145–6, 162–3,
  226; see also *kele*
pollution, 14–16, 129–31, 145–7,
  149–54, 155, 158, 159, 168–9, 290–1
position, 12–13, 23n, 200, 249
sequestering, 16, 151, 154, 155, 200–1
social structure, threat to, 226–7, 288
spirits, danger of, 12, 13, 14, 16, 131,
  145–6, 148, 150–1, 154, 156, 157,
  163, 248–9, 252
vulnerability during, 226
birthing sites
  aid-post, 18–19, 21n, 213–14, 215
  atur ghor or *chodi ghor* (Bengali, birthing
    room or hut), 146, 150, 151, 154, 163
  engi and (Anganen, mother house), 18,
    215, 219–20, 226
  forest, 12, 13, 213, 248–9, 252, 263
  home, 6, 33, 61, 68, 129, 132, 146, 150,
    151
  see also clinics; hospitals
bisnis (Tok Pisin, business), 19, 215, 219,
  224
Blacklock, M., 42–3, 44
Blanchet, T., 146–7, 149, 158
boarding schools, *see* schools
body, theories of, 53, 54–5, 74–5n, 275ff
Boer War, 35, 179
bomoh (Malay, folk healer), *see* healers
bottle-feeding, 4, 6, 32, 39, 41, 67, 70,
  124, 192, 207n
Bourdieu, P., 277

Braidotti, R., 289
breast-feeding, 2, 4, 6, 26, 27, 32, 38–9,
  41, 67, 69, 124, 134, 188, 192, 200,
  222, 234, 248, 249, 258
  colostrum, 38
  'economy of the borrowed breast', 32
  meaning of, 124, 135, 222, 234, 248
  wet-nurses, 32
bui ni gone, see midwives

caesarean, 23n, 133, 145
cannibalism, 183, 186
cash, *see bisnis*; economy
caste
  Bangladesh, 14, 15, 148–50, 155,
    169–70, 290–1
  birth and, 129–31, 169
  India, 10–11, 13–14, 16, 21, 87, 89, 90,
    92, 94–5, 96, 98, 99, 101–2, 104, 106,
    115–16, 117, 121, 127, 128–32, 134,
    136, 137, 139, 140, 291
  positionality of ethnographer and, 21,
    115, 284
Catholicism, 8, 15, 17, 18–19, 117–18,
  120–5, 128, 134, 135, 137, 147, 160,
  170–1, 196–7, 213, 215, 283
  see also missionaries; nuns; priests
cervix, 34, 167
Chatterjee, P., 125
child abuse, 70–1
child rearing, 36, 52, 56–7, 58, 68–70,
  123–4, 139, 177, 181–2, 190, 258,
  262, 264
  child-care provision, 53, 54, 192
  colonial disapproval of, 4, 5, 7, 8, 9, 36,
    38–9, 56, 58, 71, 182, 183, 186–93,
    194, 196, 199, 200, 206n
  commoditization of, 63, 284
  Islam and, 52
  kin and, 69–70, 200, 250
  manuals, 4, 63, 66, 123
  maternal deprivation theory, 123
  men and, 68–9, 70, 256, 257
  nation building and, 66
  popular culture and, 63–6
  'Westoxification' of, 71
childlessness, 58, 137–8, 193–4, 245, 264
chodi (Bengali, pollution), *see* pollution
chodi ghor, see birthing sites
Christianity
  in Bangladesh, 145, 147, 149, 150, 151,
    155, 156–7, 163, 164, 165, 169,
    170–1
  in Britain, 178, 179
  in Fiji, 202

  in India, 81ff, 114ff
  in PNG, 22n, 219, 223, 224
  in the Solomons, 239, 243, 245, 251ff
  see also Bible women; Catholicism; Jesus;
    Methodism; missionaries; nuns;
    priests; St Anthony; Virgin Mary
class
  concept of, 1, 11, 14, 15, 16, 21, 27, 31,
    41, 43, 52, 55, 82, 87, 132, 169,
    177–81, 278, 288
  middle class, 3, 11, 30, 32, 38, 43, 52,
    53, 55, 59, 60–71, 72, 87, 88, 102,
    104, 106, 127, 132, 137, 178, 179–80,
    181, 253
  upper class, 87, 101, 126, 179, 283
  working class, 9, 11, 30, 35, 40, 52, 87,
    100–1, 104, 178, 179, 180–2, 187
clinics, 4, 6, 12–13, 21n, 32, 34, 38,
    39–42, 43, 44, 66, 68, 119, 120,
    128–9, 131, 132, 138, 146, 160, 167,
    168, 170, 213–14, 215, 216, 220,
    221, 226, 232, 233, 243, 252, 263,
    291
cognatic kin, 12, 245, 247, 249, 250, 254
Collins, P., 281–2
colonial discourse on
  child rearing, *see* child rearing
  'insouciance', *see* 'insouciance'
  'lazy native', 56, 63
  marriage, *see* marriage
  maternity, *see* maternity
  population, *see* population
  sexuality, *see* sexuality
  'women's work', 82ff
  workforce, *see* workforce
colonialism
  'maternalism' of, 31, 40, 82–3, 105, 178,
    181
  see also Bible women; Catholicism;
    Christianity; clinics; education;
    emasculation; home visiting;
    midwives; missionaries; nuns; nurses;
    pacification; postcoloniality; schools
'colonizing women', 81–3, 105, 107n
  see also Bible women; Hygiene Mission;
    missionaries; nuns
Community Health Workers (Bangladesh),
    166–7
contraception, 4, 8, 19–20, 59, 61 147,
    158–60, 166, 172–3n, 179, 188, 189,
    196, 239, 242, 244, 248, 250, 253,
    256, 257–8, 261, 263–4, 266
Csordas, T., 277

dai, see midwives

dakwah (Malaysia, Islamic missionary groups), 51–2, 60, 68
see also Islam
Daniel, E., 295n
Davidoff, L. and Hall, C., 108n
Davin, A., 178–81
Decrease Report (Fiji), 182, 190–4
'degeneration', 178, 179, 186–7
depopulation, *see* population discourse
development
   concept of, 50, 59, 60, 70–1, 121, 214
   'Kerala model', 119
diarrhoea, 5, 36, 39, 41, 145, 154, 156, 164
   International Centre for Diarrhoeal Disease Research, Bangladesh, 145, 166
divorce, 58, 72, 122, 245, 247, 250, 252
Djamour, J., 58
doctors, 6, 13, 15, 16, 23n, 33, 35, 36, 39, 40, 41, 42, 58, 67, 118–19, 132, 144, 147, 158–9, 161–3, 164, 165, 168, 170, 171, 173n, 179, 283
domestic science education, 5, 7, 42–3
Douglas, M., 276
'Dravida' movement (India), 126
Dumont, L., 148–9, 276
Dureau, C., 12–13, 17–18, 19–20, 21n, 22n, 201, 239ff, 276, 280, 290
Durrad, W., 188, 189–90

eclampsia, 33, 156, 167
economy, 19, 50, 55–7, 59–60, 63, 69, 118, 131, 215, 217, 219, 243, 244, 250–1, 260, 261, 263
   see also bisnis
education, 9, 17, 30, 31, 37, 40, 41, 42–3, 52, 57, 82, 87, 88, 90–1, 98, 99, 104, 115, 116, 132, 155, 161, 165, 168, 171, 181, 182, 187, 196–7, 202, 243, 263
   see also missionaries; nuns; schools
emasculation, 8, 179, 183, 186–7
engi and, *see* birthing sites
enlightenment, 1, 2, 10, 11–14, 18, 84, 114ff, 202
epidural anaesthesia, 23n
episiotomy, 23n, 68, 133
eugenics, 35, 179–80, 187, 188
exchange, 216, 219, 227, 230–4, 248, 250, 255

family planning, *see* abortion;
   contraception; infanticide; sexuality
Female Village Workers (Bangladesh), *see* Community Health Workers

feminism, 2, 15, 20–1, 26–7, 51–5, 58, 66, 70, 71–2, 73–4n, 81, 83–4, 106, 114, 123, 126, 127, 136, 177, 201, 241–2, 275ff
Fernandez, J., 216–17, 229, 235–6n
Fiji, 4, 5, 6, 7–10, 13, 16–17, 182, 184, 186, 189, 190–202, 243, 250–1, 254, 282, 283
film, 114, 126
Firth, R., 58
folk healers, *see* healers
food taboos, 67, 134–5, 154, 155–6
Forbes, G., 109n
forceps, 133, 157
fostering, 249, 261–3
Foucault, M., 5, 10, 277
Freudian psychology, 123, 124, 125

gay theory, 277
Ginsburg, F. and Rapp, R., 278, 279
Godelier, M., 234
Grimshaw, B., 183, 186, 204n
Grimshaw, P., 81–2
Gunn, Reverend, 183
gynaecology, 23n, 114, 283

Haggis, J., 10–11, 20, 81ff, 132, 169, 283, 287
Hawaii, 266
headhunting, 186, 239, 243, 244, 250
healers, 16, 32, 44n, 145, 147, 156, 157, 158–9, 164–5, 171, 201
health centres, *see* clinics
Hertz, R., 176
Hinduism, 14, 85–6, 89, 90, 92, 93, 97, 116, 118, 122, 124, 125–6, 132, 134, 135–6, 139, 145, 147, 148–9, 150–1, 155, 156–7, 162, 163, 164, 165, 169
Hocart, A., 241, 242, 243, 247, 248, 255, 258, 260, 261
honour, 155, 158, 165
home visiting, 6, 37–9, 40, 42, 43, 100–1, 180
homoeopathy, 22n, 145, 146, 147, 158, 161
hospitals, 6, 13, 14, 16, 17, 32–3, 38, 39, 40, 41, 43, 45n, 61, 67, 68, 118–19, 120, 128–9, 131–3, 136, 147, 158, 160, 162, 164, 165, 168, 170, 173n, 220, 291
Hunt, N., 82–3
Hunter, J., 81
hybridity, 139
hygiene, 14, 37, 38, 42, 43, 57, 102, 131, 139, 146–7, 159, 165, 166, 168, 180–1, 189, 221

Hygiene Mission (Fiji), 8, 17, 196–7

ICDDR,B (International Centre for Diarrhoeal Disease Research, Bangladesh), *see* diarrhoea
identity
　Anganen, 214–17, 221–4, 226–8, 232–3
　Tamil, 125–7
　see also personhood
ijjat, see *izzat*
Im Thurn, Sir E., 186–7
India, 10–11, 13–14, 15, 16–17, 20, 81ff, 114ff, 145, 149, 154, 157, 160, 161, 169, 283, 291–2, 293–4
infant mortality, 5, 7, 9, 14, 19, 28, 34, 35–6, 37, 44, 56, 144, 148, 166, 179–82, 187, 189–90, 193, 196, 224, 239, 244, 249, 282
　National Association for the Prevention of Infant Mortality, 36
infanticide, 4, 8, 183, 187, 188–9, 193, 194, 201, 244, 248, 249, 253, 264
injections, 119, 128, 129, 158, 162, 168
'insouciance', 8, 177, 178, 183, 186, 189, 191, 197
Irigaray, L., 286, 288, 289
Islam, 3, 22n, 51–2, 58, 60, 62–3, 68, 69, 70, 71, 72, 76n, 94, 145, 146, 147, 149, 150, 151, 155, 156–7, 158, 159, 163, 164, 169, 173n
Islam, S., 158, 161, 294
izzat (Bengali, honour), *see* honour

Jackson, M., 277
Jesus, 10, 11, 87, 89, 91, 94, 99, 131, 132, 138, 219
Jolly, M., 7–10, 82–3, 105, 107n, 177ff, 280, 283, 287
　concept of 'maternalism', 82–3, 105, 178, 181
Jolly, M. and Macintyre, M., 251
Jordan, B., 278, 279, 280
　Birth in Four Cultures (1983, 1993), 278, 279

kabiraj (Bengali, folk healer), *see* healers
kastom (Tok Pisin, Solomon Islands pidgin, Bislama, tradition), 22n, 221, 257, 261, 265
Keesing, R., 16
kele (Anganen, work; labour), 222, 226
　birth and, 226
'Kerala model' of development, *see* development
kinship, 54, 55, 123, 201, 216, 223, 230,

239ff, 289
　see also luluna
Knapman, C., 196
Kottar Social Service Society (KSSS), *see* missionaries
Kristeva, J., 281, 285–6, 289, 292
　Stabat Mater, 281, 285

labour (birth), *see* birth
labour (work), see *bisnis; kele*; workforce
Lacan, J., 286
Laderman, C., 7, 32, 157, 168
'lady visitors', 101
Leach, E., 276
Lederman, R., 233–4
Levi-Strauss, C., 289
loas po isin, *see* midwives
London Missionary Society (LMS), *see* missionaries
Lukere, V., 8–9, 13, 16, 23n, 193, 194, 199, 202, 207n
luluna (Simbo, classificatory opposite sex sibling, brother (f.s.)), 19, 239, 245–8, 249, 250, 251, 254, 255, 259, 261, 264, 266–8, 290

MCH services, *see* maternal and child health services
Macintyre, M., 261
MacKenzie, M., 235n
Mahathir, 56–7, 59
Malaya, *see* Malaysia
Malaysia, 5–7, 8, 9, 18, 21n, 22n, 26ff, 50ff, 157, 168, 181, 282, 283, 284, 294
Mandelbaum, D., 137–8
Manderson, L., 2, 3, 5–7, 9, 26ff, 51, 56, 58, 71, 181–2, 282, 283
　'obstetric gaze', 2, 28
marriage, 20, 96, 98, 102, 104–6, 121–2, 126, 191, 192, 206n, 217, 223, 225, 232, 233, 239, 241, 245, 246, 247–50, 253–68
maternal and child health (MCH) services, 45n, 158, 166, 263
maternal mortality, 5, 14, 19, 33–4, 37, 44, 45n, 144, 148, 166, 167, 196, 224
'maternalism', *see* colonialism; Jolly, M.
maternity, concept of, 1–2, 26–7, 177–8, 239, 275ff
maternity leave, 34, 69
matriliny, 55, 59, 105
matrilocality, 105, 262
Mauss, M., 276
Mead, M. and Newton, N., 279

medical pluralism, 137–8
menstruation, 16, 121, 127–8, 149, 154,
    159, 165, 200, 225, 246, 290
Merrett-Balkos, L., 18–19, 20, 213ff, 276,
    288–9, 291, 293
metaphor, 216–17, 219, 221–2, 226–32,
    234, 276, 288–9, 291
Methodism, 8, 12, 20, 196–7, 243, 252–5
midwives
    Bible women (India) as, 92–3, 97
    bidan (Malay), 6, 7, 30, 31, 32, 33,
        36–7, 40, 42, 43, 44n, 61, 67, 157
    bui ni gone (Fijian), 16–17, 193, 200,
        201, 202, 208n
    dai (Bengali), 14, 15, 144ff, 290–1
    Indian rural midwives, 129–33, 169
    loas po isin (Pentecost), 200
    Midwives Act (1902), 35
    Native Obstetric Nurses (Fiji), 17, 197,
        202
    nuns as, 160, 170–1, 213–14, 220–1
    payment of, 146, 161, 163, 164, 165–6,
        169–70
    status of, 15, 16, 129–33, 149, 157,
        169–70, 201, 291
    western training, 5, 6, 7, 9, 13, 14, 17,
        36–7, 39, 67, 68, 92–3, 97, 148, 157,
        160, 165–7, 170, 197, 202, 294
    see also healers; traditional birth
        attendants
milk, *see* breast-feeding; bottle-feeding
miscarriage, 26, 33, 154, 193, 196, 244
'mission of sisterhood', 20, 21, 81ff, 287
missionaries, 7–8, 10–11, 12–13, 16,
    17–20, 43, 81ff, 117–18, 120, 125–6,
    132, 137, 170, 182–3, 187, 188–90,
    191, 195, 196–7, 199, 213–15, 219,
    220–1, 223–4, 232–3, 243, 247,
    250–68, 283, 294
    Bible women, *see* Bible women
    Church of England Zenana Missionary
        Society, 108n
    Kottar Social Service Society (KSSS),
        120, 127, 129
    Kwato mission, 188
    'lady missionaries', 86–7, 89, 96, 97, 98,
        102–5, 283
    London Missionary Society (LMS), 10,
        81ff
    'mission hegemony', 251, 253
    'missionary wives', 88, 90, 91, 92, 93,
        96, 98, 102–5, 106
    Society for the Propagation of Female
        Education in the East (SPFEE), 88–9
    'trope of emancipation', 82, 95, 106

'women's work', 81ff
Mitchell, J., 289
mobility, women's, 8, 33, 40, 93, 97–8,
    155, 195–6
modernity, 1, 2–3, 5, 15, 16, 18–19, 39,
    50ff, 115–17, 123, 127, 136–7, 139,
    292, 294
moka (Tok Pisin, ceremonial exchange,
    highlands PNG) 219, 233, 234
mongol (Anganen, road; connection) 221,
    223, 227–9, 231, 232
mother house, *see* birthing sites
mother-roasting, 6, 22n, 32
Mukkuvar (fishing caste of Kanyakumari,
    south India) 14, 15–16, 117–20,
    130–6
Munn, N., 235n

nannies, 197
nationalism, 51, 107n, 117, 121, 125–6,
    136
nau (Tok Pisin, now), see *bipo* and *nau*
net bag, 222, 228–9, 233, 234, 235n
New Zealand, 183, 189, 243
Niranjana, T., 107n
nonope (Anganen, metaphor), *see* metaphor
nu (Anganen, placenta), *see* placenta
    broader meaning of, 227–9
nuns, 8, 15, 18–19, 22n, 128, 137, 147,
    160, 165, 170–1, 196–7, 213–15,
    220–1, 224, 232–3
nurses, 5, 6, 9, 12–13, 14, 15, 16, 17, 23n,
    33, 36, 37, 38, 39, 40–1, 93, 97–8,
    118–19, 131–3, 173n, 197, 202, 252
    see also midwives; Native Obstetric
        Nurses; nuns

obstetrics
    colonial, 283
    'obstetric gaze', *see* Manderson, L.
    'primitive', 278

pacification, 19, 186, 201, 214, 242, 243,
    248, 251, 261, 268
pain
    birth and, *see* birth
    pregnancy and, 133, 134
pamaZna (Simbo, respect), 245–6
Papua New Guinea, 9, 14, 17, 18–19, 188,
    213ff, 242, 243, 244–5, 252, 258
parda (Bengali, seclusion), *see* seclusion
past, concept of, see *bipo* and *nau*; *kastom*;
    tradition
patriliny, 223, 249
patrilocality, 135, 217, 223, 231, 262

pearlshells, meaning of, 230–1
Pentecost, 188, 189, 199, 200
personhood, 201, 216–17, 219
  see also identity
phenomenology, 216, 277
Pitt-Rivers, G., 183, 187, 189, 192
place, 18–19, 200, 215, 217, 220, 224–31, 233, 291
  'base place' (Anganen), 220, 224–5, 227, 228, 229, 233
placenta, 4, 12, 33, 68, 145, 146–7, 214, 225, 228
  meaning of, 227–31, 232–3
  planting of, 7, 12, 18–19, 200, 214, 217, 219–20, 225, 229–31, 233, 249
  polluting properties of, 12, 15, 147, 149, 221, 225
  see also umbilicus
polio, 260
pollution, 14–16, 22n, 109n, 115, 129–32, 139, 145–7, 148–54, 155, 158, 159, 168–9, 171, 221, 225, 276, 290–1
  see also auspiciousness; purity
polu (Anganen, umbilicus; road), *see* umbilicus
population discourse, 5, 7–8, 9–10, 35, 59–60, 178–88, 189, 191, 197–9, 200, 202, 282;
  see also Decrease Report (Fiji); eugenics
pornography, 121
positionality of researcher, 50, 52–3, 83–5, 115–16, 241–2, 284, 287–8
postcoloniality, 1, 3, 20, 73n, 83–5, 138–40, 279–80, 293
postenlightenment discourse, 115, 292
postmodernism, 51, 73n, 76n, 234
poststructuralism, 54, 84, 289
postnatal care, 4, 12, 30, 145, 148, 151, 154, 156, 165, 169, 249, 263
  see also home visiting
postnatal restrictions, 151, 154, 155–6
postnatal hut (Simbo), 12, 249
Prakash, Fr J., 121–5
Prakash, G., 279–80
pregnancy, 1, 2, 4, 6, 7, 8, 19, 26, 27, 28, 32, 33, 34, 37, 41, 43, 61, 66, 68, 69, 115, 119, 121, 124, 128–9, 133–5, 138, 147, 151, 154, 165, 166, 170, 189, 192, 194, 223, 231, 244, 247, 248, 252, 261
priests (Catholic), 117, 120–5, 137
Prochaska, F., 108n
pronatalism, 58–60, 68, 124, 284
prostitution, 30, 33, 121, 206n, 241, 244, 247

psychoanalysis, 123, 286, 293
psychology, 4–5, 26, 27, 122–4
purdah (Urdu, seclusion), 104, 155, 158
  see also parda
purity, 115, 125, 147, 148–9, 155, 158, 171
  see also auspiciousness; pollution

Ram, K., 13–14, 15–16, 17, 21, 109n, 114ff, 160, 169, 291–2
Ranyard, E., *see* Bible women
Rich, A., 285–6
  Of Woman Born (1977), 285
Rivers, W., 183, 186, 187, 188, 241, 242, 255
roasting, *see* mother-roasting
Roberts, S., 183, 186–7, 188, 189, 190, 191
Ross, E., 276, 282
Rozario, S., 14, 15, 144ff, 276, 288, 290–1

Sacks, K., 266–8
Said, E., 84–5, 295n
St Anthony, 156–7
St Pancras School for Mothers, 181
saline, 129, 158, 162
Samoa, 243, 250, 254, 266, 267
Sangari, K. and Vaid, S., 107n
Saunders, P., 295n
savo (Simbo, postnatal hut), *see* postnatal hut
Scheffler, H., 242, 249, 255, 269n
schools, 10, 11, 17, 35, 42, 66, 69, 90–2, 95, 96, 102, 168, 171, 181, 197, 243
seclusion, 10, 96, 104, 125, 127, 155, 158, 165
Seremetakis, C., 139
Sexton, L., 233
sexuality
  abstinence, 4, 26, 183, 188, 200, 201
  Christianity and, 121–2, 124–5, 251, 252, 253
  colonial discourse on, 190–1, 193, 195–6, 206n
  extra-marital, 19, 122, 193, 244, 247, 250, 251, 252–3, 255–6, 258, 261–2
  premarital, 19, 70, 247, 248, 261–2
  regulation of, 246–7, 248, 251, 255–6, 258
  theories of, 277
  Tamil nationalism and, 124–5
Shetty, S., 283
Siddha medicine, 118, 134–5, 138

Simbo (Solomons), 12–13, 14, 17–18, 19–20, 239ff, 290, 293
Singapore, 6, 32–3, 36, 38, 39, 58
social Darwinism, 57
Society for the Propagation of Female Education in the East (SPFEE), *see* missionaries
Solomons, 20, 186, 197, 201
  see also Simbo
space, *see* place
Speiser, F., 183, 187, 188, 189, 190, 205n
Spence, L., 196
Spencer, H., 179–80
Spencer, R., 278
spirits, 222, 224–5, 232, 247
  bhut (Bengali), 145, 147, 148, 150, 151, 154, 155, 156, 159, 163–4, 169
  birth danger of, 12, 13, 14, 16, 131, 145–6, 148, 150–1, 154, 156, 157, 163, 248–9, 252
  Christian discourse on, 13, 122, 123, 224, 232, 252
Spivak, G., 20, 83, 107n
sterilization, 115
Stivens, M., 2, 3, 7, 18, 20–1, 50ff, 284, 285, 292
Stoler, A., 5, 9, 10, 28, 31, 56
Strathern, M., 216, 219, 233, 234n, 236n, 294n
structuralism, 289
sweet potato, meaning of, 217, 226, 229, 231

TBAs, *see* midwives; traditional birth attendants; WHO
Tahiti, 183, 189
Tamil Nadu (India), 15–16, 114ff
territoriality, *see* place
tetanus, 4, 5, 6, 12–13, 22n, 33, 36, 37, 119, 128, 154
Thomas, N., 251
Tonga, 189, 254, 266, 267
tradition, concept of, 15, 18, 22–3n, 50–1, 66–9, 72, 122–4, 127, 128, 136–7, 159, 178, 202, 257, 264–5, 268, 293–4
  see also bipo and *nau; kastom*
traditional birth attendants (TBAs), *see* midwives
  WHO interest in, 15, 21n, 22n, 144, 166–7, 295n

Travancore (India), 10–11, 81ff, 118, 132, 169
Trobriands, 233, 266
Turner, T., 54, 74–5n

UC, *see* United Church of Papua New Guinea and the Solomon Islands
ultrasound, 114
umbilicus, 4, 12, 15, 18–19, 22n, 45n, 67, 145–6, 149, 150, 152–3, 154, 160, 163, 165, 167, 189, 200, 214, 217, 219–23, 225, 227, 228, 232–3
United Church of Papua New Guinea and the Solomon Islands, 243, 252, 256
Usman Awang, 75n
uterus, 6, 32, 114, 133
uxorilocality, *see* matrilocality

Van Hollen, C., 279
Vance, C., 277
Vanuatu, 5, 7–8, 182, 183, 185, 187, 189, 190, 197–8, 199–200, 202, 282, 283
venereal disease, 30, 33, 34
Virgin Mary, 131, 134, 135, 219, 224, 292
virilocality, *see* patrilocality

Wagner, R., 230
weeping, 135
Weiner, A., 233, 266, 267
'Westoxification', 3, 70, 71, 72, 76n
White, H., 84–5
WHO (World Health Organization) interest in TBAs, 15, 21n, 22n, 144, 166–7, 295n
widow strangulation, 183, 205–6n
wok meri (Tok Pisin, 'women's work', rural women's movement in highlands PNG), 233, 234
'women's work', *see* missionaries
workforce, 5, 35–6, 59–60, 131, 132, 135, 137, 219, 243, 263, 282
  concerns about in Pacific, 7, 182, 183, 187, 198–9, 243
  female, 6, 9, 30–1, 32, 39, 60, 63, 69, 96, 195, 214, 215–16
  male, 32, 195, 214

YWCA, 96

zenana (India, women's quarters), 10, 11, 86–106